the GUARDIANS of the GALAXY

"We're Super Heroes."

THIS GALAXY IS NOT YOUR TOY.

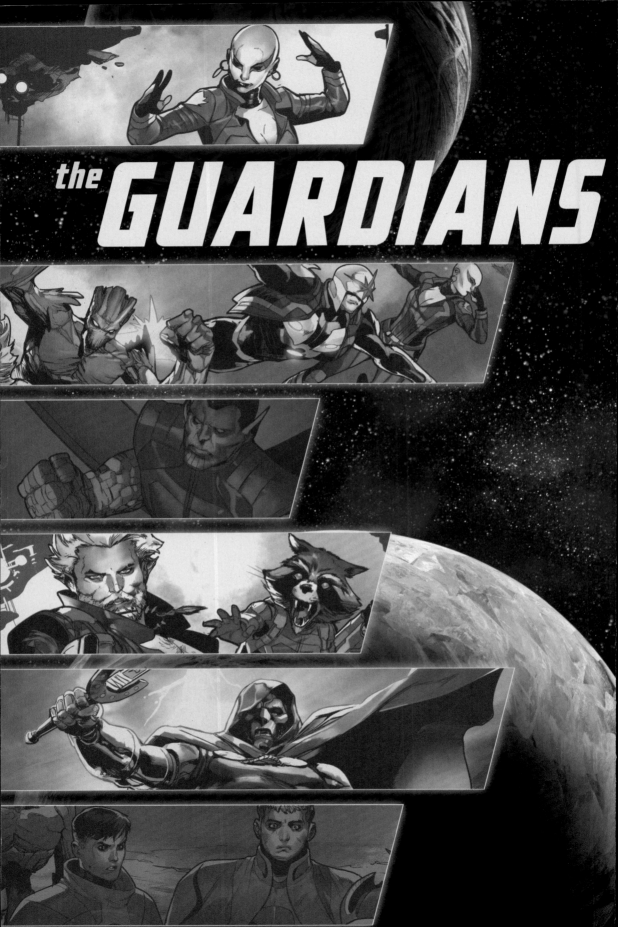

the GUARDIANS

COLLECTION EDITOR: **DANIEL KIRCHHOFFER** ASSISTANT MANAGING EDITOR: **MAIA LOY**

ASSISTANT MANAGING EDITOR: **LISA MONTALBANO** SENIOR EDITOR, SPECIAL PROJECTS: **JENNIFER GRÜNWALD**

VP PRODUCTION & SPECIAL PROJECTS: **JEFF YOUNGQUIST** BOOK DESIGNER: **STACIE ZUCKER** WITH **JAY BOWEN**

SVP PRINT, SALES & MARKETING: **DAVID GABRIEL** EDITOR IN CHIEF: **C.B. CEBULSKI**

GUARDIANS OF THE GALAXY BY AL EWING VOL. 3: WE'RE SUPER HEROES. Contains material originally published in magazine form as GUARDIANS OF THE GALAXY (2020) #13-18. First printing 2021. ISBN 978-1-302-92876-6. Published by MARVEL WORLDWIDE, INC., a subsidiary of MARVEL ENTERTAINMENT, LLC. OFFICE OF PUBLICATION: 1290 Avenue of the Americas, New York, NY 10104. © 2021 MARVEL No similarity between any of the names, characters, persons, and/or institutions in this magazine with those of any living or dead person or institution is intended, and any such similarity which may exist is purely coincidental. **Printed in Canada.** KEVIN FEIGE, Chief Creative Officer; DAN BUCKLEY, President, Marvel Entertainment; JOE QUESADA, EVP & Creative Director; DAVID BOGART, Associate Publisher & SVP of Talent Affairs; TOM BREVOORT, VP, Executive Editor; NICK LOWE, Executive Editor, VP of Content, Digital Publishing; DAVID GABRIEL, VP of Print & Digital Publishing; JEFF YOUNGQUIST, VP of Production & Special Projects; ALEX MORALES, Director of Publishing Operations; DAN EDINGTON, Managing Editor; RICKEY PURDIN, Director of Talent Relations; JENNIFER GRÜNWALD, Senior Editor, Special Projects; SUSAN CRESPI, Production Manager; STAN LEE, Chairman Emeritus. For information regarding advertising in Marvel Comics or on Marvel.com, please contact Vit DeBellis, Custom Solutions & Integrated Advertising Manager, at vdebellis@marvel.com. For Marvel subscription inquiries, please call 888-511-5480. Manufactured between 9/3/2021 and 10/5/2021 by SOLISCO PRINTERS, SCOTT, QC, CANADA.

10 9 8 7 6 5 4 3 2 1

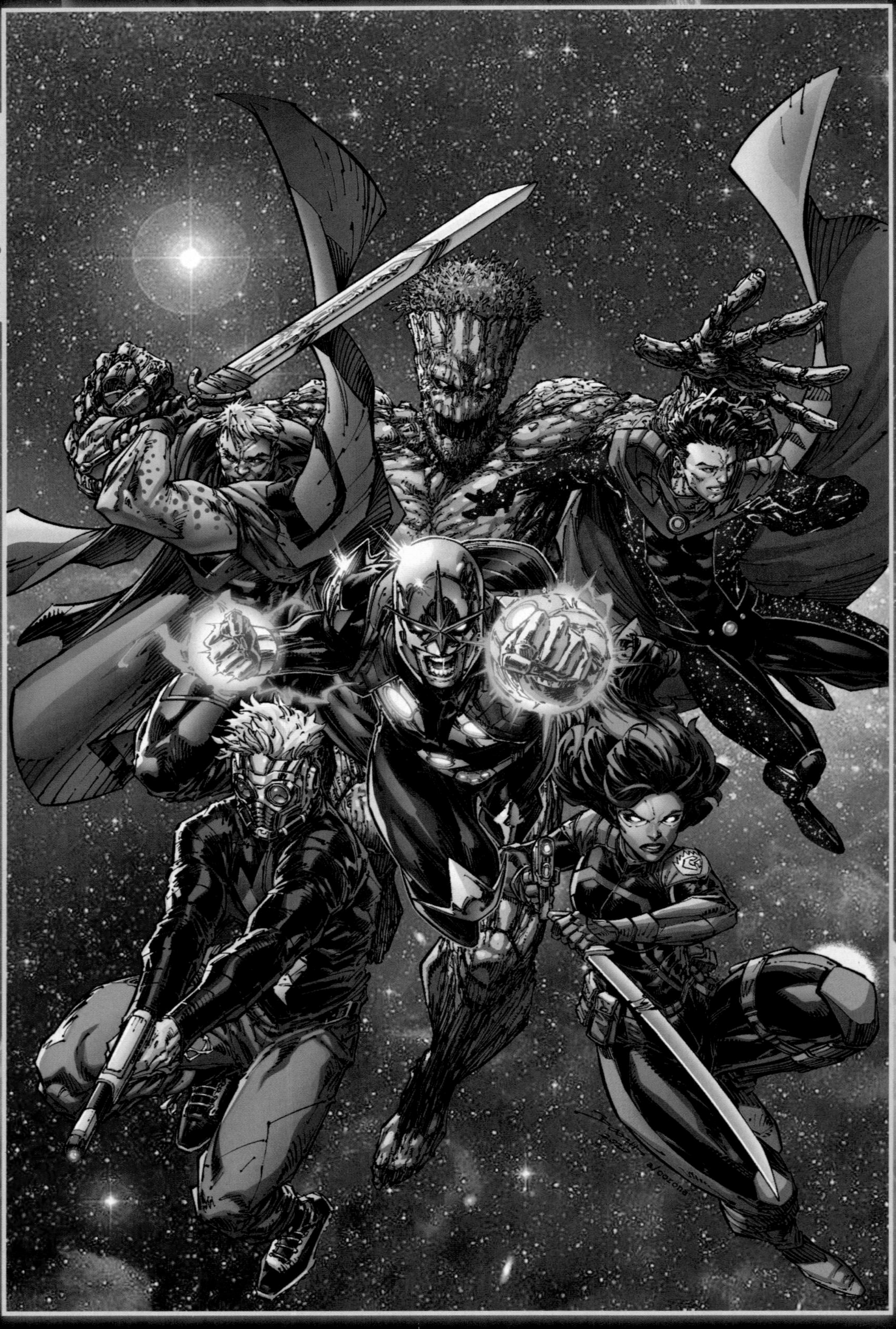

"We're super heroes."

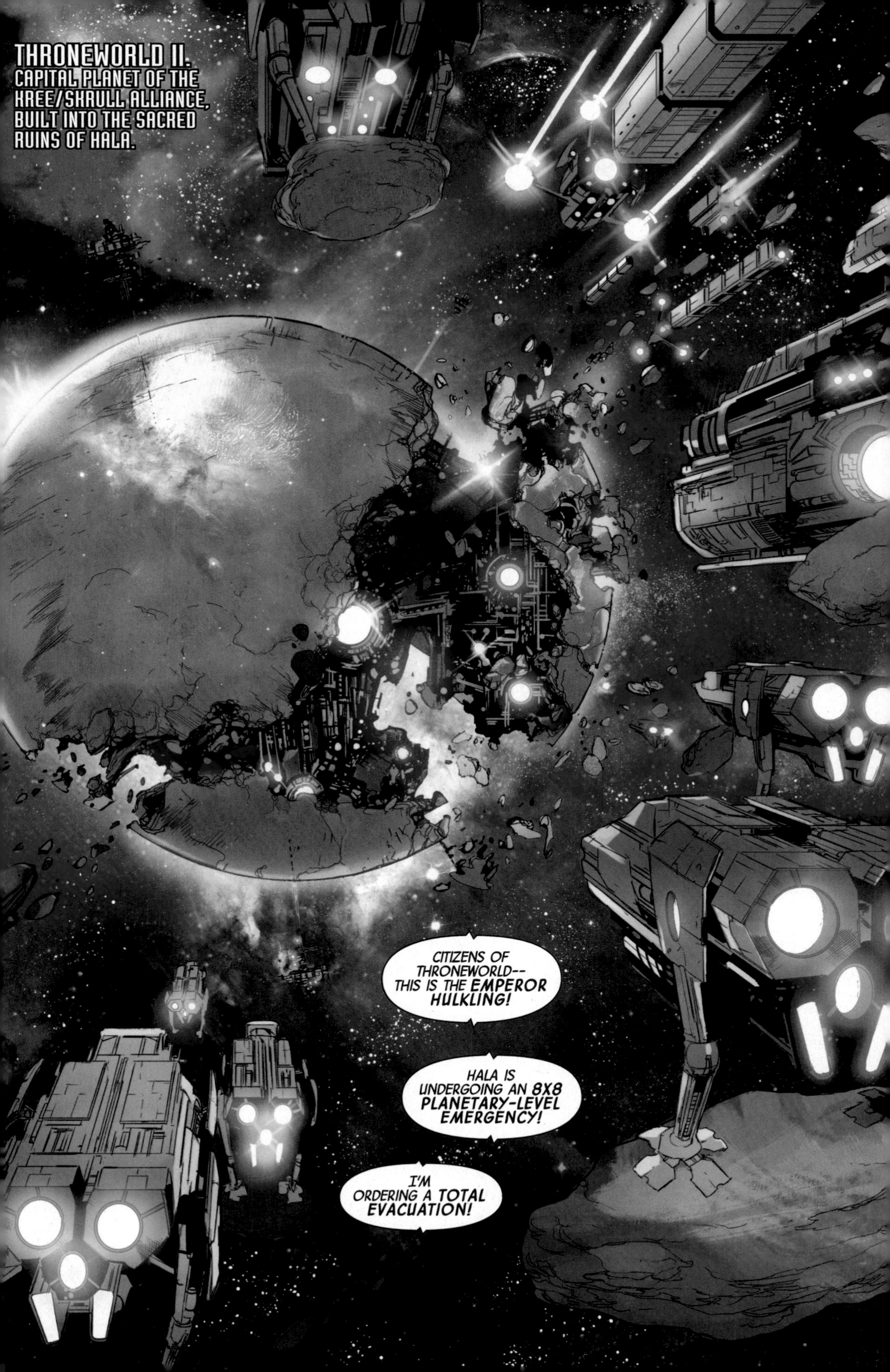
THRONEWORLD II.
CAPITAL PLANET OF THE KREE/SKRULL ALLIANCE, BUILT INTO THE SACRED RUINS OF HALA.
CITIZENS OF THRONEWORLD-- THIS IS THE EMPEROR HULKLING!
HALA IS UNDERGOING AN 8X8 PLANETARY-LEVEL EMERGENCY!
I'M ORDERING A TOTAL EVACUATION!

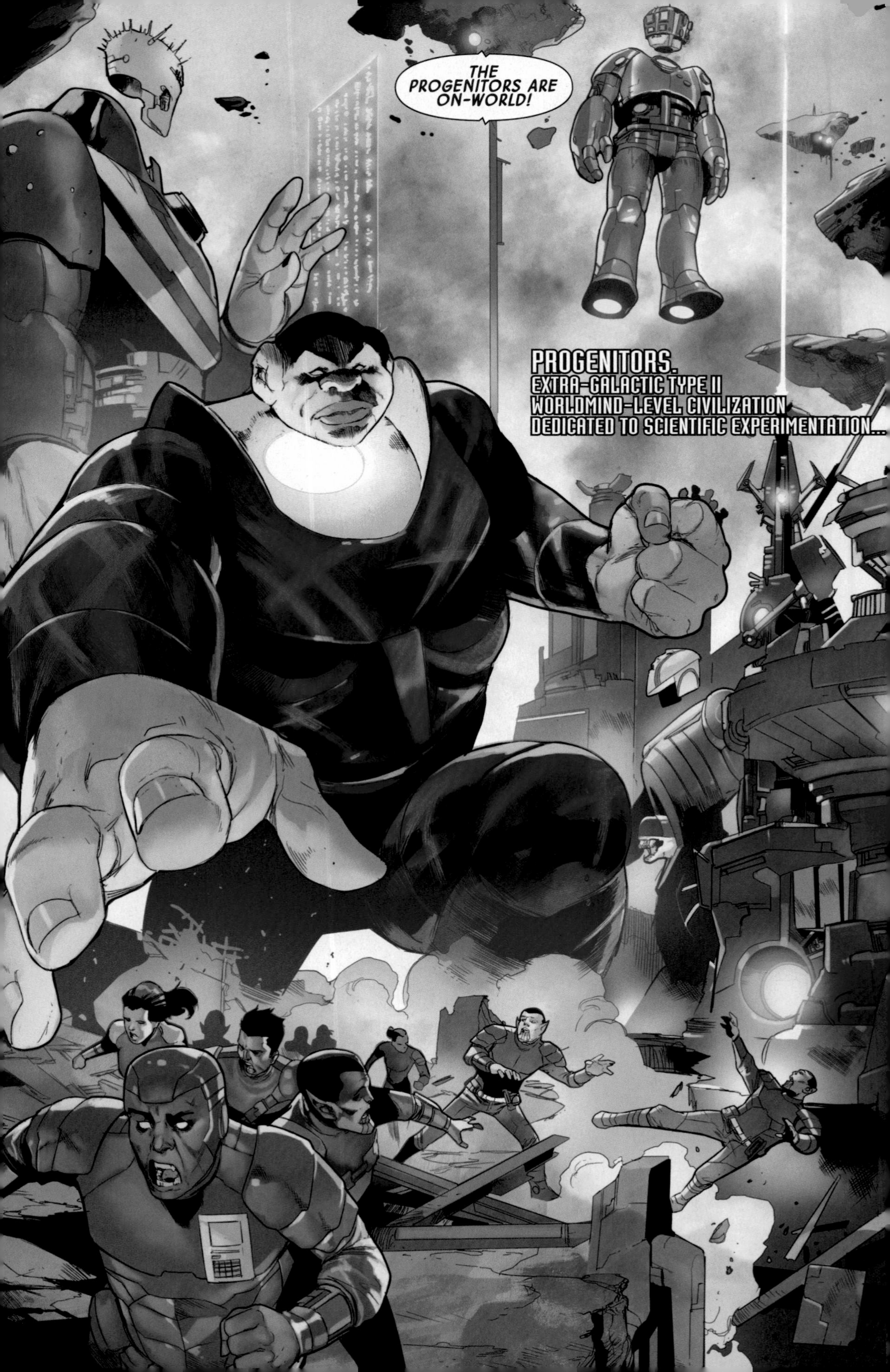
THE PROGENITORS ARE ON-WORLD!
PROGENITORS.
EXTRA-GALACTIC TYPE II
WORLDMIND-LEVEL CIVILIZATION
DEDICATED TO SCIENTIFIC EXPERIMENTATION...

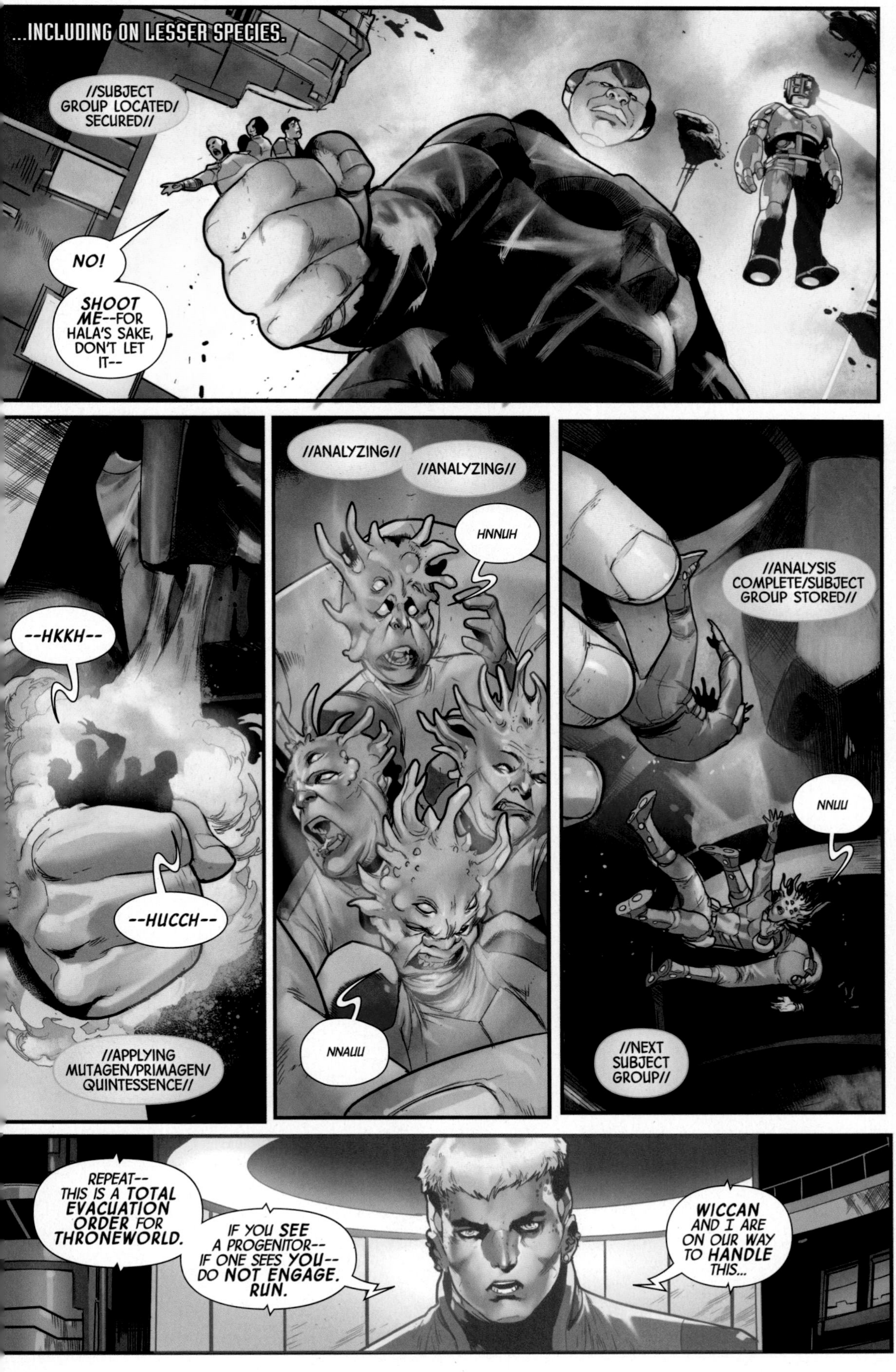
...INCLUDING ON LESSER SPECIES.
//SUBJECT GROUP LOCATED/ SECURED//
NO!
SHOOT ME--FOR HALA'S SAKE, DON'T LET IT--
--HKKH--
--HUCCH--
//APPLYING MUTAGEN/PRIMAGEN/ QUINTESSENCE//
//ANALYZING//
//ANALYZING//
HNNUH
NNAUU
//ANALYSIS COMPLETE/SUBJECT GROUP STORED//
NNUU
//NEXT SUBJECT GROUP//
REPEAT-- THIS IS A TOTAL EVACUATION ORDER FOR THRONEWORLD.
IF YOU SEE A PROGENITOR-- IF ONE SEES YOU-- DO NOT ENGAGE. RUN.
WICCAN AND I ARE ON OUR WAY TO HANDLE THIS...

"...AND WE'RE BRINGING **HELP**."

NOVA-- WE HAVE AN **SXS** ALERT FROM **THRONEWORLD**.

PROGENITOR INCURSION.

THE PROSCENIUM. INTERSTELLAR DIPLOMATIC STATION AND HEADQUARTERS FOR GALACTIC PEACEKEEPING EFFORTS.

MAKE THAT YOUR **PRIORITY**.

I **TOLD** YOU, **SUPER-SKRULL--** THAT'S NOT HOW IT **WORKS**.

WE DON'T TAKE ORDERS FROM **GALACTIC COUNCIL MEMBERS--**

THRONEWORLD: CONDITION RED. PROGENITOR INCURSION.

SOL: CONDITION YELL POTENTIAL KORV IRON MAN IS RE

--ANY MORE THAN THE **AVENGERS** TAKE ORDERS FROM **EARTH'S** NATIONS.

WE'RE NOT YOUR **SOLDIERS** OR YOUR **COPS**, WE'RE **SUPER HEROES**, GUARDING THE **GALAXY--**

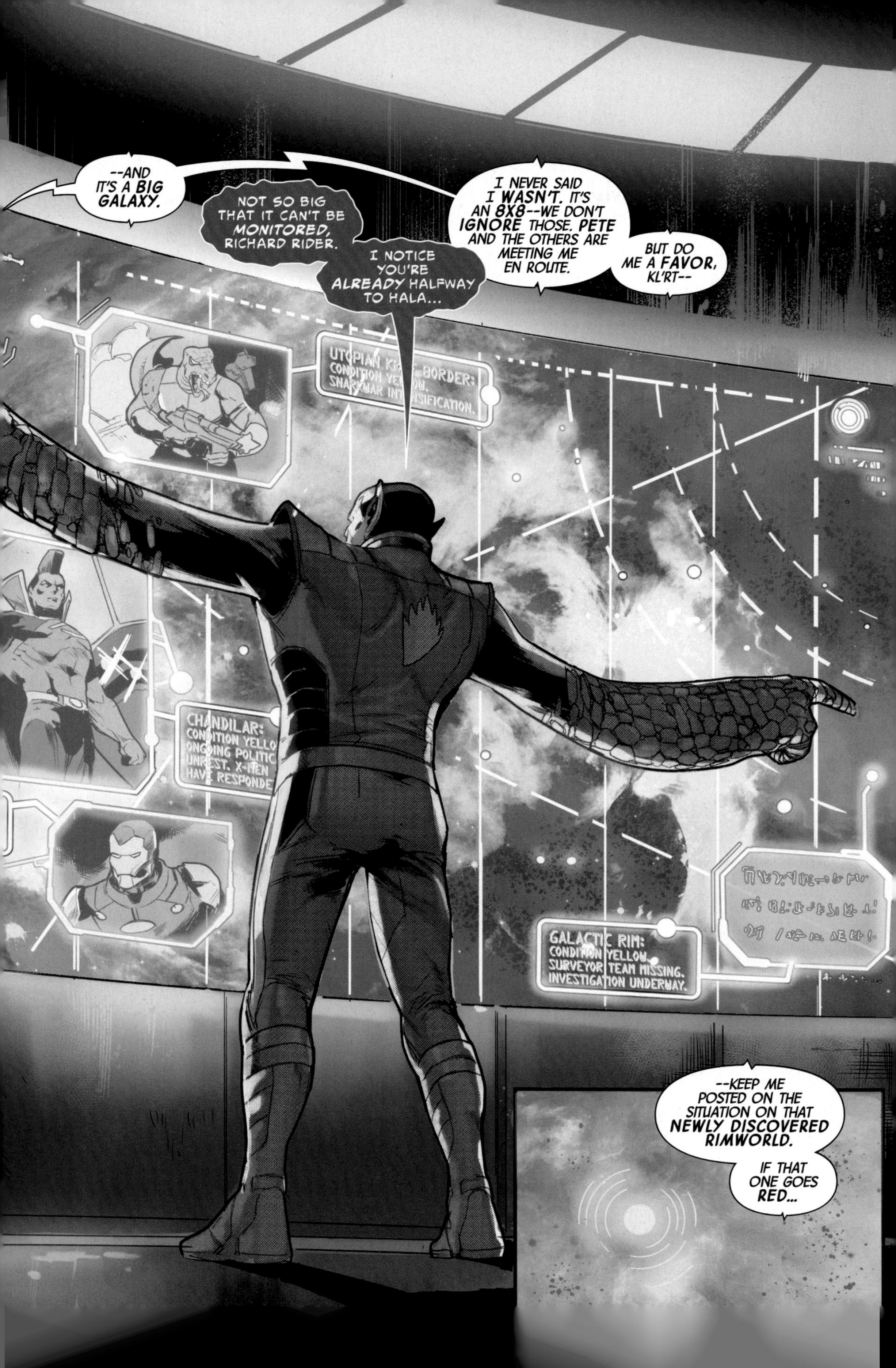

--AND IT'S A BIG GALAXY.
NOT SO BIG THAT IT CAN'T BE MONITORED, RICHARD RIDER.
I NOTICE YOU'RE ALREADY HALFWAY TO HALA...
I NEVER SAID I WASN'T. IT'S AN 8X8--WE DON'T IGNORE THOSE. PETE AND THE OTHERS ARE MEETING ME EN ROUTE.
BUT DO ME A FAVOR, KL'RT--
CONDITION YELLOW.
CHANDILAR:
GALACTIC RIM:
CONDITION YELLOW.
SURVEYOR TEAM MISSING.
INVESTIGATION UNDERWAY.
--KEEP ME POSTED ON THE SITUATION ON THAT NEWLY DISCOVERED RIMWORLD.
IF THAT ONE GOES RED...

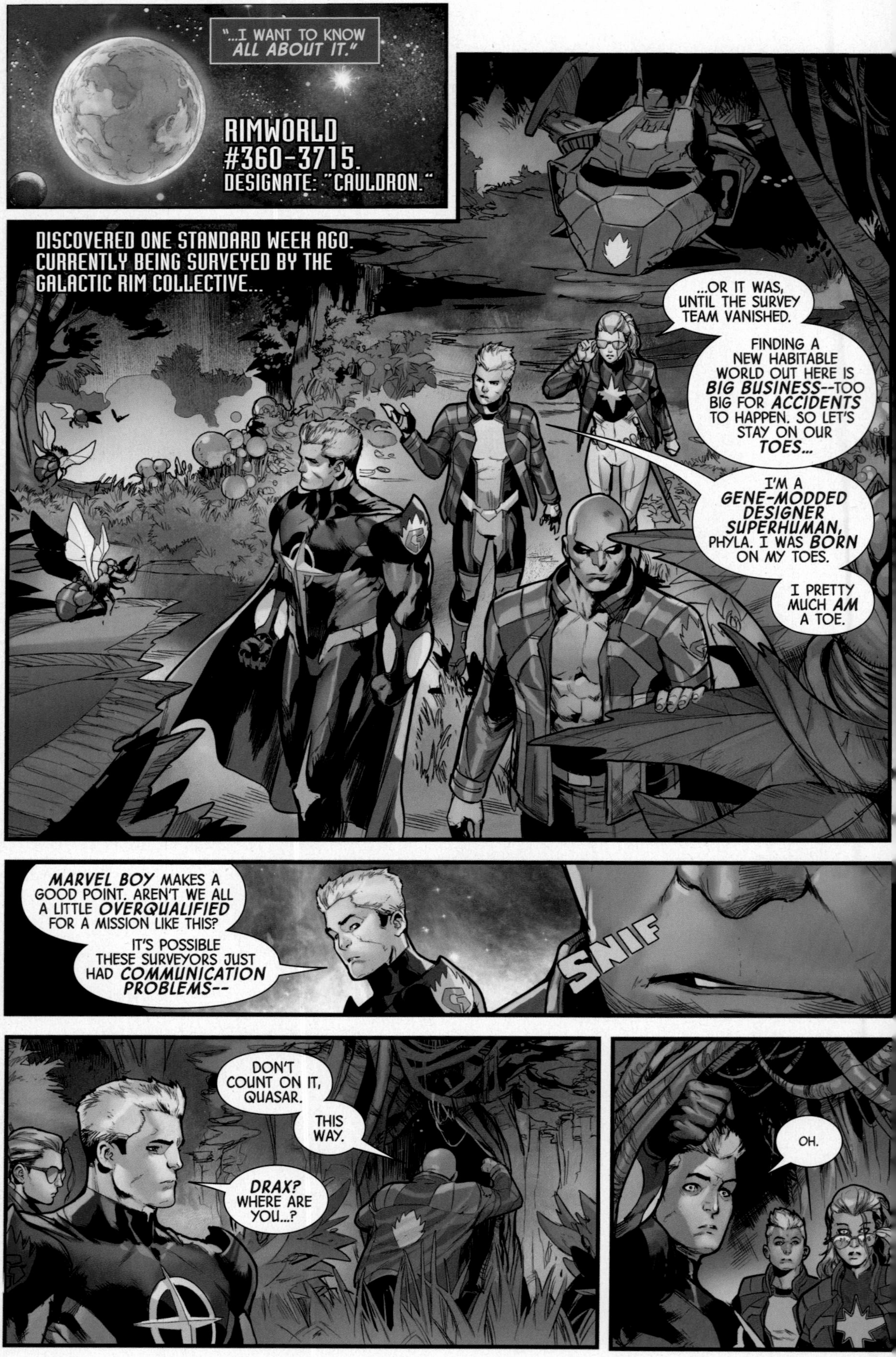
"...I WANT TO KNOW ALL ABOUT IT."
RIMWORLD #360-3715. DESIGNATE: "CAULDRON."
DISCOVERED ONE STANDARD WEEK AGO. CURRENTLY BEING SURVEYED BY THE GALACTIC RIM COLLECTIVE...
...OR IT WAS, UNTIL THE SURVEY TEAM VANISHED.
FINDING A NEW HABITABLE WORLD OUT HERE IS BIG BUSINESS--TOO BIG FOR ACCIDENTS TO HAPPEN. SO LET'S STAY ON OUR TOES...
I'M A GENE-MODDED DESIGNER SUPERHUMAN, PHYLA. I WAS BORN ON MY TOES.
I PRETTY MUCH AM A TOE.
MARVEL BOY MAKES A GOOD POINT. AREN'T WE ALL A LITTLE OVERQUALIFIED FOR A MISSION LIKE THIS?
IT'S POSSIBLE THESE SURVEYORS JUST HAD COMMUNICATION PROBLEMS--
SNIF
DON'T COUNT ON IT, QUASAR.
THIS WAY.
DRAX? WHERE ARE YOU...?
OH.

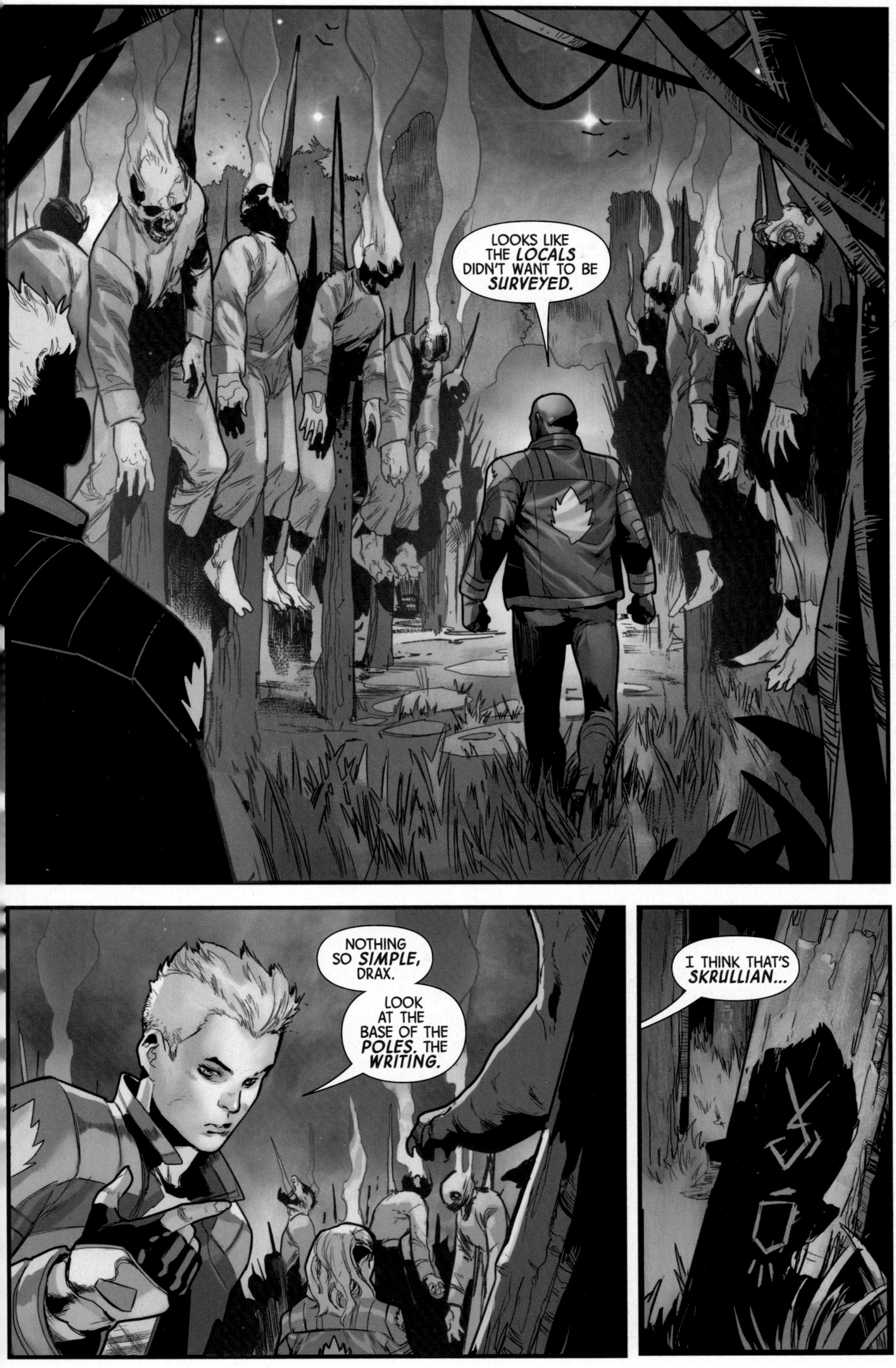
LOOKS LIKE THE LOCALS DIDN'T WANT TO BE SURVEYED.
NOTHING SO SIMPLE, DRAX.
LOOK AT THE BASE OF THE POLES. THE WRITING.
I THINK THAT'S SKRULLIAN...

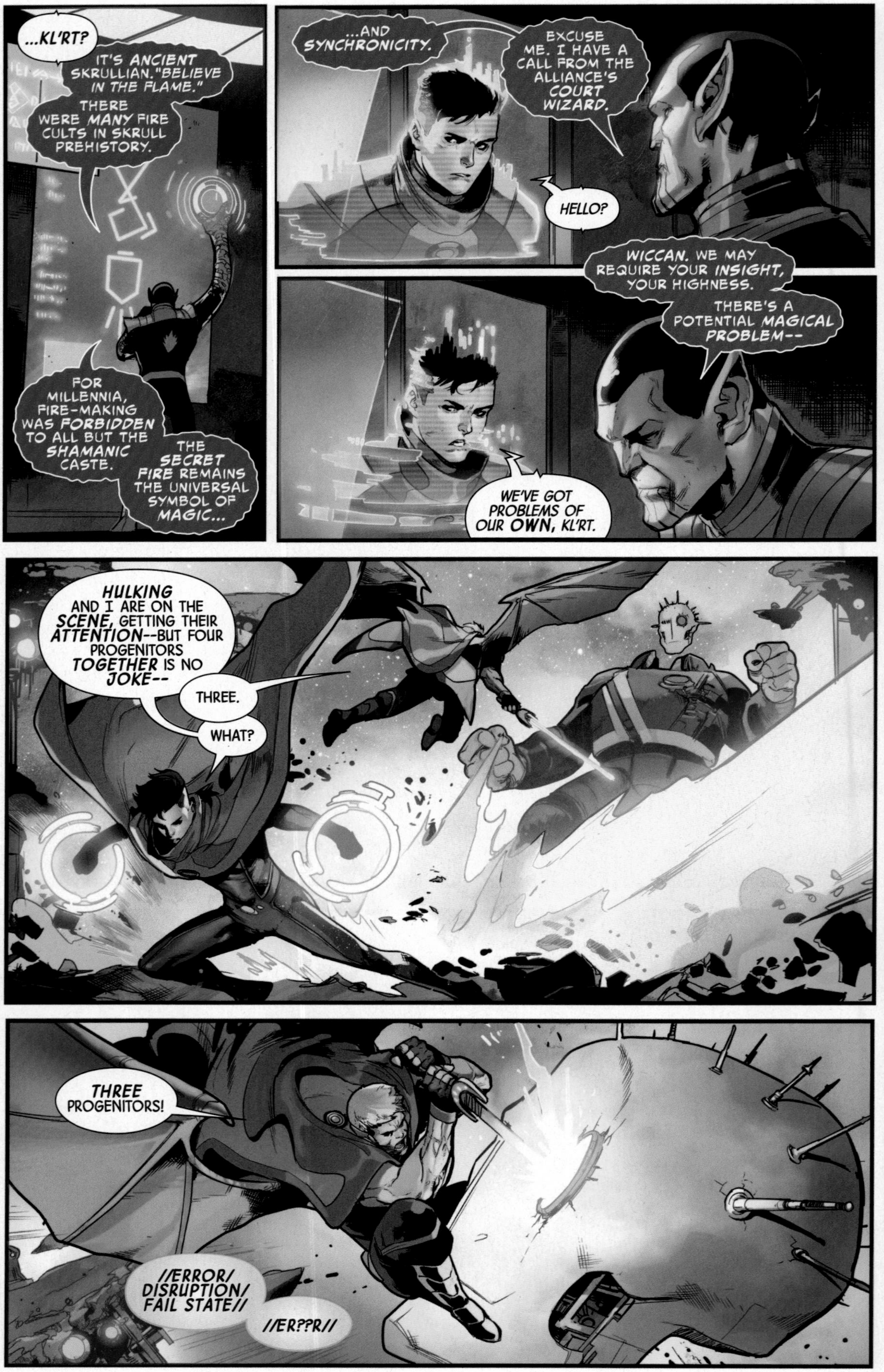
...KL'RT?
IT'S ANCIENT SKRULLIAN. "BELIEVE IN THE FLAME."
THERE WERE MANY FIRE CULTS IN SKRULL PREHISTORY.
FOR MILLENNIA, FIRE-MAKING WAS FORBIDDEN TO ALL BUT THE SHAMANIC CASTE.
THE SECRET FIRE REMAINS THE UNIVERSAL SYMBOL OF MAGIC...
...AND SYNCHRONICITY.
EXCUSE ME. I HAVE A CALL FROM THE ALLIANCE'S COURT WIZARD.
HELLO?
WICCAN. WE MAY REQUIRE YOUR INSIGHT, YOUR HIGHNESS.
THERE'S A POTENTIAL MAGICAL PROBLEM--
WE'VE GOT PROBLEMS OF OUR OWN, KL'RT.
HULKING AND I ARE ON THE SCENE, GETTING THEIR ATTENTION--BUT FOUR PROGENITORS TOGETHER IS NO JOKE--
THREE.
WHAT?
THREE PROGENITORS!
//ERROR/ DISRUPTION/ FAIL STATE//
//ER??R//

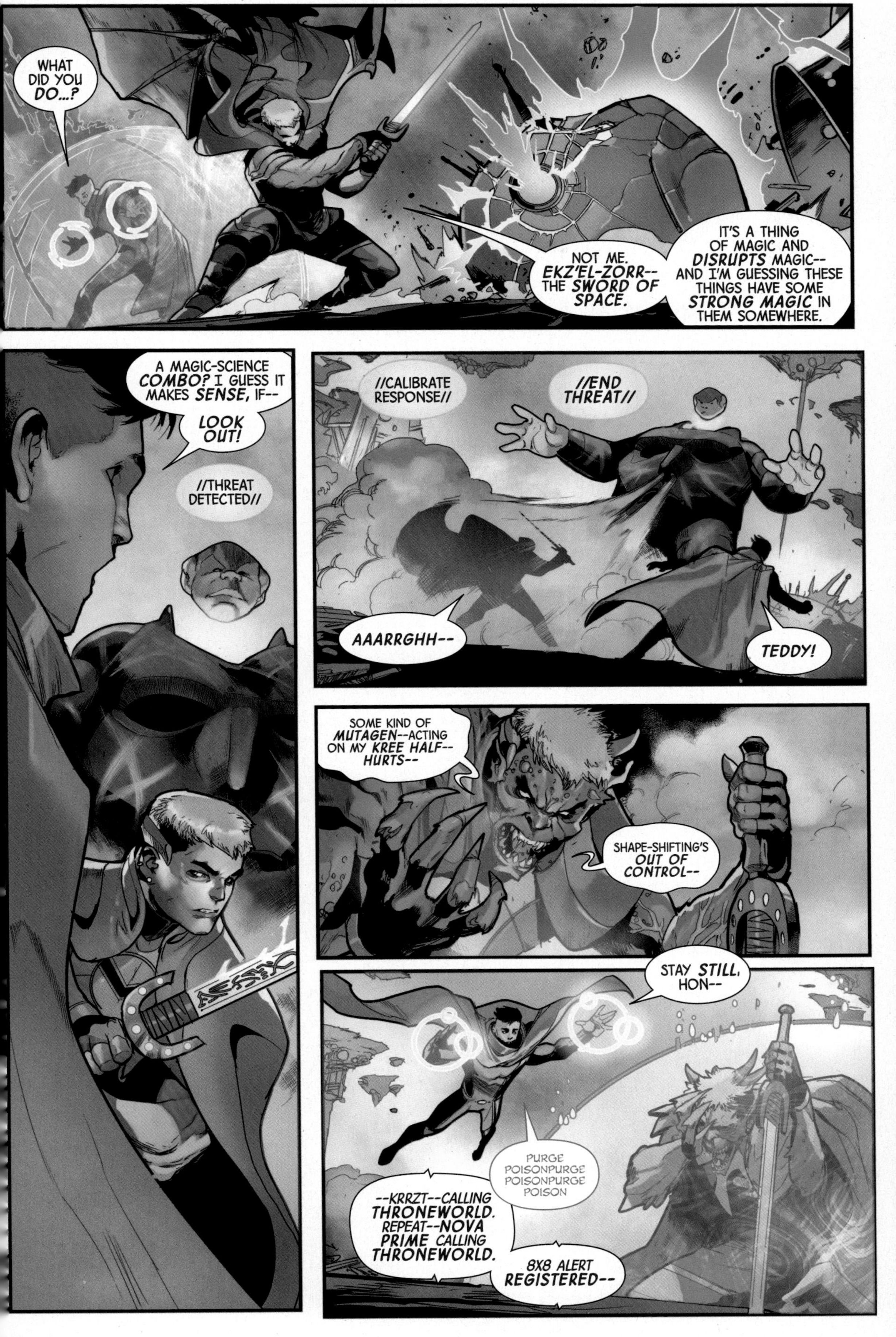
WHAT DID YOU DO...?
NOT ME. EKZ'EL-ZORR-- THE SWORD OF SPACE.
IT'S A THING OF MAGIC AND DISRUPTS MAGIC-- AND I'M GUESSING THESE THINGS HAVE SOME STRONG MAGIC IN THEM SOMEWHERE.
A MAGIC-SCIENCE COMBO? I GUESS IT MAKES SENSE, IF--
LOOK OUT!
//THREAT DETECTED//
//CALIBRATE RESPONSE//
//END THREAT//
AAARRGHH--
TEDDY!
SOME KIND OF MUTAGEN--ACTING ON MY KREE HALF-- HURTS--
SHAPE-SHIFTING'S OUT OF CONTROL--
STAY STILL, HON--
PURGE POISONPURGE POISONPURGE POISON
--KRRZT--CALLING THRONEWORLD. REPEAT--NOVA PRIME CALLING THRONEWORLD.
8X8 ALERT REGISTERED--

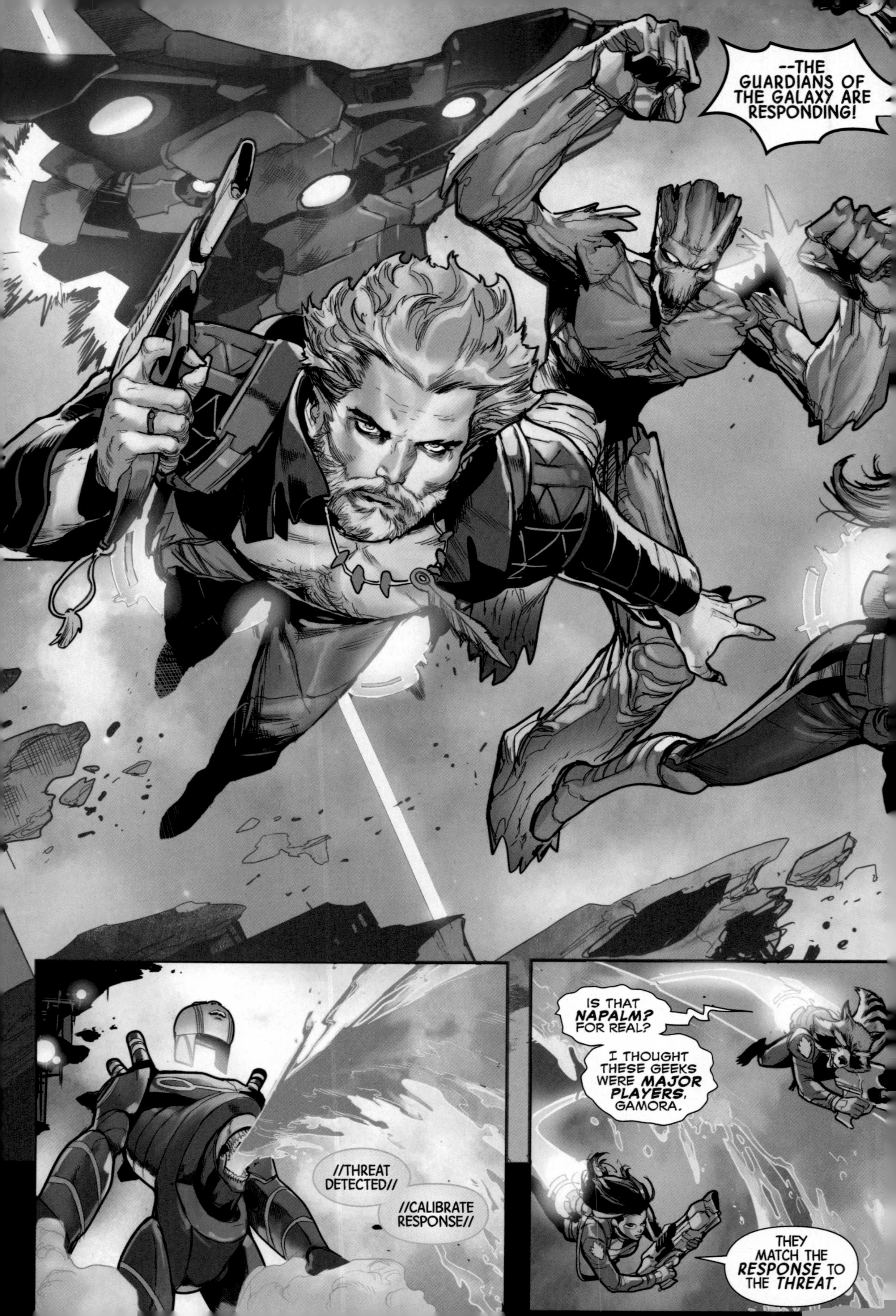
--THE GUARDIANS OF THE GALAXY ARE RESPONDING!
//THREAT DETECTED//
//CALIBRATE RESPONSE//
IS THAT NAPALM? FOR REAL?
I THOUGHT THESE GEEKS WERE MAJOR PLAYERS, GAMORA.
THEY MATCH THE RESPONSE TO THE THREAT.

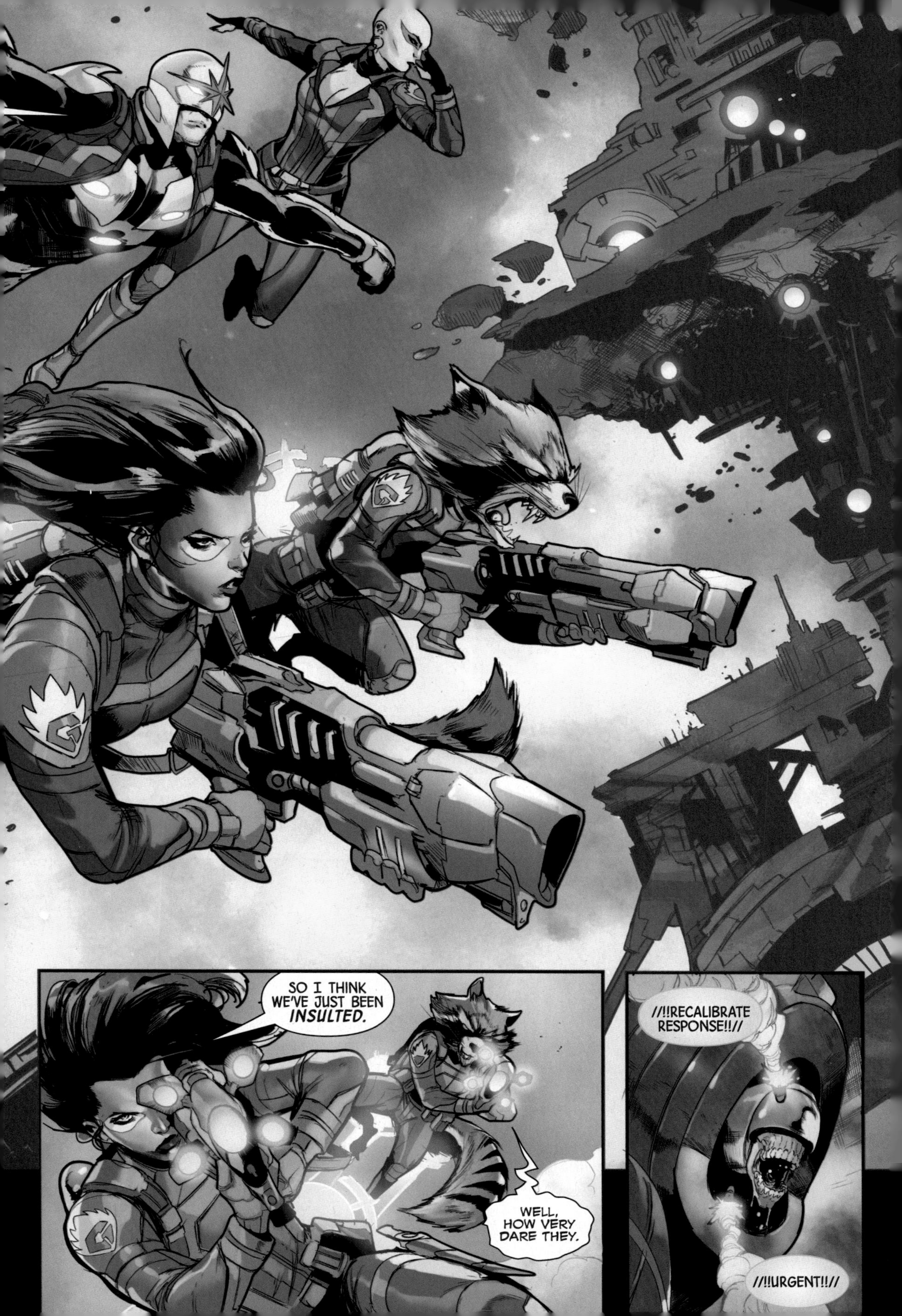
SO I THINK WE'VE JUST BEEN *INSULTED.*
WELL, HOW VERY DARE THEY.
//!!RECALIBRATE RESPONSE!!//
//!!URGENT!!//

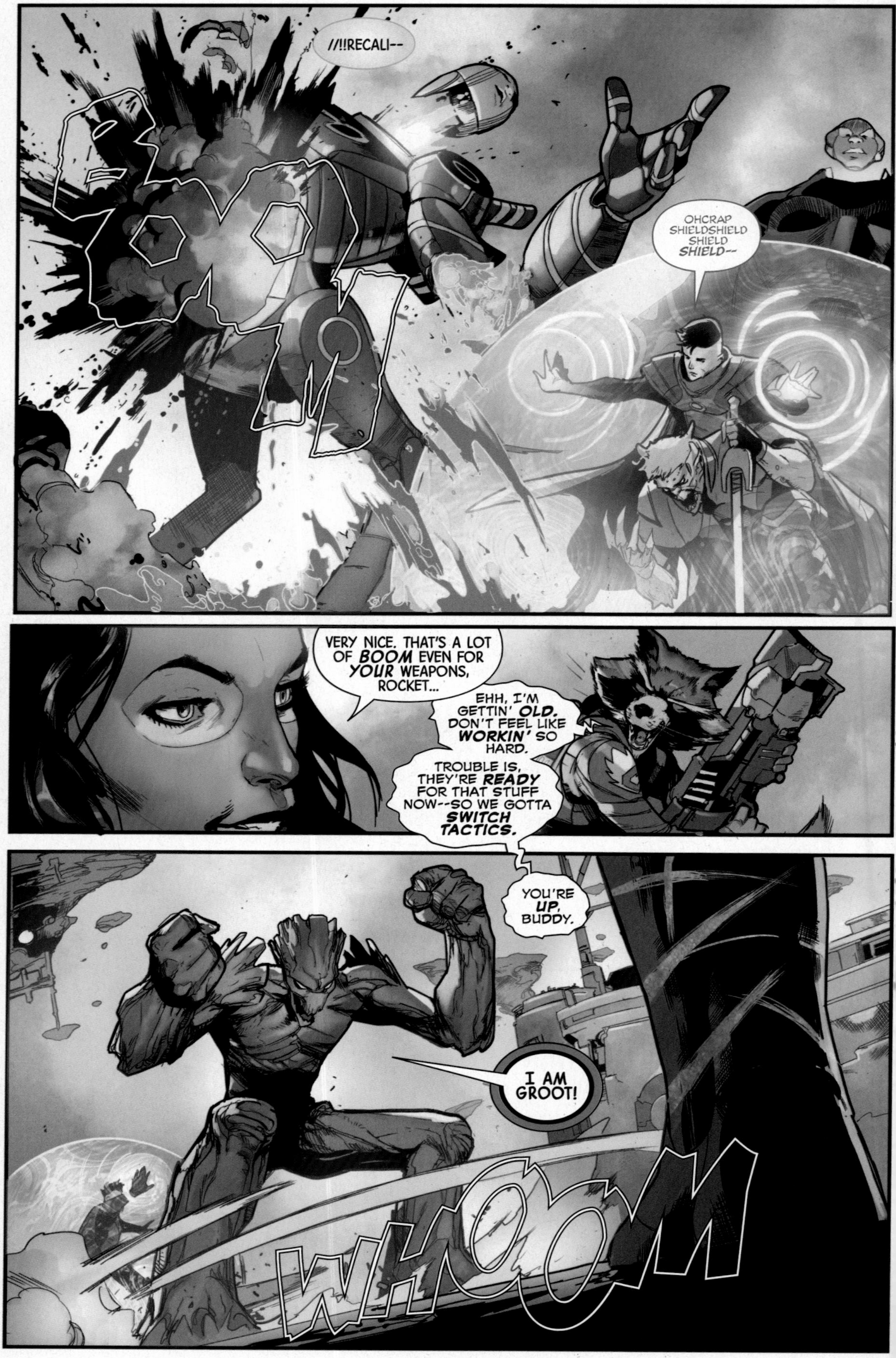
//!!RECALI--
BOOM
OHCRAP SHIELDSHIELD SHIELD SHIELD--
VERY NICE. THAT'S A LOT OF BOOM EVEN FOR YOUR WEAPONS, ROCKET...
EHH, I'M GETTIN' OLD. DON'T FEEL LIKE WORKIN' SO HARD.
TROUBLE IS, THEY'RE READY FOR THAT STUFF NOW--SO WE GOTTA SWITCH TACTICS.
YOU'RE UP, BUDDY.
I AM GROOT!
WHOOOM

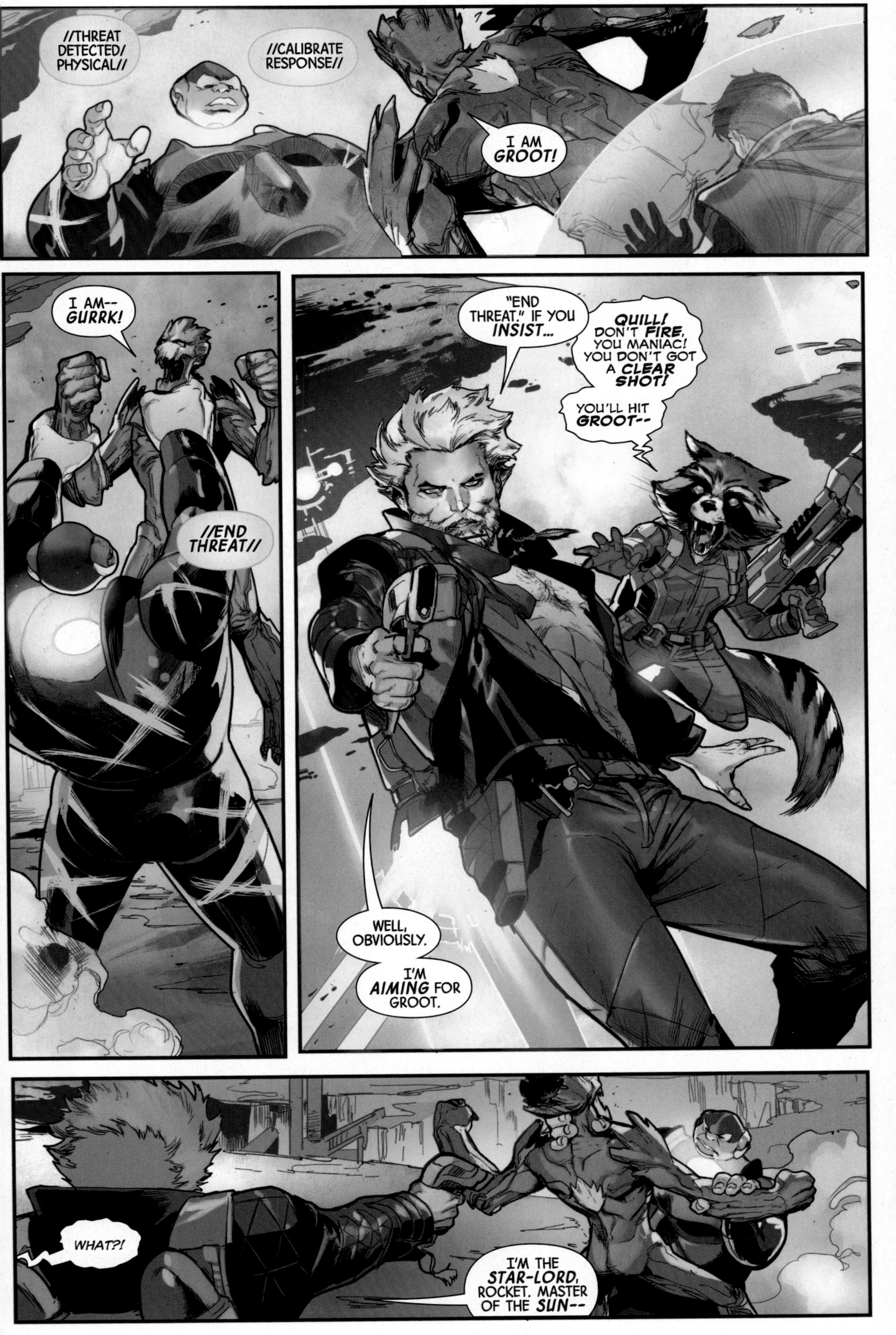
//THREAT DETECTED/ PHYSICAL//
//CALIBRATE RESPONSE//
I AM GROOT!
I AM-- GURRK!
//END THREAT//
"END THREAT." IF YOU INSIST...
QUILL! DON'T FIRE, YOU MANIAC! YOU DON'T GOT A CLEAR SHOT!
YOU'LL HIT GROOT--
WELL, OBVIOUSLY.
I'M AIMING FOR GROOT.
WHAT?!
I'M THE STAR-LORD, ROCKET. MASTER OF THE SUN--

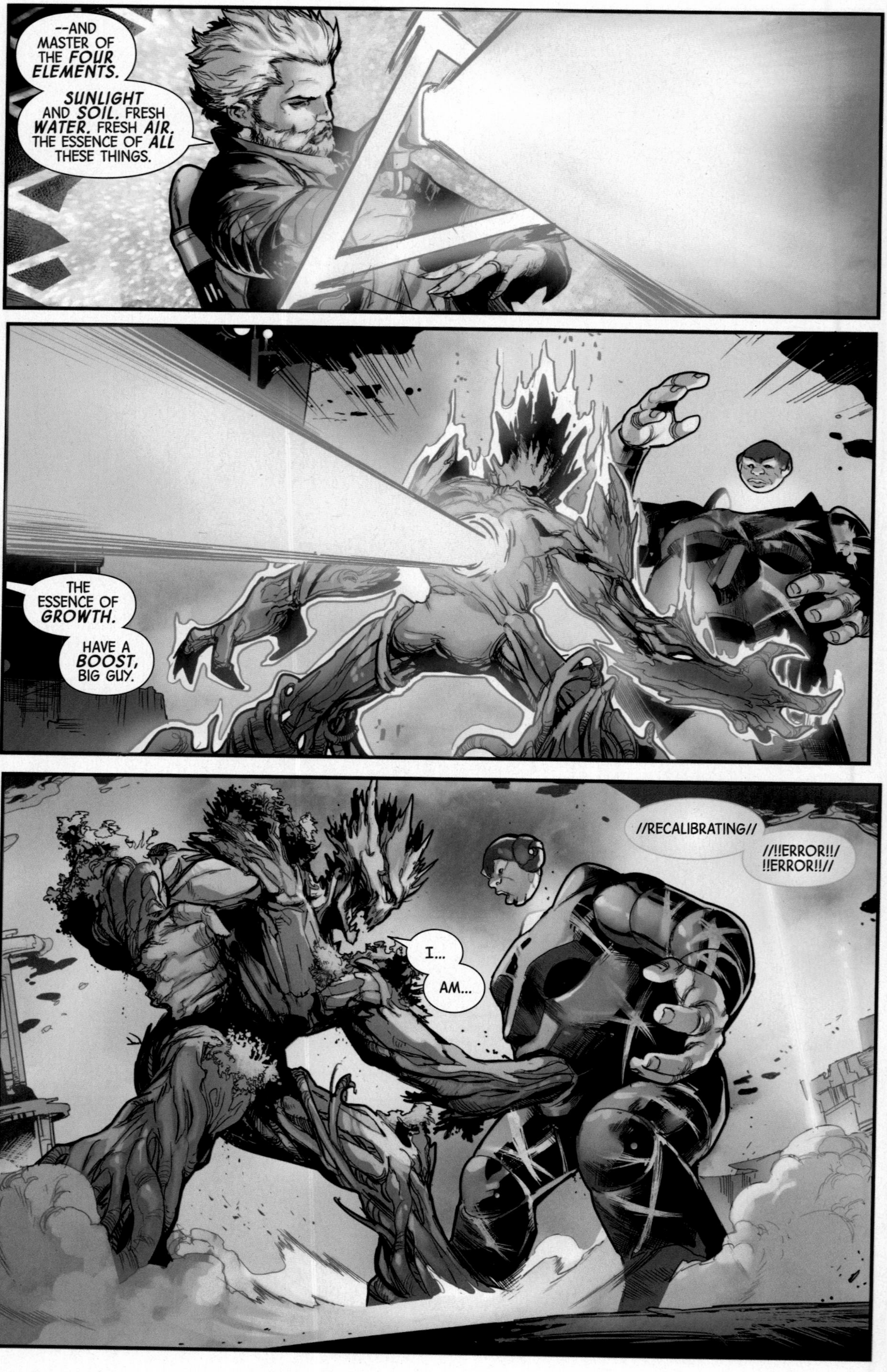

--AND MASTER OF THE FOUR ELEMENTS.
SUNLIGHT AND SOIL. FRESH WATER. FRESH AIR. THE ESSENCE OF ALL THESE THINGS.
THE ESSENCE OF GROWTH.
HAVE A BOOST, BIG GUY.
//RECALIBRATING//
//!!ERROR!!/ !!ERROR!!//
I...
AM...

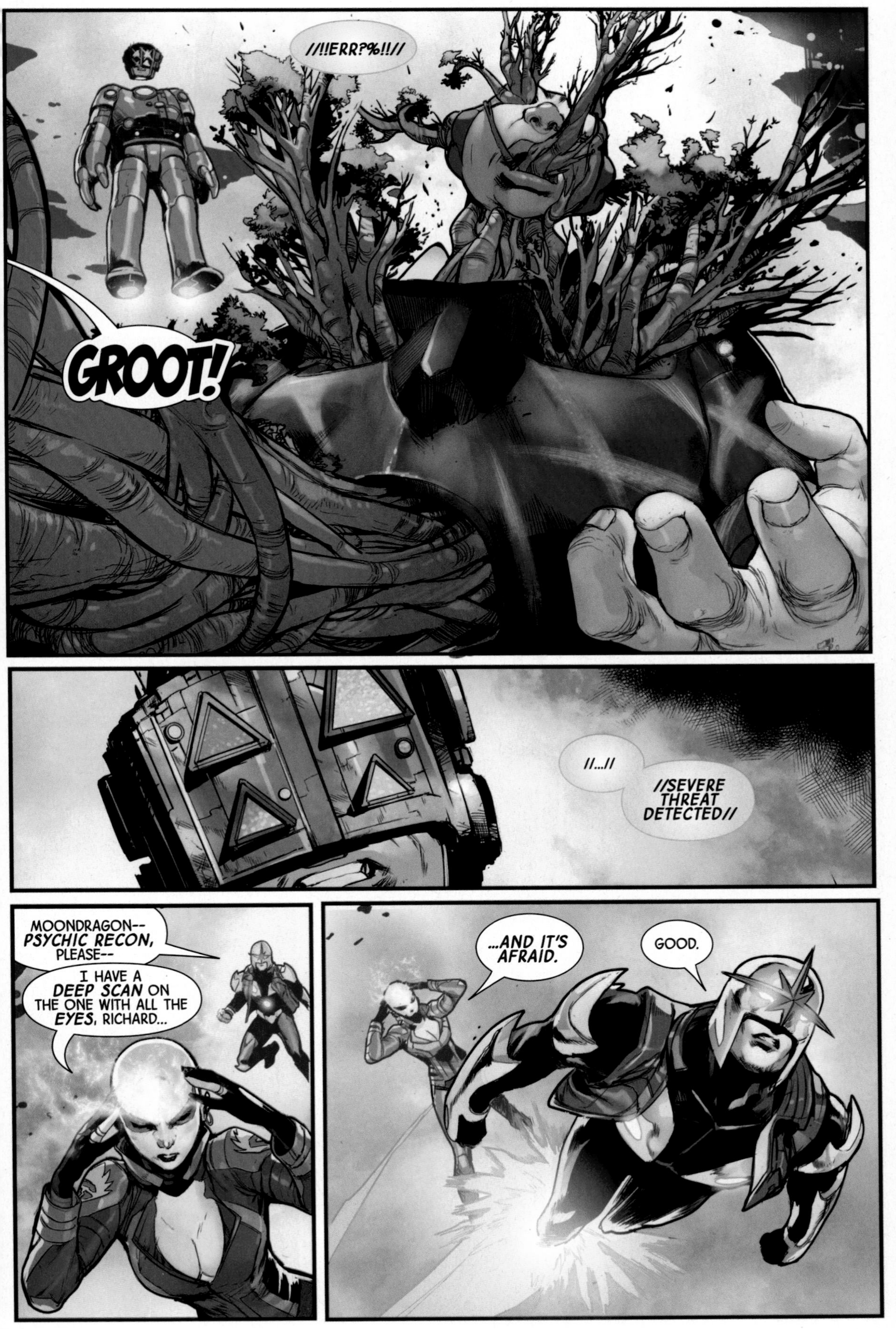
//!!ERR?%!!//
GROOT!
//...//
//SEVERE THREAT DETECTED//
MOONDRAGON-- PSYCHIC RECON, PLEASE--
I HAVE A DEEP SCAN ON THE ONE WITH ALL THE EYES, RICHARD...
...AND IT'S AFRAID.
GOOD.

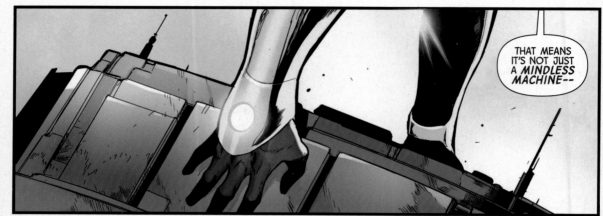

THAT MEANS IT'S NOT JUST A *MINDLESS MACHINE*--

--DESPITE *APPEARANCES.*

//ERROR//

///MAGNETIC FIELD DISTURBANCE/ DISRUPTION//

///!!INTEGRITY COMPROMISED!!//

///!!CONNECTION SEVERED!!//

///!!ERROR!!//

OH, SHUT UP WITH THAT--

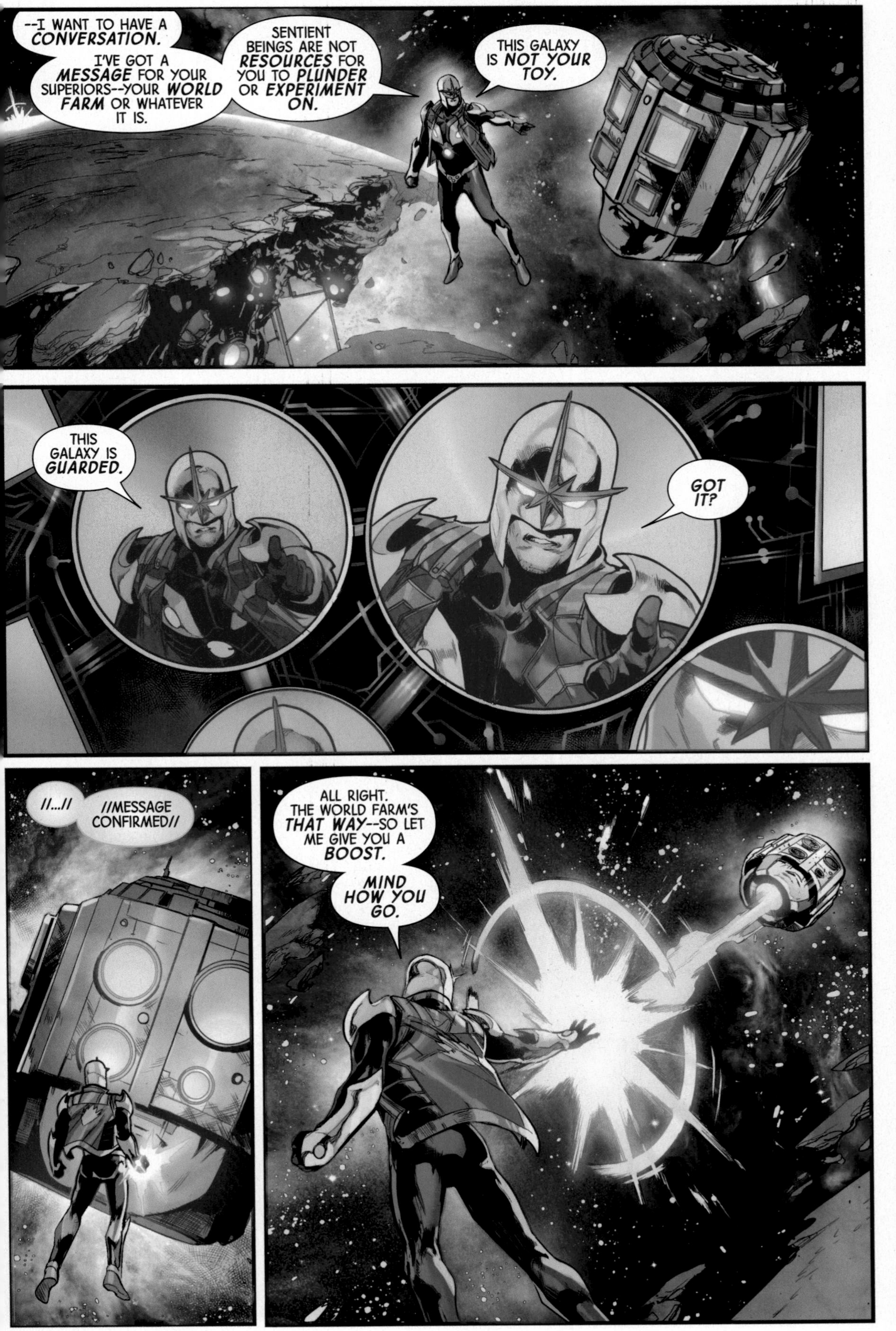
--I WANT TO HAVE A CONVERSATION.
I'VE GOT A MESSAGE FOR YOUR SUPERIORS--YOUR WORLD FARM OR WHATEVER IT IS.
SENTIENT BEINGS ARE NOT RESOURCES FOR YOU TO PLUNDER OR EXPERIMENT ON.
THIS GALAXY IS NOT YOUR TOY.
THIS GALAXY IS GUARDED.
GOT IT?
//...//
//MESSAGE CONFIRMED//
ALL RIGHT. THE WORLD FARM'S THAT WAY--SO LET ME GIVE YOU A BOOST.
MIND HOW YOU GO.

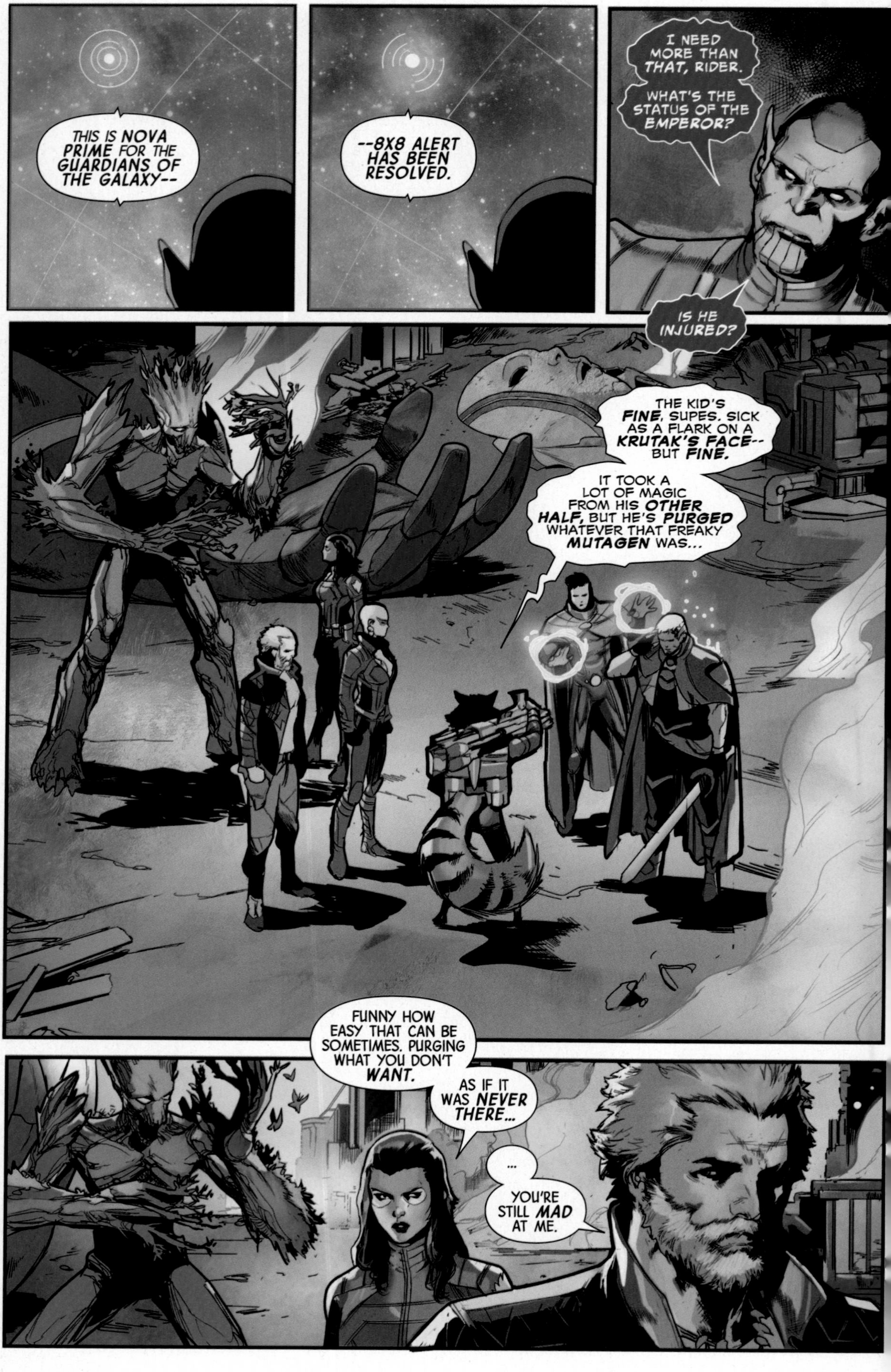
THIS IS NOVA PRIME FOR THE GUARDIANS OF THE GALAXY--
--8X8 ALERT HAS BEEN RESOLVED.
I NEED MORE THAN THAT, RIDER.
WHAT'S THE STATUS OF THE EMPEROR?
IS HE INJURED?
THE KID'S FINE, SUPES. SICK AS A FLARK ON A KRUTAK'S FACE-- BUT FINE.
IT TOOK A LOT OF MAGIC FROM HIS OTHER HALF, BUT HE'S PURGED WHATEVER THAT FREAKY MUTAGEN WAS...
FUNNY HOW EASY THAT CAN BE SOMETIMES. PURGING WHAT YOU DON'T WANT.
AS IF IT WAS NEVER THERE...
...
YOU'RE STILL MAD AT ME.

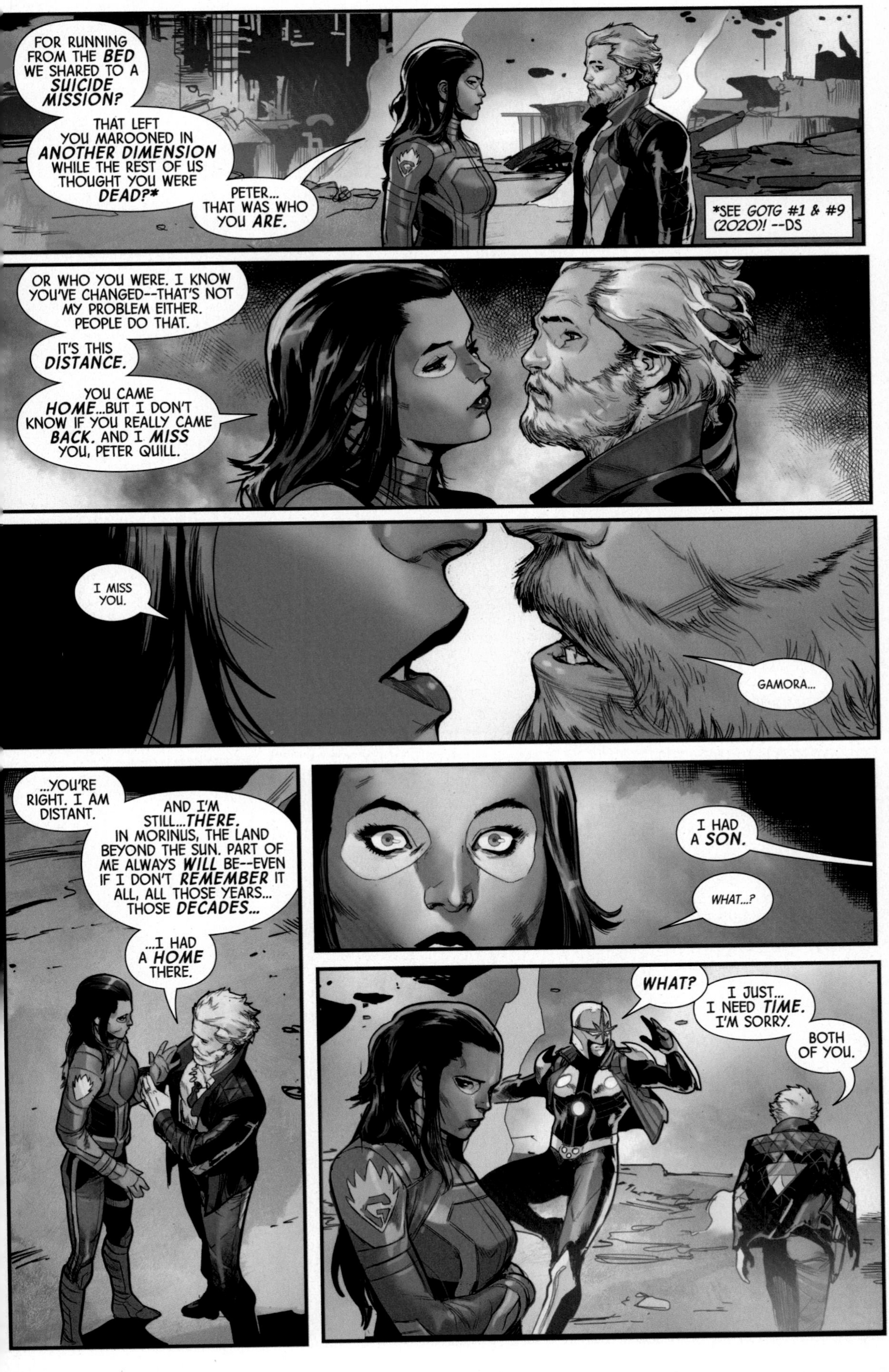
FOR RUNNING FROM THE BED WE SHARED TO A SUICIDE MISSION?
THAT LEFT YOU MAROONED IN ANOTHER DIMENSION WHILE THE REST OF US THOUGHT YOU WERE DEAD?*
PETER... THAT WAS WHO YOU ARE.
*SEE GOTG #1 & #9 (2020)! --DS
OR WHO YOU WERE. I KNOW YOU'VE CHANGED--THAT'S NOT MY PROBLEM EITHER. PEOPLE DO THAT.
IT'S THIS DISTANCE.
YOU CAME HOME...BUT I DON'T KNOW IF YOU REALLY CAME BACK. AND I MISS YOU, PETER QUILL.
I MISS YOU.
GAMORA...
...YOU'RE RIGHT. I AM DISTANT.
AND I'M STILL...THERE. IN MORINUS, THE LAND BEYOND THE SUN. PART OF ME ALWAYS WILL BE--EVEN IF I DON'T REMEMBER IT ALL, ALL THOSE YEARS... THOSE DECADES...
...I HAD A HOME THERE.
I HAD A SON.
WHAT...?
WHAT?
I JUST... I NEED TIME. I'M SORRY.
BOTH OF YOU.

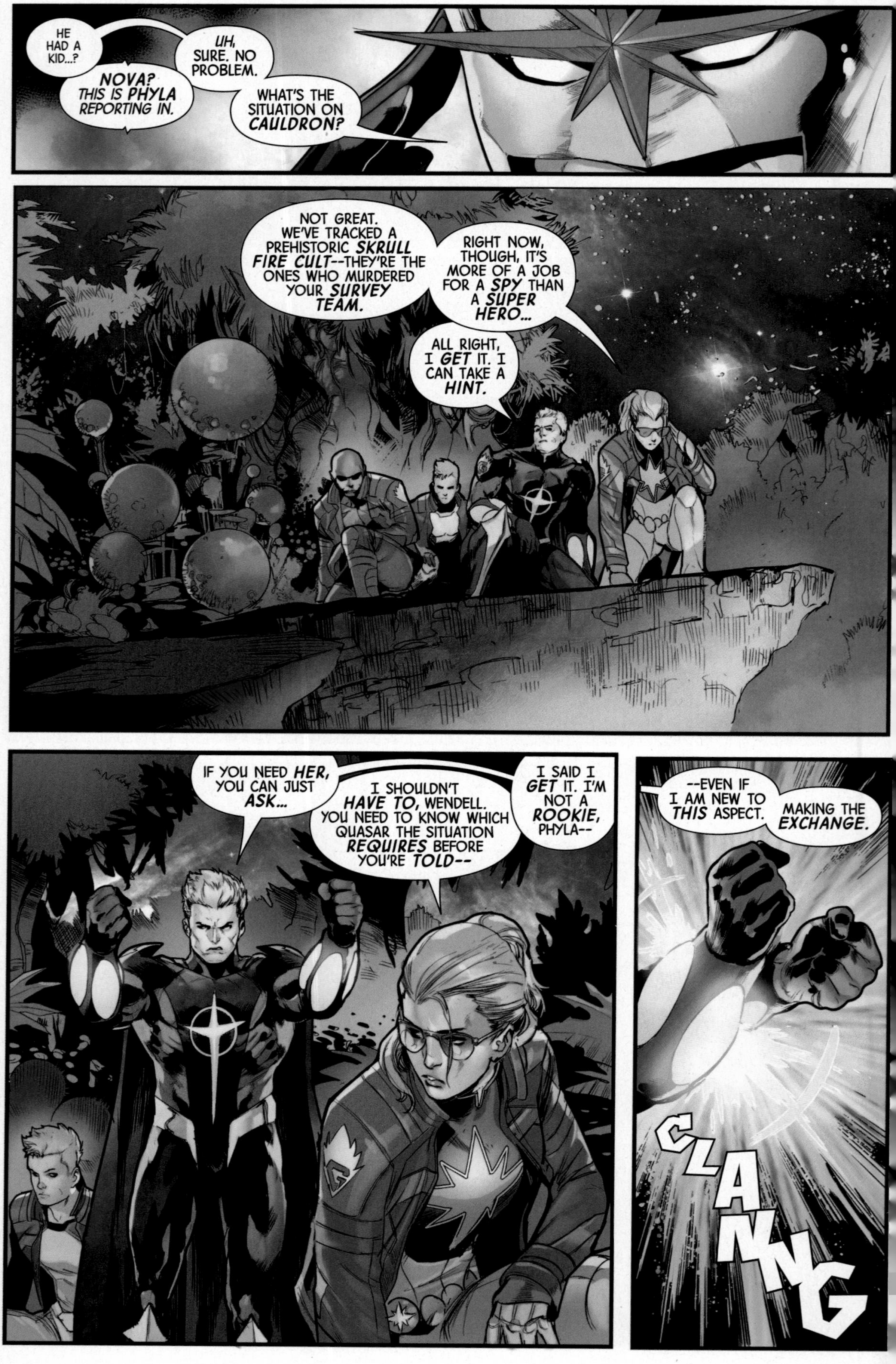

HE HAD A KID...?
NOVA? THIS IS PHYLA REPORTING IN.
UH, SURE. NO PROBLEM.
WHAT'S THE SITUATION ON CAULDRON?
NOT GREAT. WE'VE TRACKED A PREHISTORIC SKRULL FIRE CULT--THEY'RE THE ONES WHO MURDERED YOUR SURVEY TEAM.
RIGHT NOW, THOUGH, IT'S MORE OF A JOB FOR A SPY THAN A SUPER HERO...
ALL RIGHT, I GET IT. I CAN TAKE A HINT.
IF YOU NEED HER, YOU CAN JUST ASK...
I SHOULDN'T HAVE TO, WENDELL. YOU NEED TO KNOW WHICH QUASAR THE SITUATION REQUIRES BEFORE YOU'RE TOLD--
I SAID I GET IT. I'M NOT A ROOKIE, PHYLA--
--EVEN IF I AM NEW TO THIS ASPECT.
MAKING THE EXCHANGE.
CLANNNG

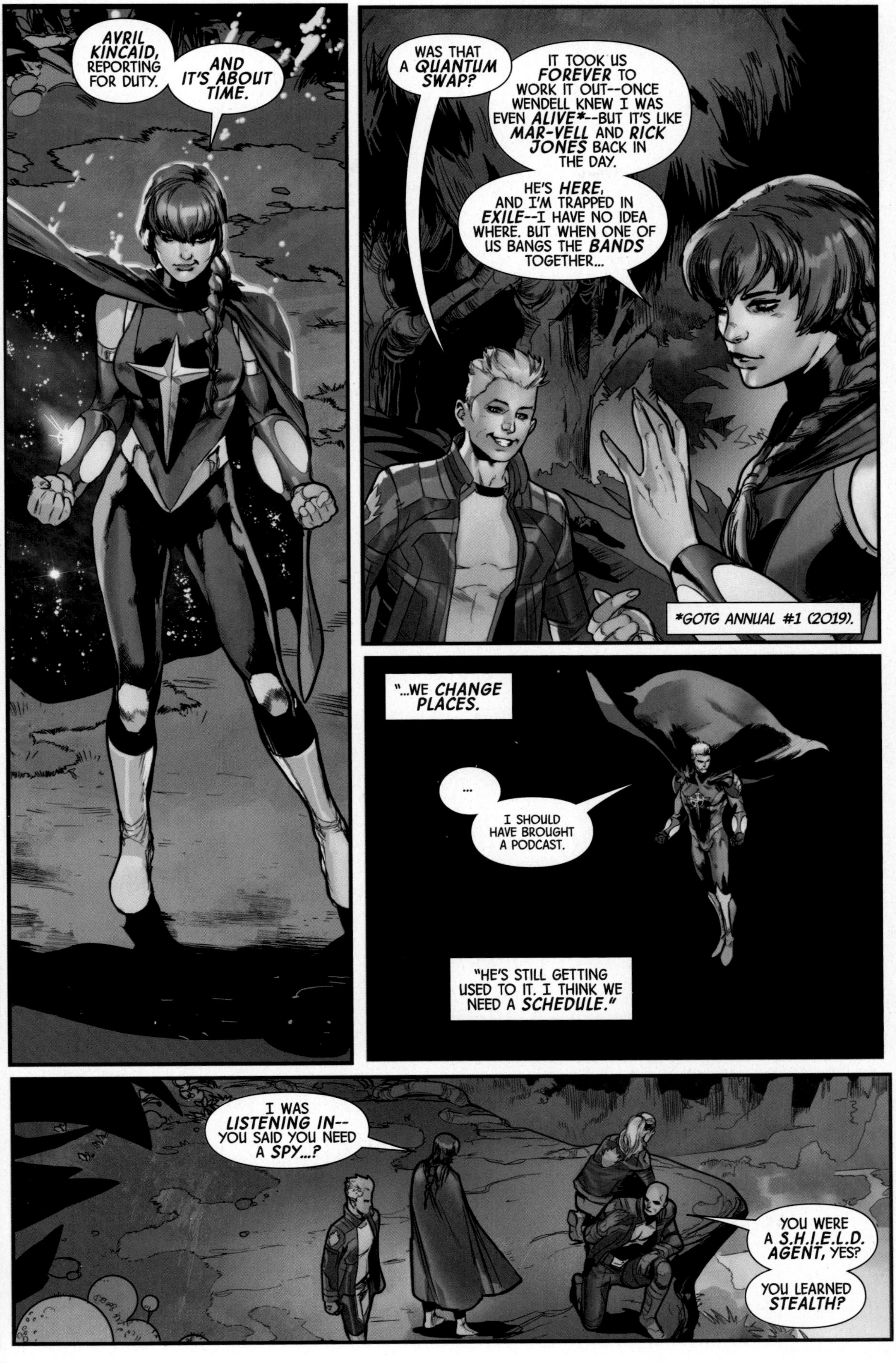
AVRIL KINCAID, REPORTING FOR DUTY.
AND IT'S ABOUT TIME.
WAS THAT A QUANTUM SWAP?
IT TOOK US FOREVER TO WORK IT OUT--ONCE WENDELL KNEW I WAS EVEN ALIVE*--BUT IT'S LIKE MAR-VELL AND RICK JONES BACK IN THE DAY.
HE'S HERE, AND I'M TRAPPED IN EXILE--I HAVE NO IDEA WHERE. BUT WHEN ONE OF US BANGS THE BANDS TOGETHER...
*GOTG ANNUAL #1 (2019).
"...WE CHANGE PLACES.
...
I SHOULD HAVE BROUGHT A PODCAST.
"HE'S STILL GETTING USED TO IT. I THINK WE NEED A SCHEDULE."
I WAS LISTENING IN--YOU SAID YOU NEED A SPY...?
YOU WERE A S.H.I.E.L.D. AGENT, YES?
YOU LEARNED STEALTH?

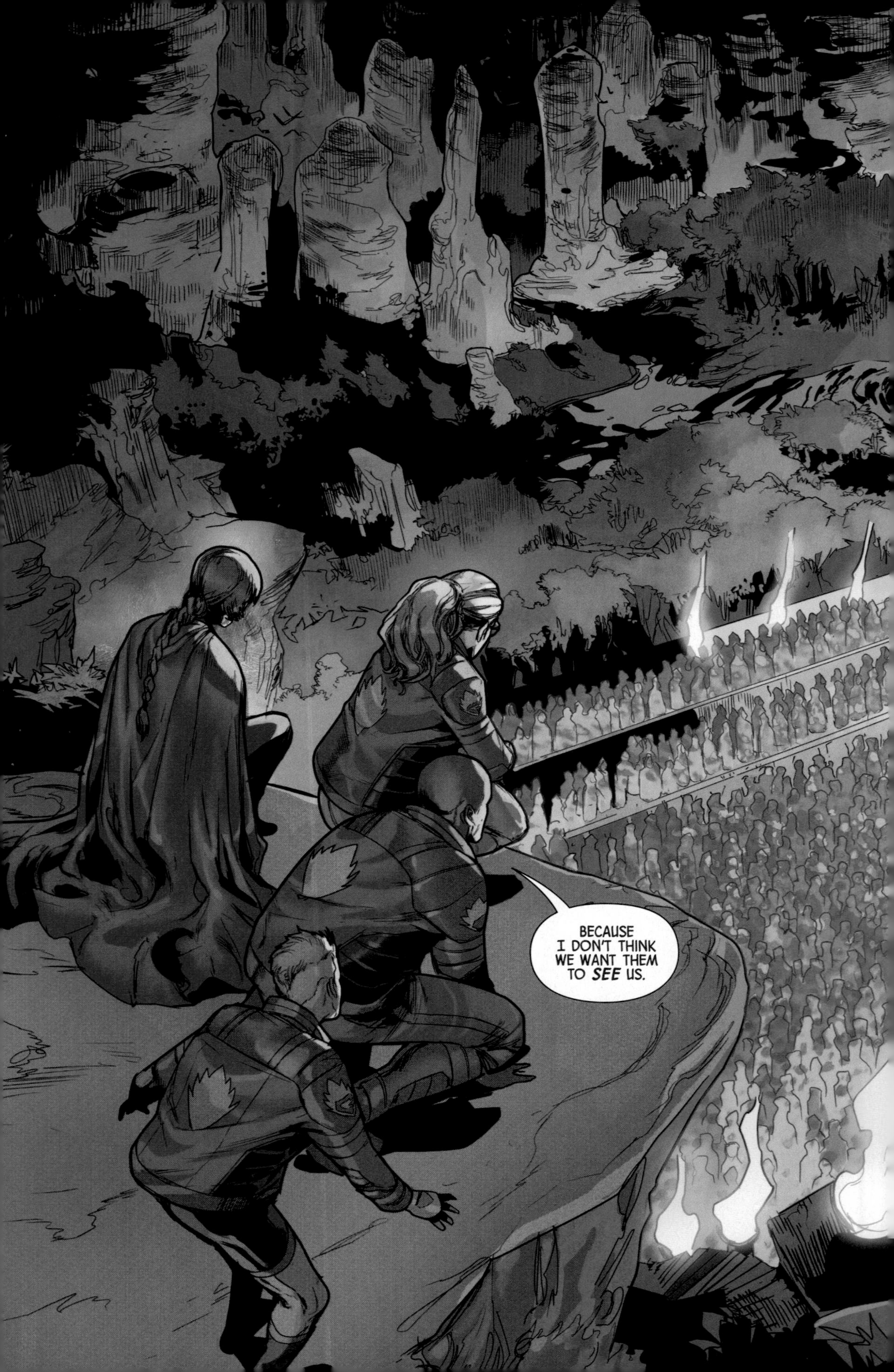
BECAUSE I DON'T THINK WE WANT THEM TO SEE US.

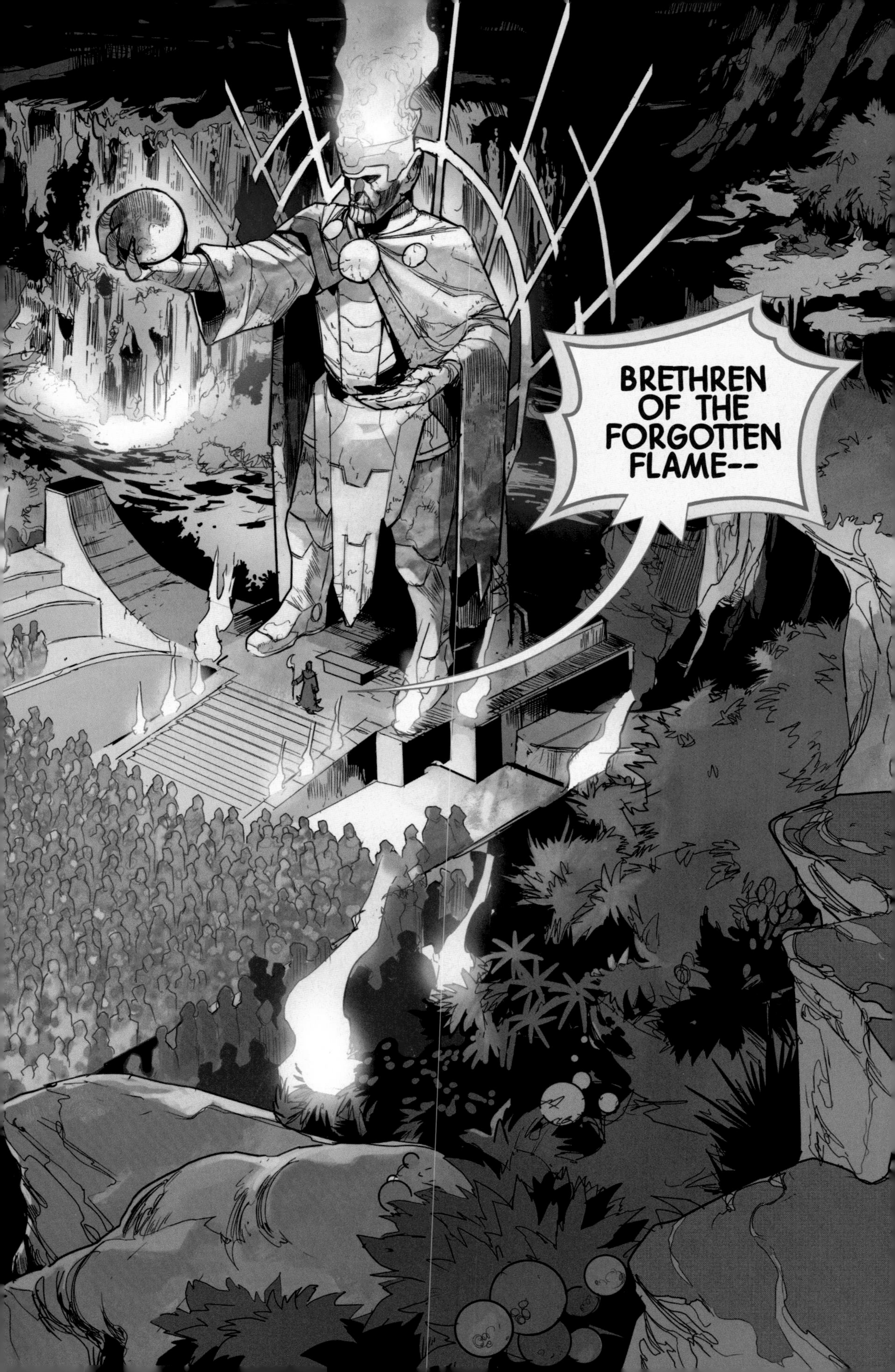
BRETHREN OF THE FORGOTTEN FLAME--

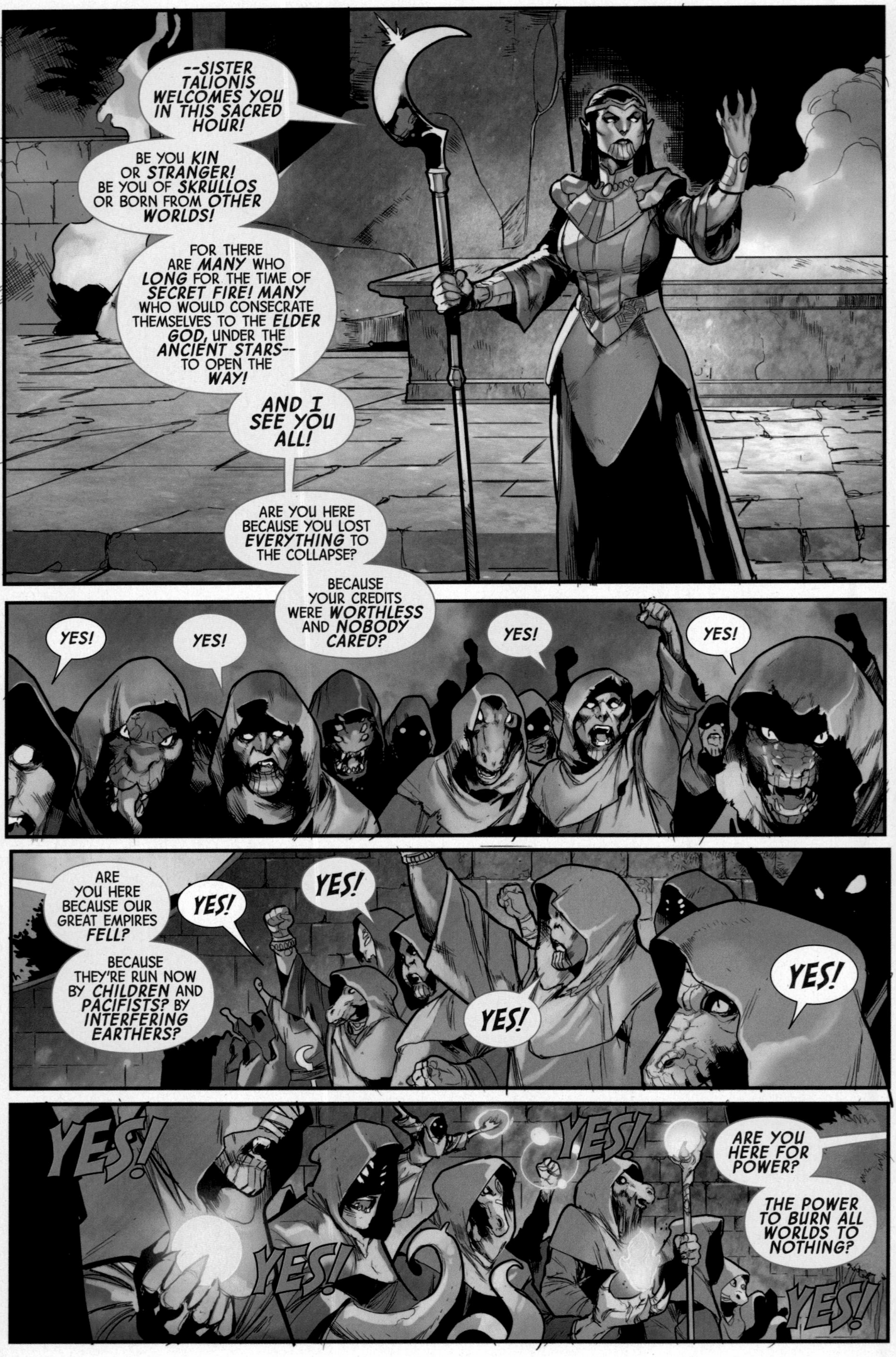
--SISTER TALIONIS WELCOMES YOU IN THIS SACRED HOUR!
BE YOU KIN OR STRANGER! BE YOU OF SKRULLOS OR BORN FROM OTHER WORLDS!
FOR THERE ARE MANY WHO LONG FOR THE TIME OF SECRET FIRE! MANY WHO WOULD CONSECRATE THEMSELVES TO THE ELDER GOD, UNDER THE ANCIENT STARS-- TO OPEN THE WAY!
AND I SEE YOU ALL!
ARE YOU HERE BECAUSE YOU LOST EVERYTHING TO THE COLLAPSE?
BECAUSE YOUR CREDITS WERE WORTHLESS AND NOBODY CARED?
YES!
YES!
YES!
YES!
ARE YOU HERE BECAUSE OUR GREAT EMPIRES FELL?
BECAUSE THEY'RE RUN NOW BY CHILDREN AND PACIFISTS? BY INTERFERING EARTHERS?
YES!
YES!
YES!
YES!
YES!
YES!
ARE YOU HERE FOR POWER?
THE POWER TO BURN ALL WORLDS TO NOTHING?
YES!
YES!

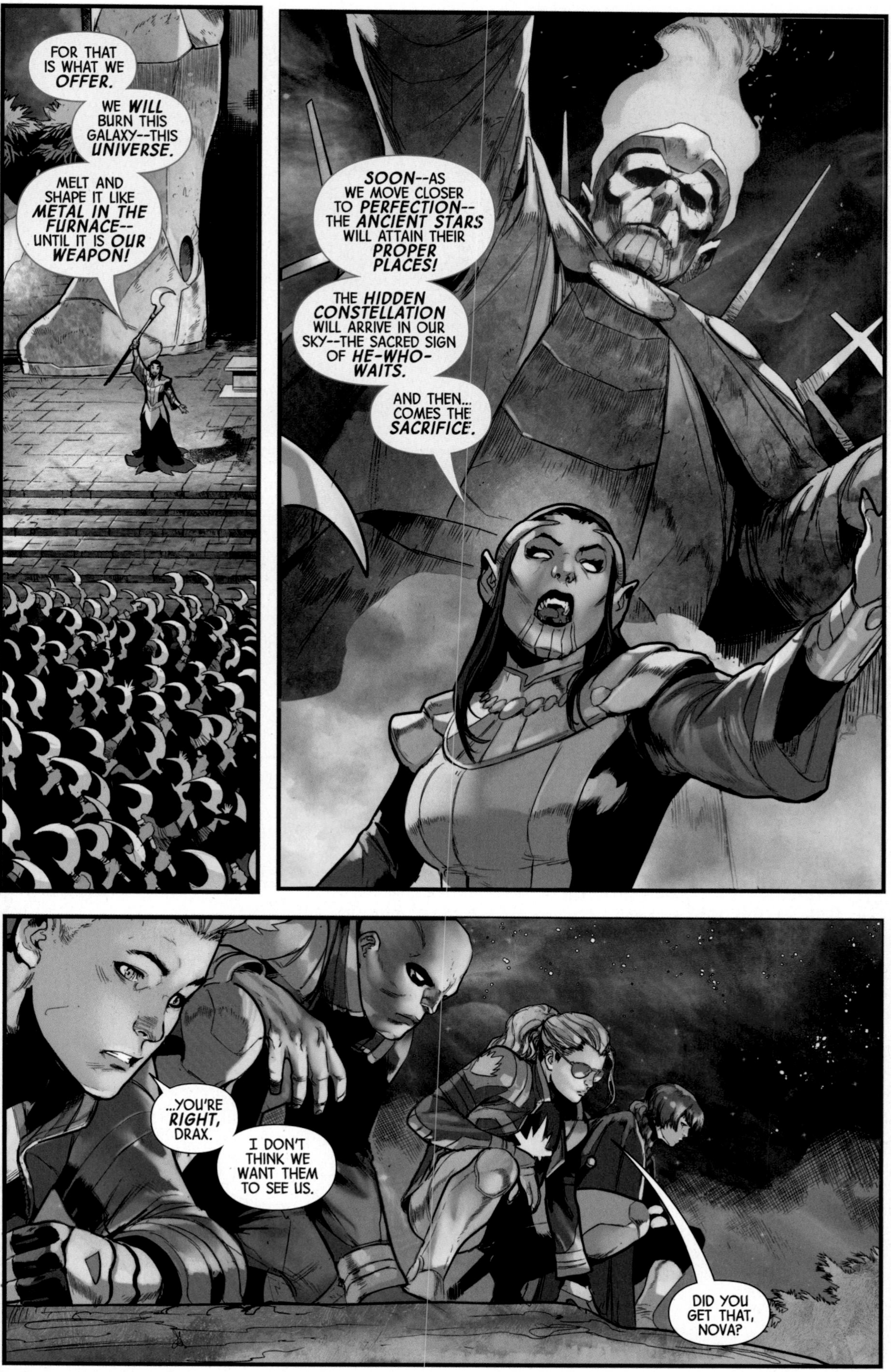

FOR THAT IS WHAT WE OFFER.
WE WILL BURN THIS GALAXY--THIS UNIVERSE.
MELT AND SHAPE IT LIKE METAL IN THE FURNACE--UNTIL IT IS OUR WEAPON!
SOON--AS WE MOVE CLOSER TO PERFECTION--THE ANCIENT STARS WILL ATTAIN THEIR PROPER PLACES!
THE HIDDEN CONSTELLATION WILL ARRIVE IN OUR SKY--THE SACRED SIGN OF HE-WHO-WAITS.
AND THEN... COMES THE SACRIFICE.
...YOU'RE RIGHT, DRAX.
I DON'T THINK WE WANT THEM TO SEE US.
DID YOU GET THAT, NOVA?

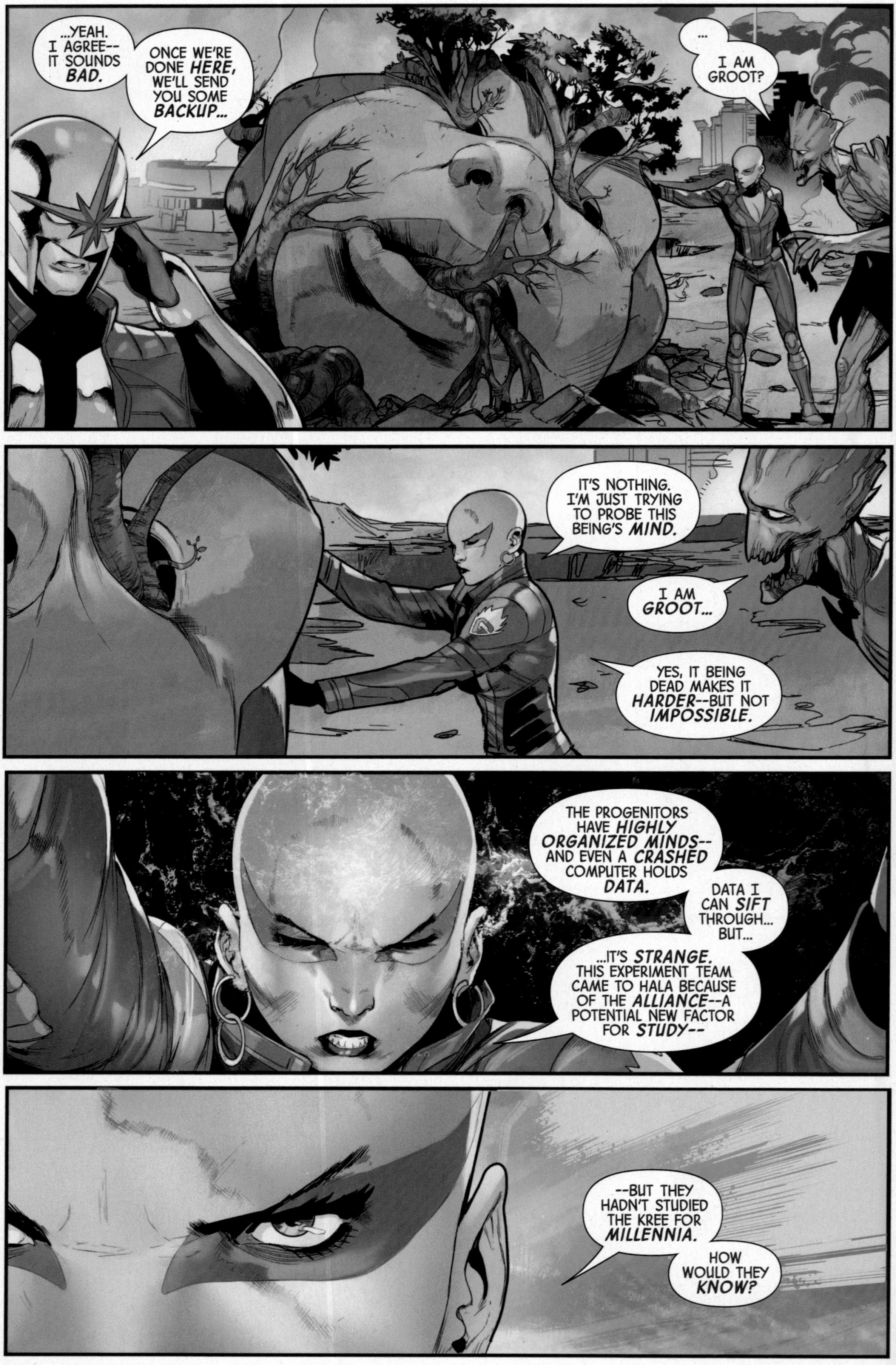
...YEAH. I AGREE-- IT SOUNDS BAD.
ONCE WE'RE DONE HERE, WE'LL SEND YOU SOME BACKUP...
...
I AM GROOT?
IT'S NOTHING. I'M JUST TRYING TO PROBE THIS BEING'S MIND.
I AM GROOT...
YES, IT BEING DEAD MAKES IT HARDER--BUT NOT IMPOSSIBLE.
THE PROGENITORS HAVE HIGHLY ORGANIZED MINDS-- AND EVEN A CRASHED COMPUTER HOLDS DATA.
DATA I CAN SIFT THROUGH... BUT...
...IT'S STRANGE. THIS EXPERIMENT TEAM CAME TO HALA BECAUSE OF THE ALLIANCE--A POTENTIAL NEW FACTOR FOR STUDY--
--BUT THEY HADN'T STUDIED THE KREE FOR MILLENNIA.
HOW WOULD THEY KNOW?

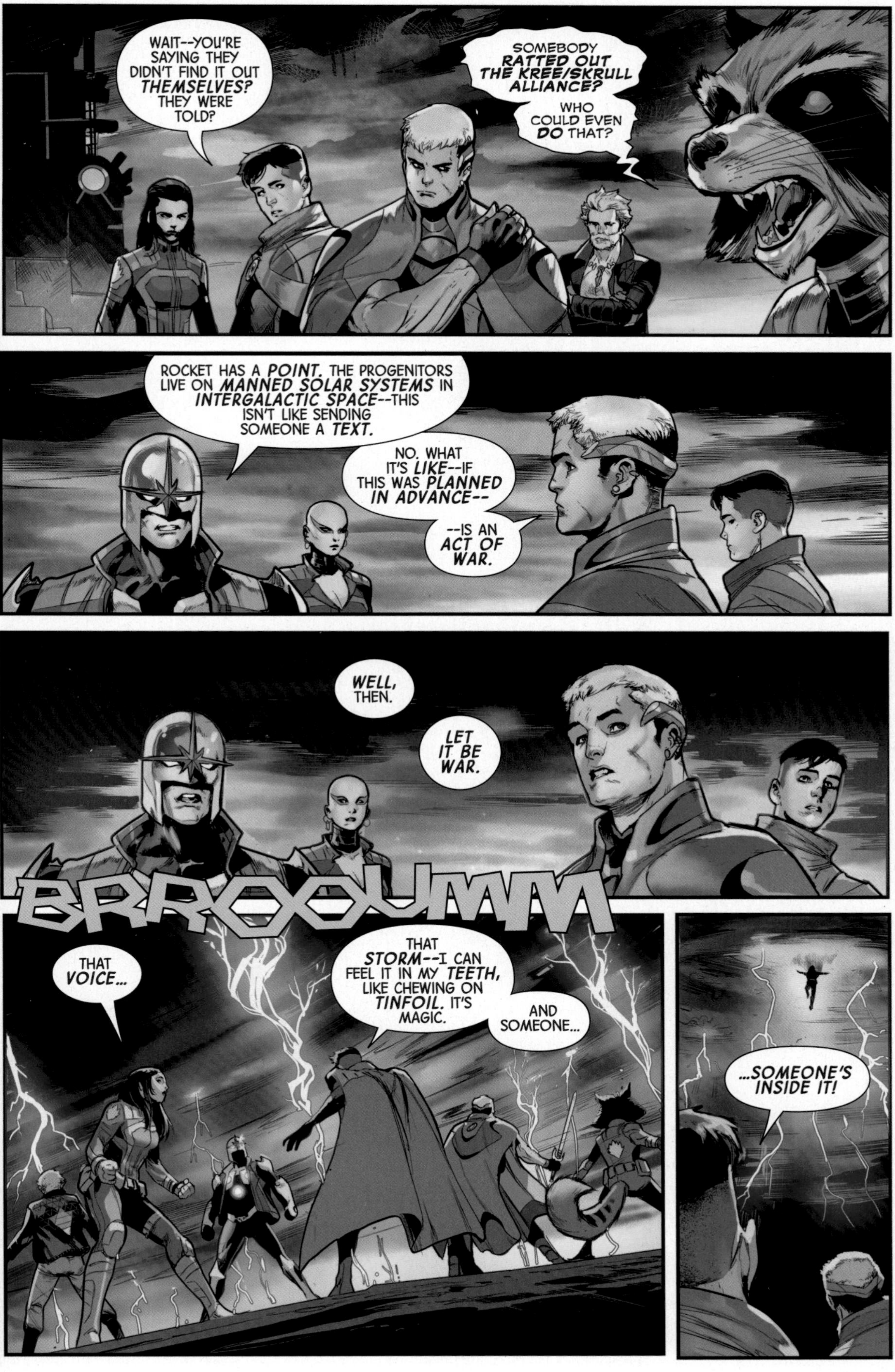
WAIT--YOU'RE SAYING THEY DIDN'T FIND IT OUT THEMSELVES? THEY WERE TOLD?
SOMEBODY RATTED OUT THE KREE/SKRULL ALLIANCE?
WHO COULD EVEN DO THAT?
ROCKET HAS A POINT. THE PROGENITORS LIVE ON MANNED SOLAR SYSTEMS IN INTERGALACTIC SPACE--THIS ISN'T LIKE SENDING SOMEONE A TEXT.
NO. WHAT IT'S LIKE--IF THIS WAS PLANNED IN ADVANCE--
--IS AN ACT OF WAR.
WELL, THEN.
LET IT BE WAR.
BRRROOUMM
THAT VOICE...
THAT STORM--I CAN FEEL IT IN MY TEETH, LIKE CHEWING ON TINFOIL. IT'S MAGIC.
AND SOMEONE...
...SOMEONE'S INSIDE IT!

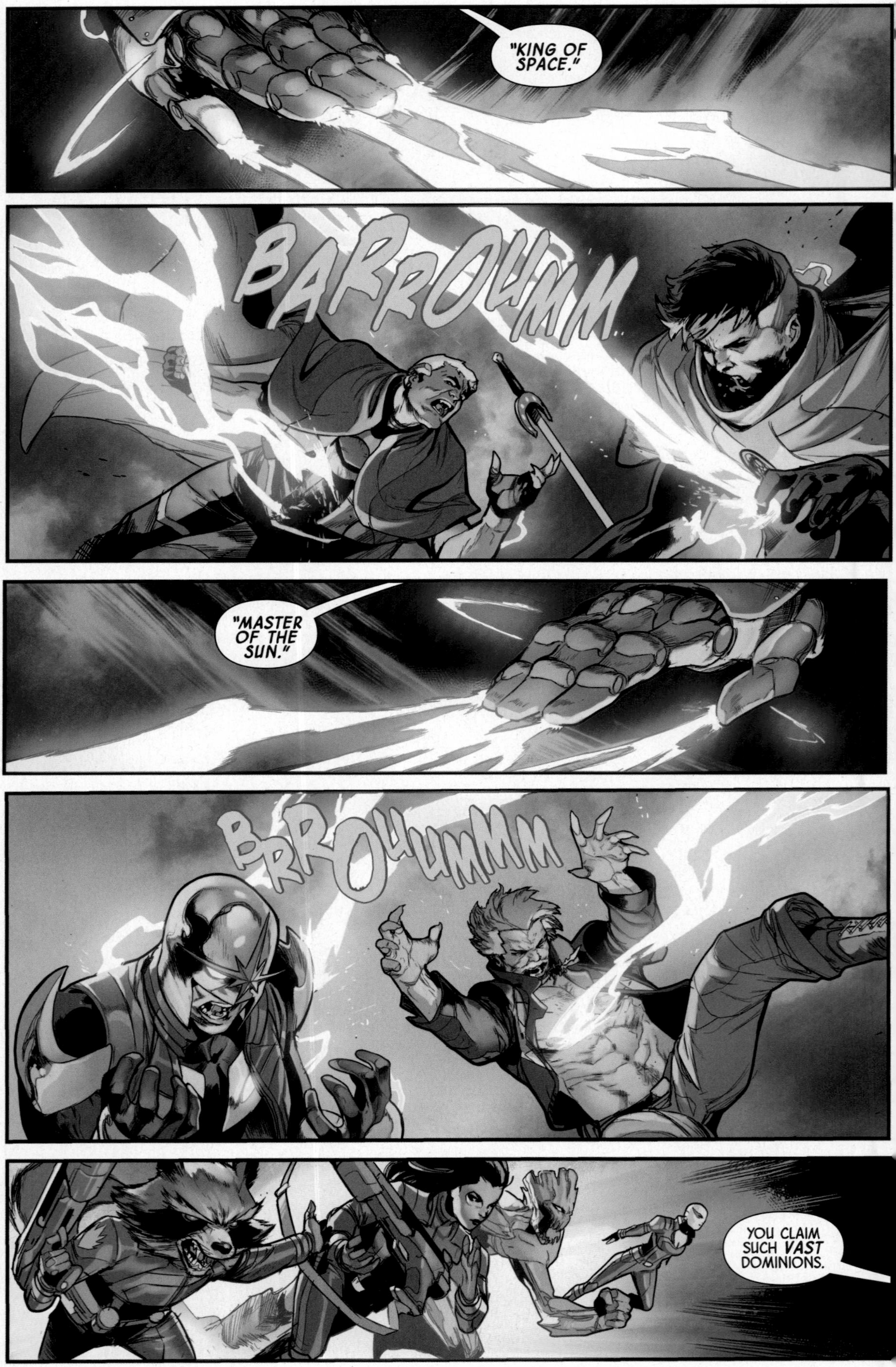
"KING OF SPACE."
BARROUMM
"MASTER OF THE SUN."
BRROUUMMM
YOU CLAIM SUCH VAST DOMINIONS.

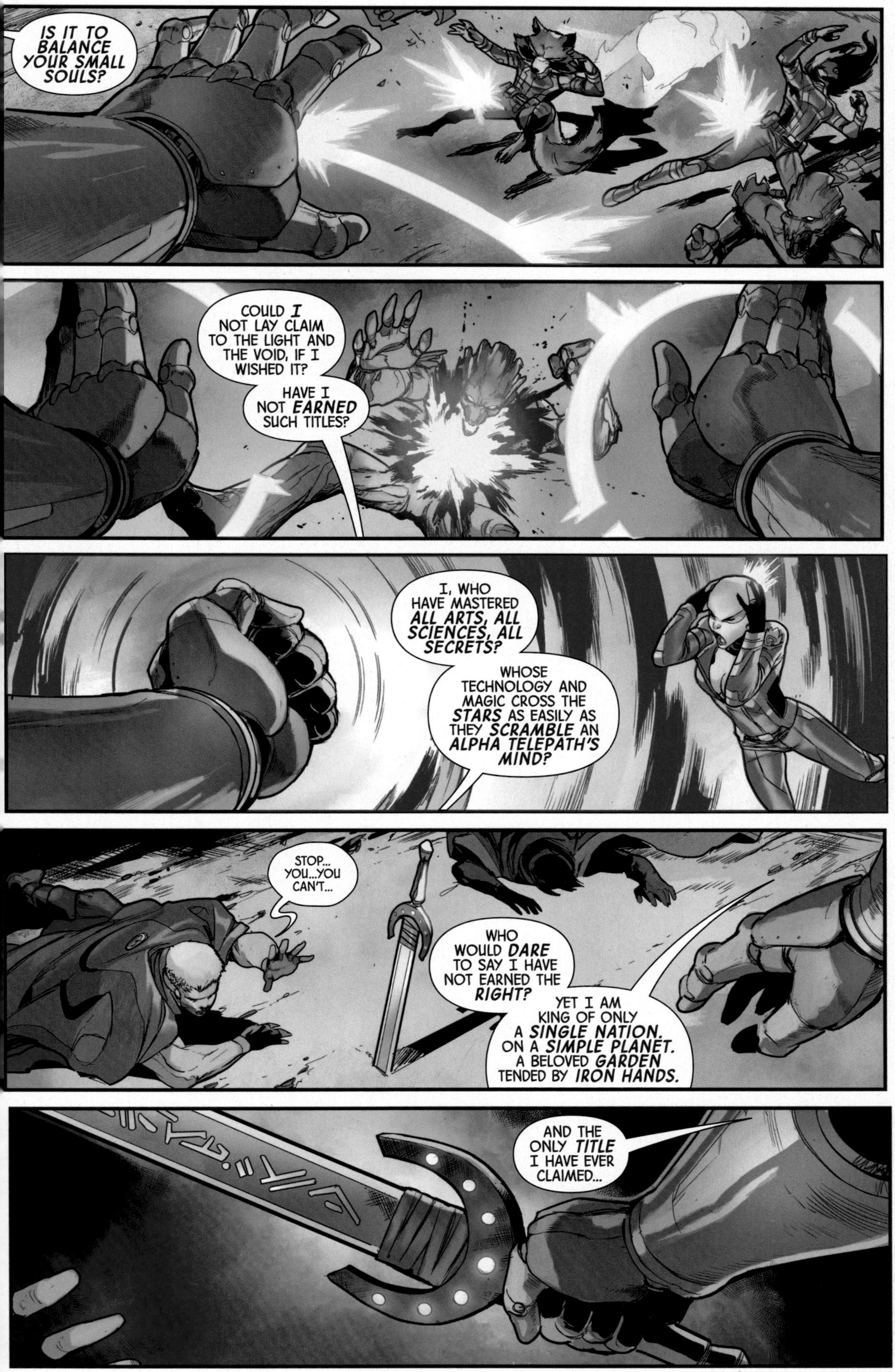
IS IT TO BALANCE YOUR SMALL SOULS?
COULD I NOT LAY CLAIM TO THE LIGHT AND THE VOID, IF I WISHED IT?
HAVE I NOT EARNED SUCH TITLES?
I, WHO HAVE MASTERED ALL ARTS, ALL SCIENCES, ALL SECRETS?
WHOSE TECHNOLOGY AND MAGIC CROSS THE STARS AS EASILY AS THEY SCRAMBLE AN ALPHA TELEPATH'S MIND?
STOP... YOU...YOU CAN'T...
WHO WOULD DARE TO SAY I HAVE NOT EARNED THE RIGHT?
YET I AM KING OF ONLY A SINGLE NATION. ON A SIMPLE PLANET. A BELOVED GARDEN TENDED BY IRON HANDS.
AND THE ONLY TITLE I HAVE EVER CLAIMED...

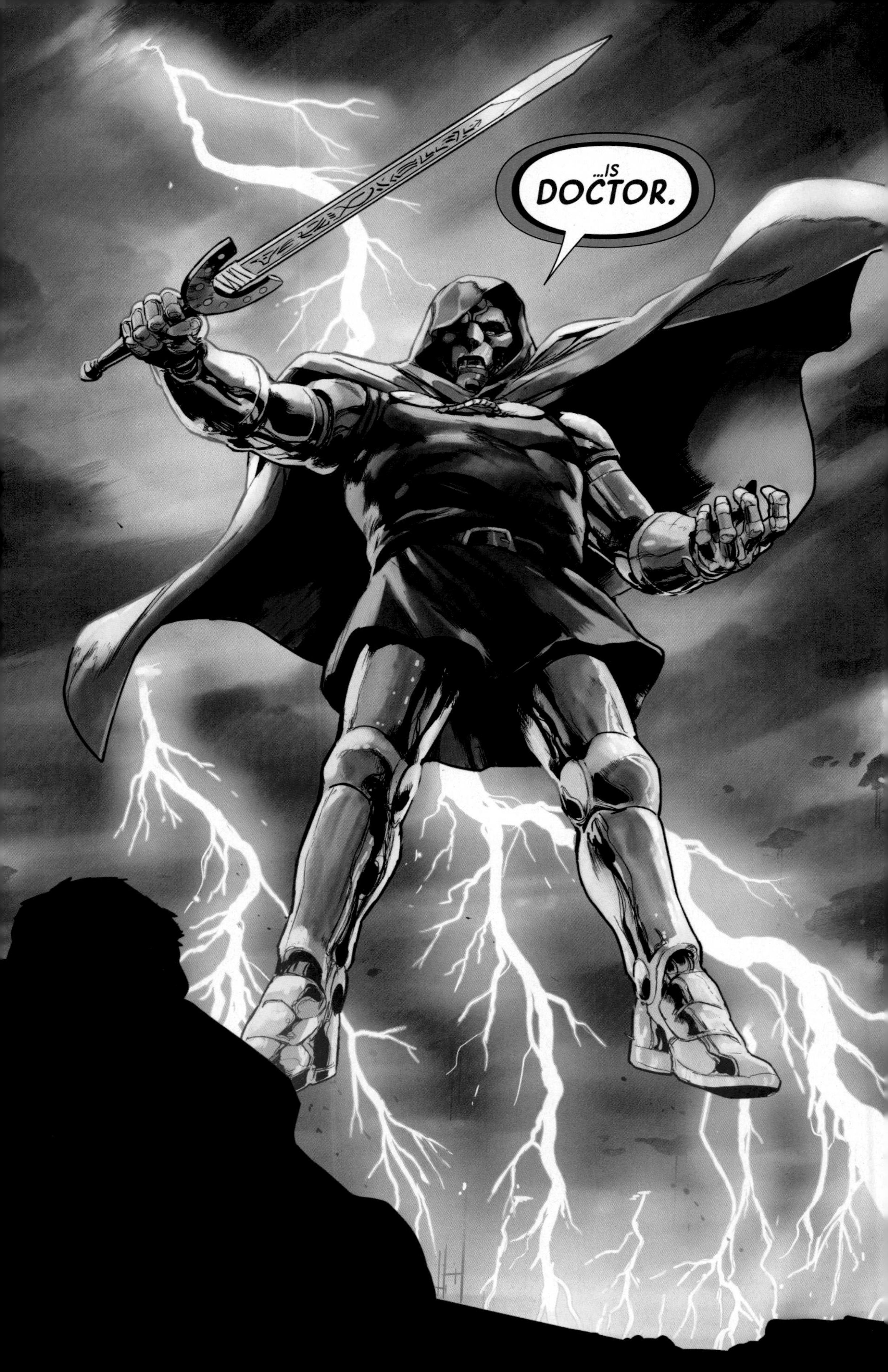
...IS DOCTOR.

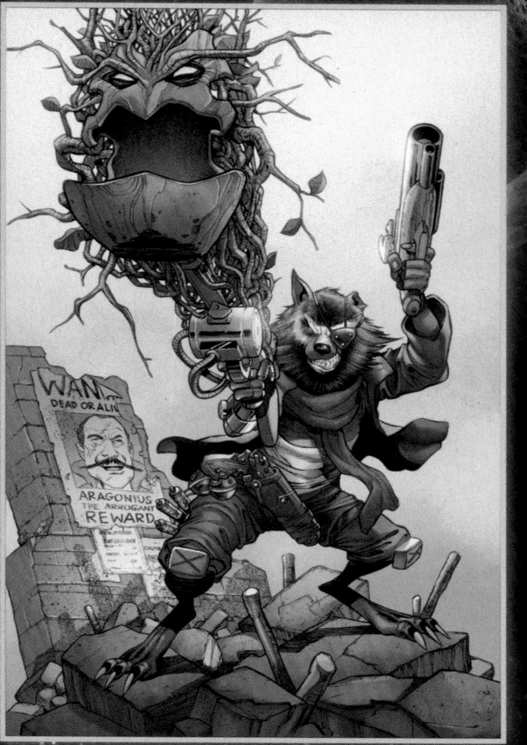
WANT
DEAD OR ALIV
ARAGONIUS
THE ARROGANT
REWARD

#13 HEROES REBORN VARIANT BY:
CARLOS PACHECO, RAFAEL FONTERIZ & RACHELLE ROSENBERG

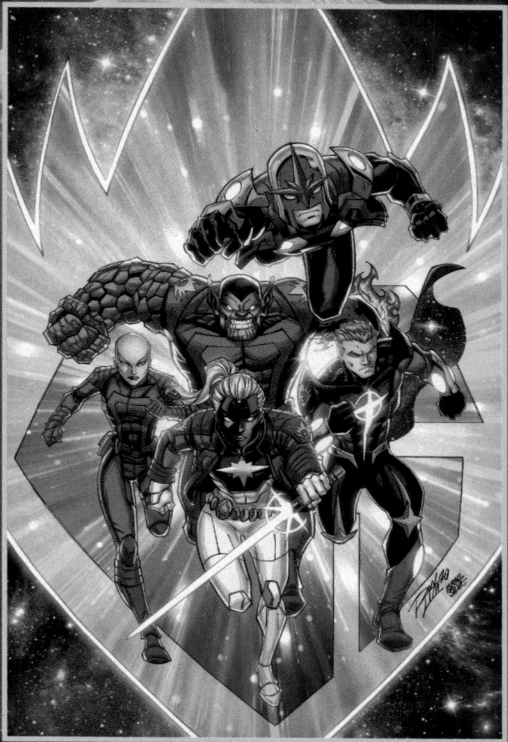

#13 VARIANT BY:
RON LIM & ISRAEL SILVA

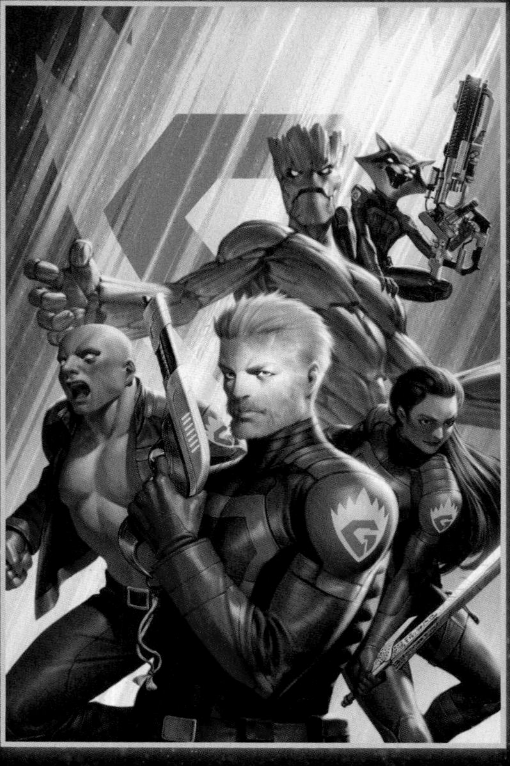

#13 VARIANT BY:
JUNGGEUN YOON

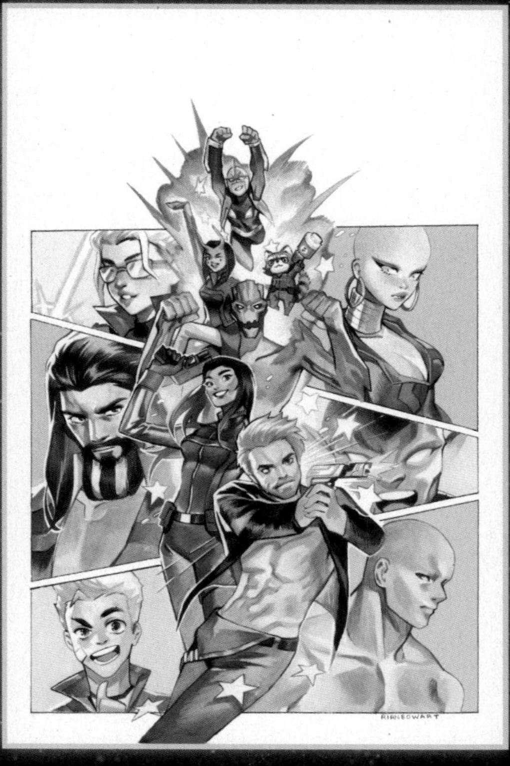
RIANGOWART

#14 VARIANT BY:
RIAN GONZALES

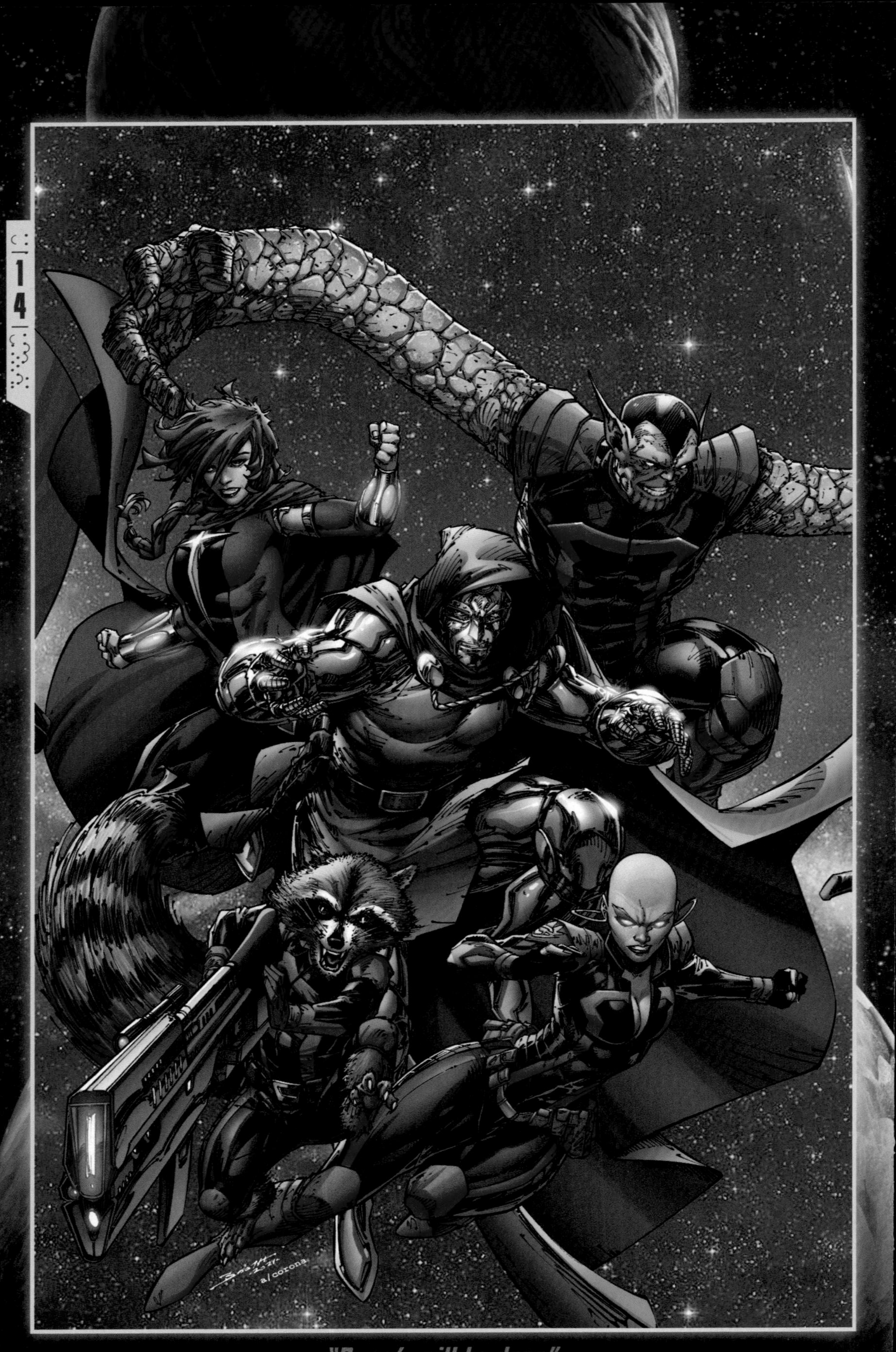

"Doom's will be done."

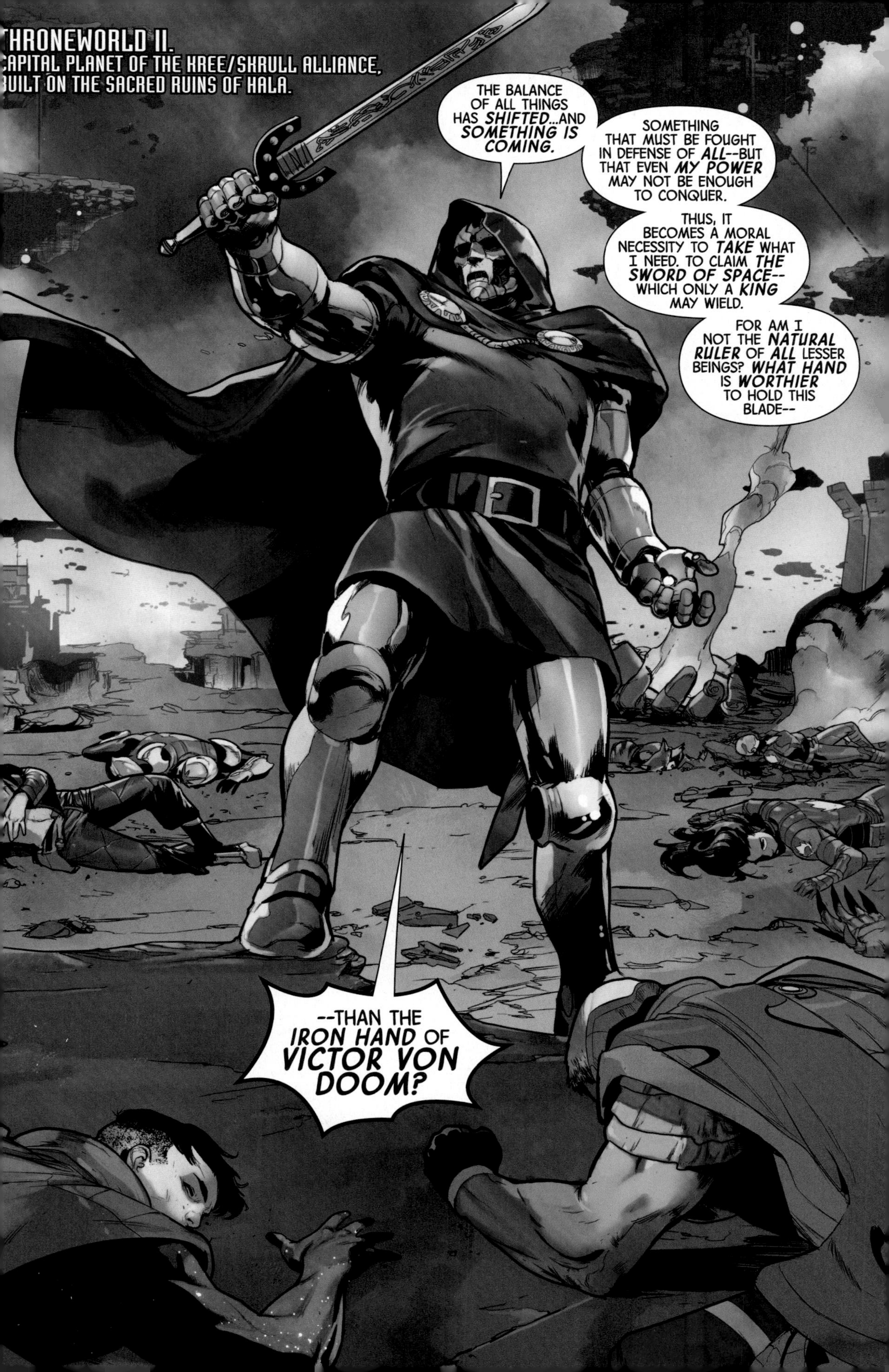
THRONEWORLD II.
CAPITAL PLANET OF THE KREE/SKRULL ALLIANCE, BUILT ON THE SACRED RUINS OF HALA.
THE BALANCE OF ALL THINGS HAS SHIFTED...AND SOMETHING IS COMING.
SOMETHING THAT MUST BE FOUGHT IN DEFENSE OF ALL--BUT THAT EVEN MY POWER MAY NOT BE ENOUGH TO CONQUER.
THUS, IT BECOMES A MORAL NECESSITY TO TAKE WHAT I NEED. TO CLAIM THE SWORD OF SPACE--WHICH ONLY A KING MAY WIELD.
FOR AM I NOT THE NATURAL RULER OF ALL LESSER BEINGS? WHAT HAND IS WORTHIER TO HOLD THIS BLADE--
--THAN THE IRON HAND OF VICTOR VON DOOM?

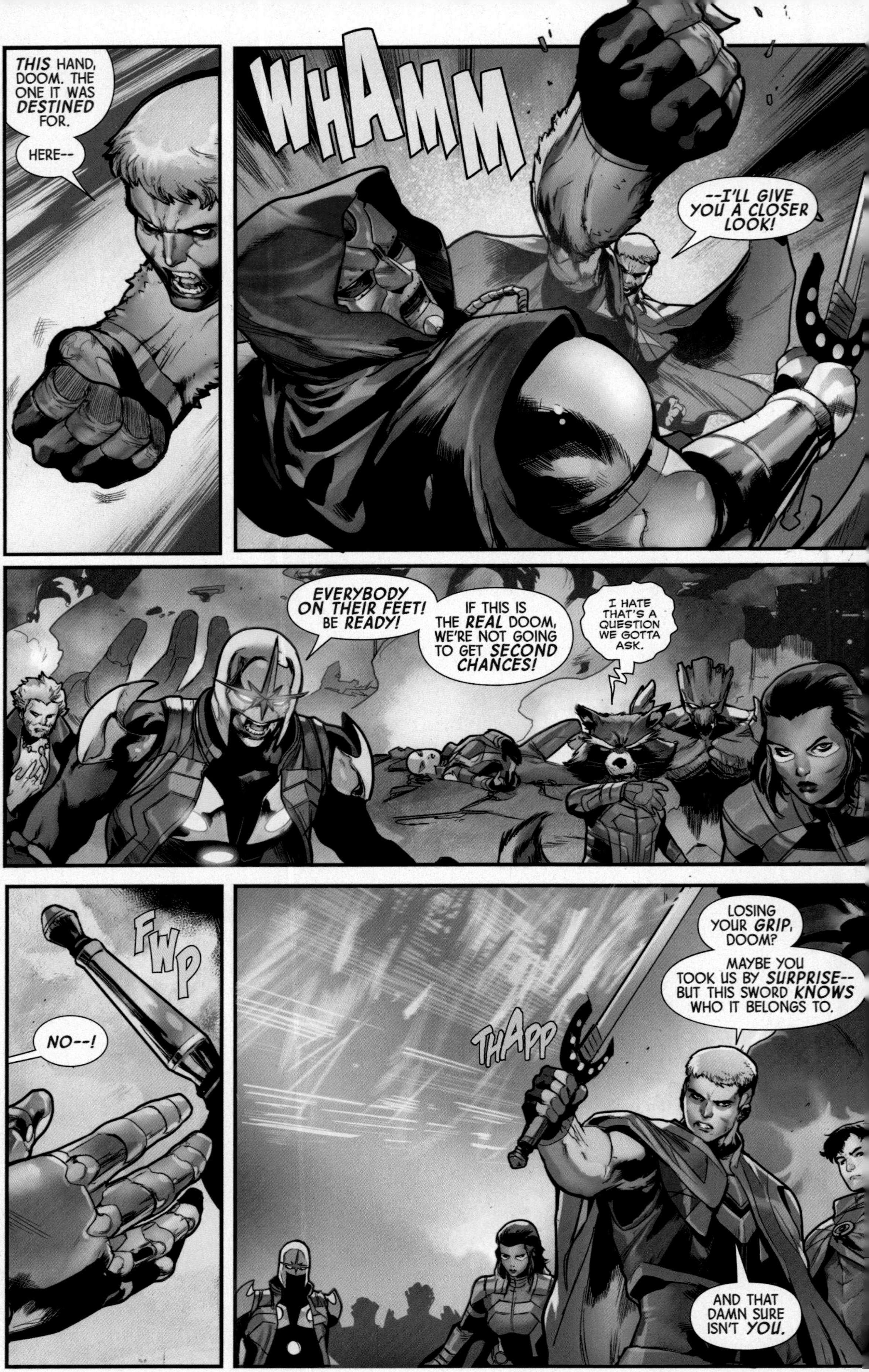
THIS HAND, DOOM. THE ONE IT WAS DESTINED FOR.
HERE--
WHAMM
--I'LL GIVE YOU A CLOSER LOOK!
EVERYBODY ON THEIR FEET! BE READY!
IF THIS IS THE REAL DOOM, WE'RE NOT GOING TO GET SECOND CHANCES!
I HATE THAT'S A QUESTION WE GOTTA ASK.
FWP
NO--!
THAPP
LOSING YOUR GRIP, DOOM?
MAYBE YOU TOOK US BY SURPRISE-- BUT THIS SWORD KNOWS WHO IT BELONGS TO.
AND THAT DAMN SURE ISN'T YOU.

NO, NO, IT SEEMS *NOT*, MR. ALTMAN.

IT SEEMS THE SWORD *KNOWS* YOU--AS WELL AS YOU KNOW *YOURSELF*.

IT'S *KAPLAN*-ALTMAN, THANK YOU.

THEN AGAIN, THE *NATURE* OF "SELF" CAN BE...

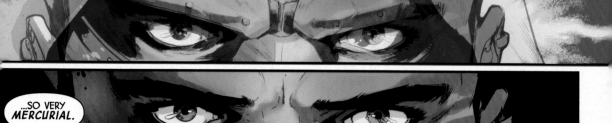

...SO VERY *MERCURIAL*.

WH-WHAT...?

DON'T YOU THINK SO, MY YOUNG FRIEND?

TEDDY?

WHAT ARE YOU *TALKING* ABOUT?

TEDDY, WHAT'S GOING...

...ON...

TEDDY ISN'T *HOME*.

EXCHANGING *MINDS* IS AN *OLD* TRICK OF MINE--AND ONE I PREFER TO *AVOID.*

BUT IT CAN PROVE *USEFUL!*

HHURK!

NO!

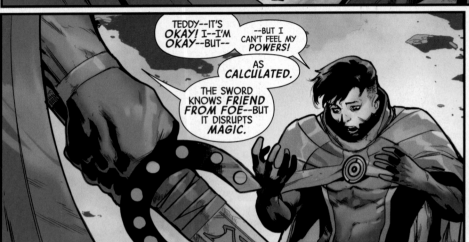

TEDDY--IT'S *OKAY!* I--I'M *OKAY*--BUT--

--BUT I CAN'T FEEL MY *POWERS!*

AS *CALCULATED.*

THE SWORD KNOWS *FRIEND FROM FOE*--BUT IT DISRUPTS *MAGIC.*

AND *ALL* REALITY WARPERS HAVE A *TOUCH* OF MAGIC IN THEM...

...AS DO *YOU,* STAR-LORD-- AND YOUR *ELEMENT GUN.*

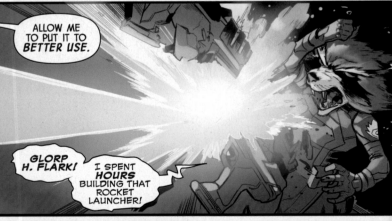

ALLOW ME TO PUT IT TO *BETTER USE.*

GLORP H. FLARK!

I SPENT *HOURS* BUILDING THAT ROCKET LAUNCHER!

HIS MISTAKE, ROCKET.

HE SHOULD HAVE HIT *MINE.*

WHOOM

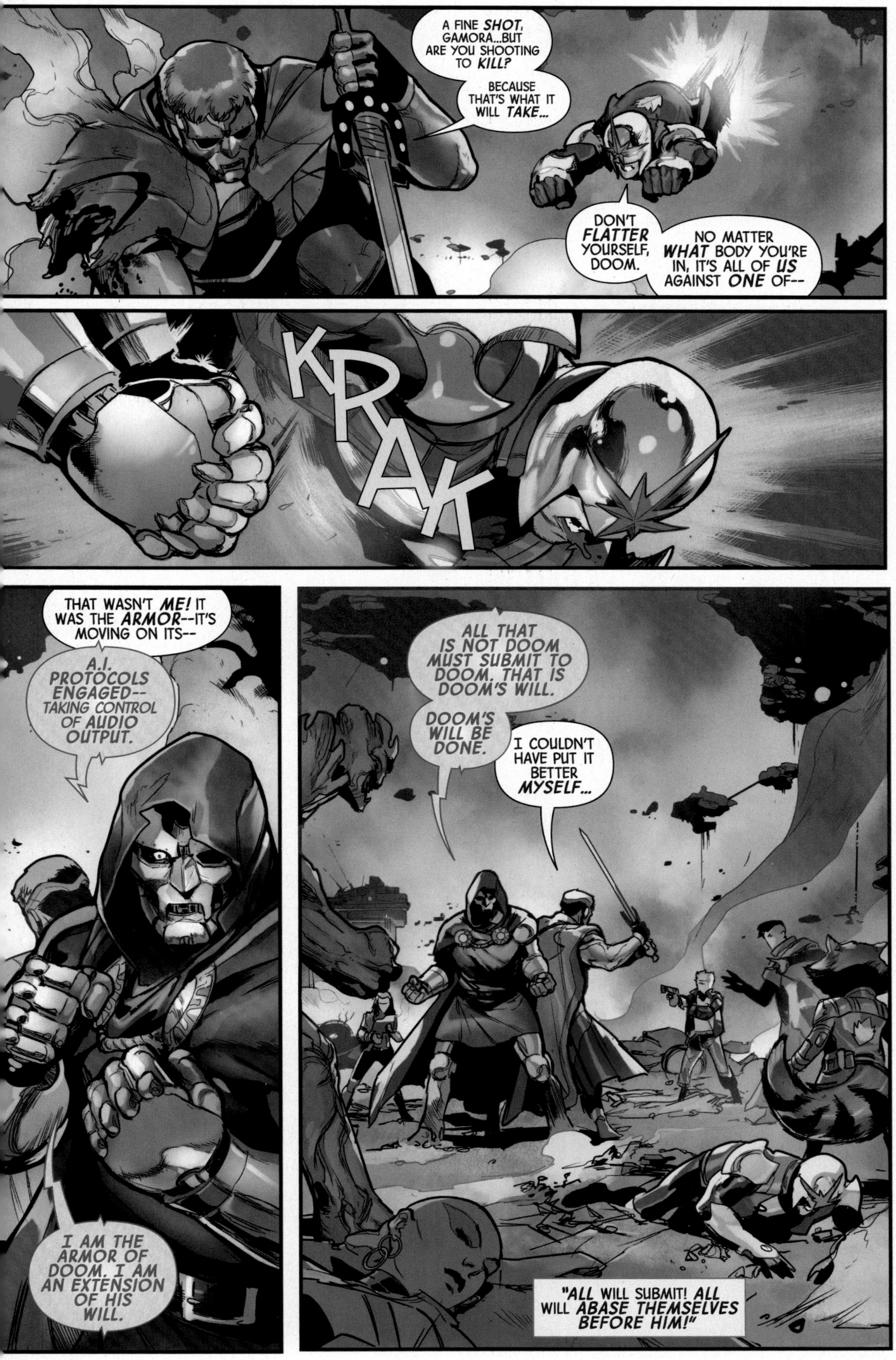
A FINE SHOT, GAMORA...BUT ARE YOU SHOOTING TO KILL?
BECAUSE THAT'S WHAT IT WILL TAKE...
DON'T FLATTER YOURSELF, DOOM.
NO MATTER WHAT BODY YOU'RE IN, IT'S ALL OF US AGAINST ONE OF--
KRAK
THAT WASN'T ME! IT WAS THE ARMOR--IT'S MOVING ON ITS--
A.I. PROTOCOLS ENGAGED-- TAKING CONTROL OF AUDIO OUTPUT.
I AM THE ARMOR OF DOOM. I AM AN EXTENSION OF HIS WILL.
ALL THAT IS NOT DOOM MUST SUBMIT TO DOOM. THAT IS DOOM'S WILL.
DOOM'S WILL BE DONE.
I COULDN'T HAVE PUT IT BETTER MYSELF...
"ALL WILL SUBMIT! ALL WILL ABASE THEMSELVES BEFORE HIM!"

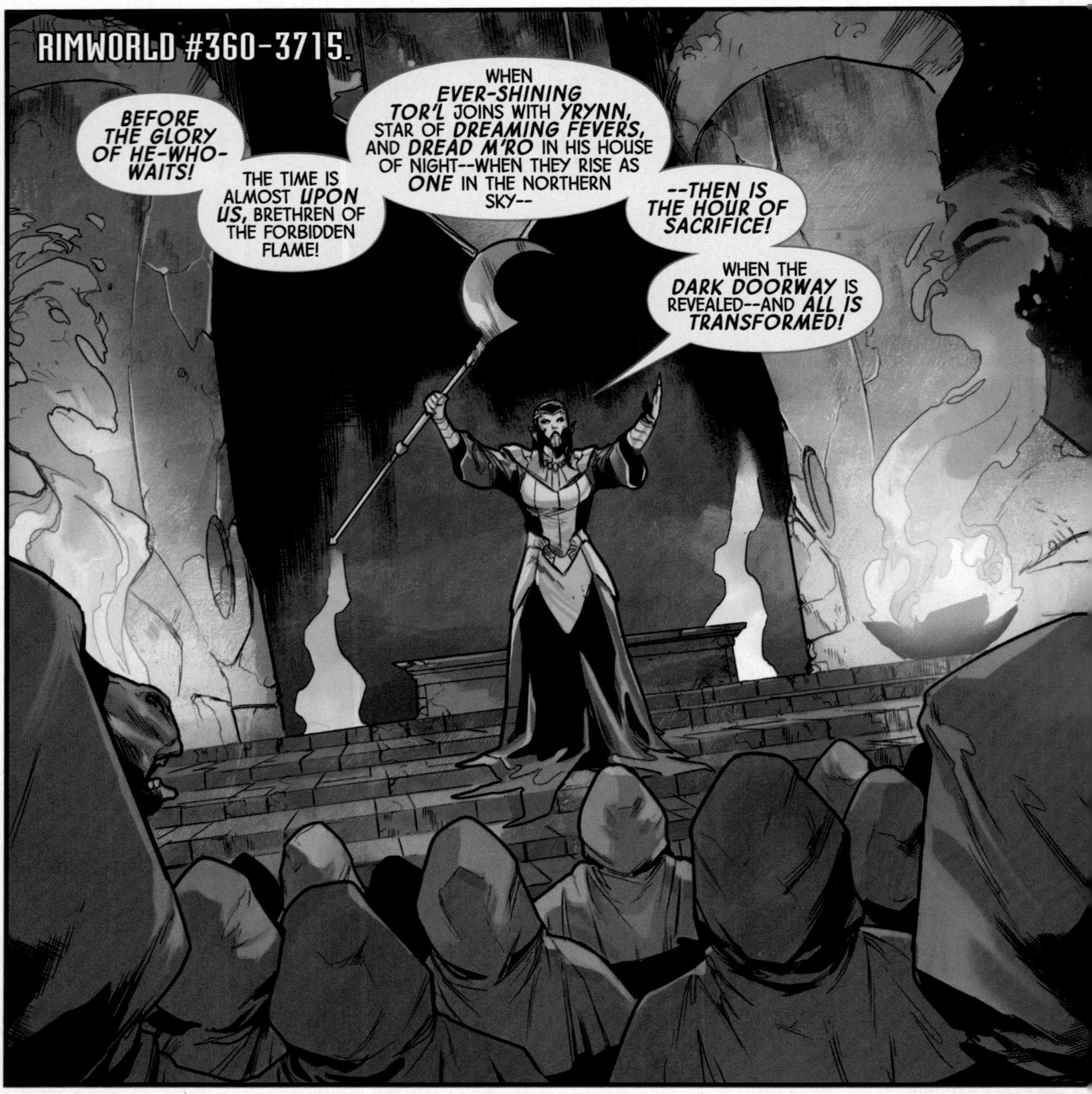
RIMWORLD #360-3715.
BEFORE THE GLORY OF HE-WHO-WAITS!
THE TIME IS ALMOST UPON US, BRETHREN OF THE FORBIDDEN FLAME!
WHEN EVER-SHINING TOR'L JOINS WITH YRYNN, STAR OF DREAMING FEVERS, AND DREAD M'RO IN HIS HOUSE OF NIGHT--WHEN THEY RISE AS ONE IN THE NORTHERN SKY--
--THEN IS THE HOUR OF SACRIFICE!
WHEN THE DARK DOORWAY IS REVEALED--AND ALL IS TRANSFORMED!

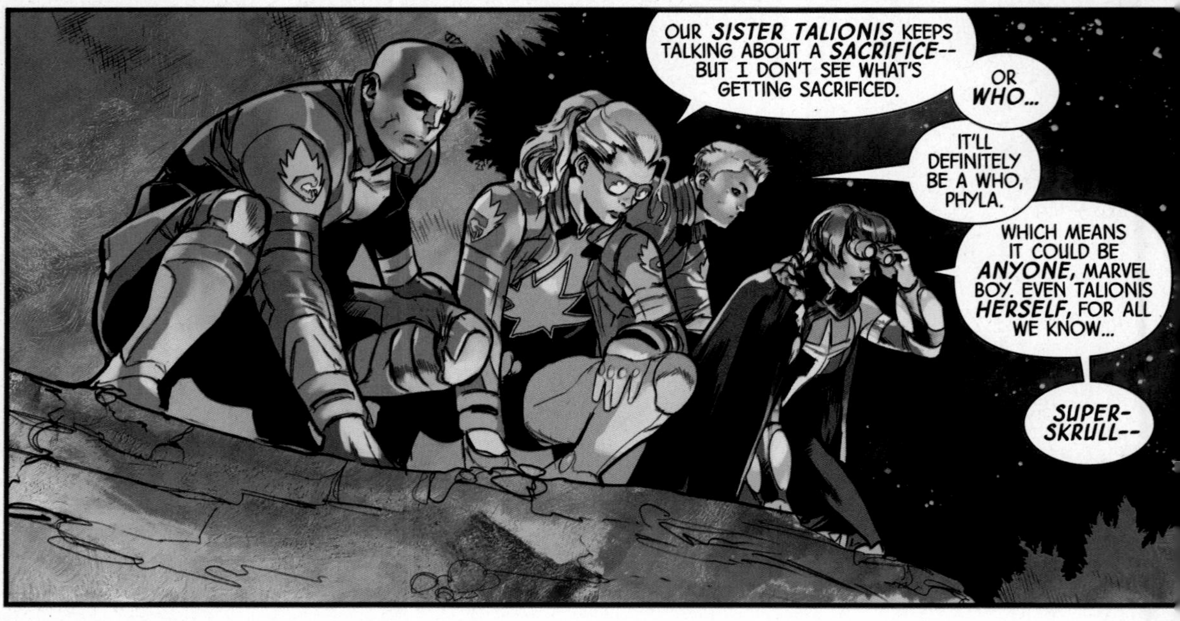
OUR SISTER TALIONIS KEEPS TALKING ABOUT A SACRIFICE-- BUT I DON'T SEE WHAT'S GETTING SACRIFICED.
OR WHO...
IT'LL DEFINITELY BE A WHO, PHYLA.
WHICH MEANS IT COULD BE ANYONE, MARVEL BOY. EVEN TALIONIS HERSELF, FOR ALL WE KNOW...
SUPER-SKRULL--

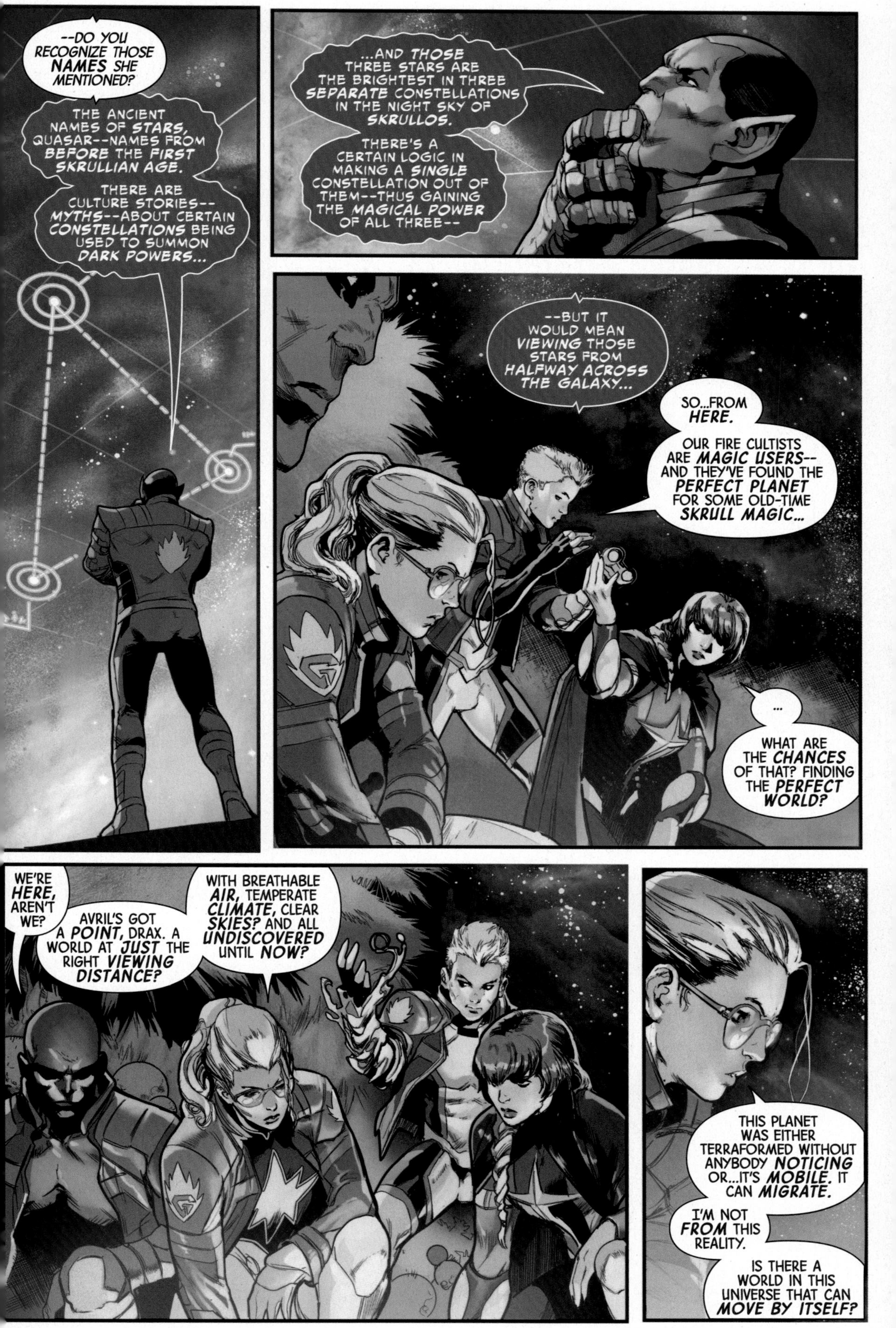
--DO YOU RECOGNIZE THOSE NAMES SHE MENTIONED?
THE ANCIENT NAMES OF STARS, QUASAR--NAMES FROM BEFORE THE FIRST SKRULLIAN AGE.
THERE ARE CULTURE STORIES--MYTHS--ABOUT CERTAIN CONSTELLATIONS BEING USED TO SUMMON DARK POWERS...
...AND THOSE THREE STARS ARE THE BRIGHTEST IN THREE SEPARATE CONSTELLATIONS IN THE NIGHT SKY OF SKRULLOS.
THERE'S A CERTAIN LOGIC IN MAKING A SINGLE CONSTELLATION OUT OF THEM--THUS GAINING THE MAGICAL POWER OF ALL THREE--
--BUT IT WOULD MEAN VIEWING THOSE STARS FROM HALFWAY ACROSS THE GALAXY...
SO...FROM HERE.
OUR FIRE CULTISTS ARE MAGIC USERS--AND THEY'VE FOUND THE PERFECT PLANET FOR SOME OLD-TIME SKRULL MAGIC...
...
WHAT ARE THE CHANCES OF THAT? FINDING THE PERFECT WORLD?
WE'RE HERE, AREN'T WE?
AVRIL'S GOT A POINT, DRAX. A WORLD AT JUST THE RIGHT VIEWING DISTANCE?
WITH BREATHABLE AIR, TEMPERATE CLIMATE, CLEAR SKIES? AND ALL UNDISCOVERED UNTIL NOW?
THIS PLANET WAS EITHER TERRAFORMED WITHOUT ANYBODY NOTICING OR...IT'S MOBILE. IT CAN MIGRATE.
I'M NOT FROM THIS REALITY.
IS THERE A WORLD IN THIS UNIVERSE THAT CAN MOVE BY ITSELF?

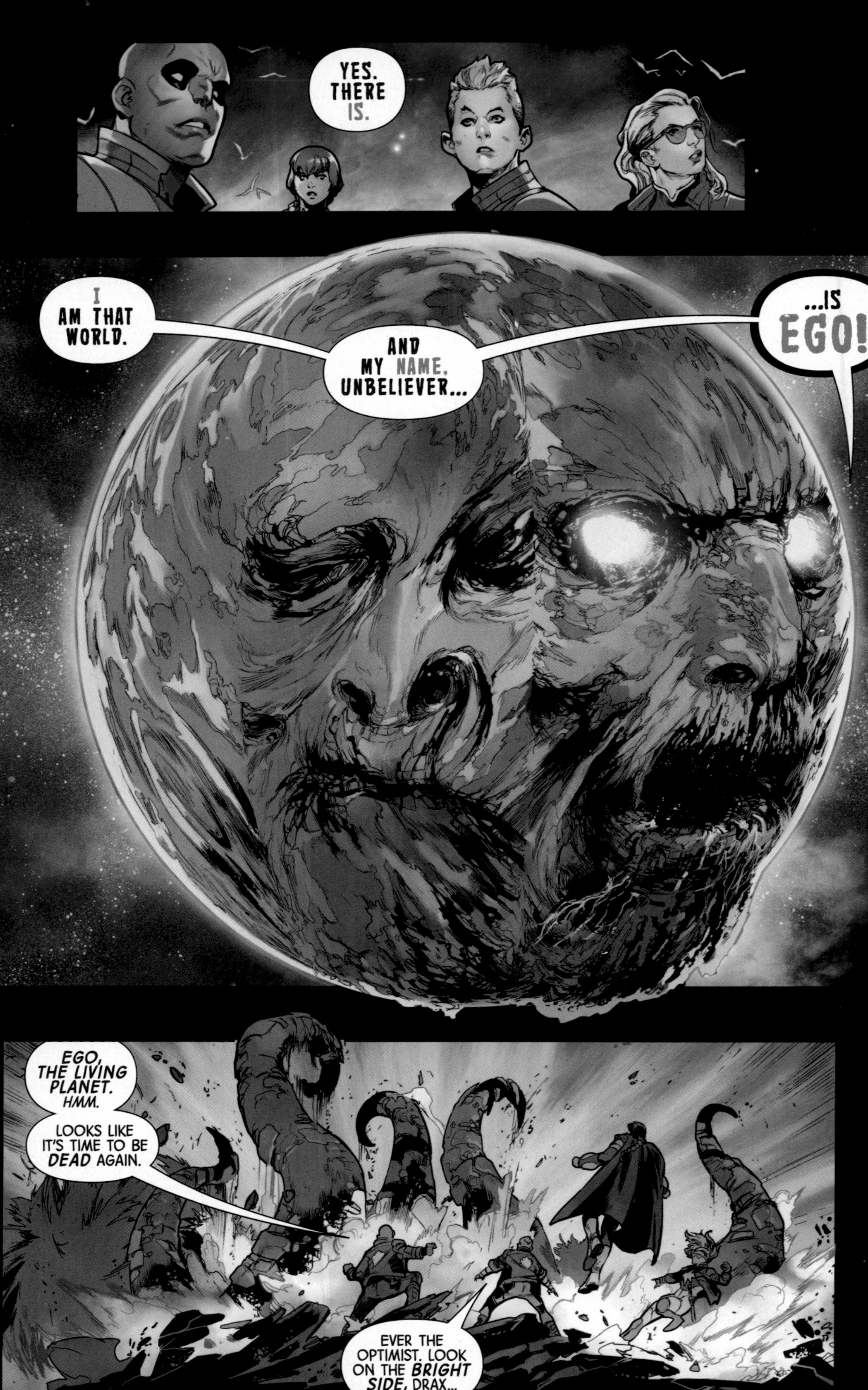
YES. THERE IS.
I AM THAT WORLD.
AND MY NAME, UNBELIEVER...
...IS EGO!
EGO, THE LIVING PLANET. HMM.
LOOKS LIKE IT'S TIME TO BE DEAD AGAIN.
EVER THE OPTIMIST. LOOK ON THE BRIGHT SIDE, DRAX...

"...THINGS CAN ALWAYS GET *WORSE*."

I AM AN EXTENSION OF DOOM'S WILL. DOOM'S WILL BE DONE.

I AM GROOT!

THEN YOU ARE NOT DOOM AND MUST SUBMIT TO DOOM.

I AM AN EXTENSION OF DOOM'S--

WE GET IT! CAN YOU *SHUT YOUR GUY UP* ALREADY, DOC?

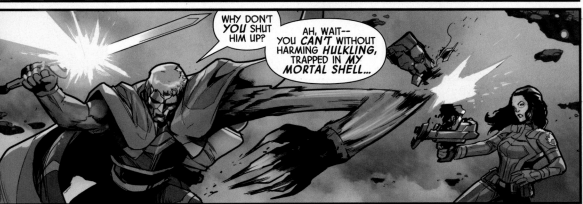

WHY DON'T *YOU* SHUT HIM UP?

AH, WAIT-- YOU *CAN'T* WITHOUT HARMING *HULKLING*, TRAPPED IN *MY MORTAL SHELL*...

BESIDES, IT ONLY SPEAKS THE *TRUTH*. THE SUIT'S A.I. *IS* AN EXTENSION OF MY WILL--JUST AS MY *ROBOTS* ARE.

THEY ARE MY *HANDS*, MY *EYES*, MY *WORK* IN THE WORLD. THEY ARE *THEMSELVES*... BUT *THEY ARE ALSO ME.*

I THINK YOUR ROBOTS ARE A LITTLE *MORE* LIKE YOU THAN *YOU* ARE RIGHT NOW...

GOOD.

KEEP PUSHING THAT BUTTON, PETER.

MOONDRAGON...?

DOOM'S ARMOR HAS A TELEPATHIC SCRAMBLER--I'VE BEEN PLAYING POSSUM SO HE DOESN'T SCRAMBLE ME AGAIN.

BUT I *DO HAVE A PLAN*...

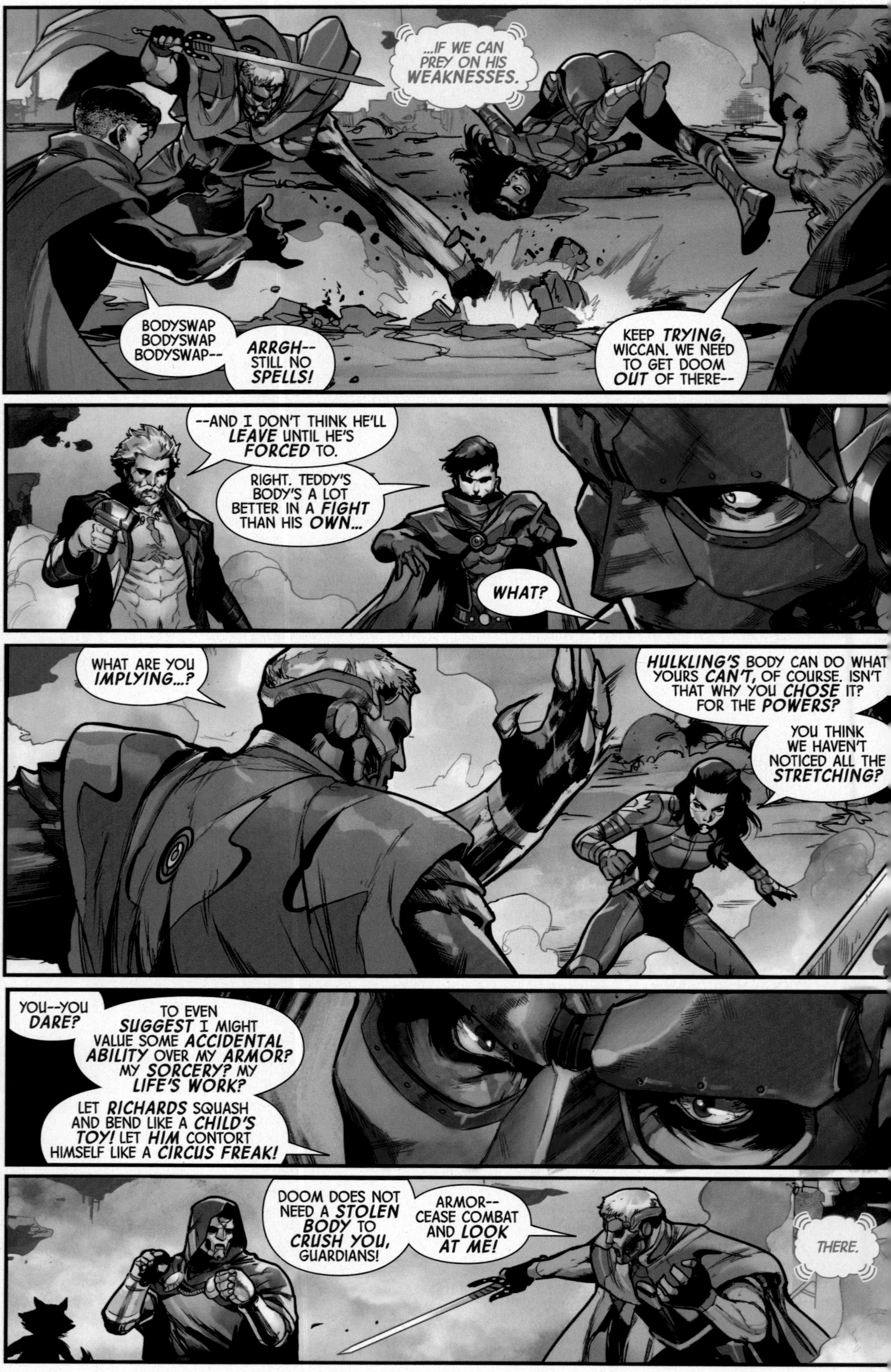
...IF WE CAN PREY ON HIS WEAKNESSES.
BODYSWAP BODYSWAP BODYSWAP--
ARRGH-- STILL NO SPELLS!
KEEP TRYING, WICCAN. WE NEED TO GET DOOM OUT OF THERE--
--AND I DON'T THINK HE'LL LEAVE UNTIL HE'S FORCED TO.
RIGHT. TEDDY'S BODY'S A LOT BETTER IN A FIGHT THAN HIS OWN...
WHAT?
WHAT ARE YOU IMPLYING...?
HULKLING'S BODY CAN DO WHAT YOURS CAN'T, OF COURSE. ISN'T THAT WHY YOU CHOSE IT? FOR THE POWERS?
YOU THINK WE HAVEN'T NOTICED ALL THE STRETCHING?
YOU--YOU DARE?
TO EVEN SUGGEST I MIGHT VALUE SOME ACCIDENTAL ABILITY OVER MY ARMOR? MY SORCERY? MY LIFE'S WORK?
LET RICHARDS SQUASH AND BEND LIKE A CHILD'S TOY! LET HIM CONTORT HIMSELF LIKE A CIRCUS FREAK!
DOOM DOES NOT NEED A STOLEN BODY TO CRUSH YOU, GUARDIANS!
ARMOR-- CEASE COMBAT AND LOOK AT ME!
THERE.

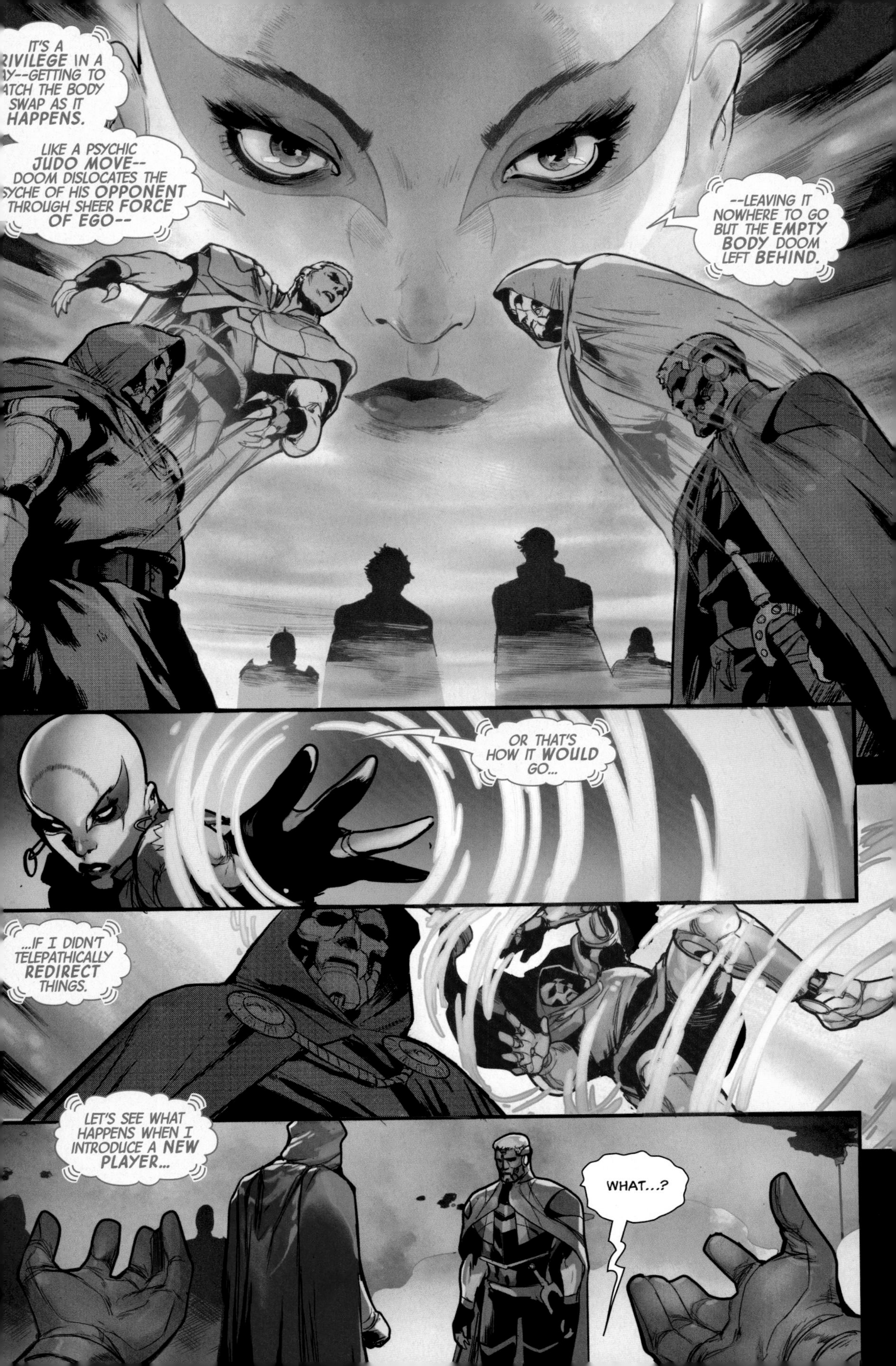

IT'S A
RIVILEGE IN A
AY--GETTING TO
ATCH THE BODY
SWAP AS IT
HAPPENS.
LIKE A PSYCHIC JUDO MOVE--DOOM DISLOCATES THE SYCHE OF HIS OPPONENT THROUGH SHEER FORCE OF EGO--
--LEAVING IT NOWHERE TO GO BUT THE EMPTY BODY DOOM LEFT BEHIND.
OR THAT'S HOW IT WOULD GO...
...IF I DIDN'T TELEPATHICALLY REDIRECT THINGS.
LET'S SEE WHAT HAPPENS WHEN I INTRODUCE A NEW PLAYER...
WHAT...?

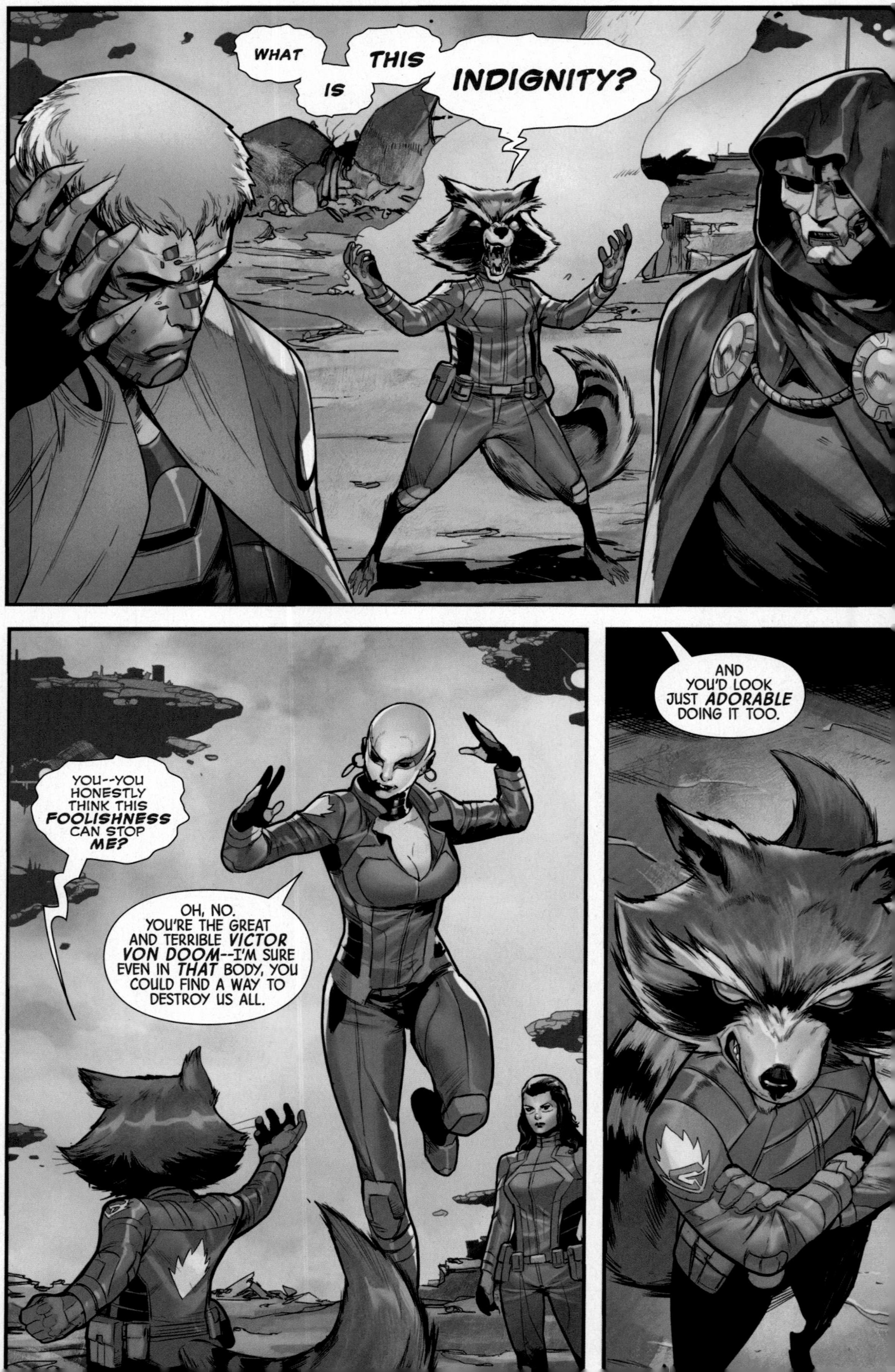
WHAT IS THIS INDIGNITY?
YOU--YOU HONESTLY THINK THIS FOOLISHNESS CAN STOP ME?
OH, NO. YOU'RE THE GREAT AND TERRIBLE VICTOR VON DOOM--I'M SURE EVEN IN THAT BODY, YOU COULD FIND A WAY TO DESTROY US ALL.
AND YOU'D LOOK JUST ADORABLE DOING IT TOO.

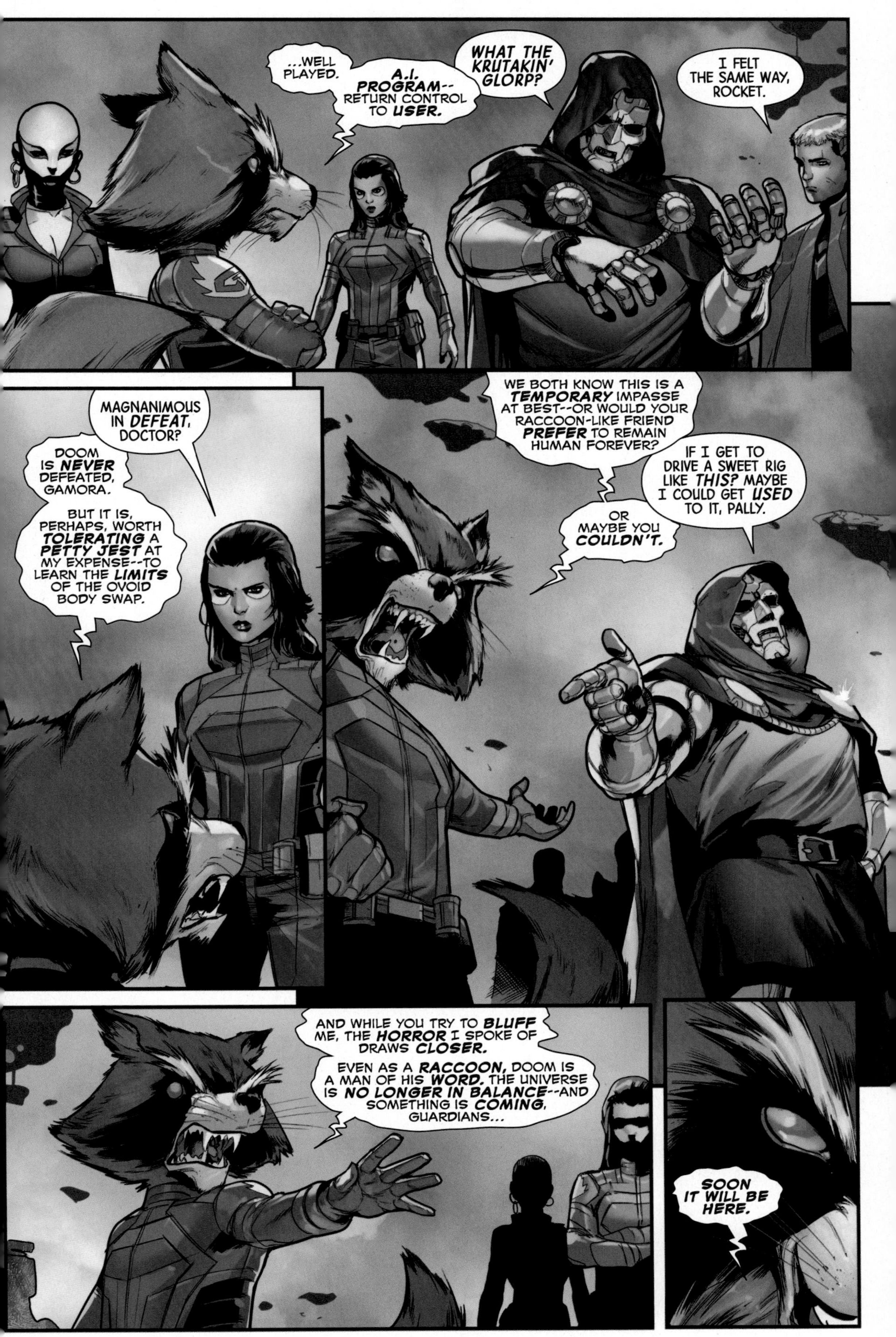
...WELL PLAYED.
A.I. PROGRAM-- RETURN CONTROL TO USER.
WHAT THE KRUTAKIN' GLORP?
I FELT THE SAME WAY, ROCKET.
MAGNANIMOUS IN DEFEAT, DOCTOR?
DOOM IS NEVER DEFEATED, GAMORA.
BUT IT IS, PERHAPS, WORTH TOLERATING A PETTY JEST AT MY EXPENSE--TO LEARN THE LIMITS OF THE OVOID BODY SWAP.
WE BOTH KNOW THIS IS A TEMPORARY IMPASSE AT BEST--OR WOULD YOUR RACCOON-LIKE FRIEND PREFER TO REMAIN HUMAN FOREVER?
OR MAYBE YOU COULDN'T.
IF I GET TO DRIVE A SWEET RIG LIKE THIS? MAYBE I COULD GET USED TO IT, PALLY.
AND WHILE YOU TRY TO BLUFF ME, THE HORROR I SPOKE OF DRAWS CLOSER.
EVEN AS A RACCOON, DOOM IS A MAN OF HIS WORD. THE UNIVERSE IS NO LONGER IN BALANCE--AND SOMETHING IS COMING, GUARDIANS...
SOON IT WILL BE HERE.

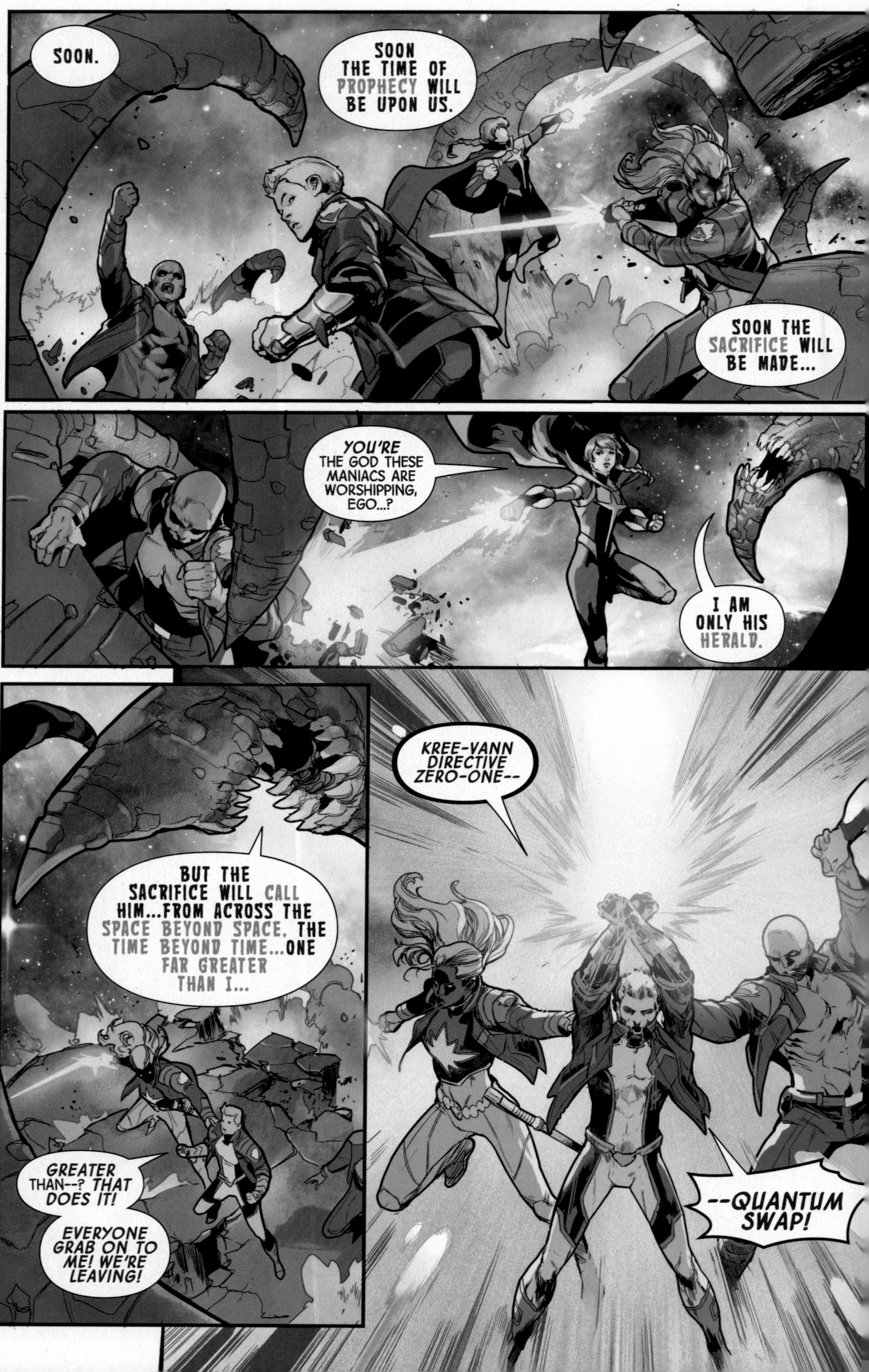
SOON.
SOON THE TIME OF PROPHECY WILL BE UPON US.
SOON THE SACRIFICE WILL BE MADE...
YOU'RE THE GOD THESE MANIACS ARE WORSHIPPING, EGO...?
I AM ONLY HIS HERALD.
BUT THE SACRIFICE WILL CALL HIM...FROM ACROSS THE SPACE BEYOND SPACE, THE TIME BEYOND TIME...ONE FAR GREATER THAN I...
GREATER THAN--? THAT DOES IT!
EVERYONE GRAB ON TO ME! WE'RE LEAVING!
KREE-VANN DIRECTIVE ZERO-ONE--
--QUANTUM SWAP!

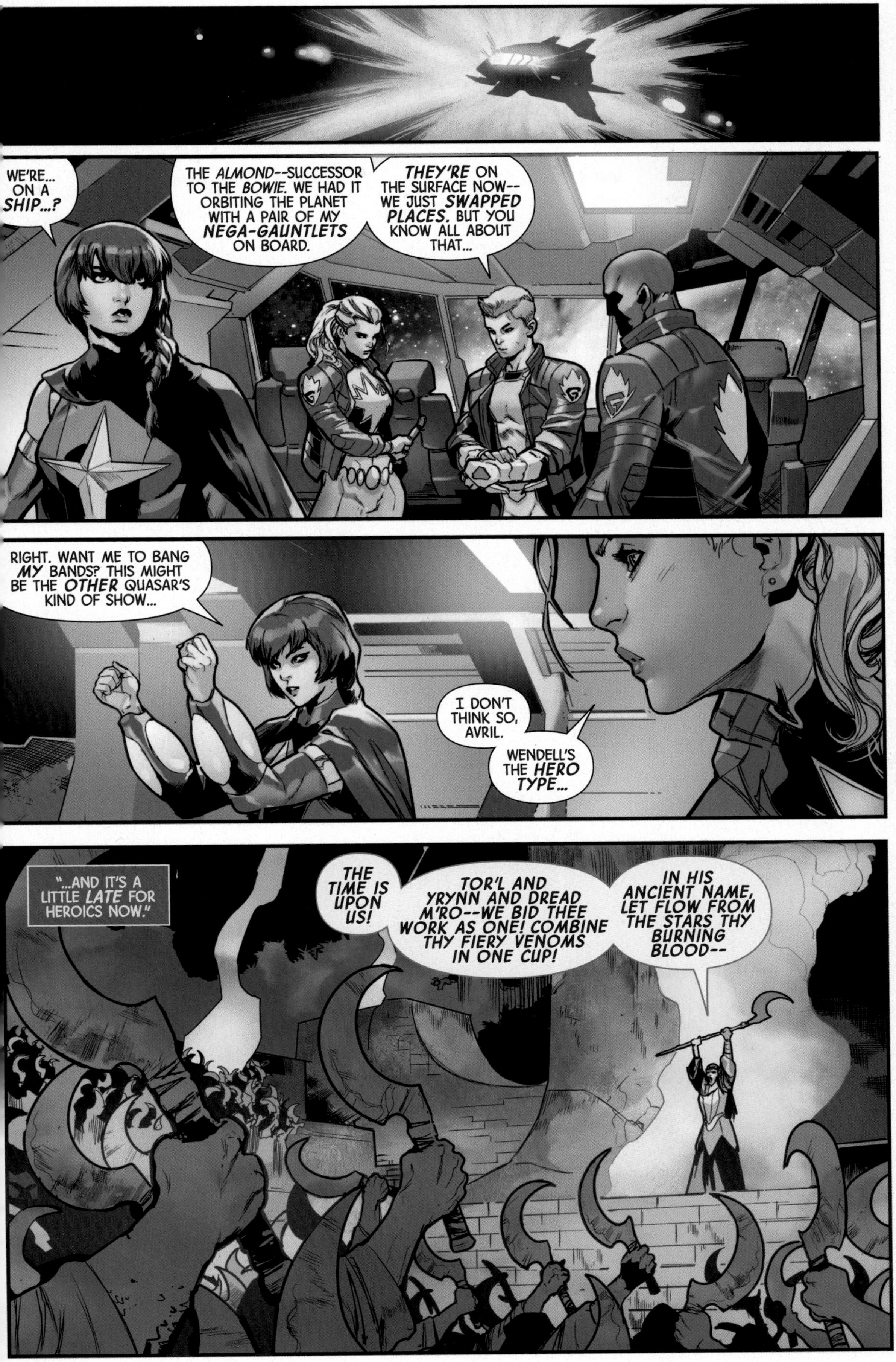
WE'RE... ON A SHIP...?
THE ALMOND--SUCCESSOR TO THE BOWIE. WE HAD IT ORBITING THE PLANET WITH A PAIR OF MY NEGA-GAUNTLETS ON BOARD.
THEY'RE ON THE SURFACE NOW-- WE JUST SWAPPED PLACES. BUT YOU KNOW ALL ABOUT THAT...
RIGHT. WANT ME TO BANG MY BANDS? THIS MIGHT BE THE OTHER QUASAR'S KIND OF SHOW...
I DON'T THINK SO, AVRIL.
WENDELL'S THE HERO TYPE...
"...AND IT'S A LITTLE LATE FOR HEROICS NOW."
THE TIME IS UPON US!
TOR'L AND YRYNN AND DREAD M'RO--WE BID THEE WORK AS ONE! COMBINE THY FIERY VENOMS IN ONE CUP!
IN HIS ANCIENT NAME, LET FLOW FROM THE STARS THY BURNING BLOOD--

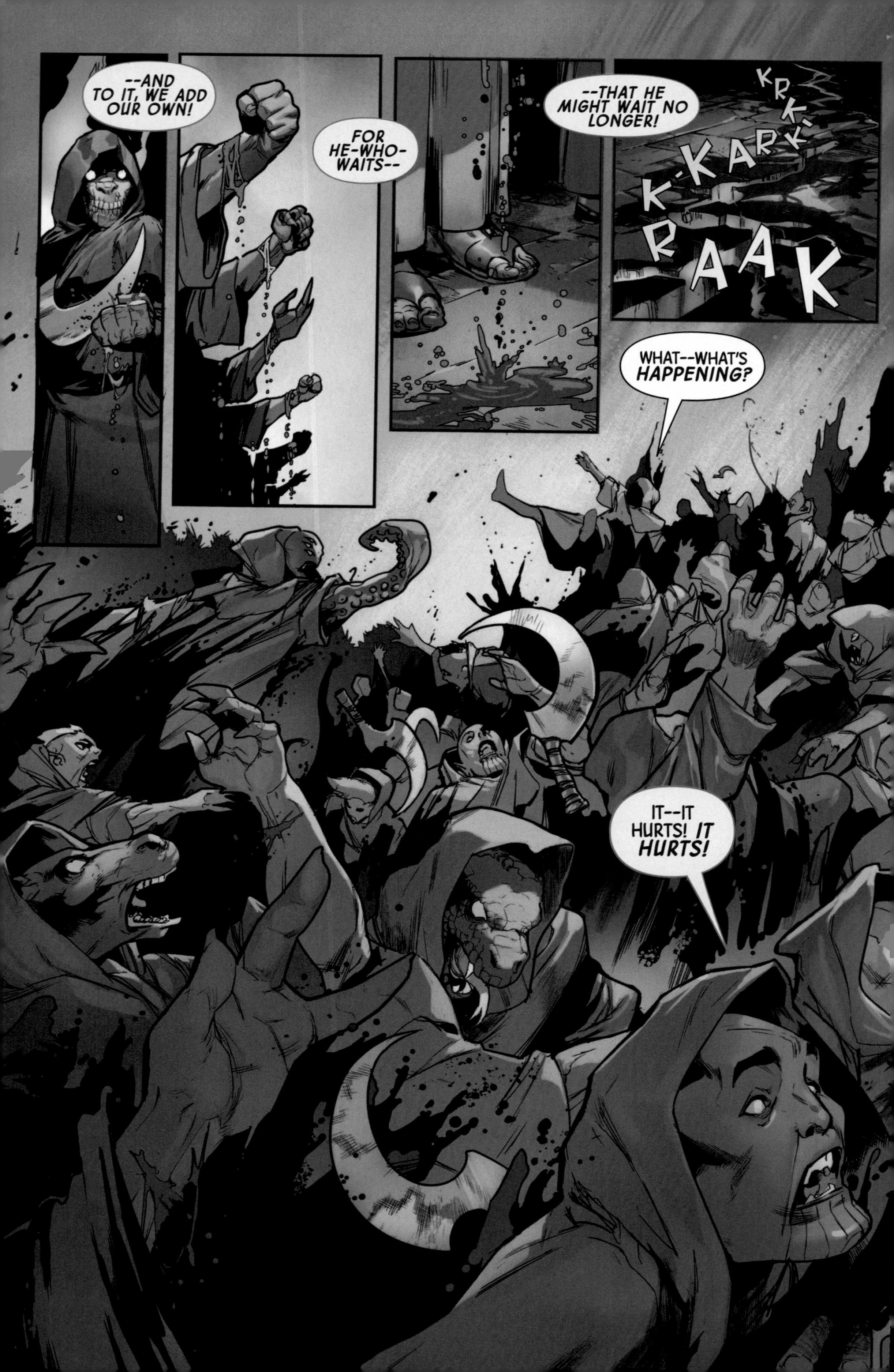
--AND TO IT, WE ADD OUR OWN!
FOR HE-WHO-WAITS--
--THAT HE MIGHT WAIT NO LONGER!
KRK-K-KARK-
RAAK
WHAT--WHAT'S HAPPENING?
IT--IT HURTS! IT HURTS!

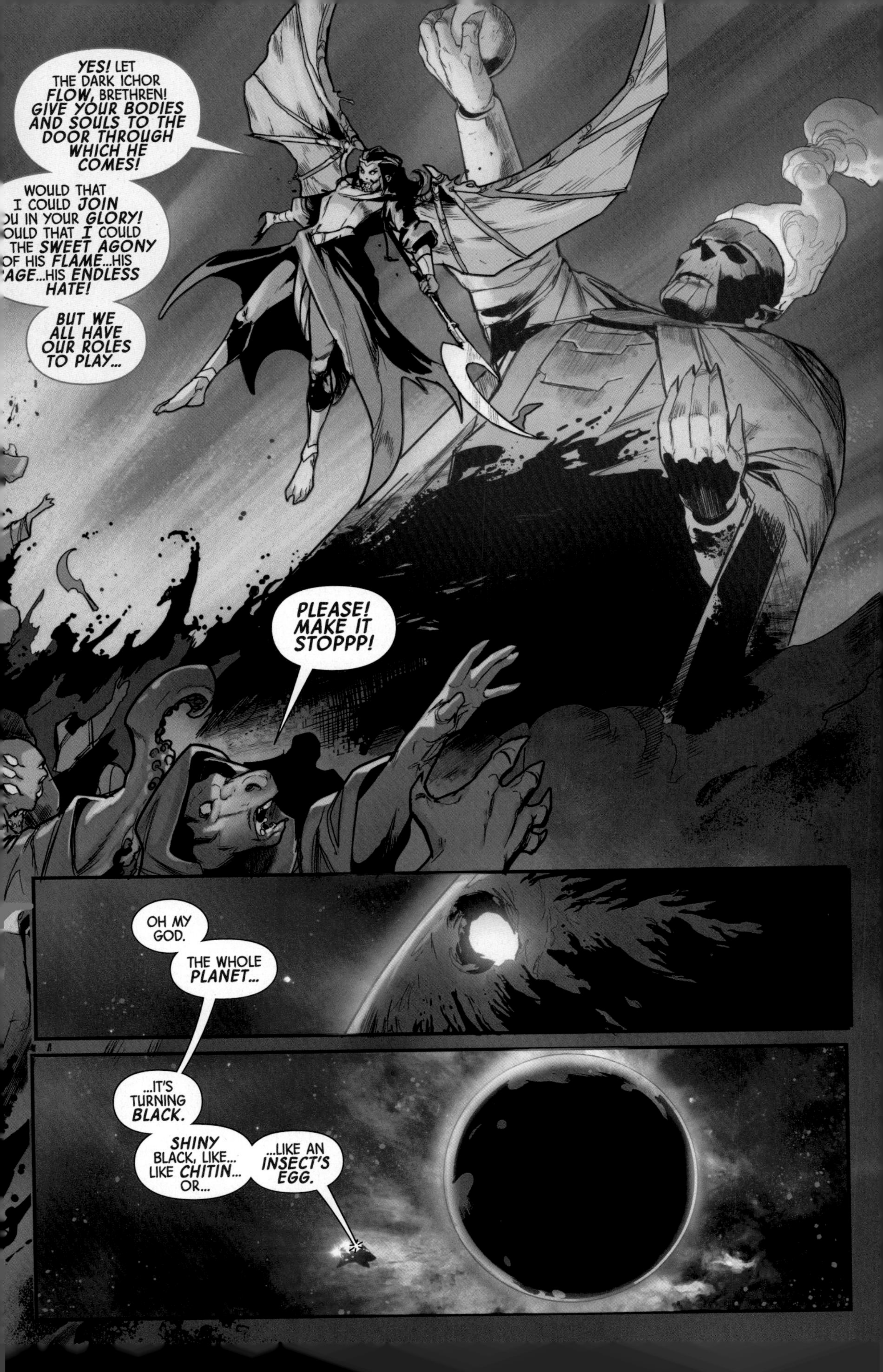
YES! LET THE DARK ICHOR FLOW, BRETHREN! GIVE YOUR BODIES AND SOULS TO THE DOOR THROUGH WHICH HE COMES!
WOULD THAT I COULD JOIN OU IN YOUR GLORY! OULD THAT I COULD THE SWEET AGONY OF HIS FLAME...HIS AGE...HIS ENDLESS HATE!
BUT WE ALL HAVE OUR ROLES TO PLAY...
PLEASE! MAKE IT STOPPP!
OH MY GOD.
THE WHOLE PLANET...
...IT'S TURNING BLACK.
SHINY BLACK, LIKE... LIKE CHITIN... OR...
...LIKE AN INSECT'S EGG.

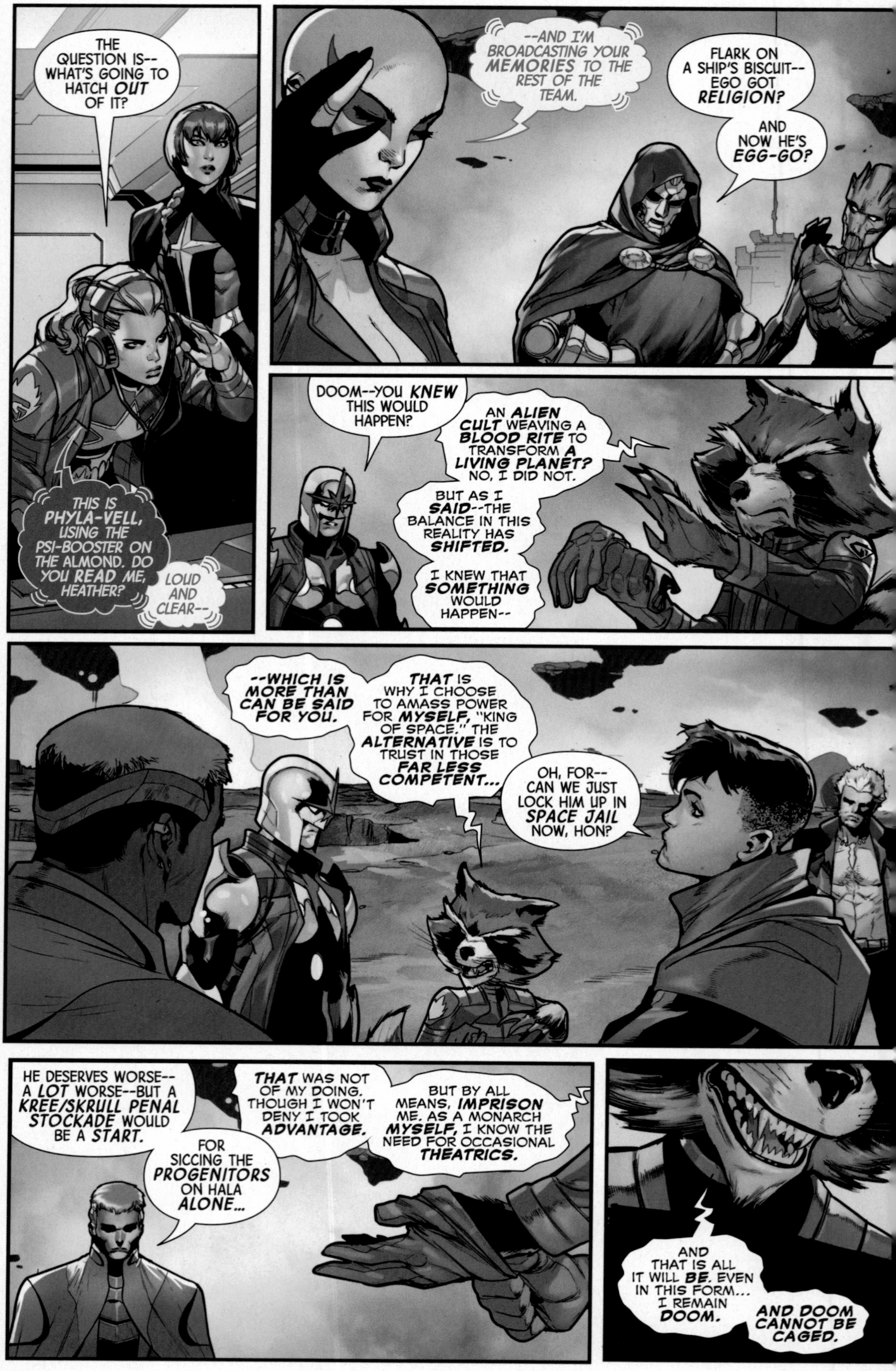
THE QUESTION IS-- WHAT'S GOING TO HATCH OUT OF IT?
THIS IS PHYLA-VELL, USING THE PSI-BOOSTER ON THE ALMOND. DO YOU READ ME, HEATHER?
LOUD AND CLEAR--
--AND I'M BROADCASTING YOUR MEMORIES TO THE REST OF THE TEAM.
FLARK ON A SHIP'S BISCUIT-- EGO GOT RELIGION?
AND NOW HE'S EGG-GO?
DOOM--YOU KNEW THIS WOULD HAPPEN?
AN ALIEN CULT WEAVING A BLOOD RITE TO TRANSFORM A LIVING PLANET? NO, I DID NOT.
BUT AS I SAID--THE BALANCE IN THIS REALITY HAS SHIFTED.
I KNEW THAT SOMETHING WOULD HAPPEN--
--WHICH IS MORE THAN CAN BE SAID FOR YOU.
THAT IS WHY I CHOOSE TO AMASS POWER FOR MYSELF, "KING OF SPACE." THE ALTERNATIVE IS TO TRUST IN THOSE FAR LESS COMPETENT...
OH, FOR-- CAN WE JUST LOCK HIM UP IN SPACE JAIL NOW, HON?
HE DESERVES WORSE-- A LOT WORSE--BUT A KREE/SKRULL PENAL STOCKADE WOULD BE A START.
FOR SICCING THE PROGENITORS ON HALA ALONE...
THAT WAS NOT OF MY DOING. THOUGH I WON'T DENY I TOOK ADVANTAGE.
BUT BY ALL MEANS, IMPRISON ME. AS A MONARCH MYSELF, I KNOW THE NEED FOR OCCASIONAL THEATRICS.
AND THAT IS ALL IT WILL BE. EVEN IN THIS FORM... I REMAIN DOOM.
AND DOOM CANNOT BE CAGED.

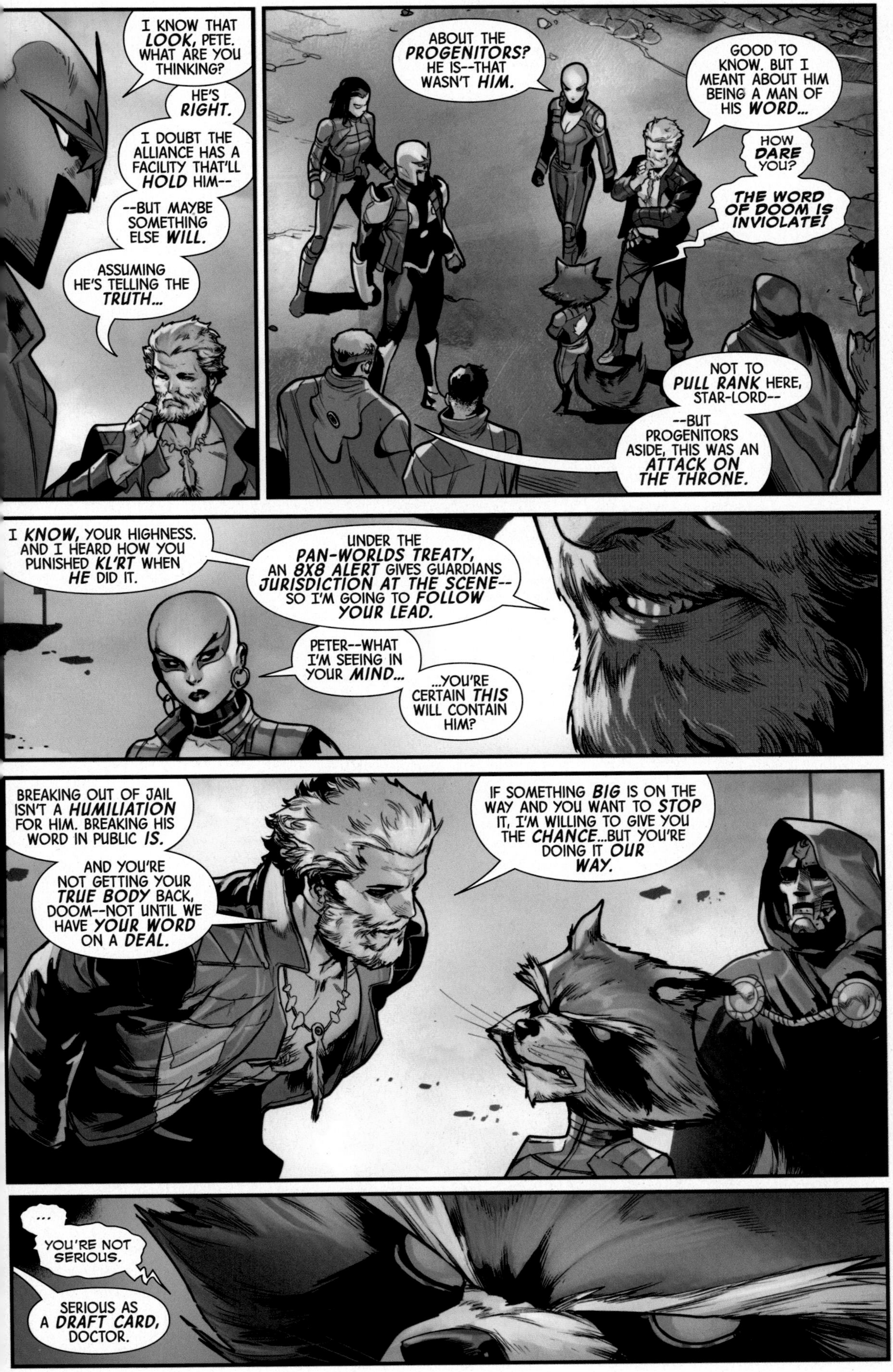
I KNOW THAT LOOK, PETE. WHAT ARE YOU THINKING?
HE'S RIGHT.
I DOUBT THE ALLIANCE HAS A FACILITY THAT'LL HOLD HIM--
--BUT MAYBE SOMETHING ELSE WILL.
ASSUMING HE'S TELLING THE TRUTH...
ABOUT THE PROGENITORS? HE IS--THAT WASN'T HIM.
GOOD TO KNOW. BUT I MEANT ABOUT HIM BEING A MAN OF HIS WORD...
HOW DARE YOU?
THE WORD OF DOOM IS INVIOLATE!
NOT TO PULL RANK HERE, STAR-LORD--
--BUT PROGENITORS ASIDE, THIS WAS AN ATTACK ON THE THRONE.
I KNOW, YOUR HIGHNESS. AND I HEARD HOW YOU PUNISHED KL'RT WHEN HE DID IT.
UNDER THE PAN-WORLDS TREATY, AN 8X8 ALERT GIVES GUARDIANS JURISDICTION AT THE SCENE-- SO I'M GOING TO FOLLOW YOUR LEAD.
PETER--WHAT I'M SEEING IN YOUR MIND...
...YOU'RE CERTAIN THIS WILL CONTAIN HIM?
BREAKING OUT OF JAIL ISN'T A HUMILIATION FOR HIM. BREAKING HIS WORD IN PUBLIC IS.
AND YOU'RE NOT GETTING YOUR TRUE BODY BACK, DOOM--NOT UNTIL WE HAVE YOUR WORD ON A DEAL.
IF SOMETHING BIG IS ON THE WAY AND YOU WANT TO STOP IT, I'M WILLING TO GIVE YOU THE CHANCE...BUT YOU'RE DOING IT OUR WAY.
...
YOU'RE NOT SERIOUS.
SERIOUS AS A DRAFT CARD, DOCTOR.

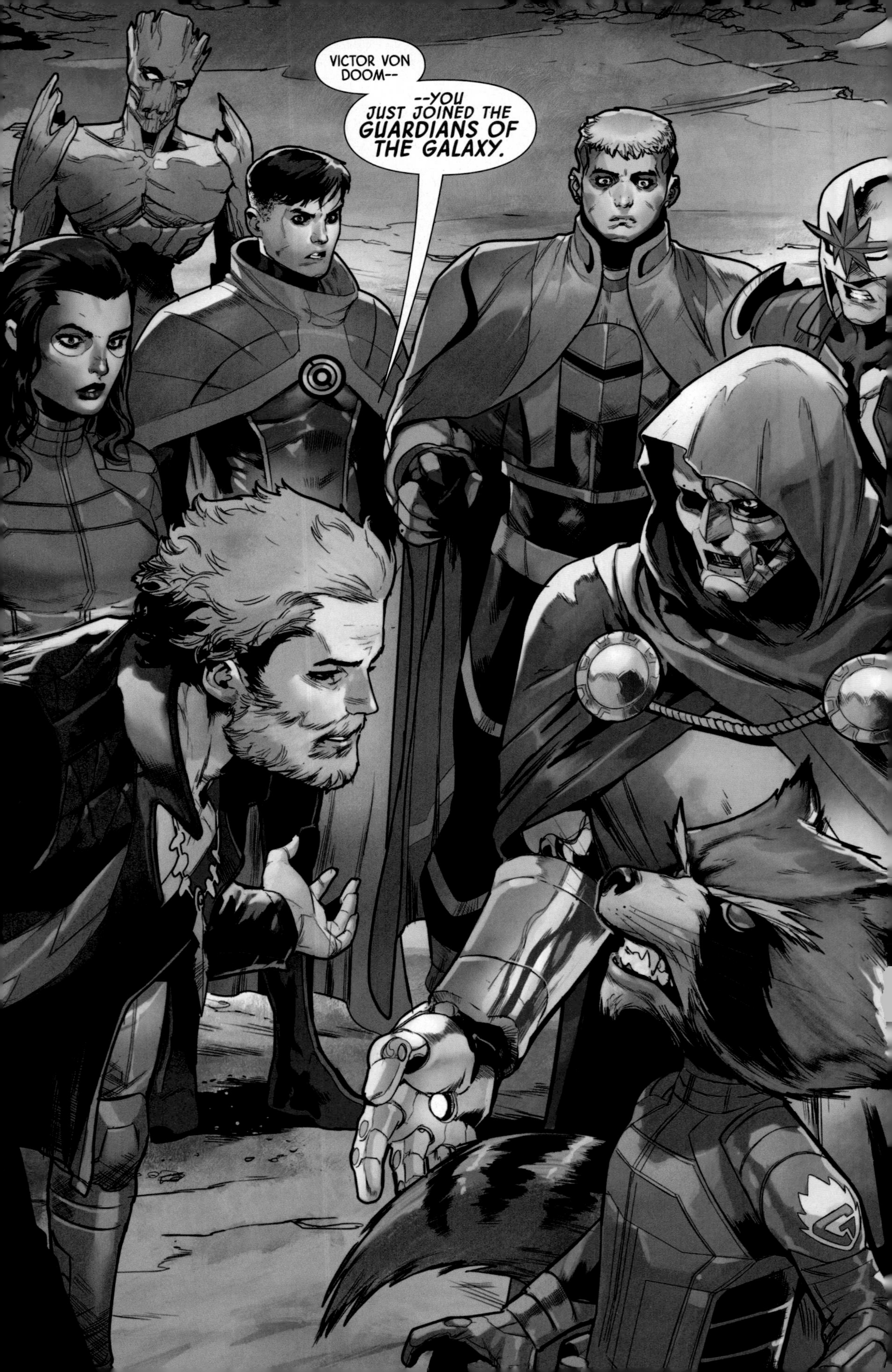
VICTOR VON DOOM--
--YOU JUST JOINED THE GUARDIANS OF THE GALAXY.

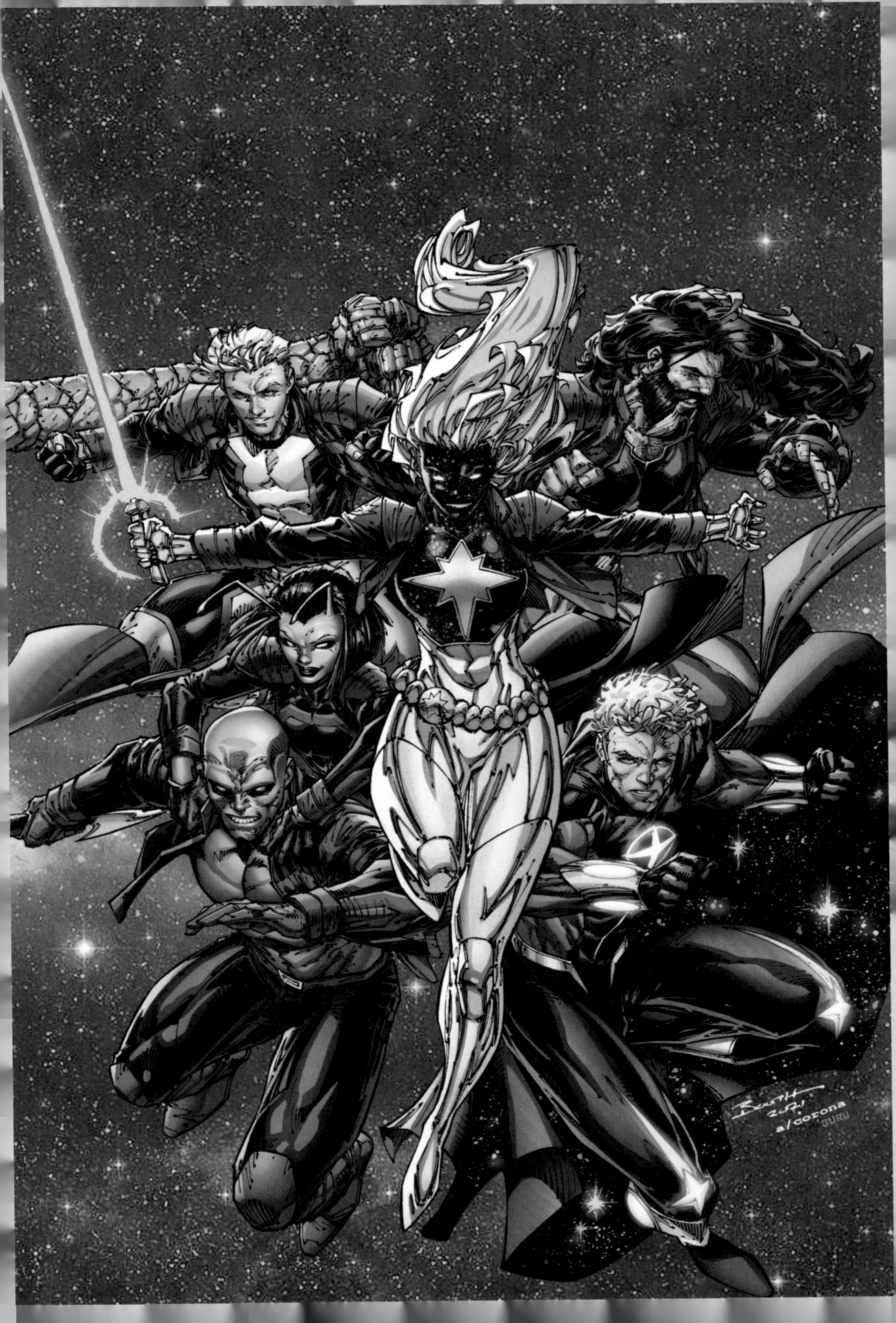

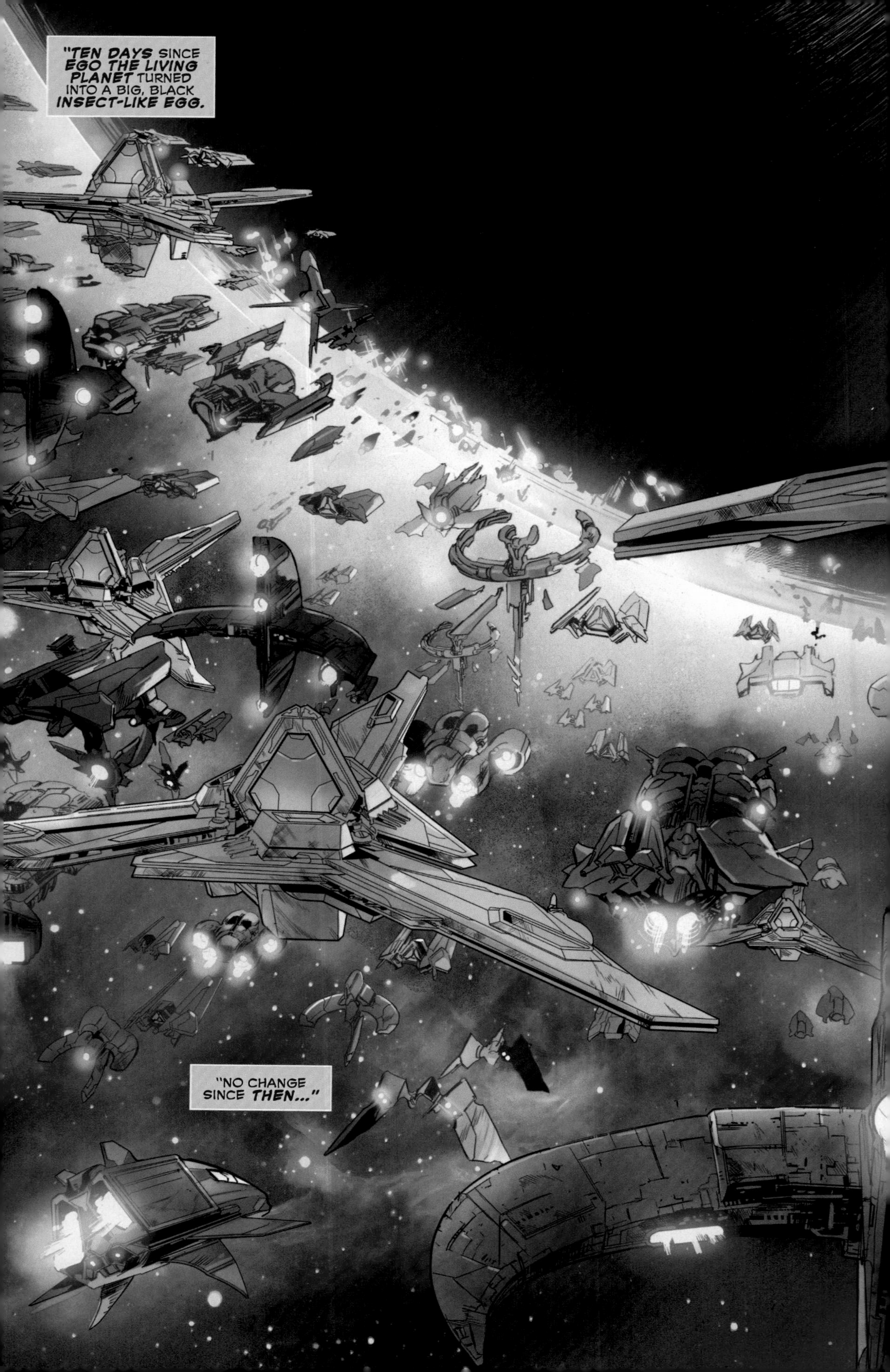
"TEN DAYS SINCE EGO THE LIVING PLANET TURNED INTO A BIG, BLACK INSECT-LIKE EGG.
"NO CHANGE SINCE THEN..."

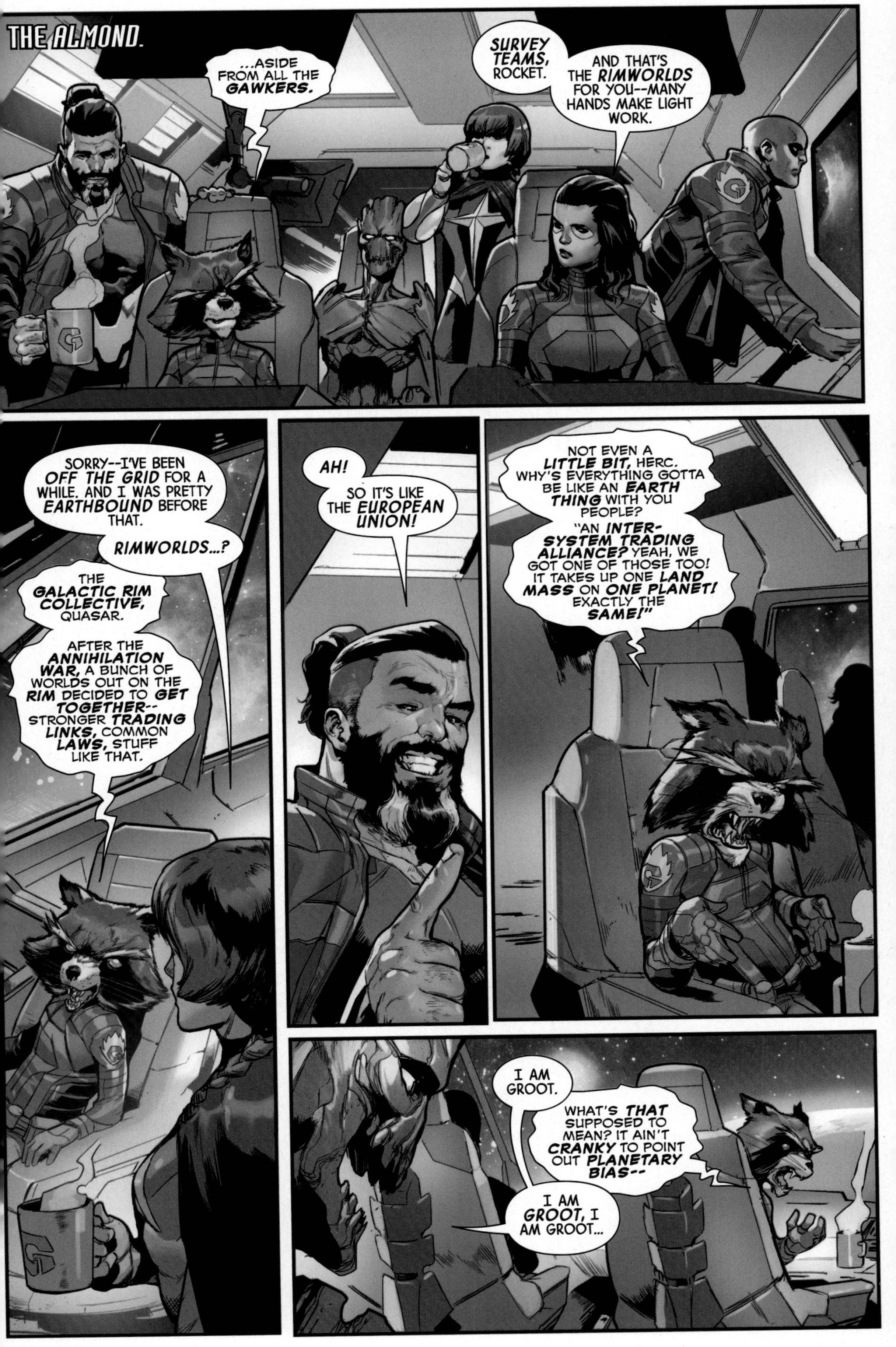
THE ALMOND.
...ASIDE FROM ALL THE GAWKERS.
SURVEY TEAMS, ROCKET.
AND THAT'S THE RIMWORLDS FOR YOU--MANY HANDS MAKE LIGHT WORK.
SORRY--I'VE BEEN OFF THE GRID FOR A WHILE. AND I WAS PRETTY EARTHBOUND BEFORE THAT.
RIMWORLDS...?
THE GALACTIC RIM COLLECTIVE, QUASAR.
AFTER THE ANNIHILATION WAR, A BUNCH OF WORLDS OUT ON THE RIM DECIDED TO GET TOGETHER--STRONGER TRADING LINKS, COMMON LAWS, STUFF LIKE THAT.
AH!
SO IT'S LIKE THE EUROPEAN UNION!
NOT EVEN A LITTLE BIT, HERC. WHY'S EVERYTHING GOTTA BE LIKE AN EARTH THING WITH YOU PEOPLE?
"AN INTER-SYSTEM TRADING ALLIANCE? YEAH, WE GOT ONE OF THOSE TOO! IT TAKES UP ONE LAND MASS ON ONE PLANET! EXACTLY THE SAME!"
I AM GROOT.
WHAT'S THAT SUPPOSED TO MEAN? IT AIN'T CRANKY TO POINT OUT PLANETARY BIAS--
I AM GROOT, I AM GROOT...

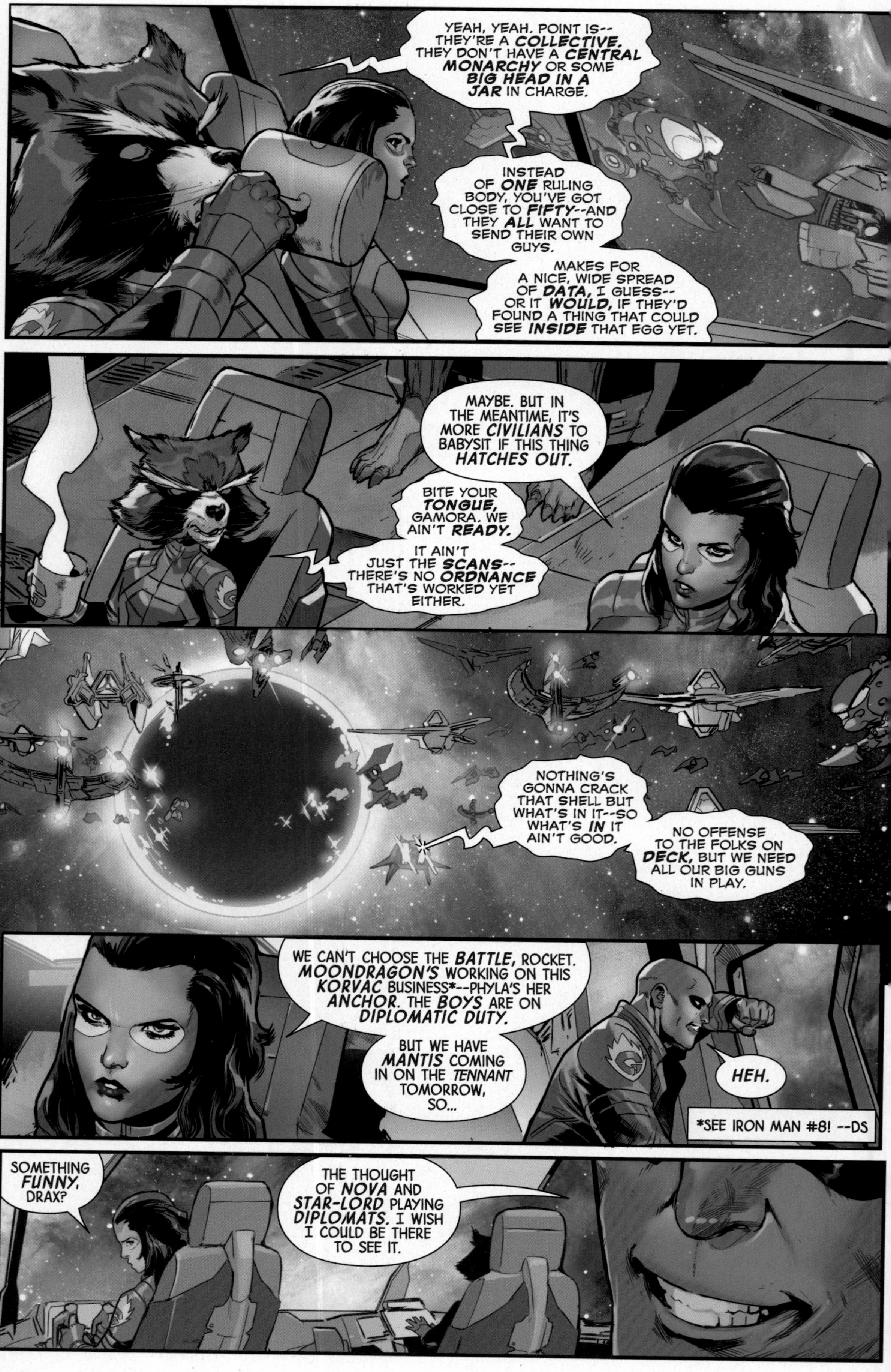
YEAH, YEAH. POINT IS-- THEY'RE A COLLECTIVE. THEY DON'T HAVE A CENTRAL MONARCHY OR SOME BIG HEAD IN A JAR IN CHARGE.
INSTEAD OF ONE RULING BODY, YOU'VE GOT CLOSE TO FIFTY--AND THEY ALL WANT TO SEND THEIR OWN GUYS.
MAKES FOR A NICE, WIDE SPREAD OF DATA, I GUESS-- OR IT WOULD, IF THEY'D FOUND A THING THAT COULD SEE INSIDE THAT EGG YET.
MAYBE. BUT IN THE MEANTIME, IT'S MORE CIVILIANS TO BABYSIT IF THIS THING HATCHES OUT.
BITE YOUR TONGUE, GAMORA. WE AIN'T READY.
IT AIN'T JUST THE SCANS-- THERE'S NO ORDNANCE THAT'S WORKED YET EITHER.
NOTHING'S GONNA CRACK THAT SHELL BUT WHAT'S IN IT--SO WHAT'S IN IT AIN'T GOOD.
NO OFFENSE TO THE FOLKS ON DECK, BUT WE NEED ALL OUR BIG GUNS IN PLAY.
WE CAN'T CHOOSE THE BATTLE, ROCKET. MOONDRAGON'S WORKING ON THIS KORVAC BUSINESS*--PHYLA'S HER ANCHOR. THE BOYS ARE ON DIPLOMATIC DUTY.
BUT WE HAVE MANTIS COMING IN ON THE TENNANT TOMORROW, SO...
HEH.
*SEE IRON MAN #8! --DS
SOMETHING FUNNY, DRAX?
THE THOUGHT OF NOVA AND STAR-LORD PLAYING DIPLOMATS. I WISH I COULD BE THERE TO SEE IT.

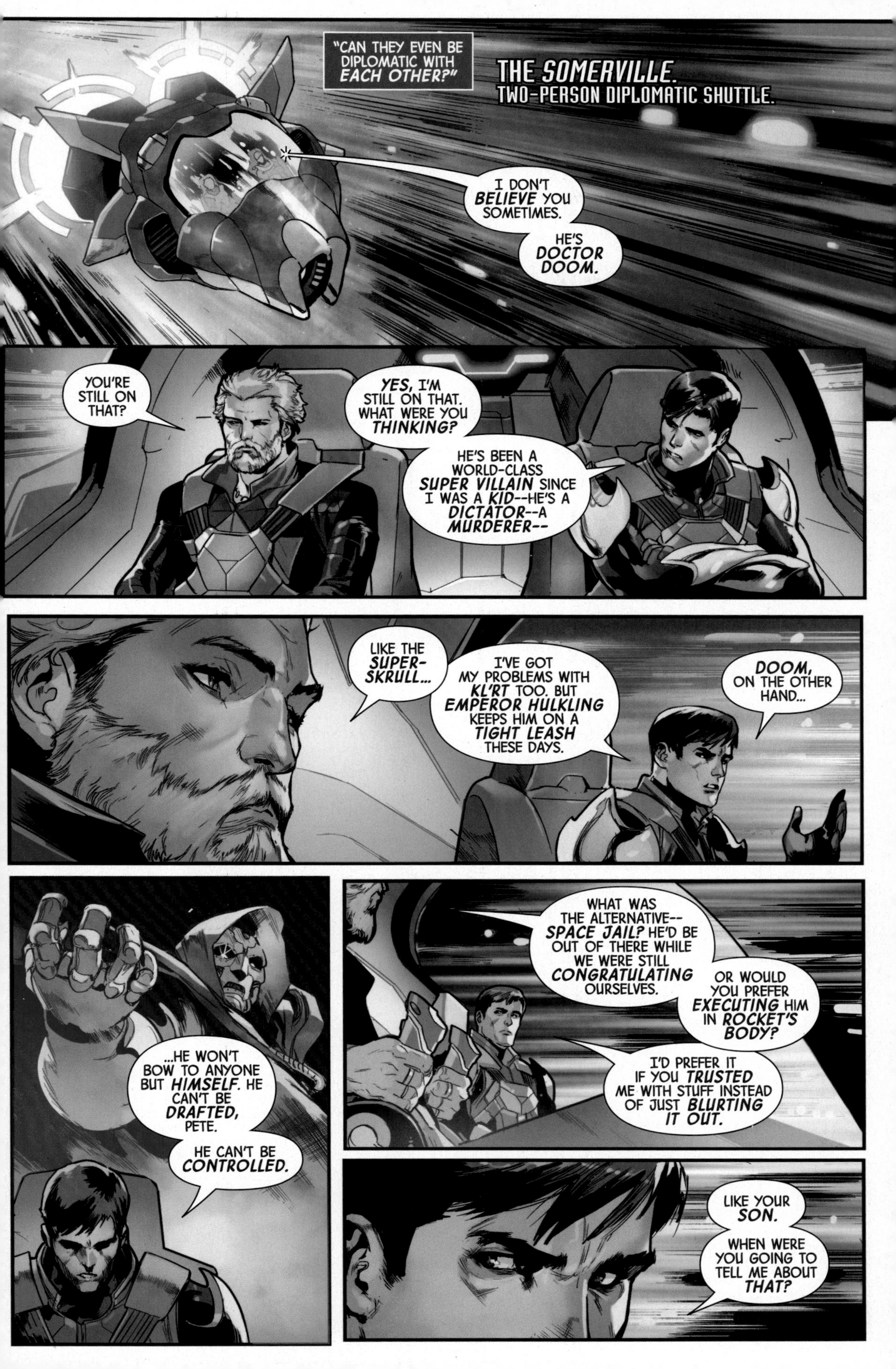
"CAN THEY EVEN BE DIPLOMATIC WITH EACH OTHER?"
THE SOMERVILLE. TWO-PERSON DIPLOMATIC SHUTTLE.
I DON'T BELIEVE YOU SOMETIMES.
HE'S DOCTOR DOOM.
YOU'RE STILL ON THAT?
YES, I'M STILL ON THAT. WHAT WERE YOU THINKING?
HE'S BEEN A WORLD-CLASS SUPER VILLAIN SINCE I WAS A KID--HE'S A DICTATOR--A MURDERER--
LIKE THE SUPER-SKRULL...
I'VE GOT MY PROBLEMS WITH KL'RT TOO. BUT EMPEROR HULKLING KEEPS HIM ON A TIGHT LEASH THESE DAYS.
DOOM, ON THE OTHER HAND...
...HE WON'T BOW TO ANYONE BUT HIMSELF. HE CAN'T BE DRAFTED, PETE.
HE CAN'T BE CONTROLLED.
WHAT WAS THE ALTERNATIVE--SPACE JAIL? HE'D BE OUT OF THERE WHILE WE WERE STILL CONGRATULATING OURSELVES.
OR WOULD YOU PREFER EXECUTING HIM IN ROCKET'S BODY?
I'D PREFER IT IF YOU TRUSTED ME WITH STUFF INSTEAD OF JUST BLURTING IT OUT.
LIKE YOUR SON.
WHEN WERE YOU GOING TO TELL ME ABOUT THAT?

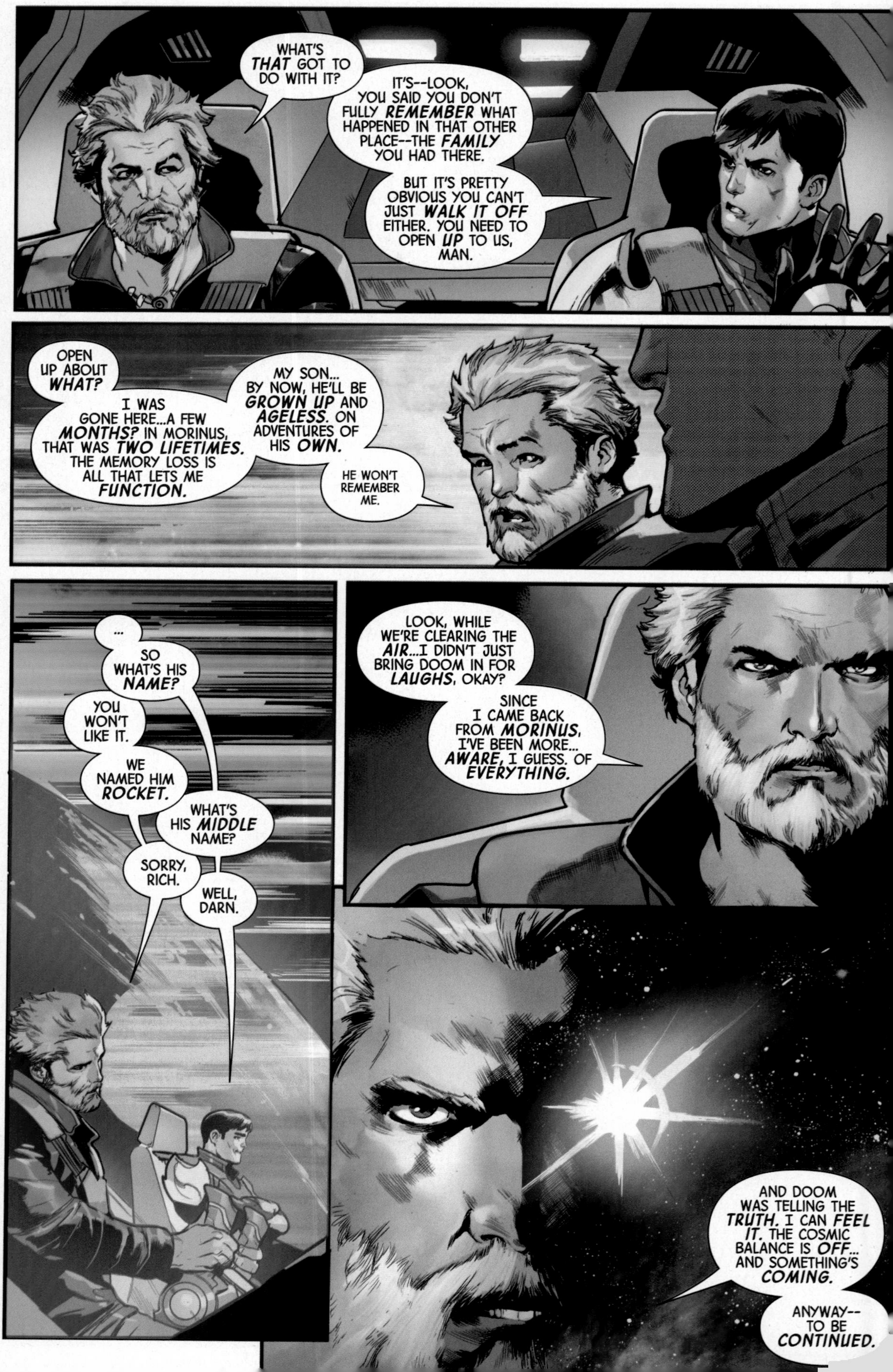
WHAT'S THAT GOT TO DO WITH IT?
IT'S--LOOK, YOU SAID YOU DON'T FULLY REMEMBER WHAT HAPPENED IN THAT OTHER PLACE--THE FAMILY YOU HAD THERE.
BUT IT'S PRETTY OBVIOUS YOU CAN'T JUST WALK IT OFF EITHER. YOU NEED TO OPEN UP TO US, MAN.
OPEN UP ABOUT WHAT?
I WAS GONE HERE...A FEW MONTHS? IN MORINUS, THAT WAS TWO LIFETIMES. THE MEMORY LOSS IS ALL THAT LETS ME FUNCTION.
MY SON... BY NOW, HE'LL BE GROWN UP AND AGELESS. ON ADVENTURES OF HIS OWN.
HE WON'T REMEMBER ME.
...
SO WHAT'S HIS NAME?
YOU WON'T LIKE IT.
WE NAMED HIM ROCKET.
WHAT'S HIS MIDDLE NAME?
SORRY, RICH.
WELL, DARN.
LOOK, WHILE WE'RE CLEARING THE AIR...I DIDN'T JUST BRING DOOM IN FOR LAUGHS, OKAY?
SINCE I CAME BACK FROM MORINUS, I'VE BEEN MORE... AWARE, I GUESS. OF EVERYTHING.
AND DOOM WAS TELLING THE TRUTH. I CAN FEEL IT. THE COSMIC BALANCE IS OFF... AND SOMETHING'S COMING.
ANYWAY-- TO BE CONTINUED.

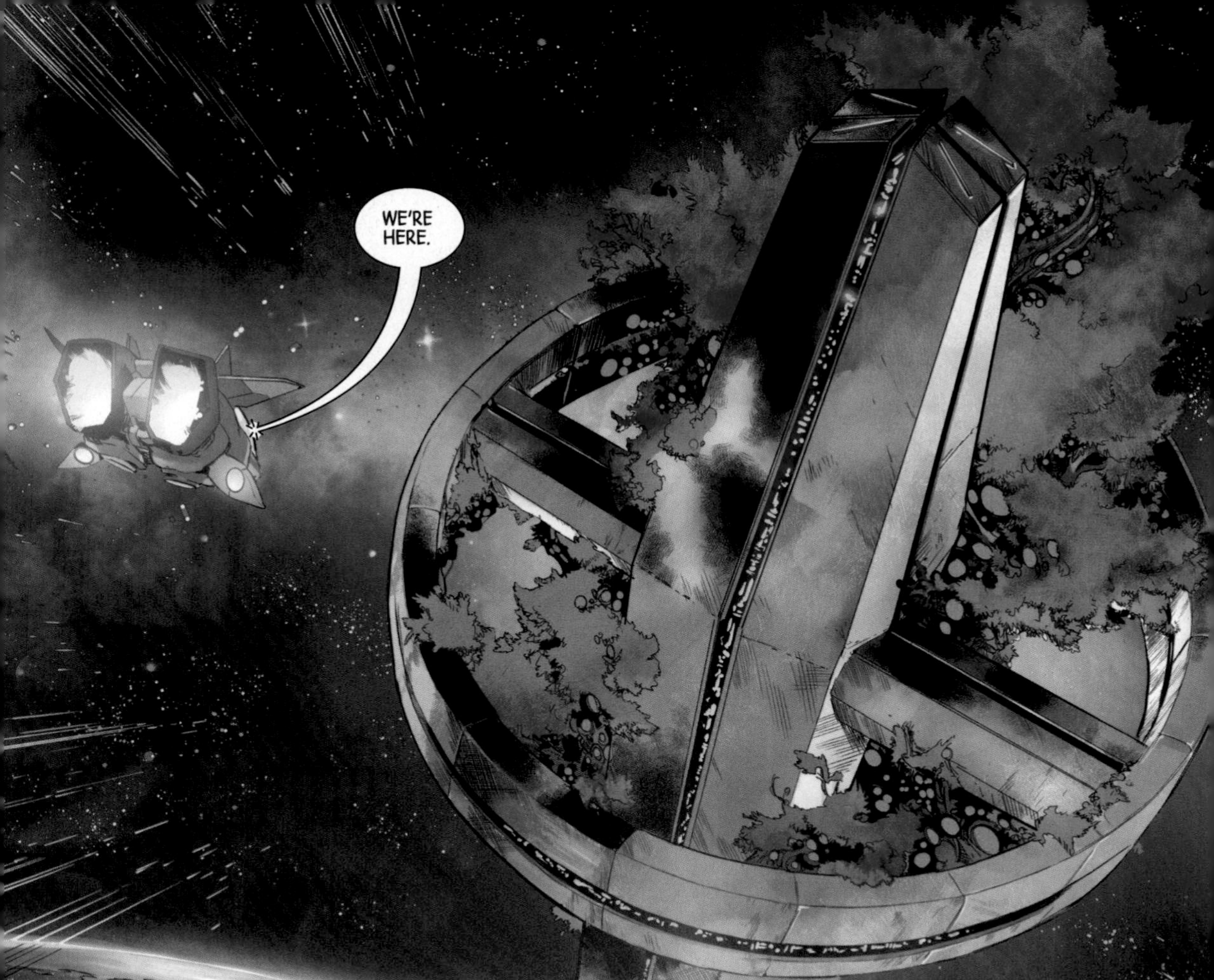
WE'RE HERE.
THIS IS THE **HANGAR,** SOMERVILLE. YOU'RE ON **RADAR** AND YOUR TRAJECTORY IS **MAPPED.**
WELCOME TO **S.W.O.R.D.,** GENTLEMEN--**HOPE YOU SURVIVE THE EXPERIENCE.**

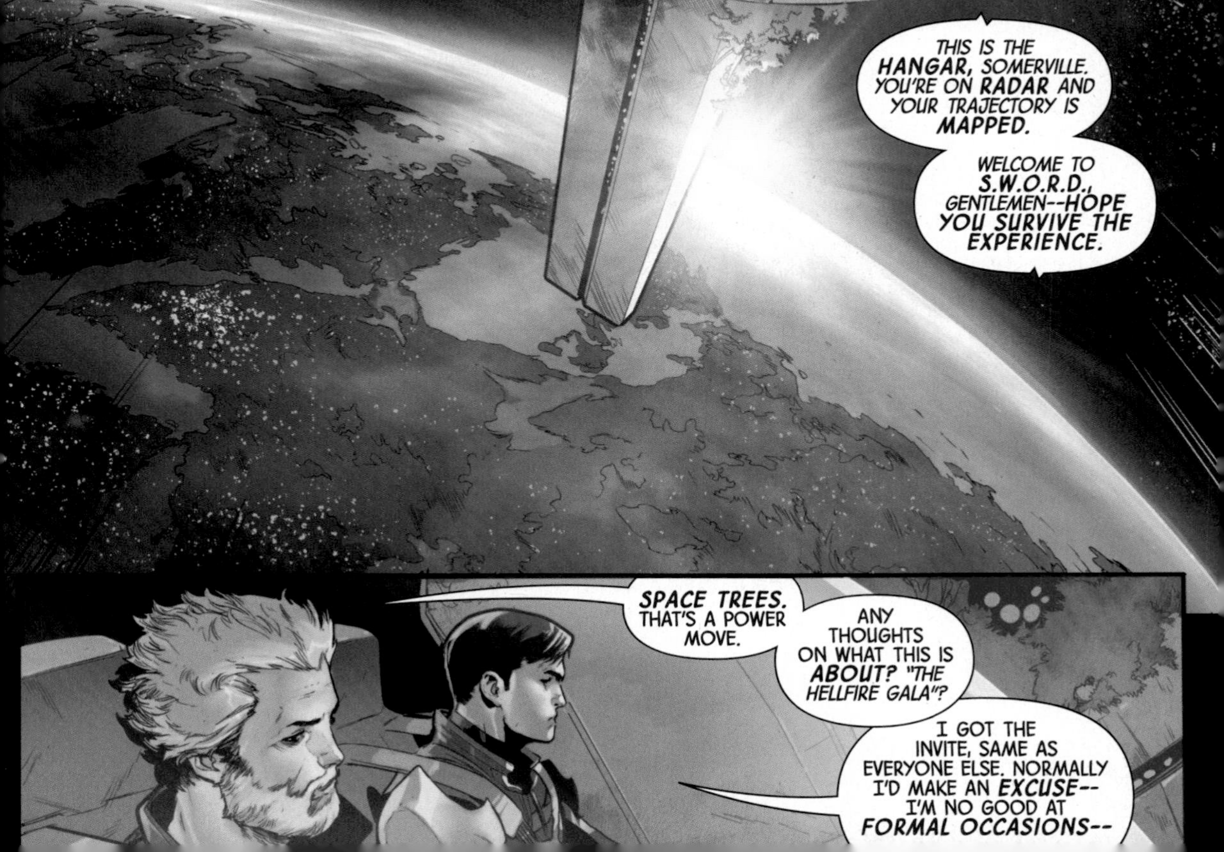
SPACE TREES. THAT'S A POWER MOVE.
ANY THOUGHTS ON WHAT THIS IS ***ABOUT?*** "THE HELLFIRE GALA"?
I GOT THE INVITE, SAME AS EVERYONE ELSE. NORMALLY I'D MAKE AN ***EXCUSE***-- I'M NO GOOD AT ***FORMAL OCCASIONS***--

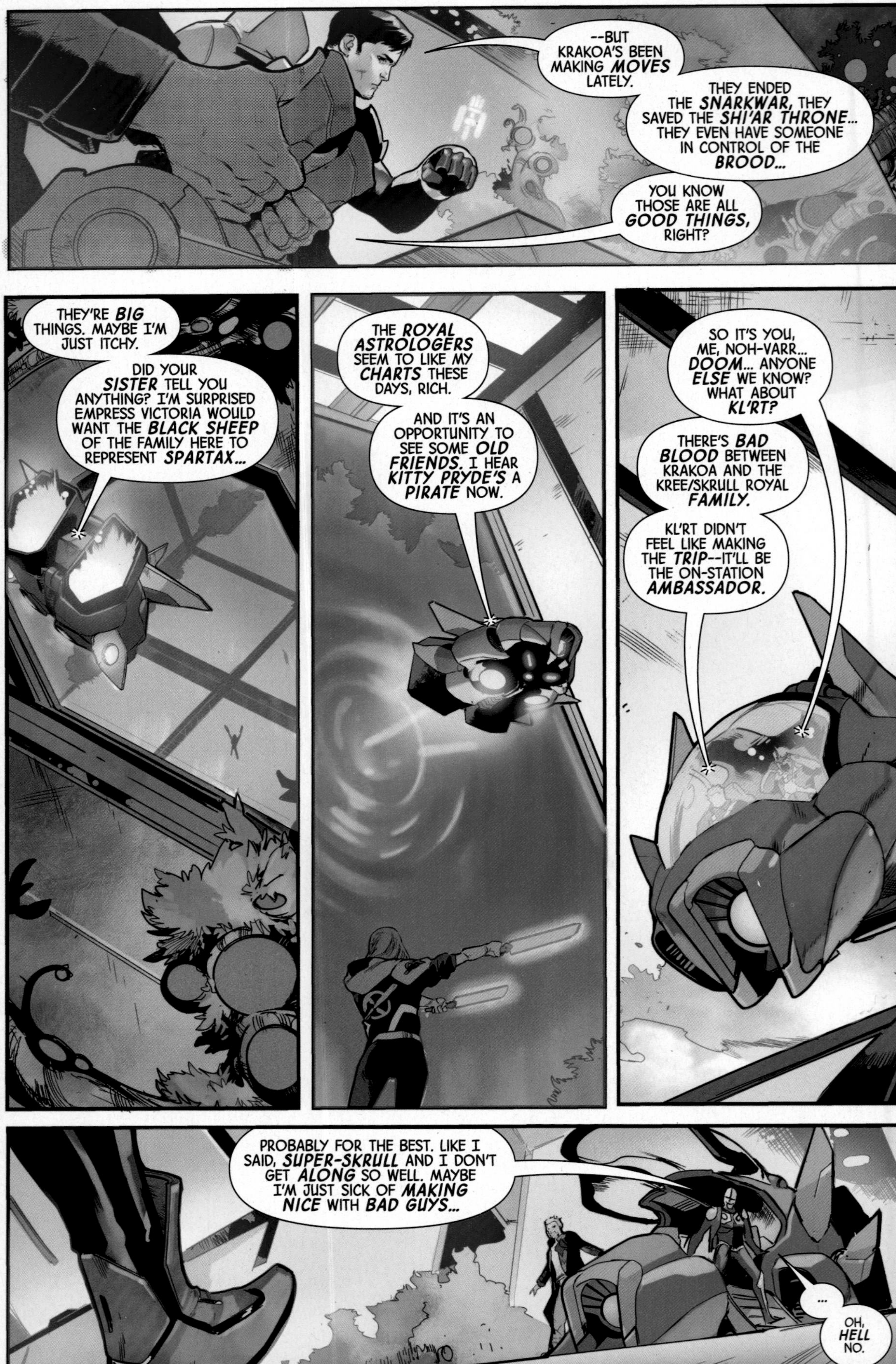
--BUT KRAKOA'S BEEN MAKING MOVES LATELY.
THEY ENDED THE SNARKWAR, THEY SAVED THE SHI'AR THRONE... THEY EVEN HAVE SOMEONE IN CONTROL OF THE BROOD...
YOU KNOW THOSE ARE ALL GOOD THINGS, RIGHT?
THEY'RE BIG THINGS. MAYBE I'M JUST ITCHY.
DID YOUR SISTER TELL YOU ANYTHING? I'M SURPRISED EMPRESS VICTORIA WOULD WANT THE BLACK SHEEP OF THE FAMILY HERE TO REPRESENT SPARTAX...
THE ROYAL ASTROLOGERS SEEM TO LIKE MY CHARTS THESE DAYS, RICH.
AND IT'S AN OPPORTUNITY TO SEE SOME OLD FRIENDS. I HEAR KITTY PRYDE'S A PIRATE NOW.
SO IT'S YOU, ME, NOH-VARR... DOOM... ANYONE ELSE WE KNOW? WHAT ABOUT KL'RT?
THERE'S BAD BLOOD BETWEEN KRAKOA AND THE KREE/SKRULL ROYAL FAMILY.
KL'RT DIDN'T FEEL LIKE MAKING THE TRIP--IT'LL BE THE ON-STATION AMBASSADOR.
PROBABLY FOR THE BEST. LIKE I SAID, SUPER-SKRULL AND I DON'T GET ALONG SO WELL. MAYBE I'M JUST SICK OF MAKING NICE WITH BAD GUYS...
...
OH, HELL NO.

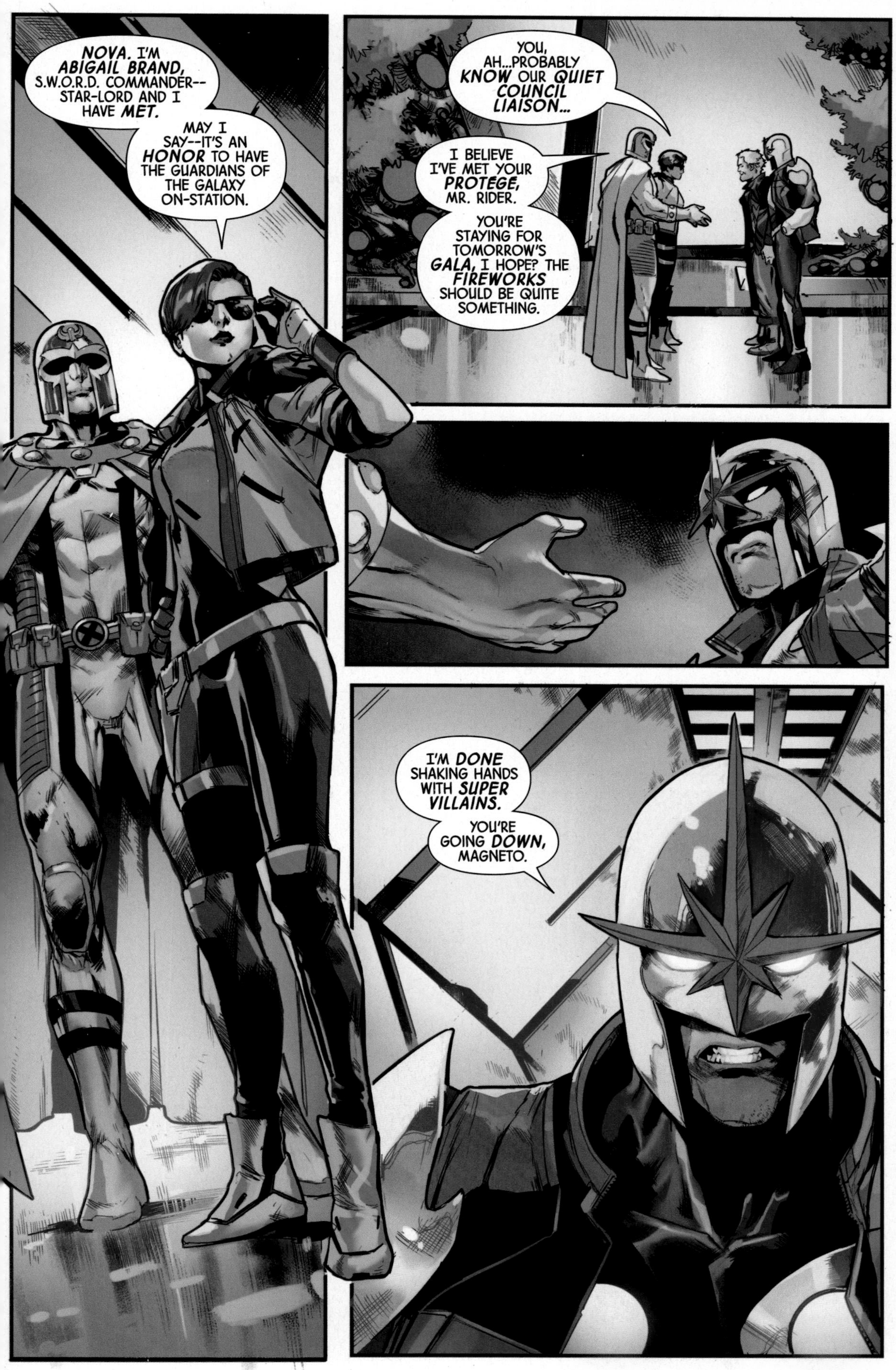
NOVA. I'M ABIGAIL BRAND, S.W.O.R.D. COMMANDER-- STAR-LORD AND I HAVE MET.
MAY I SAY--IT'S AN HONOR TO HAVE THE GUARDIANS OF THE GALAXY ON-STATION.
YOU, AH...PROBABLY KNOW OUR QUIET COUNCIL LIAISON...
I BELIEVE I'VE MET YOUR PROTEGE, MR. RIDER.
YOU'RE STAYING FOR TOMORROW'S GALA, I HOPE? THE FIREWORKS SHOULD BE QUITE SOMETHING.
I'M DONE SHAKING HANDS WITH SUPER VILLAINS.
YOU'RE GOING DOWN, MAGNETO.

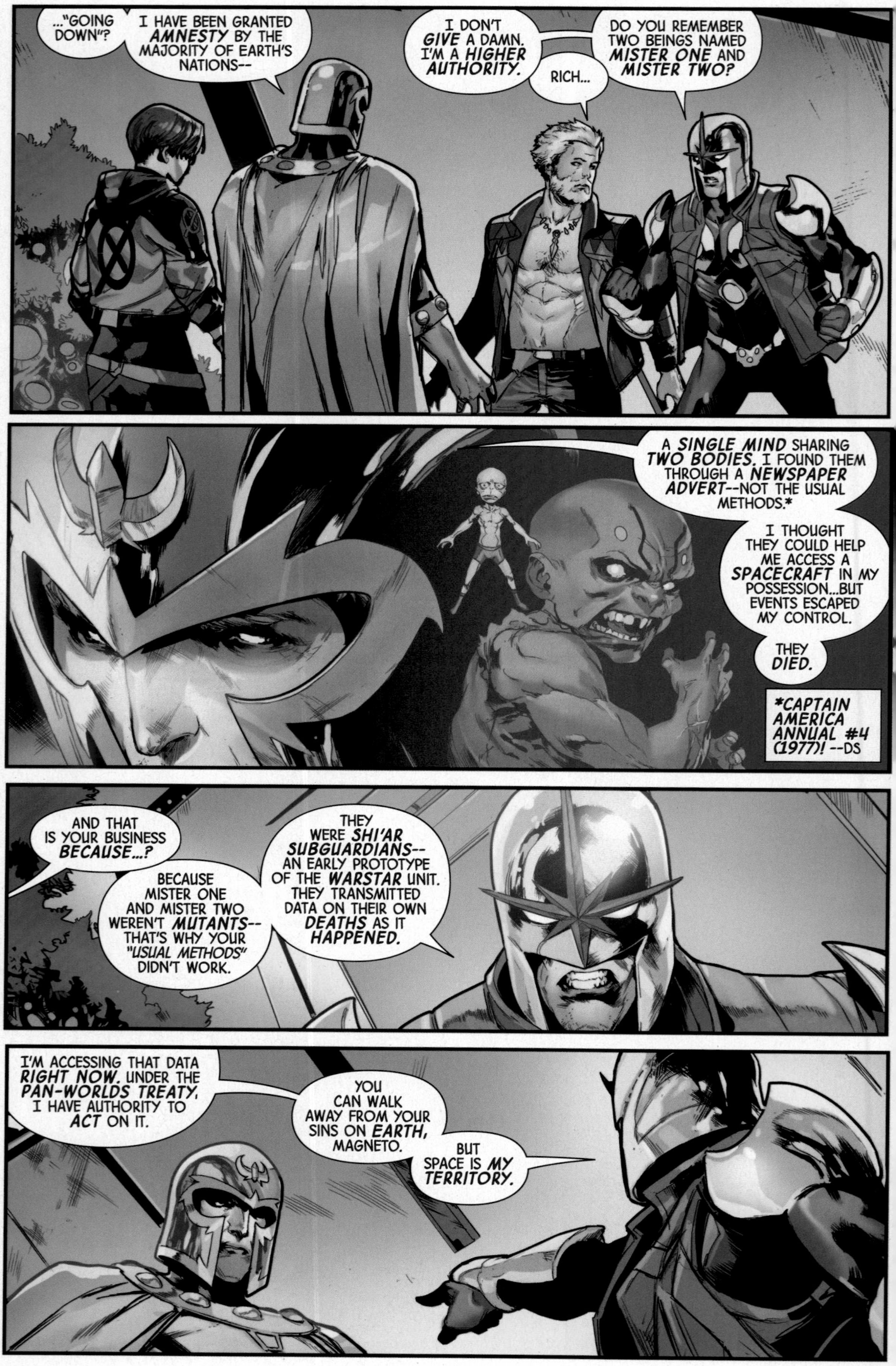
..."GOING DOWN"?
I HAVE BEEN GRANTED AMNESTY BY THE MAJORITY OF EARTH'S NATIONS--
I DON'T GIVE A DAMN. I'M A HIGHER AUTHORITY.
RICH...
DO YOU REMEMBER TWO BEINGS NAMED MISTER ONE AND MISTER TWO?
A SINGLE MIND SHARING TWO BODIES. I FOUND THEM THROUGH A NEWSPAPER ADVERT--NOT THE USUAL METHODS.*
I THOUGHT THEY COULD HELP ME ACCESS A SPACECRAFT IN MY POSSESSION...BUT EVENTS ESCAPED MY CONTROL.
THEY DIED.
*CAPTAIN AMERICA ANNUAL #4 (1977)! --DS
AND THAT IS YOUR BUSINESS BECAUSE...?
BECAUSE MISTER ONE AND MISTER TWO WEREN'T MUTANTS-- THAT'S WHY YOUR "USUAL METHODS" DIDN'T WORK.
THEY WERE SHI'AR SUBGUARDIANS-- AN EARLY PROTOTYPE OF THE WARSTAR UNIT. THEY TRANSMITTED DATA ON THEIR OWN DEATHS AS IT HAPPENED.
I'M ACCESSING THAT DATA RIGHT NOW. UNDER THE PAN-WORLDS TREATY, I HAVE AUTHORITY TO ACT ON IT.
YOU CAN WALK AWAY FROM YOUR SINS ON EARTH, MAGNETO.
BUT SPACE IS MY TERRITORY.

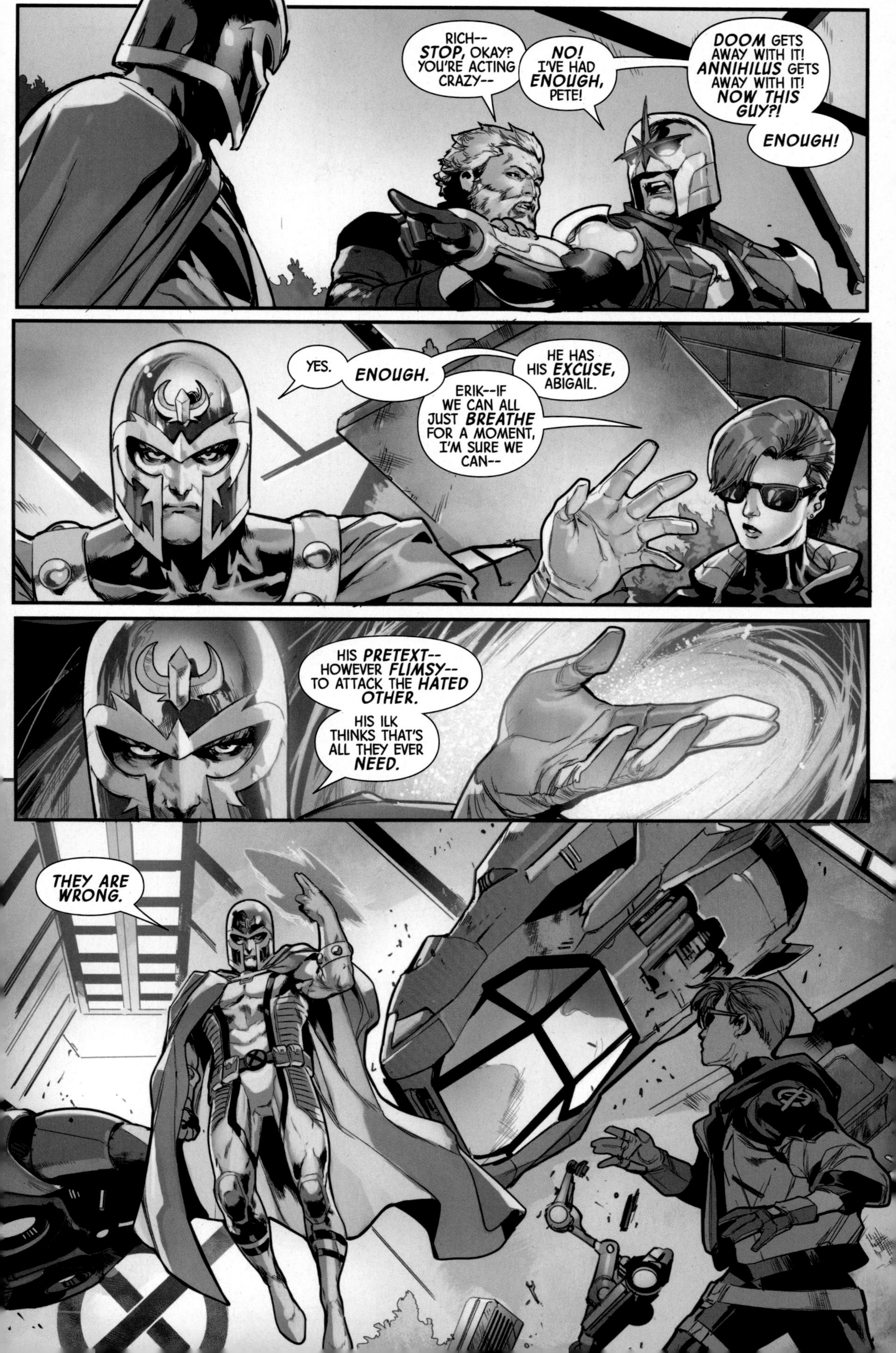
RICH-- STOP, OKAY? YOU'RE ACTING CRAZY--
NO! I'VE HAD ENOUGH, PETE!
DOOM GETS AWAY WITH IT! ANNIHILUS GETS AWAY WITH IT! NOW THIS GUY?!
ENOUGH!
YES.
ENOUGH.
HE HAS HIS EXCUSE, ABIGAIL.
ERIK--IF WE CAN ALL JUST BREATHE FOR A MOMENT, I'M SURE WE CAN--
HIS PRETEXT-- HOWEVER FLIMSY-- TO ATTACK THE HATED OTHER.
HIS ILK THINKS THAT'S ALL THEY EVER NEED.
THEY ARE WRONG.

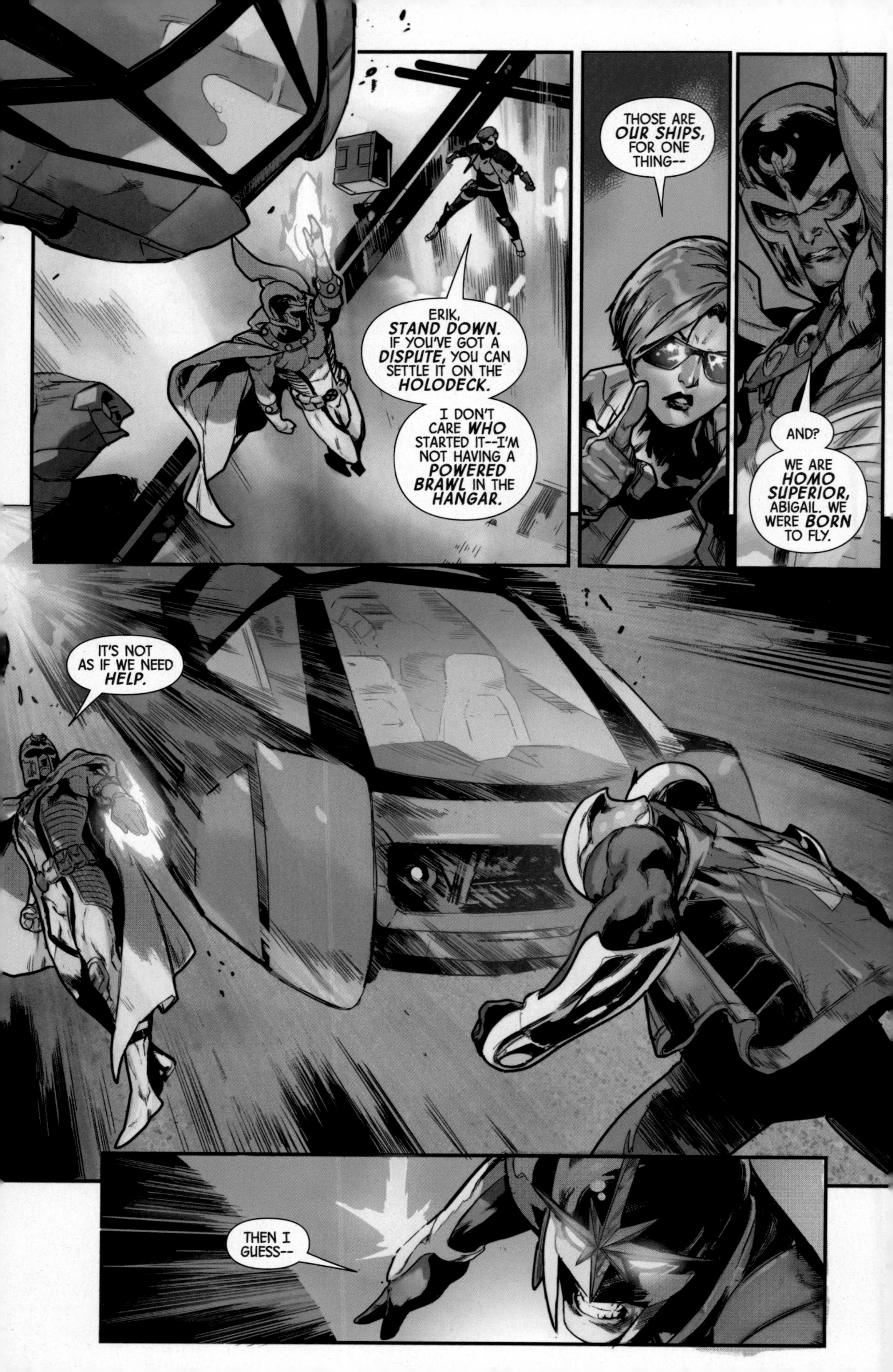
ERIK, STAND DOWN. IF YOU'VE GOT A DISPUTE, YOU CAN SETTLE IT ON THE HOLODECK.
I DON'T CARE WHO STARTED IT--I'M NOT HAVING A POWERED BRAWL IN THE HANGAR.
THOSE ARE OUR SHIPS, FOR ONE THING--
AND?
WE ARE HOMO SUPERIOR, ABIGAIL. WE WERE BORN TO FLY.
IT'S NOT AS IF WE NEED HELP.
THEN I GUESS--

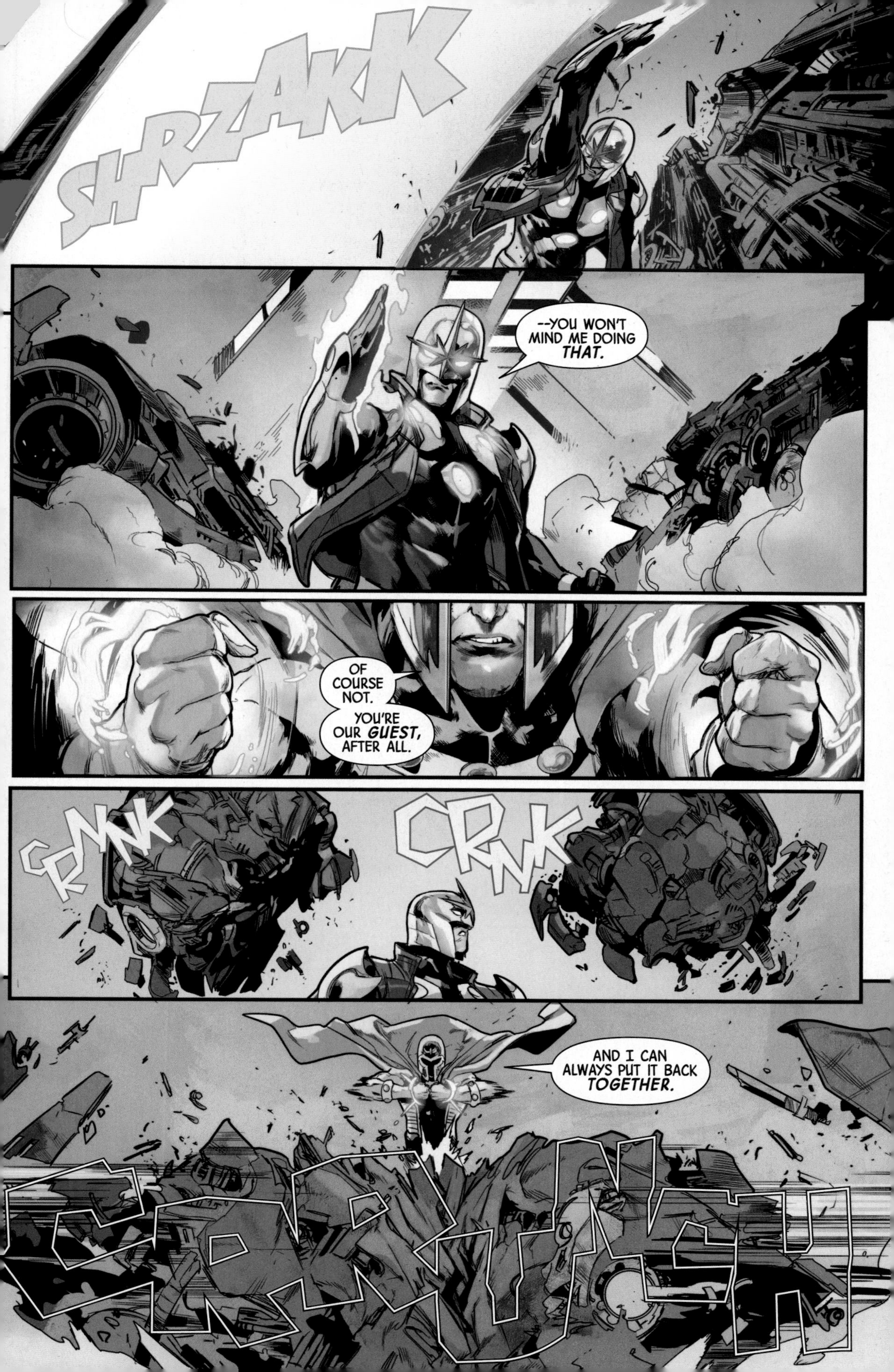
SHRZAKK
--YOU WON'T MIND ME DOING THAT.
OF COURSE NOT.
YOU'RE OUR GUEST, AFTER ALL.
CRNK
CRNK
AND I CAN ALWAYS PUT IT BACK TOGETHER.
CRRUNCH

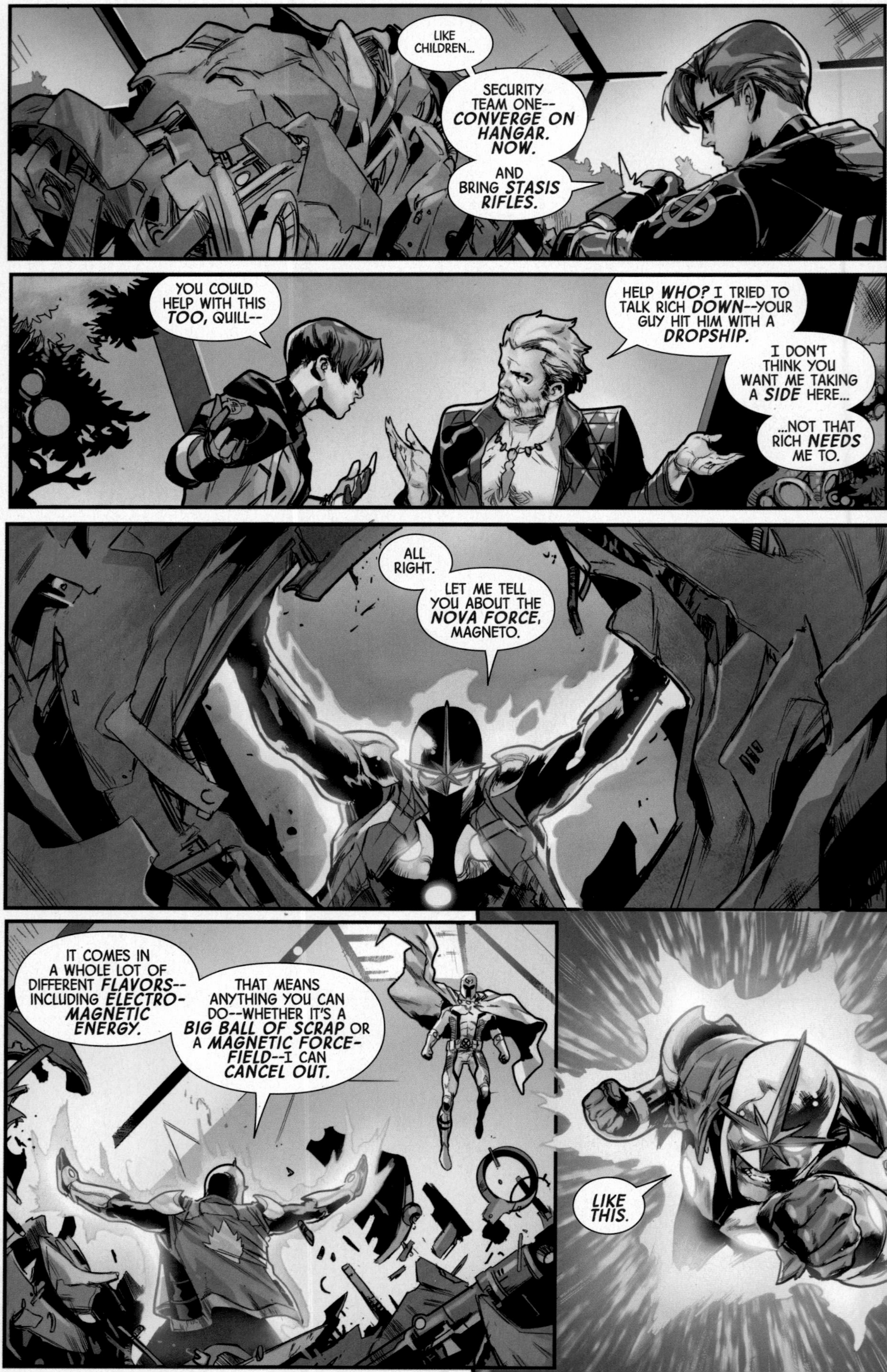
LIKE CHILDREN...
SECURITY TEAM ONE-- CONVERGE ON HANGAR. NOW.
AND BRING STASIS RIFLES.
YOU COULD HELP WITH THIS TOO, QUILL--
HELP WHO? I TRIED TO TALK RICH DOWN--YOUR GUY HIT HIM WITH A DROPSHIP.
I DON'T THINK YOU WANT ME TAKING A SIDE HERE...
...NOT THAT RICH NEEDS ME TO.
ALL RIGHT.
LET ME TELL YOU ABOUT THE NOVA FORCE, MAGNETO.
IT COMES IN A WHOLE LOT OF DIFFERENT FLAVORS-- INCLUDING ELECTRO-MAGNETIC ENERGY.
THAT MEANS ANYTHING YOU CAN DO--WHETHER IT'S A BIG BALL OF SCRAP OR A MAGNETIC FORCE-FIELD--I CAN CANCEL OUT.
LIKE THIS.

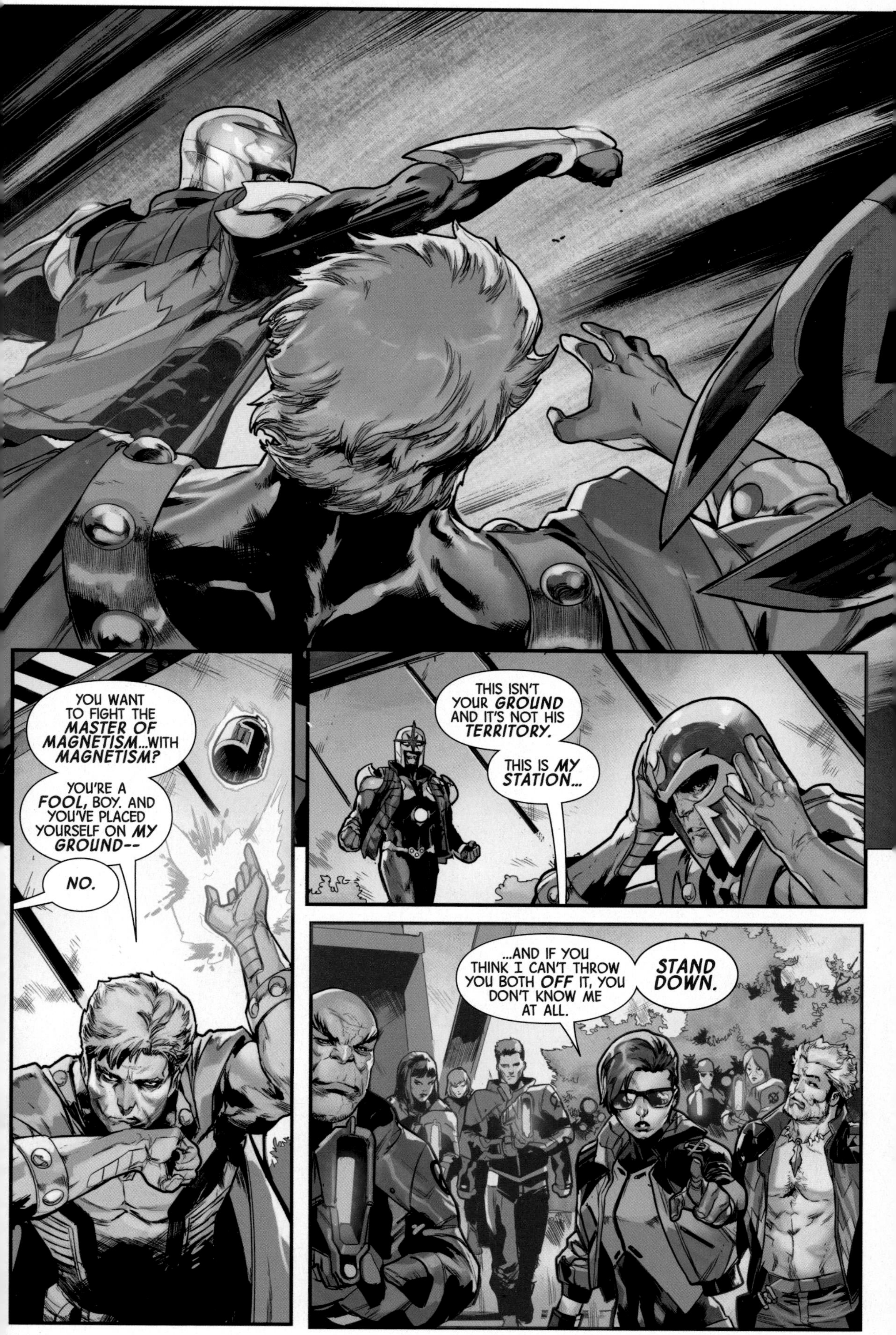
YOU WANT TO FIGHT THE MASTER OF MAGNETISM...WITH MAGNETISM?
YOU'RE A FOOL, BOY. AND YOU'VE PLACED YOURSELF ON MY GROUND--
NO.
THIS ISN'T YOUR GROUND AND IT'S NOT HIS TERRITORY.
THIS IS MY STATION...
...AND IF YOU THINK I CAN'T THROW YOU BOTH OFF IT, YOU DON'T KNOW ME AT ALL.
STAND DOWN.

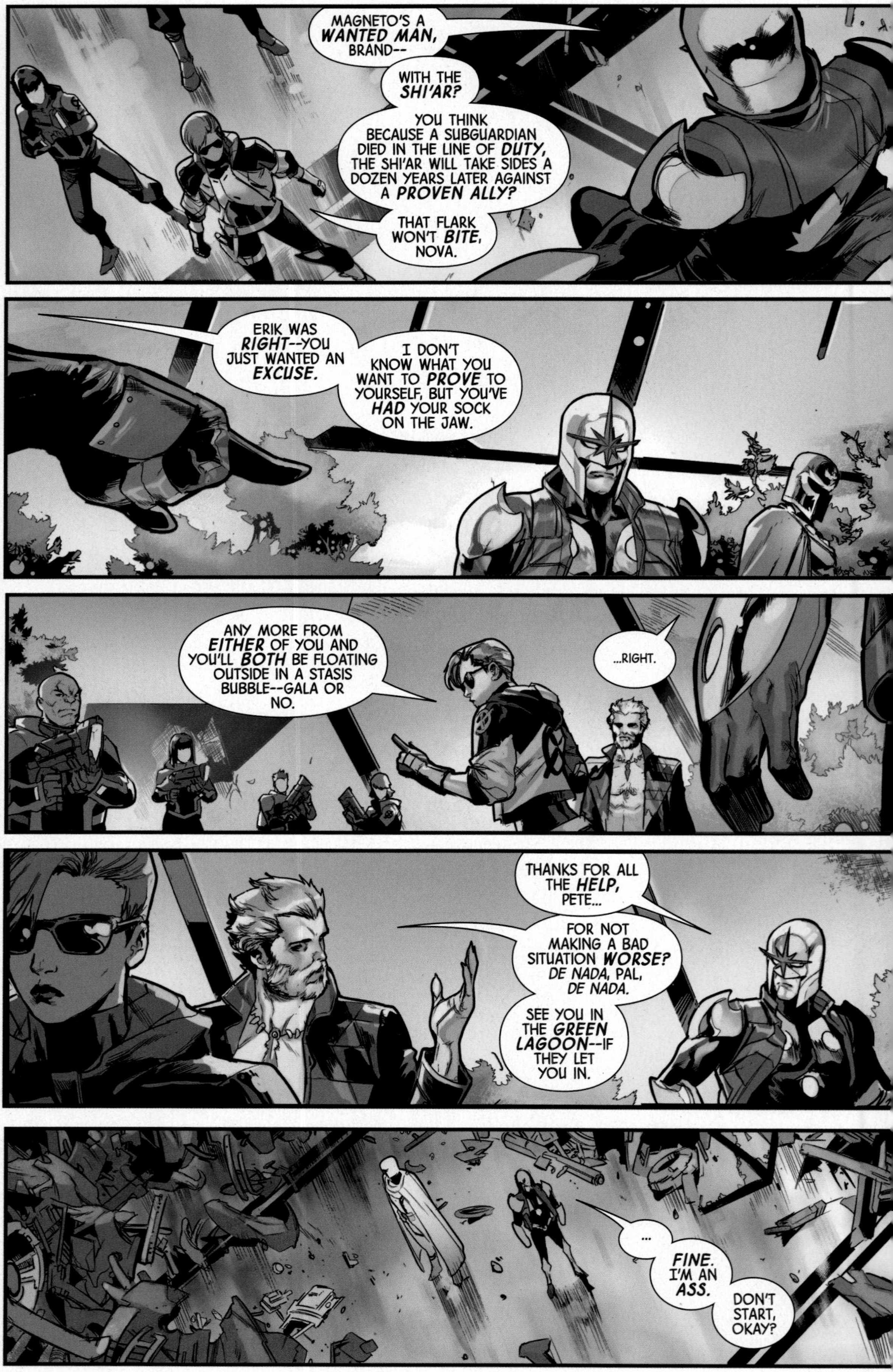
MAGNETO'S A WANTED MAN, BRAND--
WITH THE SHI'AR?
YOU THINK BECAUSE A SUBGUARDIAN DIED IN THE LINE OF DUTY, THE SHI'AR WILL TAKE SIDES A DOZEN YEARS LATER AGAINST A PROVEN ALLY?
THAT FLARK WON'T BITE, NOVA.
ERIK WAS RIGHT--YOU JUST WANTED AN EXCUSE.
I DON'T KNOW WHAT YOU WANT TO PROVE TO YOURSELF, BUT YOU'VE HAD YOUR SOCK ON THE JAW.
ANY MORE FROM EITHER OF YOU AND YOU'LL BOTH BE FLOATING OUTSIDE IN A STASIS BUBBLE--GALA OR NO.
...RIGHT.
THANKS FOR ALL THE HELP, PETE...
FOR NOT MAKING A BAD SITUATION WORSE? DE NADA, PAL, DE NADA.
SEE YOU IN THE GREEN LAGOON--IF THEY LET YOU IN.
...
FINE. I'M AN ASS.
DON'T START, OKAY?

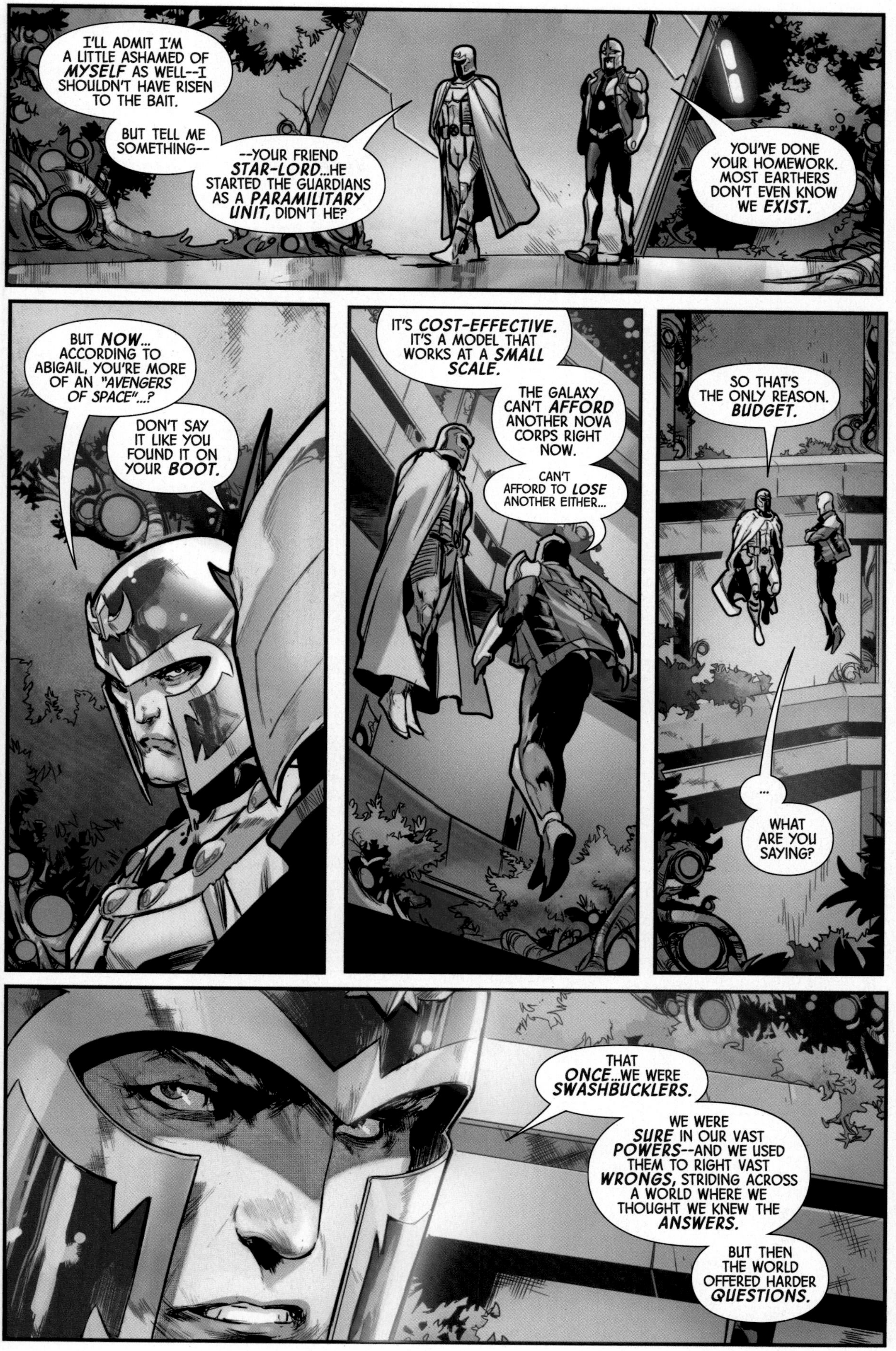
I'LL ADMIT I'M A LITTLE ASHAMED OF MYSELF AS WELL--I SHOULDN'T HAVE RISEN TO THE BAIT.
BUT TELL ME SOMETHING--
--YOUR FRIEND STAR-LORD...HE STARTED THE GUARDIANS AS A PARAMILITARY UNIT, DIDN'T HE?
YOU'VE DONE YOUR HOMEWORK. MOST EARTHERS DON'T EVEN KNOW WE EXIST.
BUT NOW... ACCORDING TO ABIGAIL, YOU'RE MORE OF AN "AVENGERS OF SPACE"...?
DON'T SAY IT LIKE YOU FOUND IT ON YOUR BOOT.
IT'S COST-EFFECTIVE. IT'S A MODEL THAT WORKS AT A SMALL SCALE.
THE GALAXY CAN'T AFFORD ANOTHER NOVA CORPS RIGHT NOW.
CAN'T AFFORD TO LOSE ANOTHER EITHER...
SO THAT'S THE ONLY REASON. BUDGET.
...
WHAT ARE YOU SAYING?
THAT ONCE...WE WERE SWASHBUCKLERS.
WE WERE SURE IN OUR VAST POWERS--AND WE USED THEM TO RIGHT VAST WRONGS, STRIDING ACROSS A WORLD WHERE WE THOUGHT WE KNEW THE ANSWERS.
BUT THEN THE WORLD OFFERED HARDER QUESTIONS.

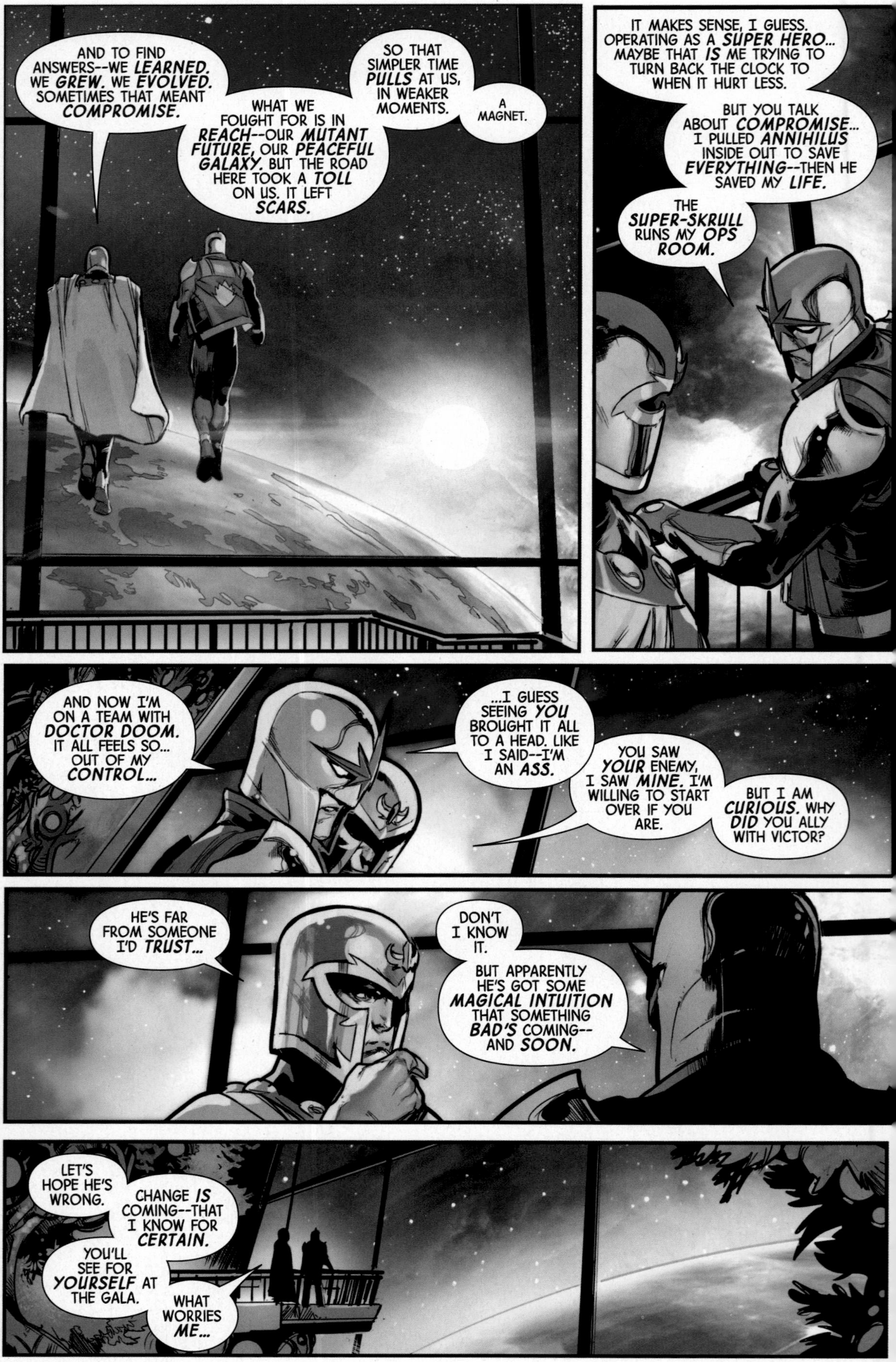
AND TO FIND ANSWERS--WE LEARNED. WE GREW. WE EVOLVED. SOMETIMES THAT MEANT COMPROMISE.
WHAT WE FOUGHT FOR IS IN REACH--OUR MUTANT FUTURE, OUR PEACEFUL GALAXY. BUT THE ROAD HERE TOOK A TOLL ON US. IT LEFT SCARS.
SO THAT SIMPLER TIME PULLS AT US, IN WEAKER MOMENTS.
A MAGNET.
IT MAKES SENSE, I GUESS. OPERATING AS A SUPER HERO... MAYBE THAT IS ME TRYING TO TURN BACK THE CLOCK TO WHEN IT HURT LESS.
BUT YOU TALK ABOUT COMPROMISE... I PULLED ANNIHILUS INSIDE OUT TO SAVE EVERYTHING--THEN HE SAVED MY LIFE.
THE SUPER-SKRULL RUNS MY OPS ROOM.
AND NOW I'M ON A TEAM WITH DOCTOR DOOM. IT ALL FEELS SO... OUT OF MY CONTROL...
...I GUESS SEEING YOU BROUGHT IT ALL TO A HEAD. LIKE I SAID--I'M AN ASS.
YOU SAW YOUR ENEMY, I SAW MINE. I'M WILLING TO START OVER IF YOU ARE.
BUT I AM CURIOUS. WHY DID YOU ALLY WITH VICTOR?
HE'S FAR FROM SOMEONE I'D TRUST...
DON'T I KNOW IT.
BUT APPARENTLY HE'S GOT SOME MAGICAL INTUITION THAT SOMETHING BAD'S COMING--AND SOON.
LET'S HOPE HE'S WRONG.
CHANGE IS COMING--THAT I KNOW FOR CERTAIN.
YOU'LL SEE FOR YOURSELF AT THE GALA.
WHAT WORRIES ME...

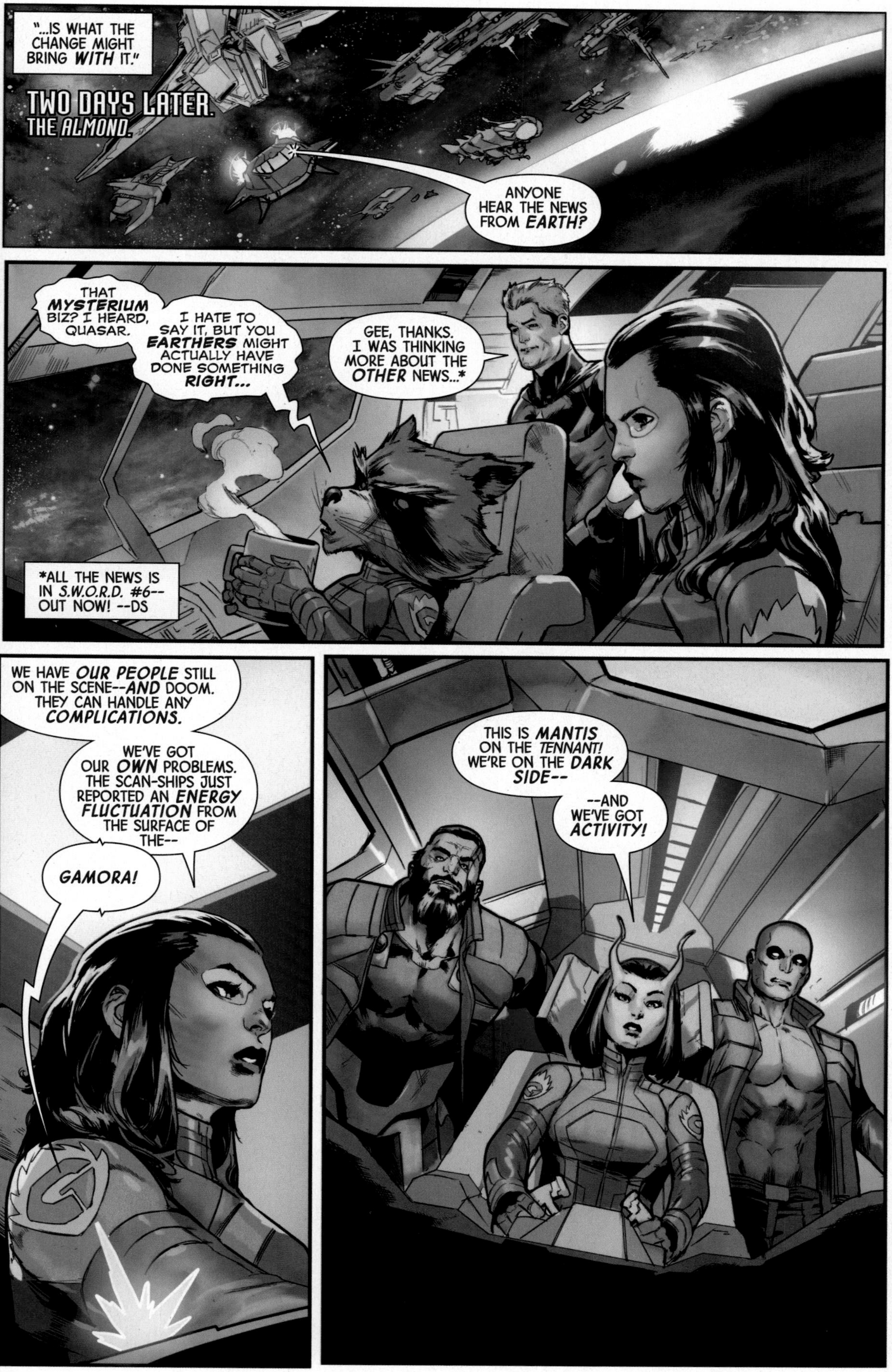
"...IS WHAT THE CHANGE MIGHT BRING WITH IT."
TWO DAYS LATER. THE ALMOND.
ANYONE HEAR THE NEWS FROM EARTH?
THAT MYSTERIUM BIZ? I HEARD, QUASAR.
I HATE TO SAY IT, BUT YOU EARTHERS MIGHT ACTUALLY HAVE DONE SOMETHING RIGHT...
GEE, THANKS. I WAS THINKING MORE ABOUT THE OTHER NEWS...*
*ALL THE NEWS IS IN S.W.O.R.D. #6-- OUT NOW! --DS
WE HAVE OUR PEOPLE STILL ON THE SCENE--AND DOOM. THEY CAN HANDLE ANY COMPLICATIONS.
WE'VE GOT OUR OWN PROBLEMS. THE SCAN-SHIPS JUST REPORTED AN ENERGY FLUCTUATION FROM THE SURFACE OF THE--
GAMORA!
THIS IS MANTIS ON THE TENNANT! WE'RE ON THE DARK SIDE--
--AND WE'VE GOT ACTIVITY!

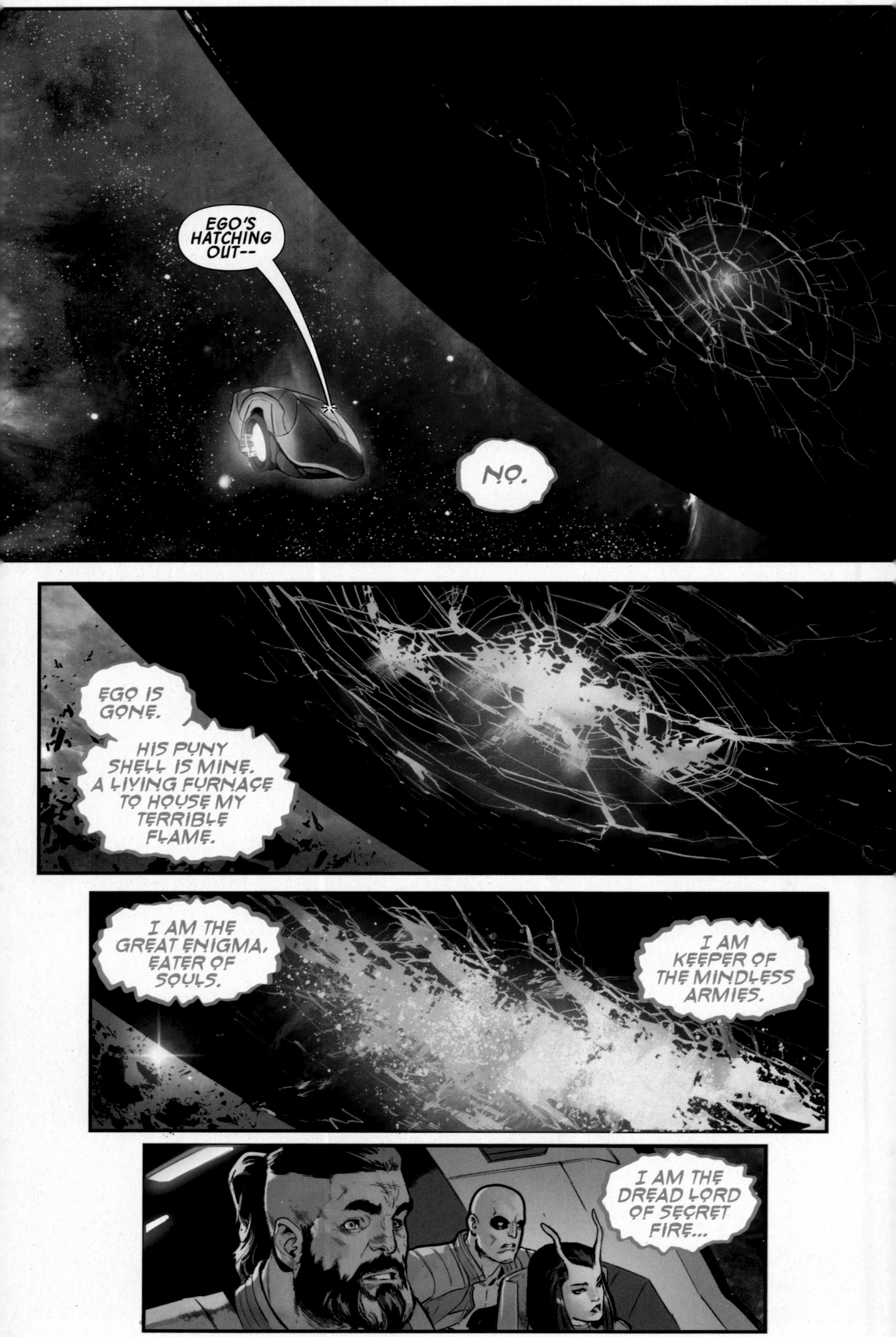
EGO'S HATCHING OUT--
NO.
EGO IS GONE.
HIS PUNY SHELL IS MINE. A LIVING FURNACE TO HOUSE MY TERRIBLE FLAME.
I AM THE GREAT ENIGMA, EATER OF SOULS.
I AM KEEPER OF THE MINDLESS ARMIES.
I AM THE DREAD LORD OF SECRET FIRE...

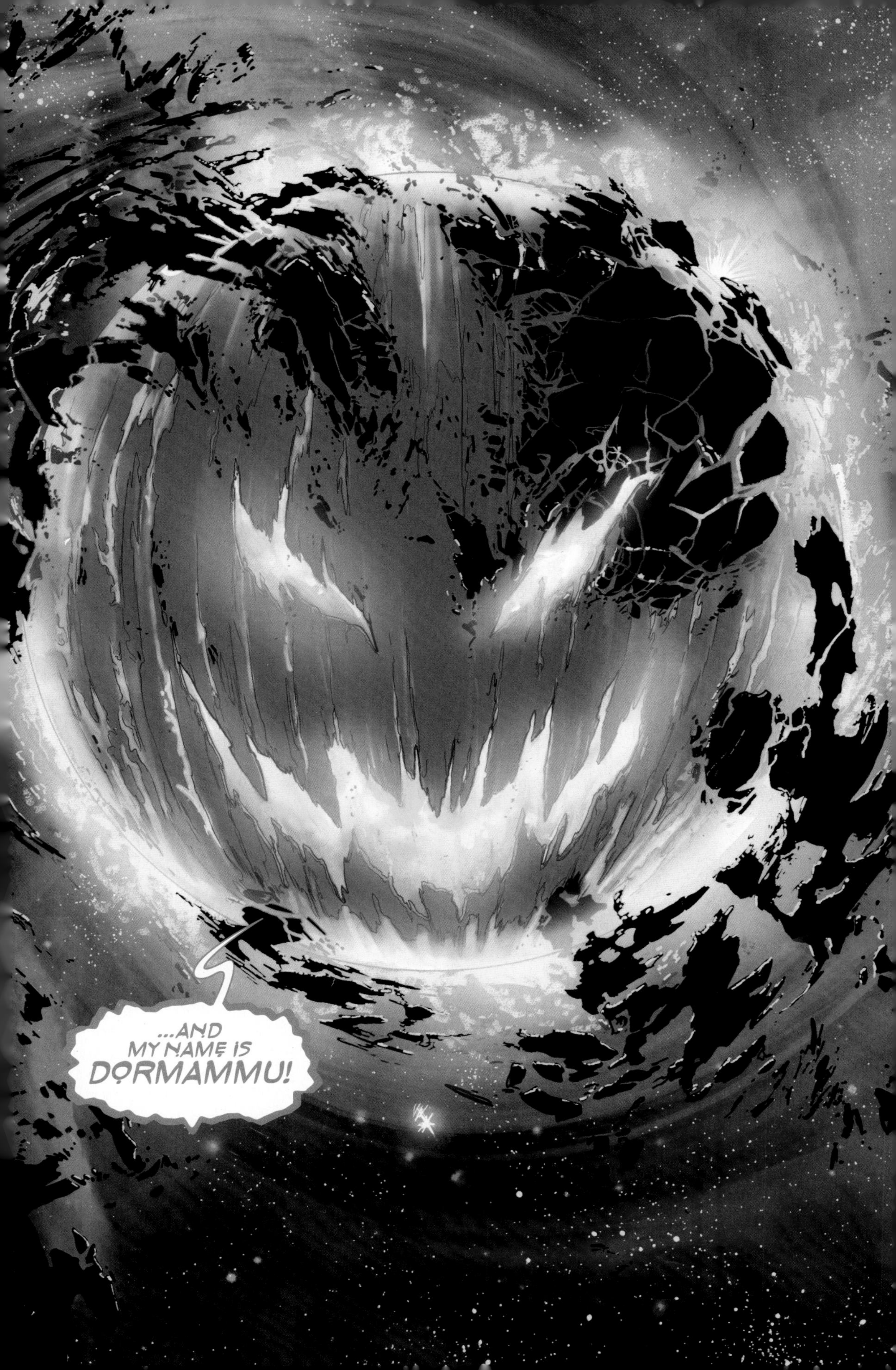
...AND MY NAME IS DORMAMMU!

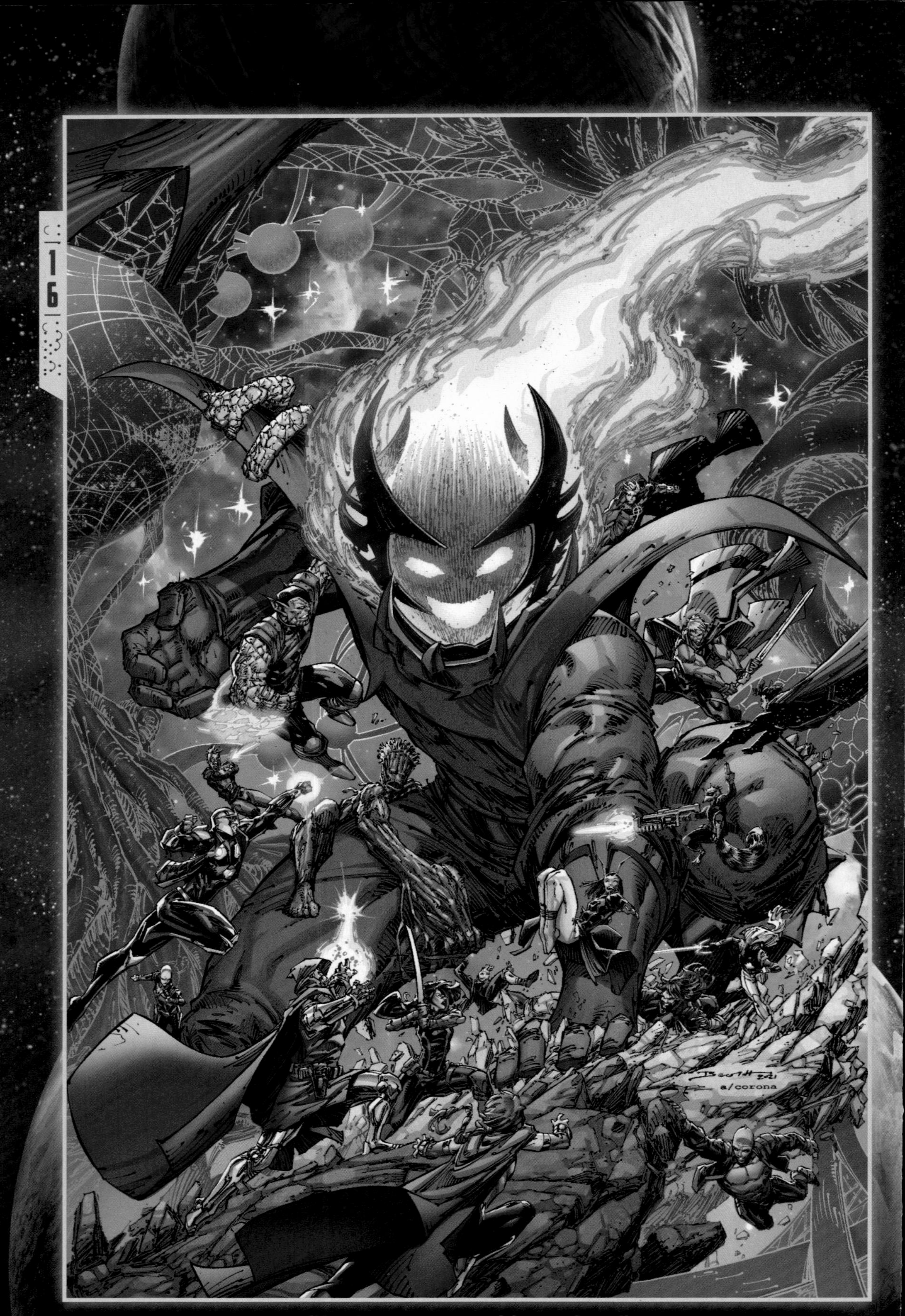
16

"Look upon me and know fear."

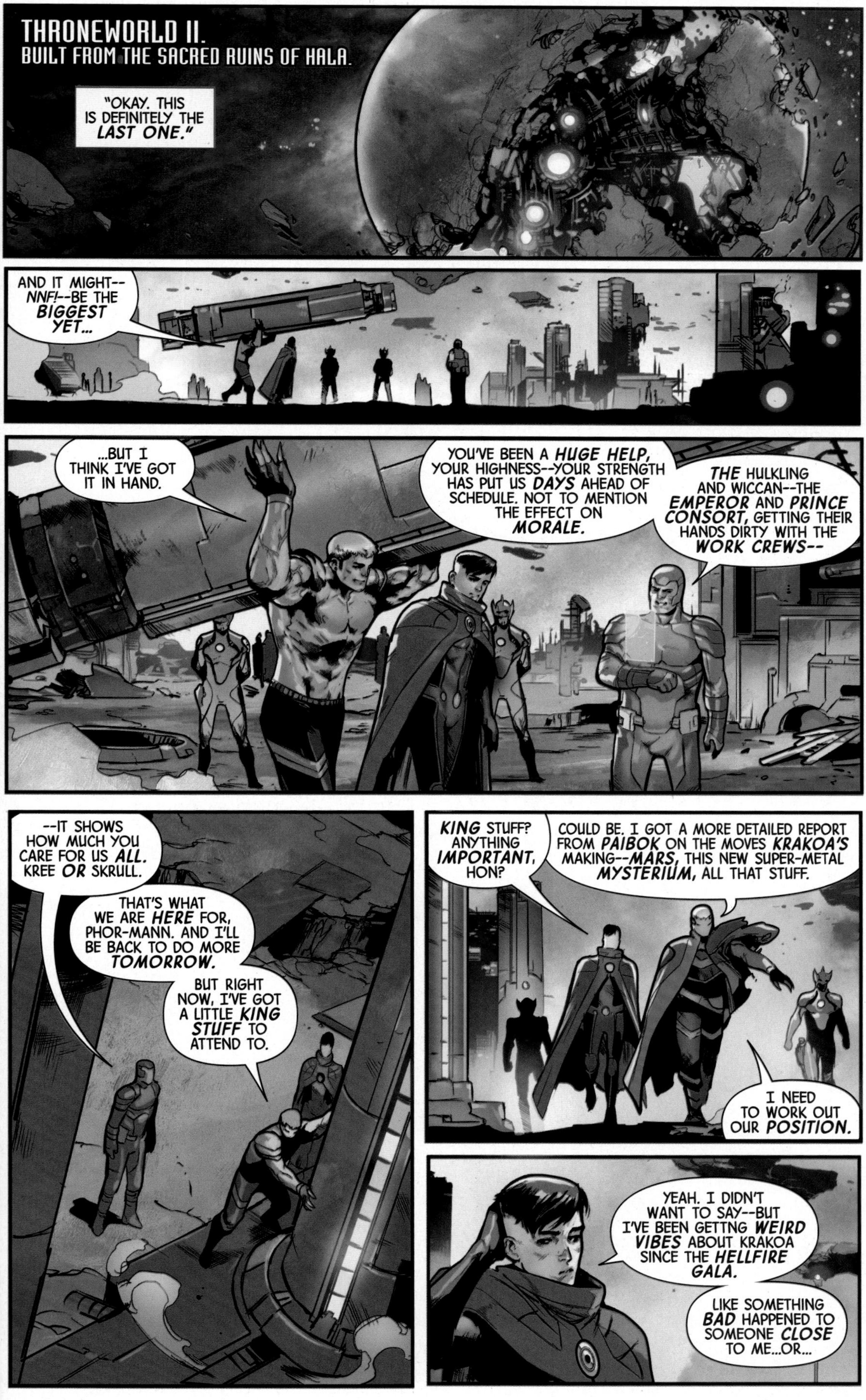
THRONEWORLD II.
BUILT FROM THE SACRED RUINS OF HALA.
"OKAY. THIS IS DEFINITELY THE LAST ONE."
AND IT MIGHT-- NNF!--BE THE BIGGEST YET...
...BUT I THINK I'VE GOT IT IN HAND.
YOU'VE BEEN A HUGE HELP, YOUR HIGHNESS--YOUR STRENGTH HAS PUT US DAYS AHEAD OF SCHEDULE. NOT TO MENTION THE EFFECT ON MORALE.
THE HULKLING AND WICCAN--THE EMPEROR AND PRINCE CONSORT, GETTING THEIR HANDS DIRTY WITH THE WORK CREWS--
--IT SHOWS HOW MUCH YOU CARE FOR US ALL. KREE OR SKRULL.
THAT'S WHAT WE ARE HERE FOR, PHOR-MANN. AND I'LL BE BACK TO DO MORE TOMORROW.
BUT RIGHT NOW, I'VE GOT A LITTLE KING STUFF TO ATTEND TO.
KING STUFF? ANYTHING IMPORTANT, HON?
COULD BE. I GOT A MORE DETAILED REPORT FROM PAIBOK ON THE MOVES KRAKOA'S MAKING--MARS, THIS NEW SUPER-METAL MYSTERIUM, ALL THAT STUFF.
I NEED TO WORK OUT OUR POSITION.
YEAH. I DIDN'T WANT TO SAY--BUT I'VE BEEN GETTNG WEIRD VIBES ABOUT KRAKOA SINCE THE HELLFIRE GALA.
LIKE SOMETHING BAD HAPPENED TO SOMEONE CLOSE TO ME...OR...

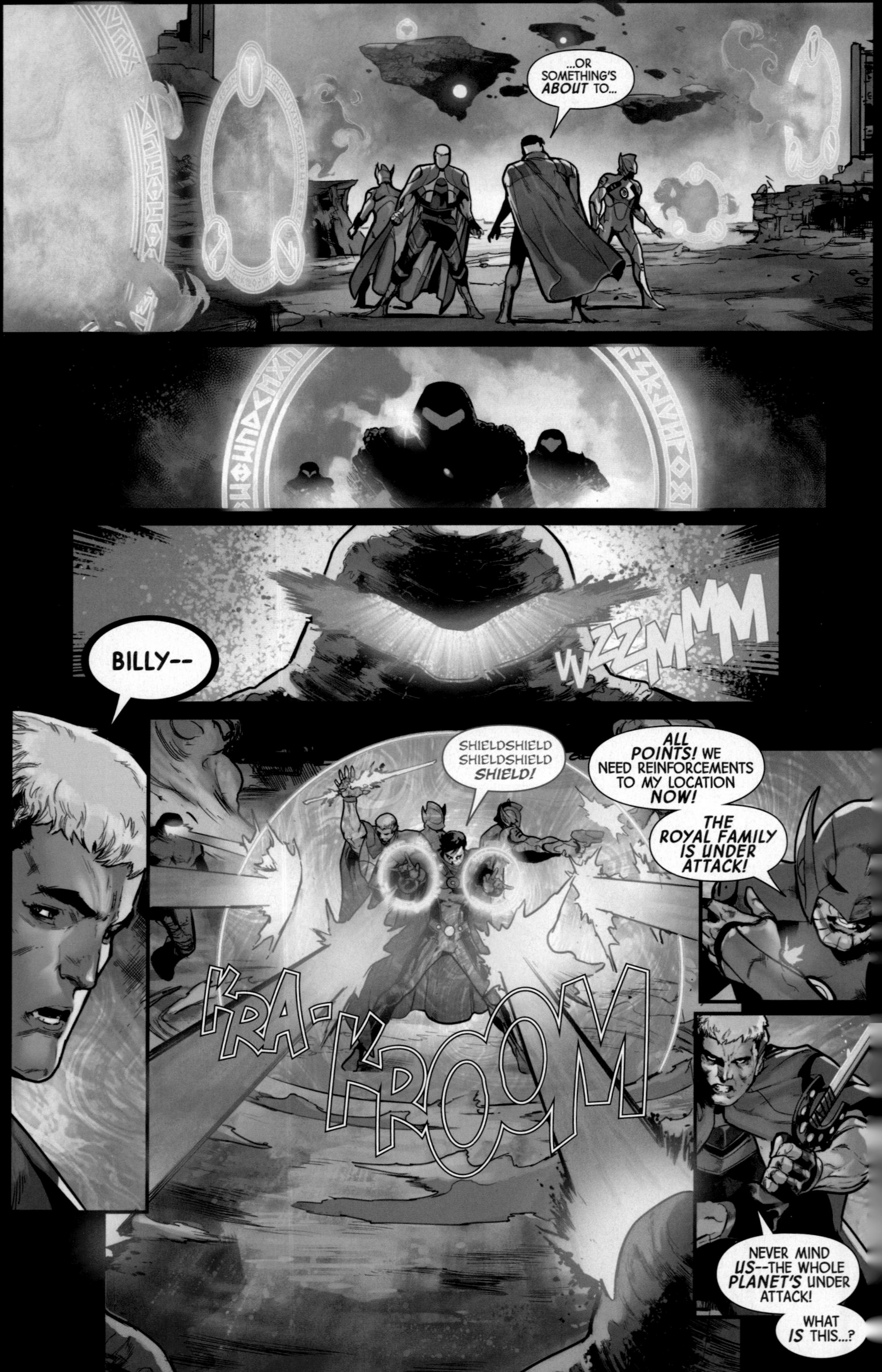
...OR SOMETHING'S ABOUT TO...
BILLY--
VVZZZMMMM
SHIELDSHIELD SHIELDSHIELD SHIELD!
ALL POINTS! WE NEED REINFORCEMENTS TO MY LOCATION NOW!
THE ROYAL FAMILY IS UNDER ATTACK!
KRA-KROOOM
NEVER MIND US--THE WHOLE PLANET'S UNDER ATTACK!
WHAT IS THIS...?

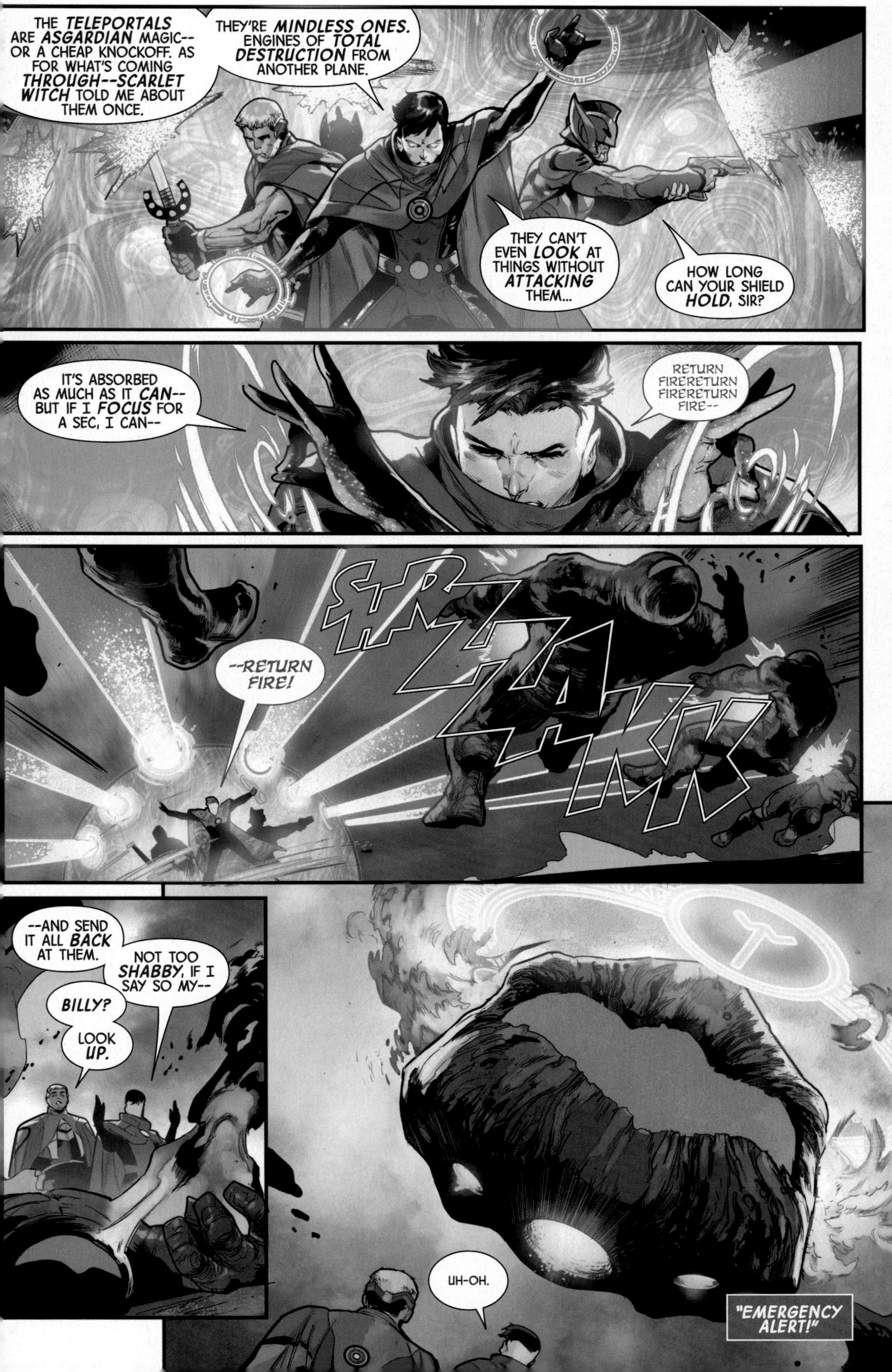
THE TELEPORTALS ARE ASGARDIAN MAGIC-- OR A CHEAP KNOCKOFF. AS FOR WHAT'S COMING THROUGH--SCARLET WITCH TOLD ME ABOUT THEM ONCE.
THEY'RE MINDLESS ONES. ENGINES OF TOTAL DESTRUCTION FROM ANOTHER PLANE.
THEY CAN'T EVEN LOOK AT THINGS WITHOUT ATTACKING THEM...
HOW LONG CAN YOUR SHIELD HOLD, SIR?
IT'S ABSORBED AS MUCH AS IT CAN-- BUT IF I FOCUS FOR A SEC, I CAN--
RETURN FIRERETURN FIRERETURN FIRE--
SHRZAKK
--RETURN FIRE!
--AND SEND IT ALL BACK AT THEM.
NOT TOO SHABBY, IF I SAY SO MY--
BILLY?
LOOK UP.
UH-OH.
"EMERGENCY ALERT!"

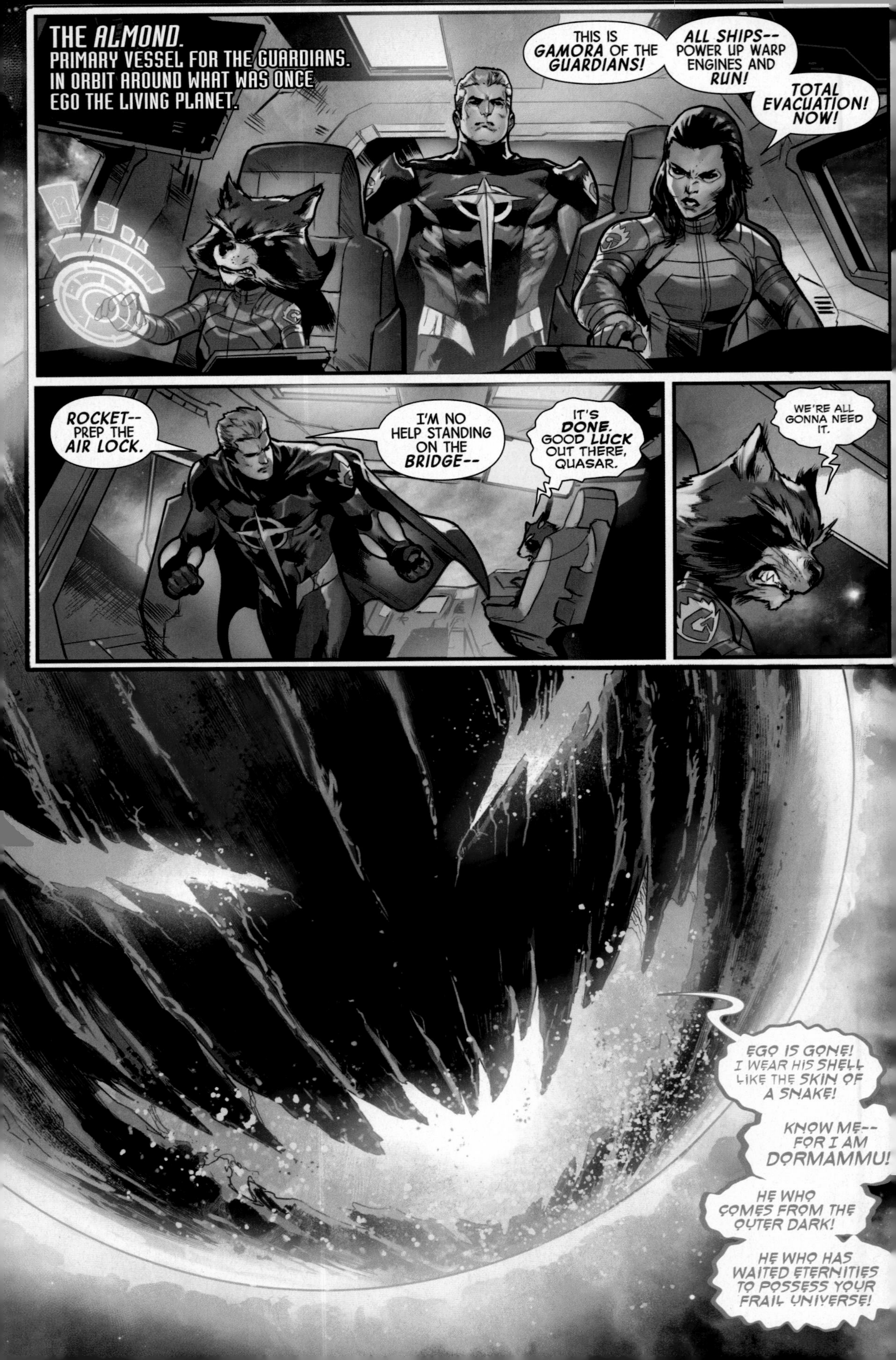
THE ALMOND.
PRIMARY VESSEL FOR THE GUARDIANS.
IN ORBIT AROUND WHAT WAS ONCE
EGO THE LIVING PLANET.
THIS IS GAMORA OF THE GUARDIANS!
ALL SHIPS-- POWER UP WARP ENGINES AND RUN!
TOTAL EVACUATION! NOW!
ROCKET-- PREP THE AIR LOCK.
I'M NO HELP STANDING ON THE BRIDGE--
IT'S DONE. GOOD LUCK OUT THERE, QUASAR.
WE'RE ALL GONNA NEED IT.
EGO IS GONE! I WEAR HIS SHELL LIKE THE SKIN OF A SNAKE!
KNOW ME-- FOR I AM DORMAMMU!
HE WHO COMES FROM THE OUTER DARK!
HE WHO HAS WAITED ETERNITIES TO POSSESS YOUR FRAIL UNIVERSE!

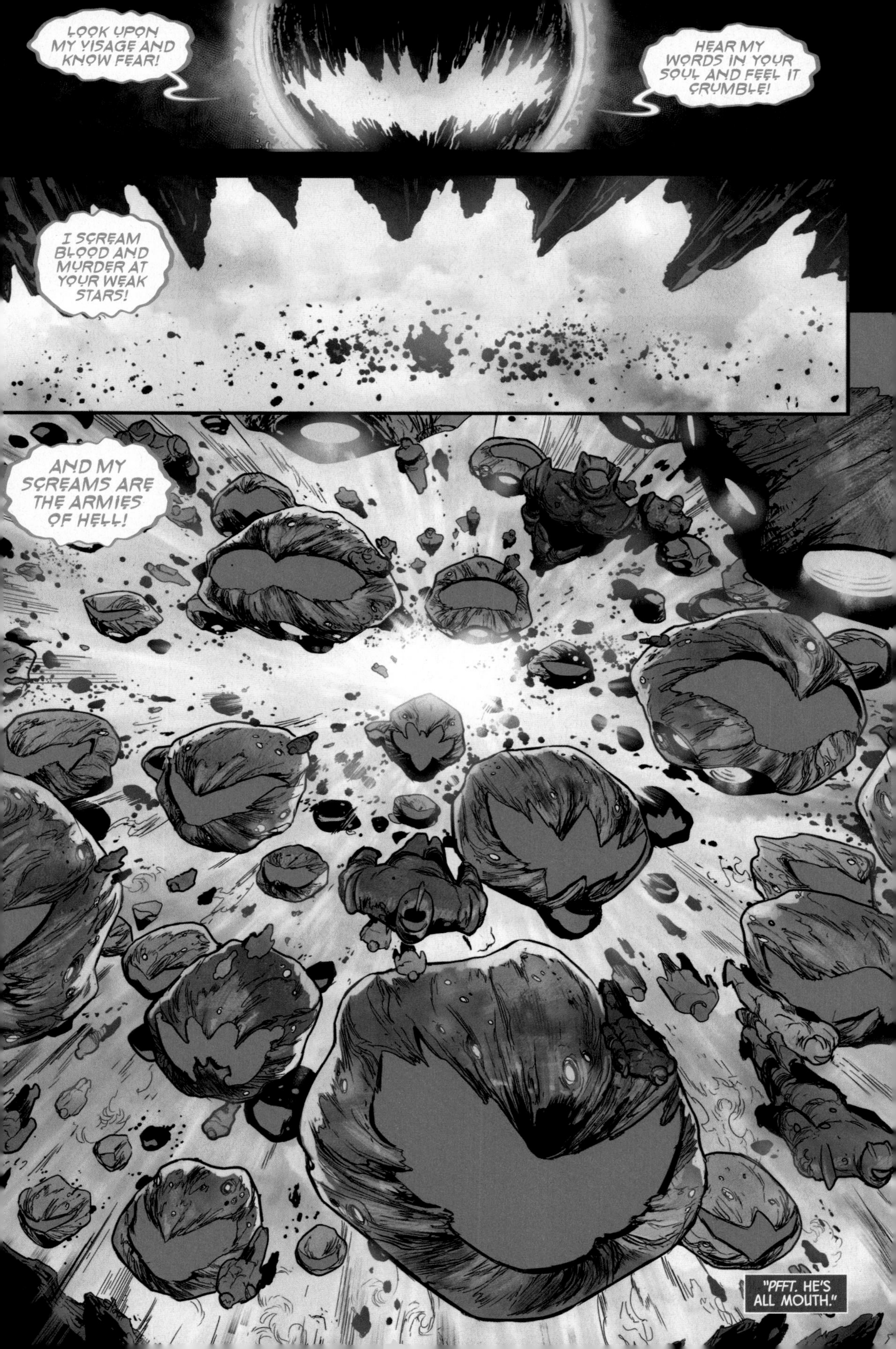
LOOK UPON MY VISAGE AND KNOW FEAR!
HEAR MY WORDS IN YOUR SOUL AND FEEL IT CRUMBLE!
I SCREAM BLOOD AND MURDER AT YOUR WEAK STARS!
AND MY SCREAMS ARE THE ARMIES OF HELL!
"PFFT. HE'S ALL MOUTH."

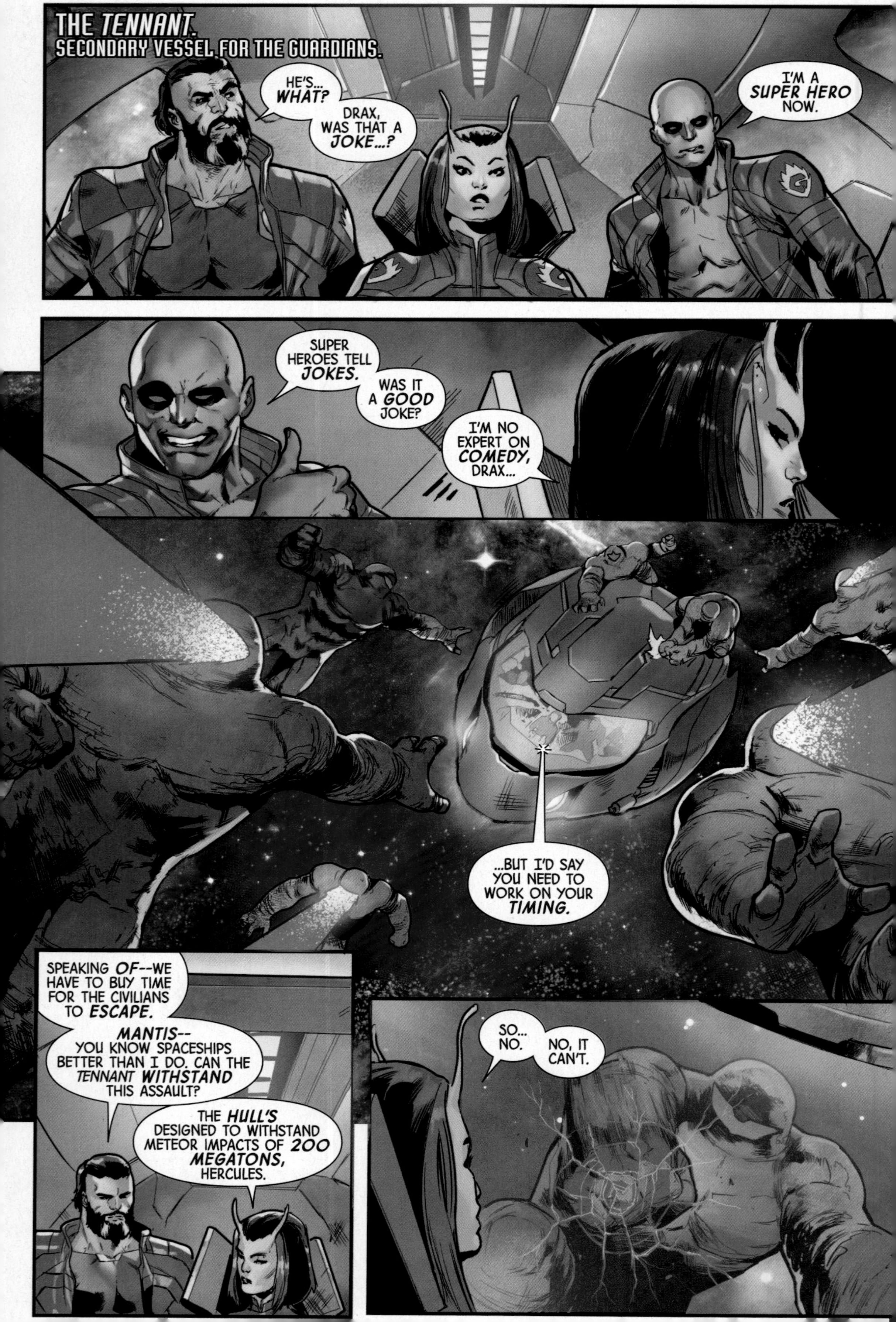
THE TENNANT.
SECONDARY VESSEL FOR THE GUARDIANS.
HE'S... WHAT?
DRAX, WAS THAT A JOKE...?
I'M A SUPER HERO NOW.
SUPER HEROES TELL JOKES.
WAS IT A GOOD JOKE?
I'M NO EXPERT ON COMEDY, DRAX...
...BUT I'D SAY YOU NEED TO WORK ON YOUR TIMING.
SPEAKING OF--WE HAVE TO BUY TIME FOR THE CIVILIANS TO ESCAPE.
MANTIS-- YOU KNOW SPACESHIPS BETTER THAN I DO. CAN THE TENNANT WITHSTAND THIS ASSAULT?
THE HULL'S DESIGNED TO WITHSTAND METEOR IMPACTS OF 200 MEGATONS, HERCULES.
SO... NO.
NO, IT CAN'T.

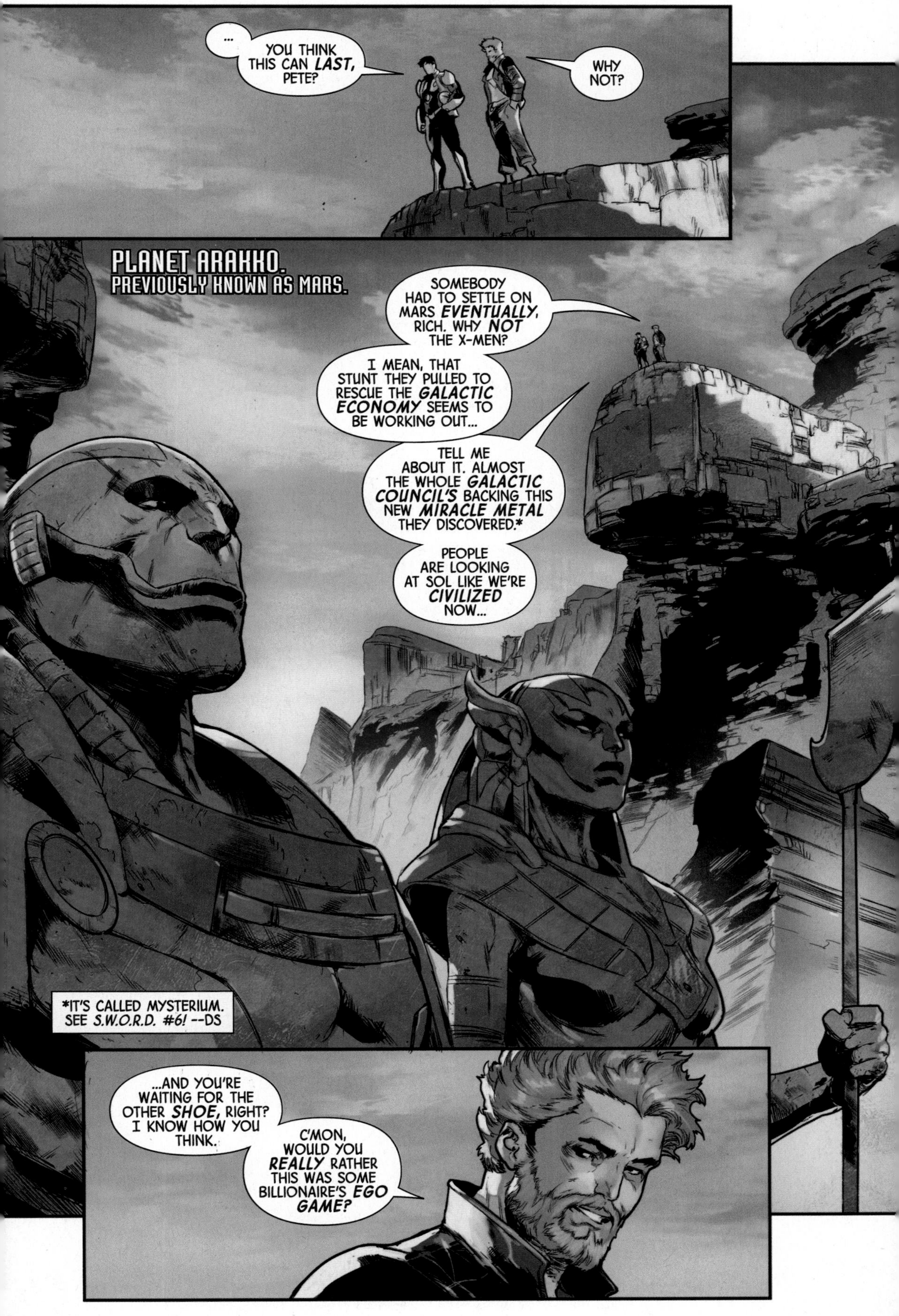

...
YOU THINK THIS CAN LAST, PETE?
WHY NOT?
PLANET ARAKKO. PREVIOUSLY KNOWN AS MARS.
SOMEBODY HAD TO SETTLE ON MARS EVENTUALLY, RICH. WHY NOT THE X-MEN?
I MEAN, THAT STUNT THEY PULLED TO RESCUE THE GALACTIC ECONOMY SEEMS TO BE WORKING OUT...
TELL ME ABOUT IT. ALMOST THE WHOLE GALACTIC COUNCIL'S BACKING THIS NEW MIRACLE METAL THEY DISCOVERED.*
PEOPLE ARE LOOKING AT SOL LIKE WE'RE CIVILIZED NOW...
*IT'S CALLED MYSTERIUM. SEE S.W.O.R.D. #6! --DS
...AND YOU'RE WAITING FOR THE OTHER SHOE, RIGHT? I KNOW HOW YOU THINK.
C'MON, WOULD YOU REALLY RATHER THIS WAS SOME BILLIONAIRE'S EGO GAME?

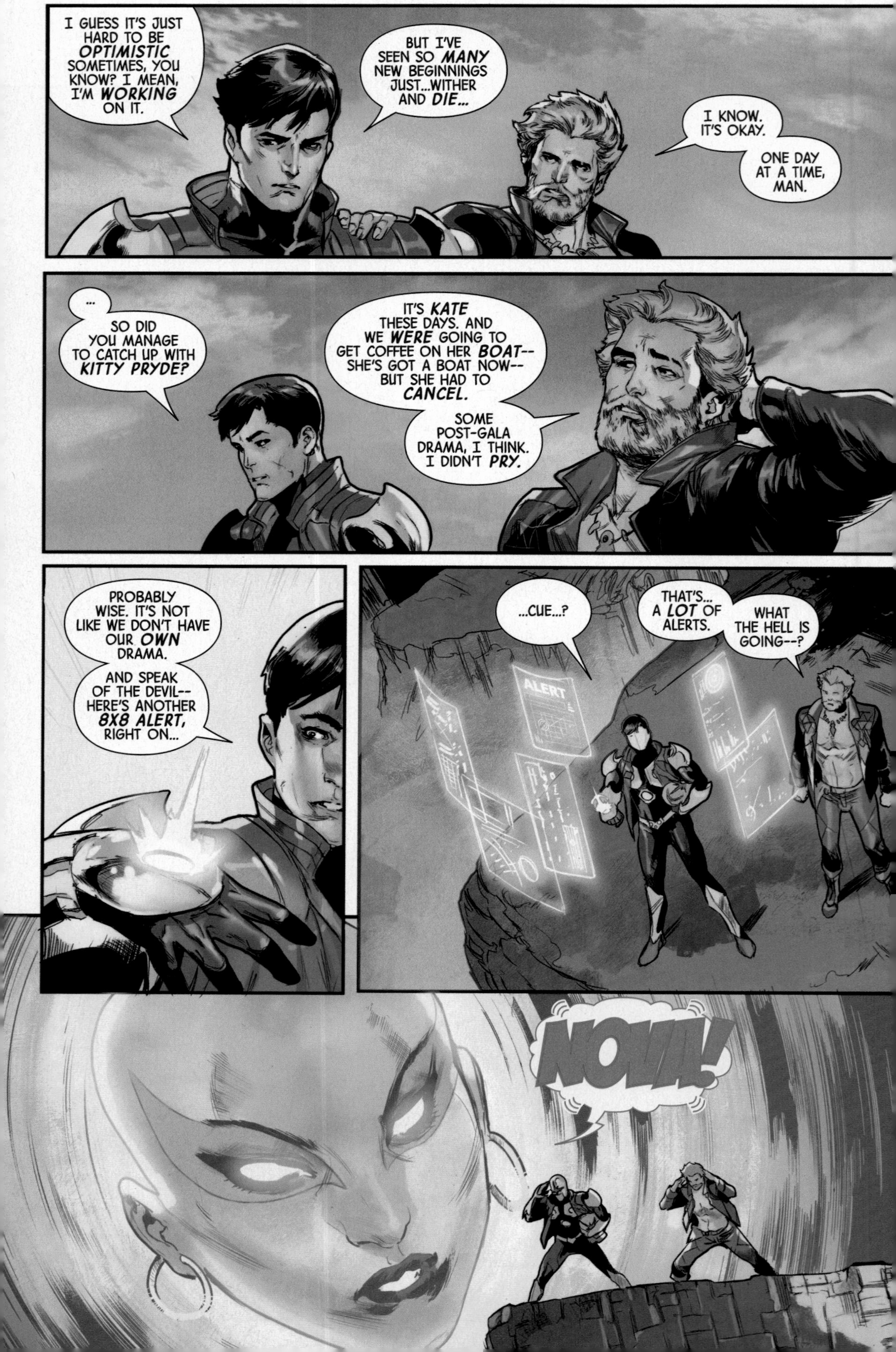
I GUESS IT'S JUST HARD TO BE OPTIMISTIC SOMETIMES, YOU KNOW? I MEAN, I'M WORKING ON IT.
BUT I'VE SEEN SO MANY NEW BEGINNINGS JUST...WITHER AND DIE...
I KNOW. IT'S OKAY.
ONE DAY AT A TIME, MAN.
...
SO DID YOU MANAGE TO CATCH UP WITH KITTY PRYDE?
IT'S KATE THESE DAYS. AND WE WERE GOING TO GET COFFEE ON HER BOAT-- SHE'S GOT A BOAT NOW-- BUT SHE HAD TO CANCEL.
SOME POST-GALA DRAMA, I THINK. I DIDN'T PRY.
PROBABLY WISE. IT'S NOT LIKE WE DON'T HAVE OUR OWN DRAMA.
AND SPEAK OF THE DEVIL-- HERE'S ANOTHER 8X8 ALERT, RIGHT ON...
...CUE...?
THAT'S... A LOT OF ALERTS.
WHAT THE HELL IS GOING--?
ALERT
NOW!

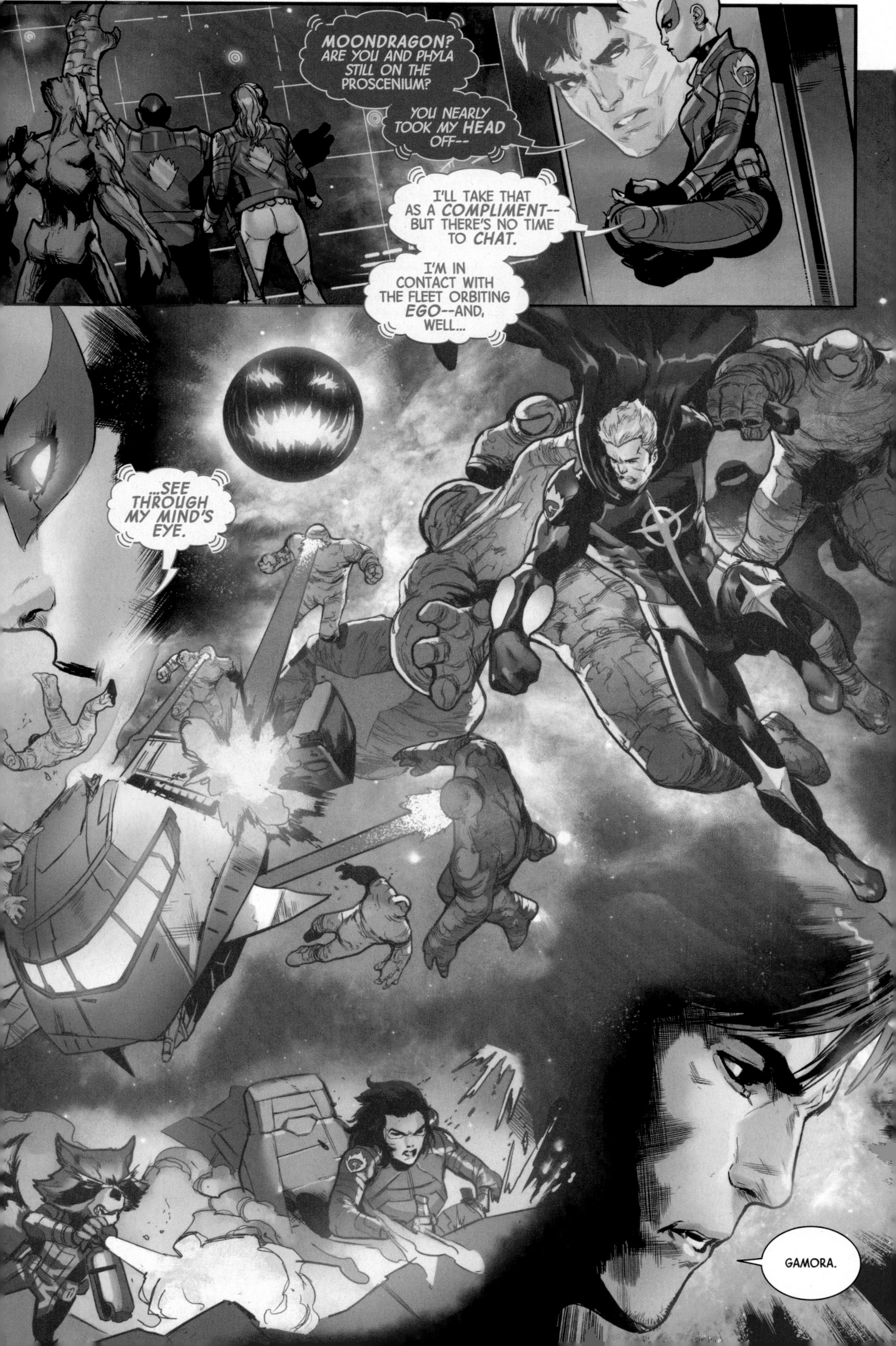
MOONDRAGON? ARE YOU AND PHYLA STILL ON THE PROSCENIUM?
YOU NEARLY TOOK MY HEAD OFF--
I'LL TAKE THAT AS A COMPLIMENT-- BUT THERE'S NO TIME TO CHAT.
I'M IN CONTACT WITH THE FLEET ORBITING EGO--AND, WELL...
...SEE THROUGH MY MIND'S EYE.
GAMORA.

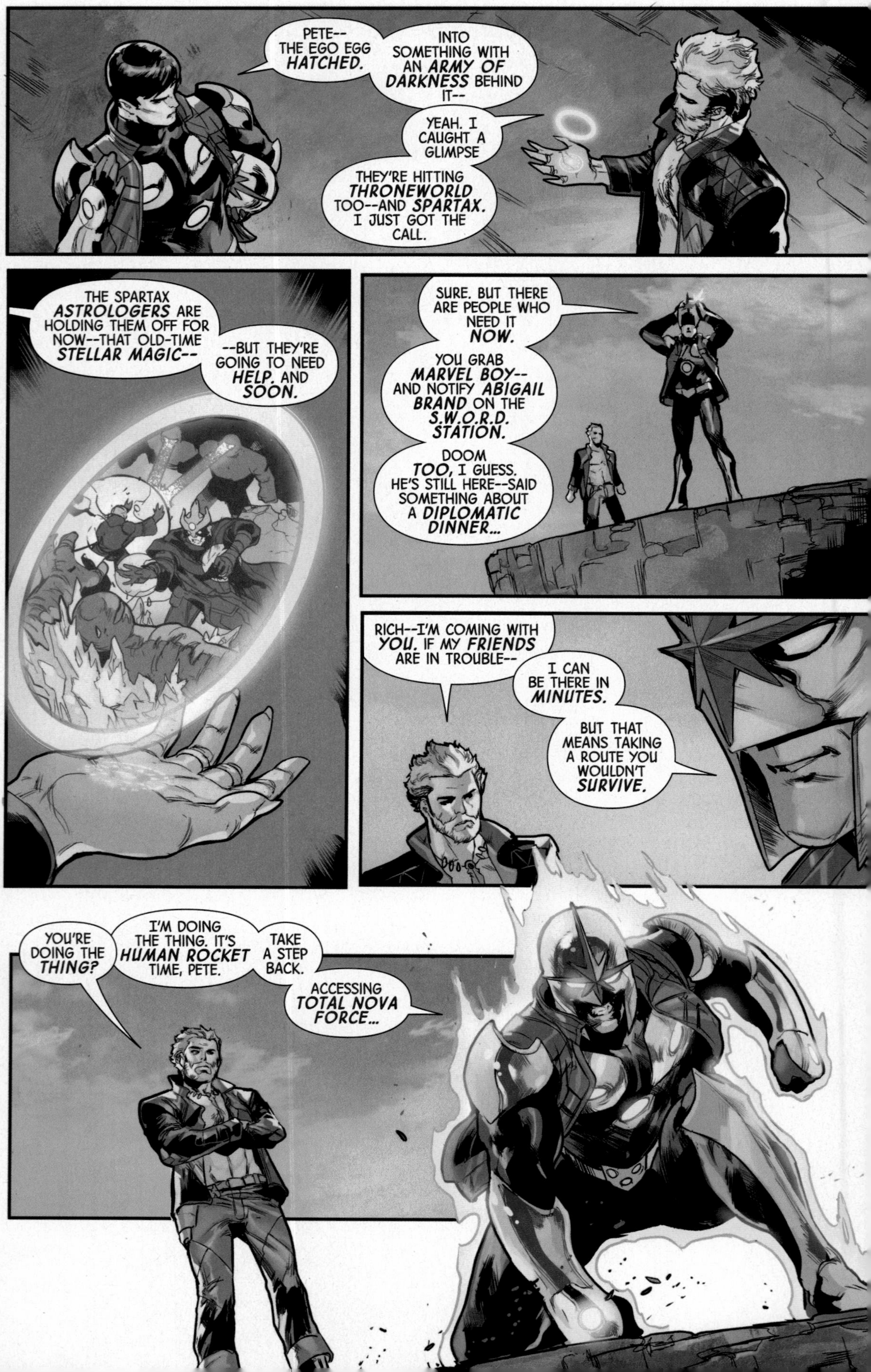
PETE-- THE EGO EGG HATCHED.
INTO SOMETHING WITH AN ARMY OF DARKNESS BEHIND IT--
YEAH. I CAUGHT A GLIMPSE
THEY'RE HITTING THRONEWORLD TOO--AND SPARTAX. I JUST GOT THE CALL.
THE SPARTAX ASTROLOGERS ARE HOLDING THEM OFF FOR NOW--THAT OLD-TIME STELLAR MAGIC--
--BUT THEY'RE GOING TO NEED HELP. AND SOON.
SURE. BUT THERE ARE PEOPLE WHO NEED IT NOW.
YOU GRAB MARVEL BOY--AND NOTIFY ABIGAIL BRAND ON THE S.W.O.R.D. STATION.
DOOM TOO, I GUESS. HE'S STILL HERE--SAID SOMETHING ABOUT A DIPLOMATIC DINNER...
RICH--I'M COMING WITH YOU. IF MY FRIENDS ARE IN TROUBLE--
I CAN BE THERE IN MINUTES.
BUT THAT MEANS TAKING A ROUTE YOU WOULDN'T SURVIVE.
YOU'RE DOING THE THING?
I'M DOING THE THING. IT'S HUMAN ROCKET TIME, PETE.
TAKE A STEP BACK.
ACCESSING TOTAL NOVA FORCE...

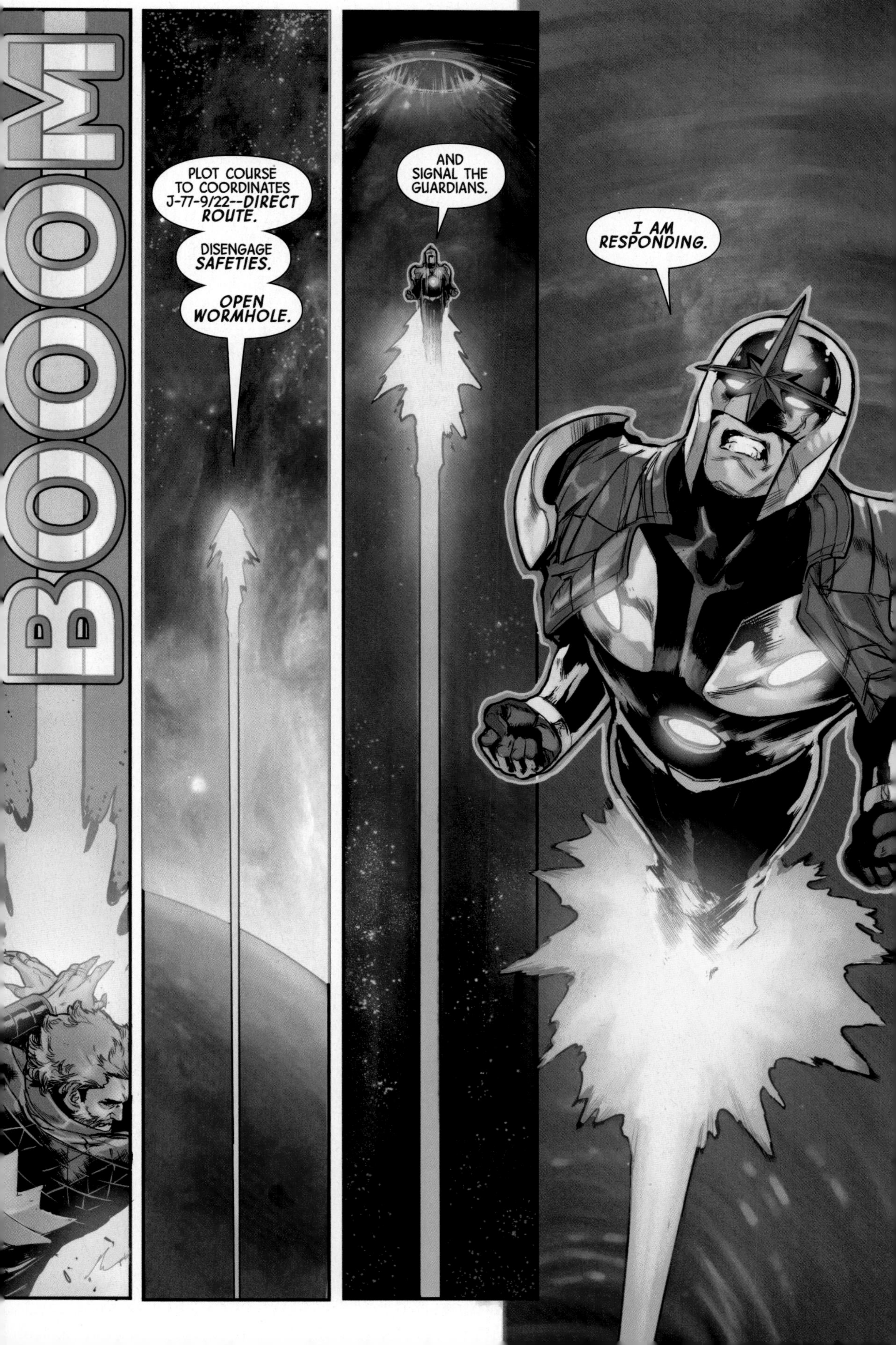
BOOOM!
PLOT COURSE TO COORDINATES J-77-9/22--DIRECT ROUTE.
DISENGAGE SAFETIES.
OPEN WORMHOLE.
AND SIGNAL THE GUARDIANS.
I AM RESPONDING.

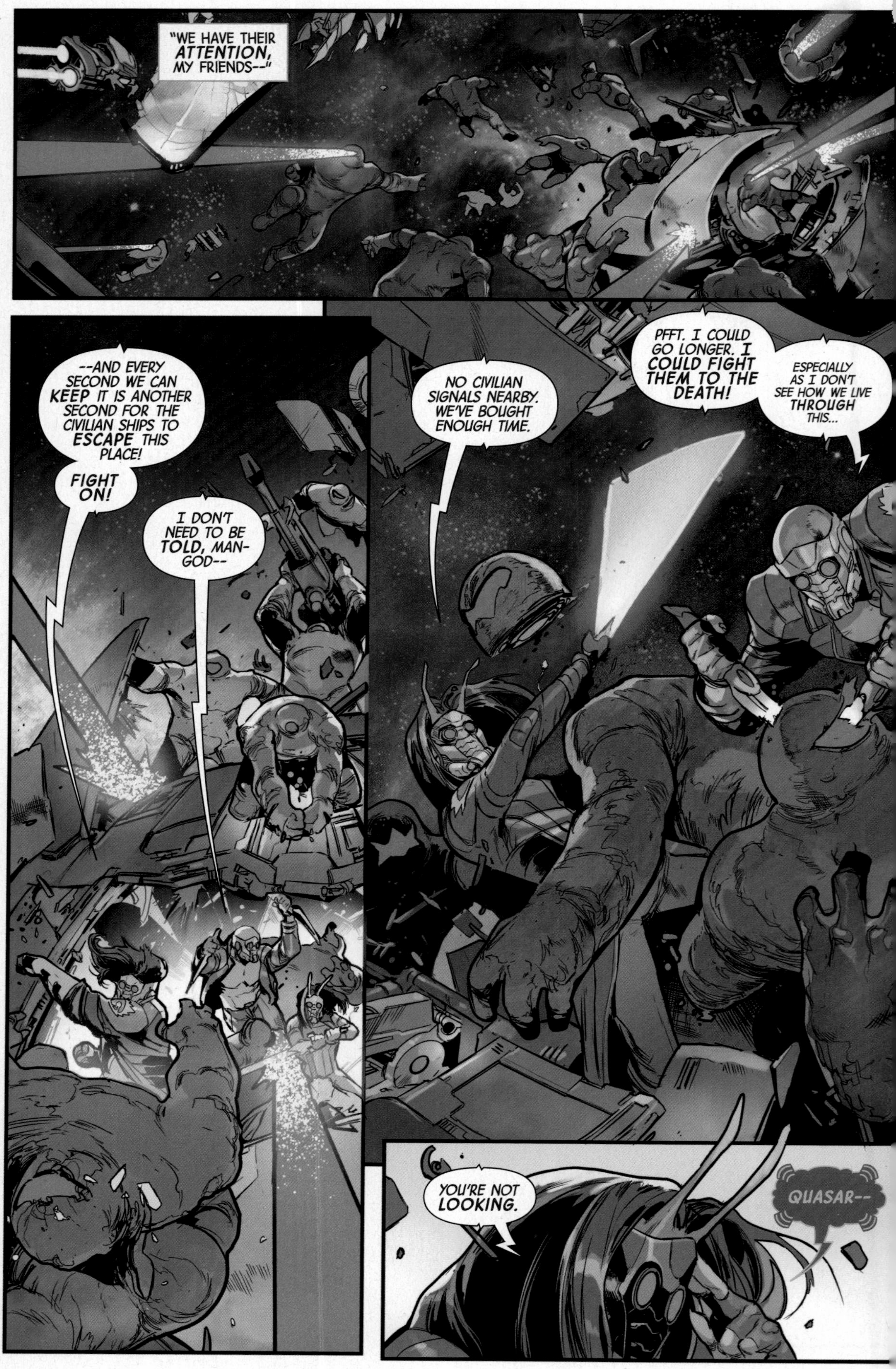
"WE HAVE THEIR ATTENTION, MY FRIENDS--"
--AND EVERY SECOND WE CAN KEEP IT IS ANOTHER SECOND FOR THE CIVILIAN SHIPS TO ESCAPE THIS PLACE!
FIGHT ON!
I DON'T NEED TO BE TOLD, MAN-GOD--
NO CIVILIAN SIGNALS NEARBY. WE'VE BOUGHT ENOUGH TIME.
PFFT. I COULD GO LONGER. I COULD FIGHT THEM TO THE DEATH!
ESPECIALLY AS I DON'T SEE HOW WE LIVE THROUGH THIS...
YOU'RE NOT LOOKING.
QUASAR--

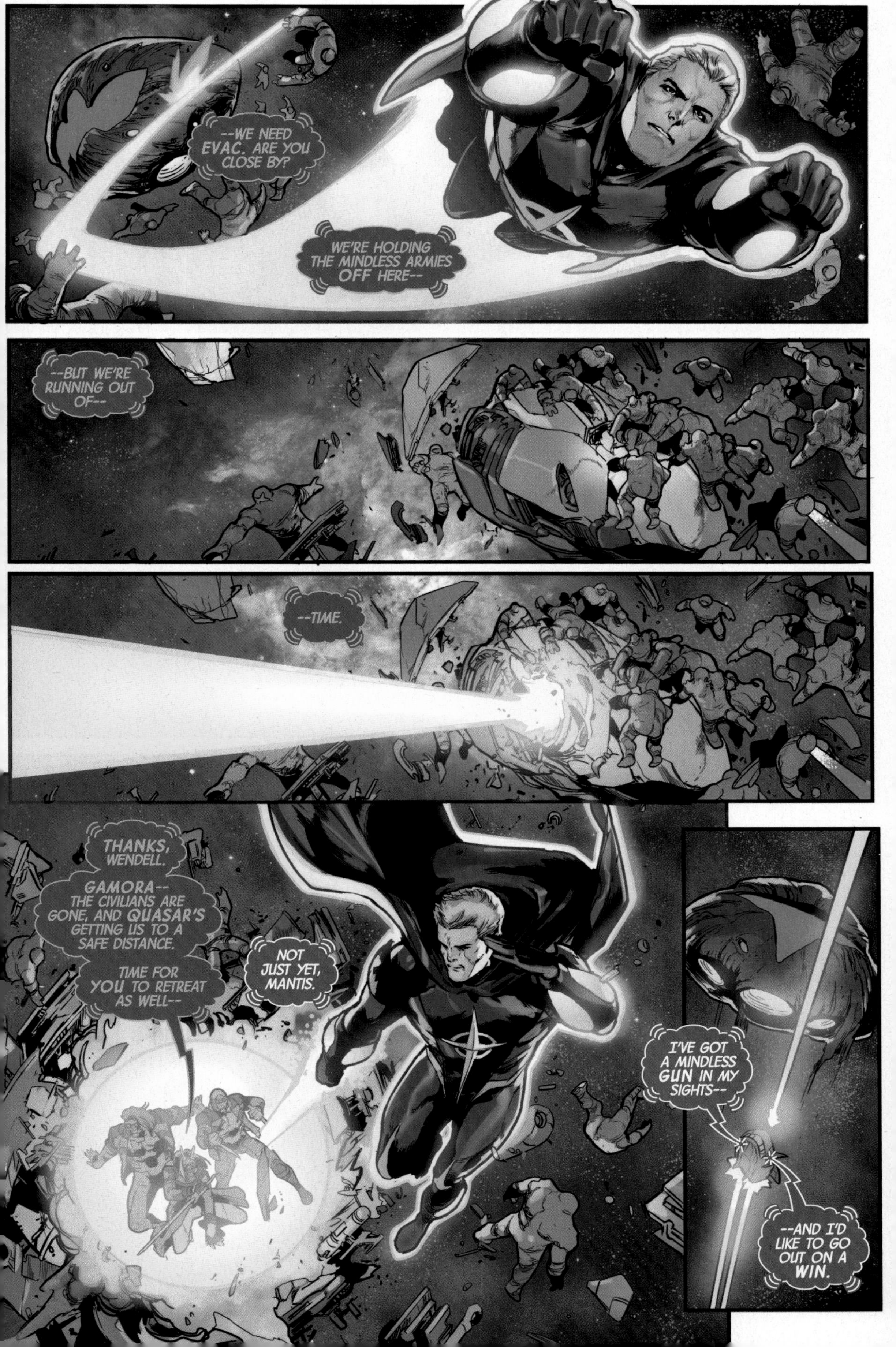
--WE NEED EVAC. ARE YOU CLOSE BY?
WE'RE HOLDING THE MINDLESS ARMIES OFF HERE--
--BUT WE'RE RUNNING OUT OF--
--TIME.
THANKS, WENDELL.
GAMORA-- THE CIVILIANS ARE GONE, AND QUASAR'S GETTING US TO A SAFE DISTANCE.
TIME FOR YOU TO RETREAT AS WELL--
NOT JUST YET, MANTIS.
I'VE GOT A MINDLESS GUN IN MY SIGHTS--
--AND I'D LIKE TO GO OUT ON A WIN.

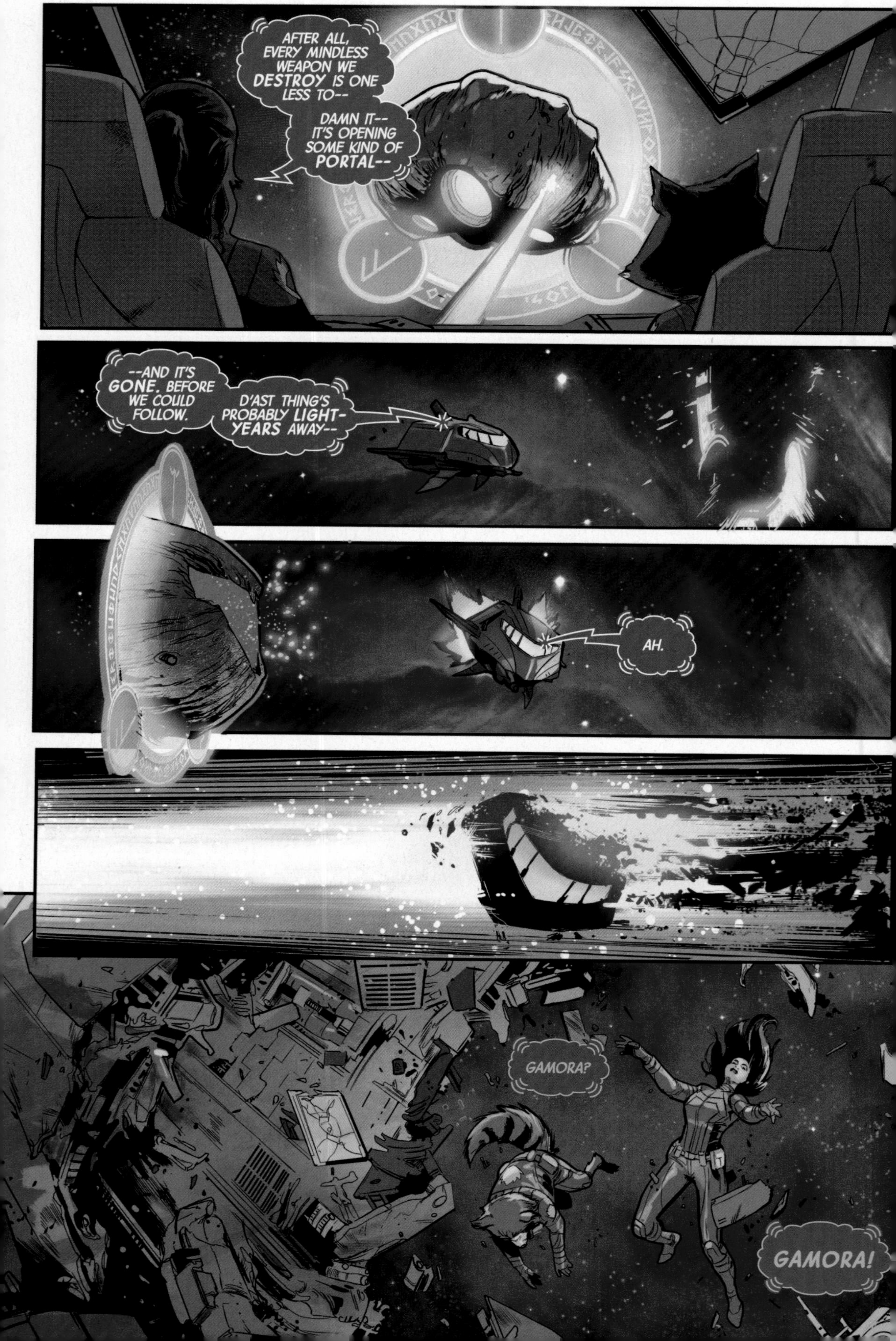

AFTER ALL, EVERY MINDLESS WEAPON WE DESTROY IS ONE LESS TO--
DAMN IT-- IT'S OPENING SOME KIND OF PORTAL--
--AND IT'S GONE. BEFORE WE COULD FOLLOW.
D'AST THING'S PROBABLY LIGHT-YEARS AWAY--
AH.
GAMORA?
GAMORA!

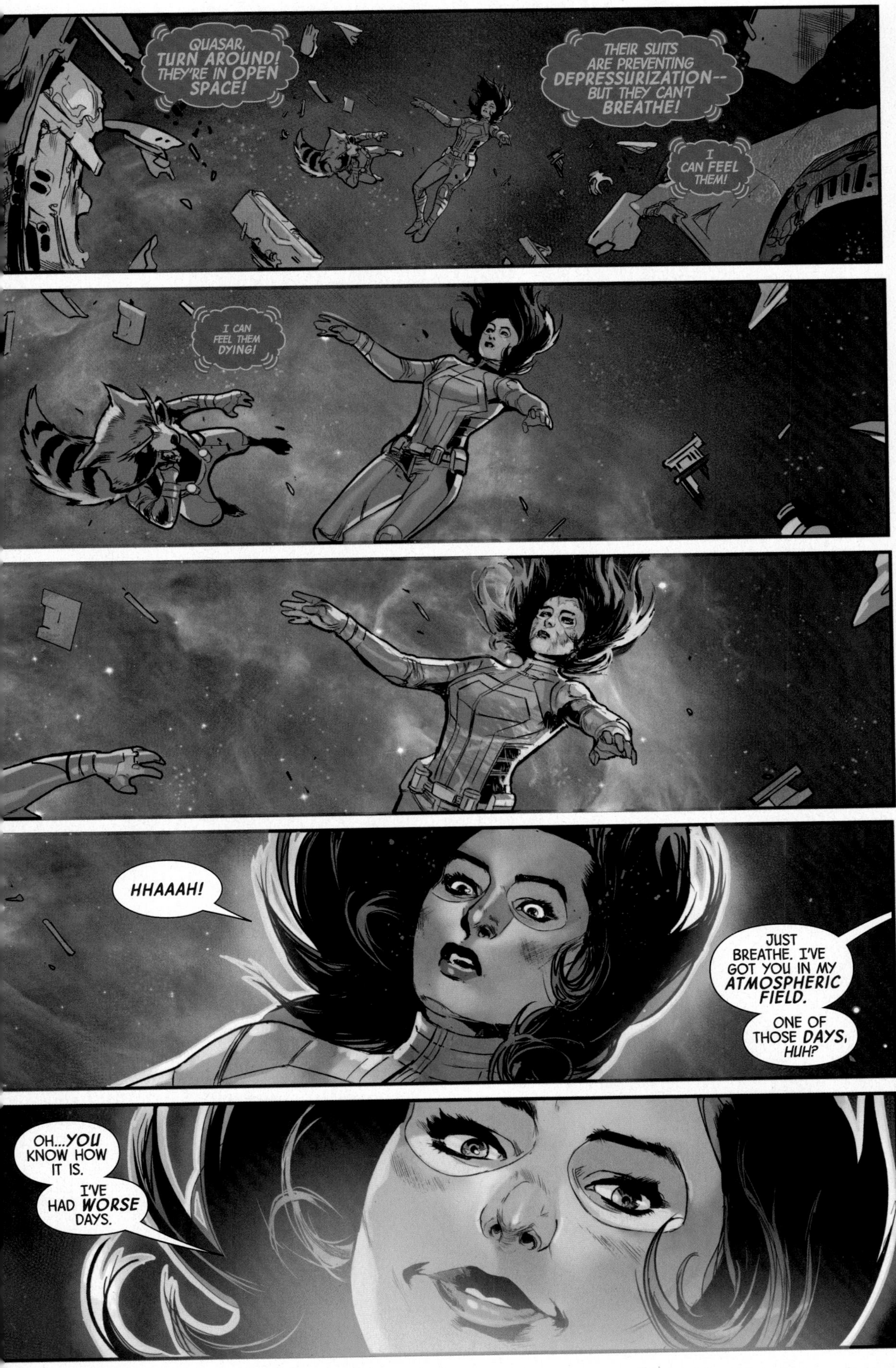
QUASAR, TURN AROUND! THEY'RE IN OPEN SPACE!
THEIR SUITS ARE PREVENTING DEPRESSURIZATION-- BUT THEY CAN'T BREATHE!
I CAN FEEL THEM!
I CAN FEEL THEM DYING!
HHAAAH!
JUST BREATHE. I'VE GOT YOU IN MY ATMOSPHERIC FIELD.
ONE OF THOSE DAYS, HUH?
OH...YOU KNOW HOW IT IS.
I'VE HAD WORSE DAYS.

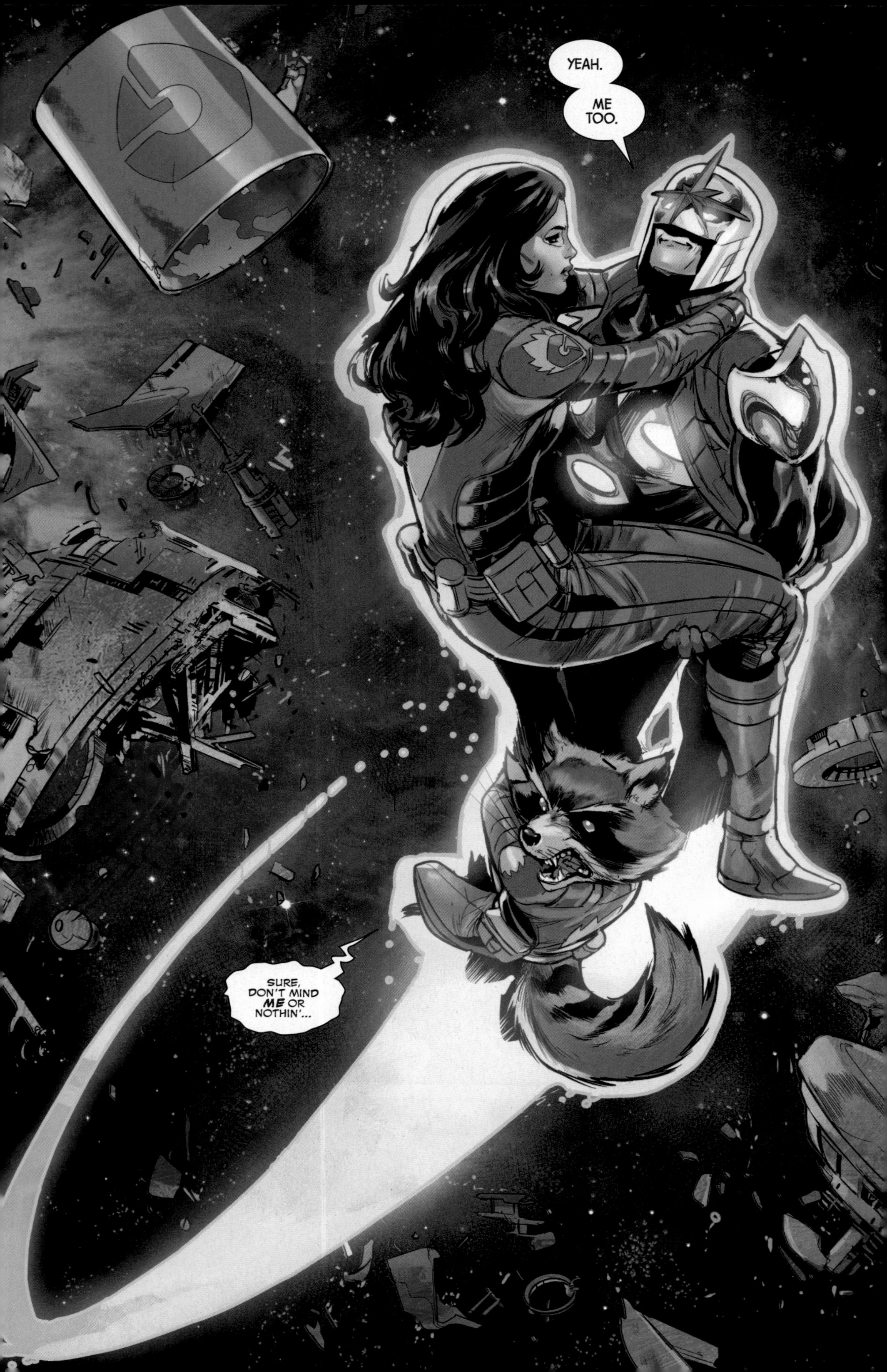
YEAH.
ME TOO.
SURE, DON'T MIND ME OR NOTHIN'...

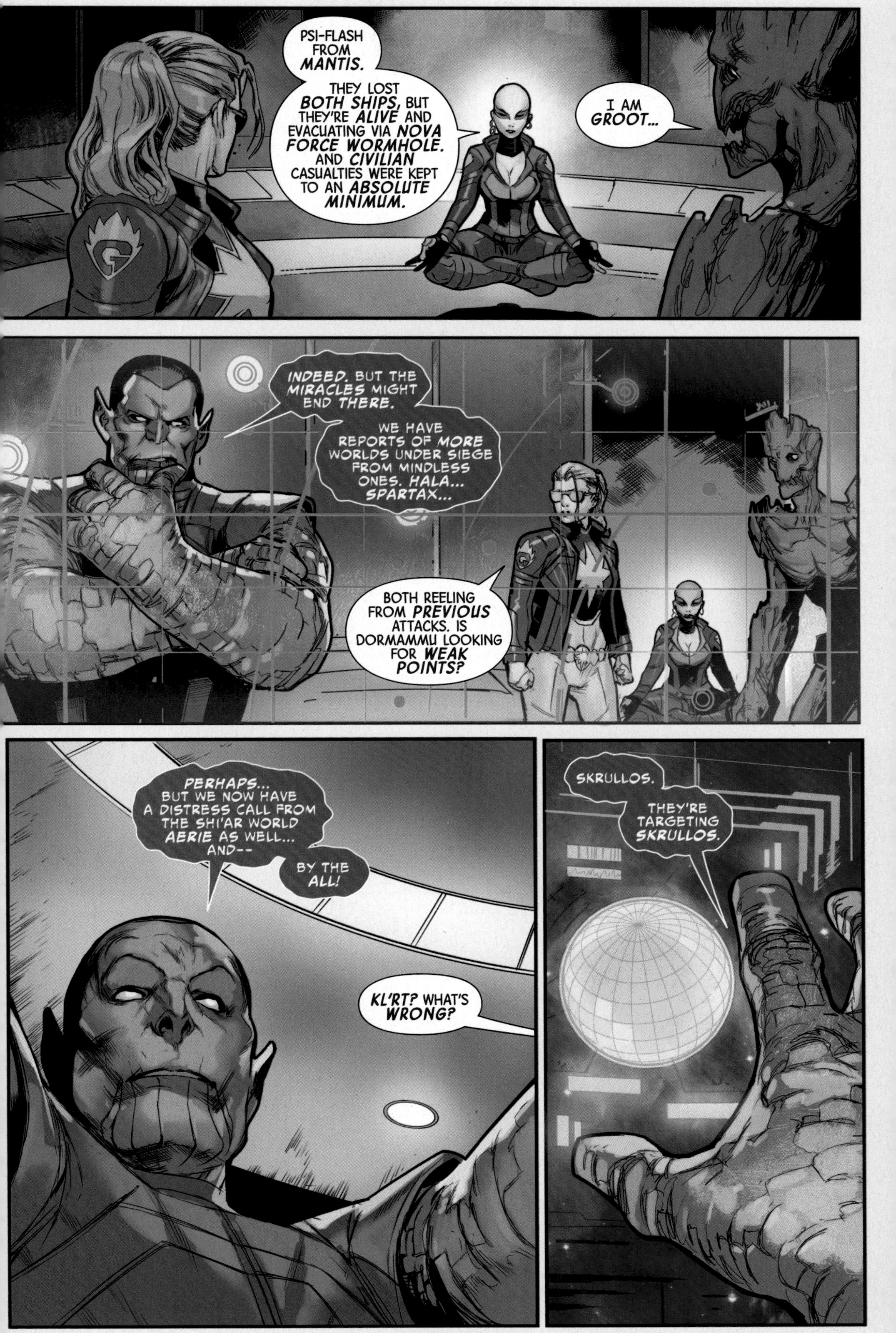

PSI-FLASH FROM MANTIS.
THEY LOST BOTH SHIPS, BUT THEY'RE ALIVE AND EVACUATING VIA NOVA FORCE WORMHOLE. AND CIVILIAN CASUALTIES WERE KEPT TO AN ABSOLUTE MINIMUM.
I AM GROOT...
INDEED. BUT THE MIRACLES MIGHT END THERE.
WE HAVE REPORTS OF MORE WORLDS UNDER SIEGE FROM MINDLESS ONES. HALA... SPARTAX...
BOTH REELING FROM PREVIOUS ATTACKS. IS DORMAMMU LOOKING FOR WEAK POINTS?
PERHAPS... BUT WE NOW HAVE A DISTRESS CALL FROM THE SHI'AR WORLD AERIE AS WELL... AND--
BY THE ALL!
KL'RT? WHAT'S WRONG?
SKRULLOS.
THEY'RE TARGETING SKRULLOS.

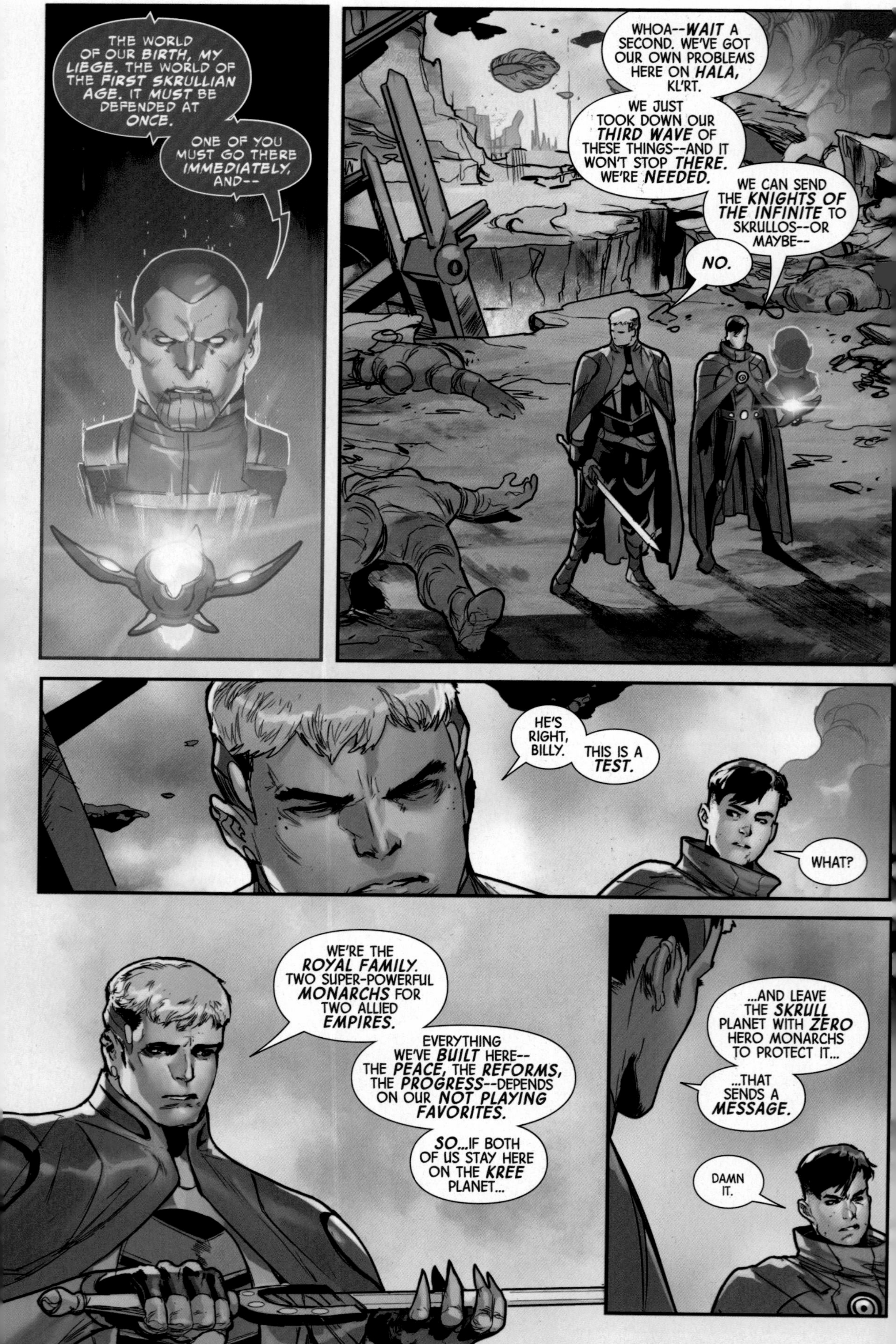
THE WORLD OF OUR BIRTH, MY LIEGE. THE WORLD OF THE FIRST SKRULLIAN AGE. IT MUST BE DEFENDED AT ONCE.
ONE OF YOU MUST GO THERE IMMEDIATELY, AND--
WHOA--WAIT A SECOND. WE'VE GOT OUR OWN PROBLEMS HERE ON HALA, KL'RT.
WE JUST TOOK DOWN OUR THIRD WAVE OF THESE THINGS--AND IT WON'T STOP THERE. WE'RE NEEDED.
WE CAN SEND THE KNIGHTS OF THE INFINITE TO SKRULLOS--OR MAYBE--
NO.
HE'S RIGHT, BILLY.
THIS IS A TEST.
WHAT?
WE'RE THE ROYAL FAMILY. TWO SUPER-POWERFUL MONARCHS FOR TWO ALLIED EMPIRES.
EVERYTHING WE'VE BUILT HERE-- THE PEACE, THE REFORMS, THE PROGRESS--DEPENDS ON OUR NOT PLAYING FAVORITES.
SO...IF BOTH OF US STAY HERE ON THE KREE PLANET...
...AND LEAVE THE SKRULL PLANET WITH ZERO HERO MONARCHS TO PROTECT IT...
...THAT SENDS A MESSAGE.
DAMN IT.

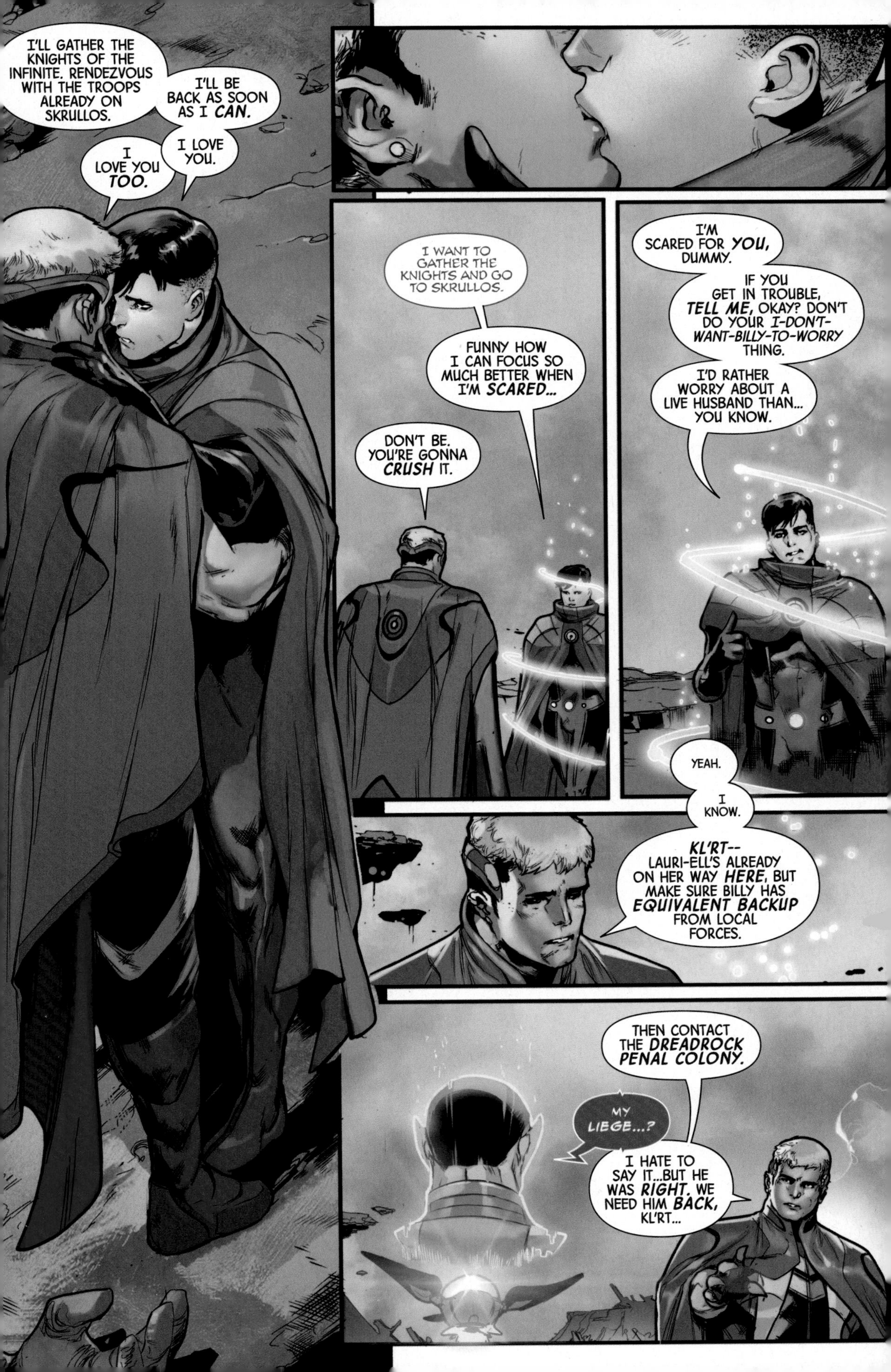
I'LL GATHER THE KNIGHTS OF THE INFINITE. RENDEZVOUS WITH THE TROOPS ALREADY ON SKRULLOS.
I'LL BE BACK AS SOON AS I CAN.
I LOVE YOU.
I LOVE YOU TOO.
I WANT TO GATHER THE KNIGHTS AND GO TO SKRULLOS.
FUNNY HOW I CAN FOCUS SO MUCH BETTER WHEN I'M SCARED...
DON'T BE. YOU'RE GONNA CRUSH IT.
I'M SCARED FOR YOU, DUMMY.
IF YOU GET IN TROUBLE, TELL ME, OKAY? DON'T DO YOUR I-DON'T-WANT-BILLY-TO-WORRY THING.
I'D RATHER WORRY ABOUT A LIVE HUSBAND THAN... YOU KNOW.
YEAH.
I KNOW.
KL'RT-- LAURI-ELL'S ALREADY ON HER WAY HERE, BUT MAKE SURE BILLY HAS EQUIVALENT BACKUP FROM LOCAL FORCES.
THEN CONTACT THE DREADROCK PENAL COLONY.
MY LIEGE...?
I HATE TO SAY IT...BUT HE WAS RIGHT. WE NEED HIM BACK, KL'RT...

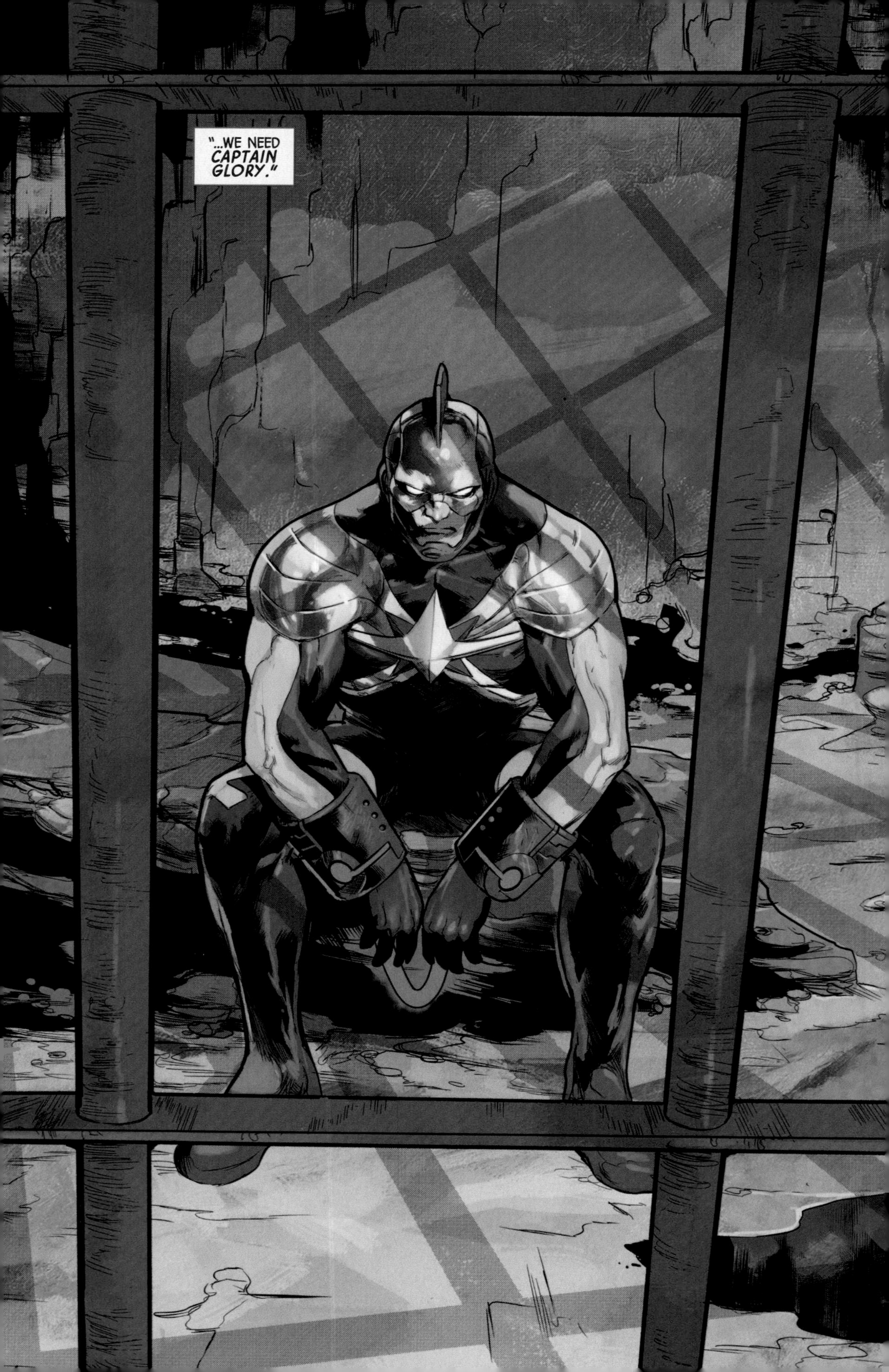
"...WE NEED CAPTAIN GLORY."

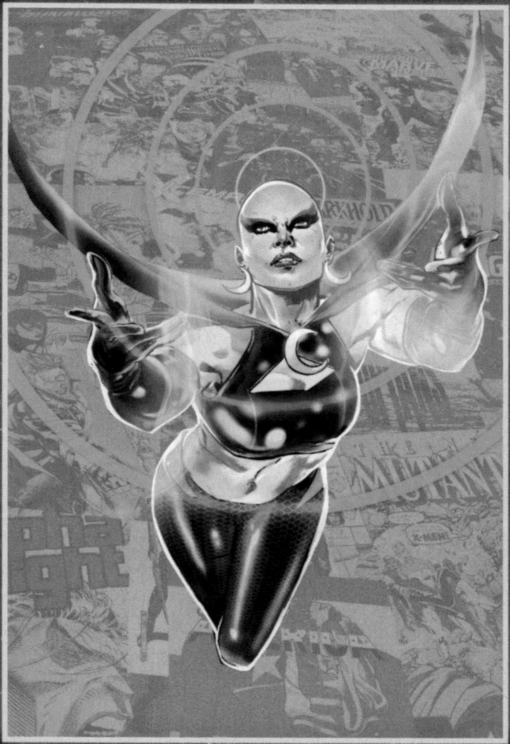

#15 PRIDE MONTH VARIANT BY:
PHIL JIMENEZ & FEDERICO BLEE

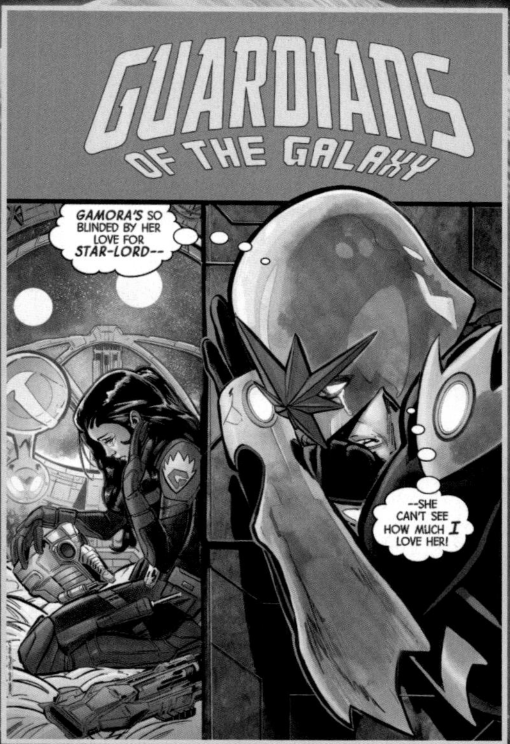
GUARDIANS
OF THE GALAXY
GAMORA'S SO BLINDED BY HER LOVE FOR STAR-LORD--
--SHE CAN'T SEE HOW MUCH I LOVE HER!

#16 VARIANT BY:
PHIL JIMENEZ & RACHELLE ROSENBERG

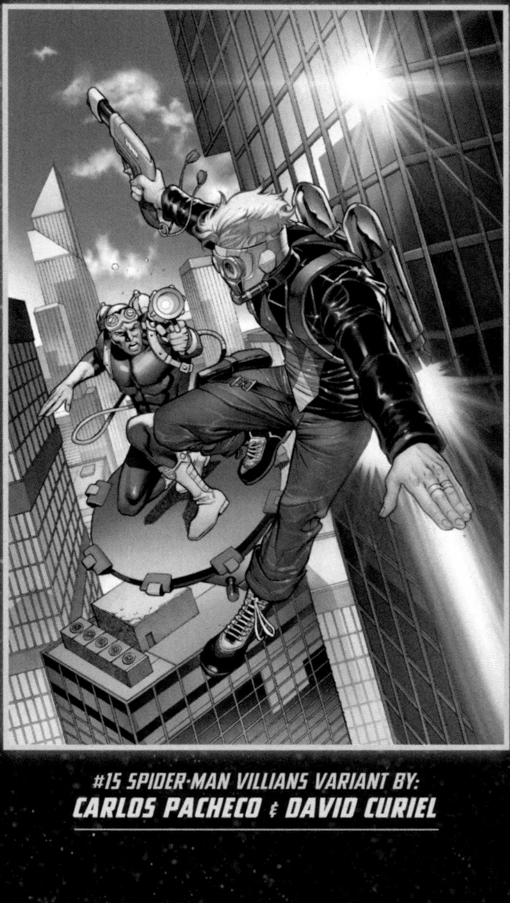

#15 SPIDER-MAN VILLIANS VARIANT BY:
CARLOS PACHECO & DAVID CURIEL

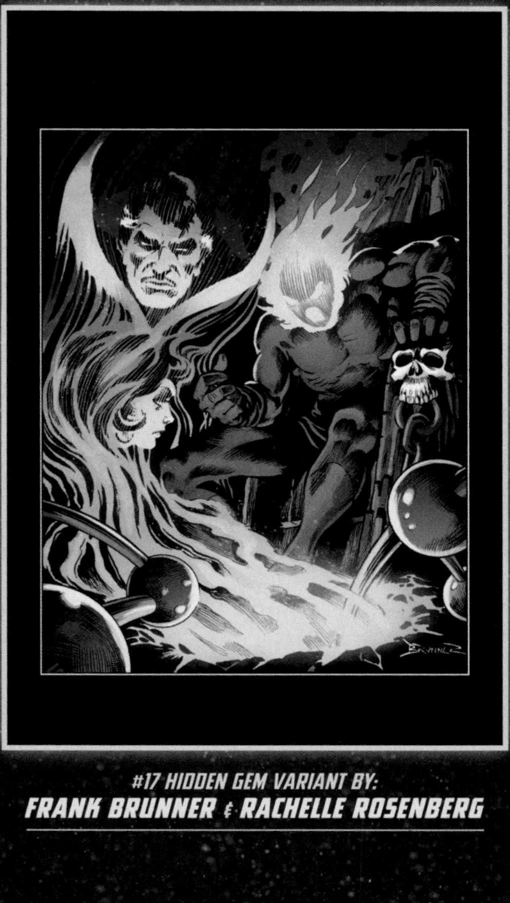

#17 HIDDEN GEM VARIANT BY:
FRANK BRUNNER & RACHELLE ROSENBERG

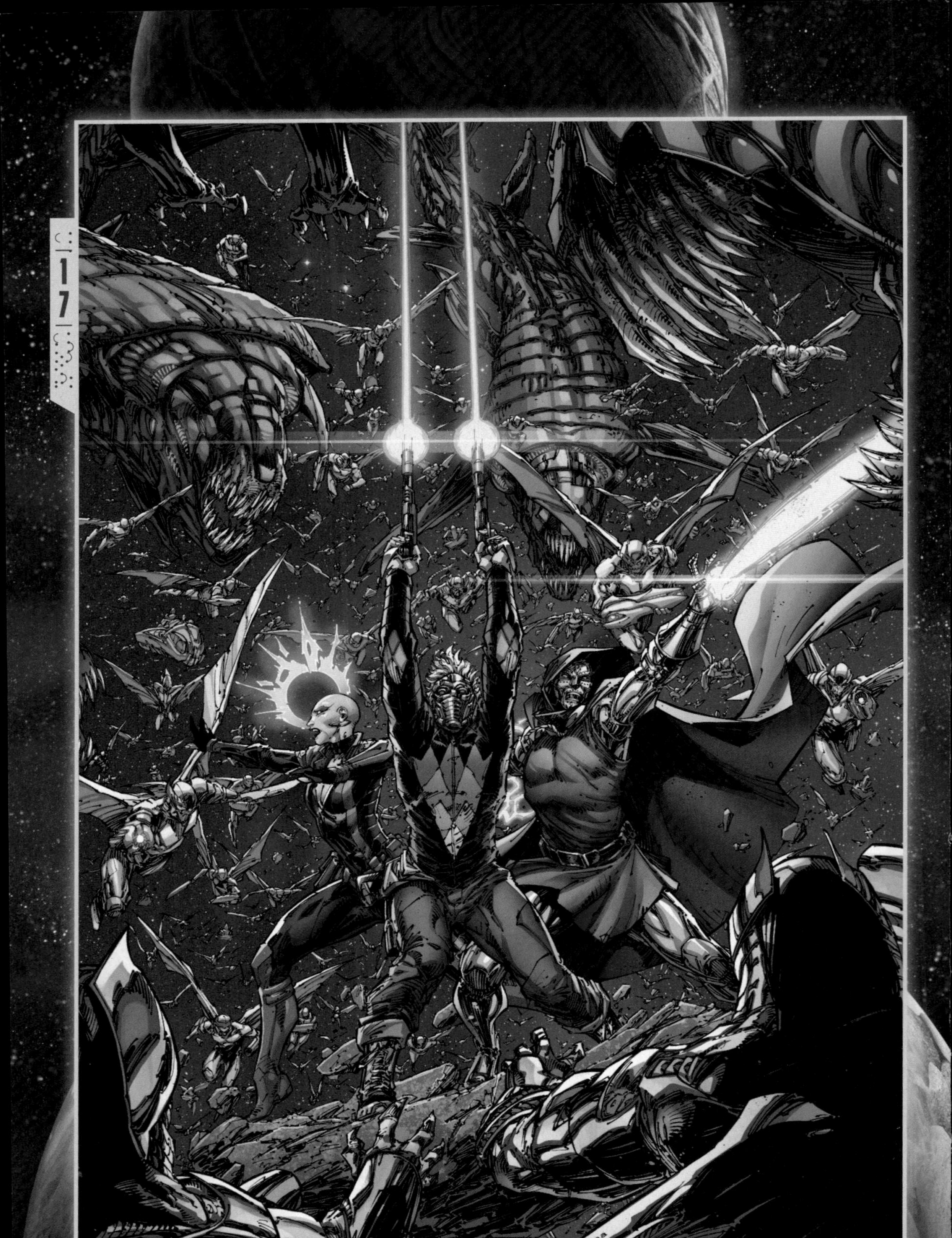
17

"Dormammu is in control."

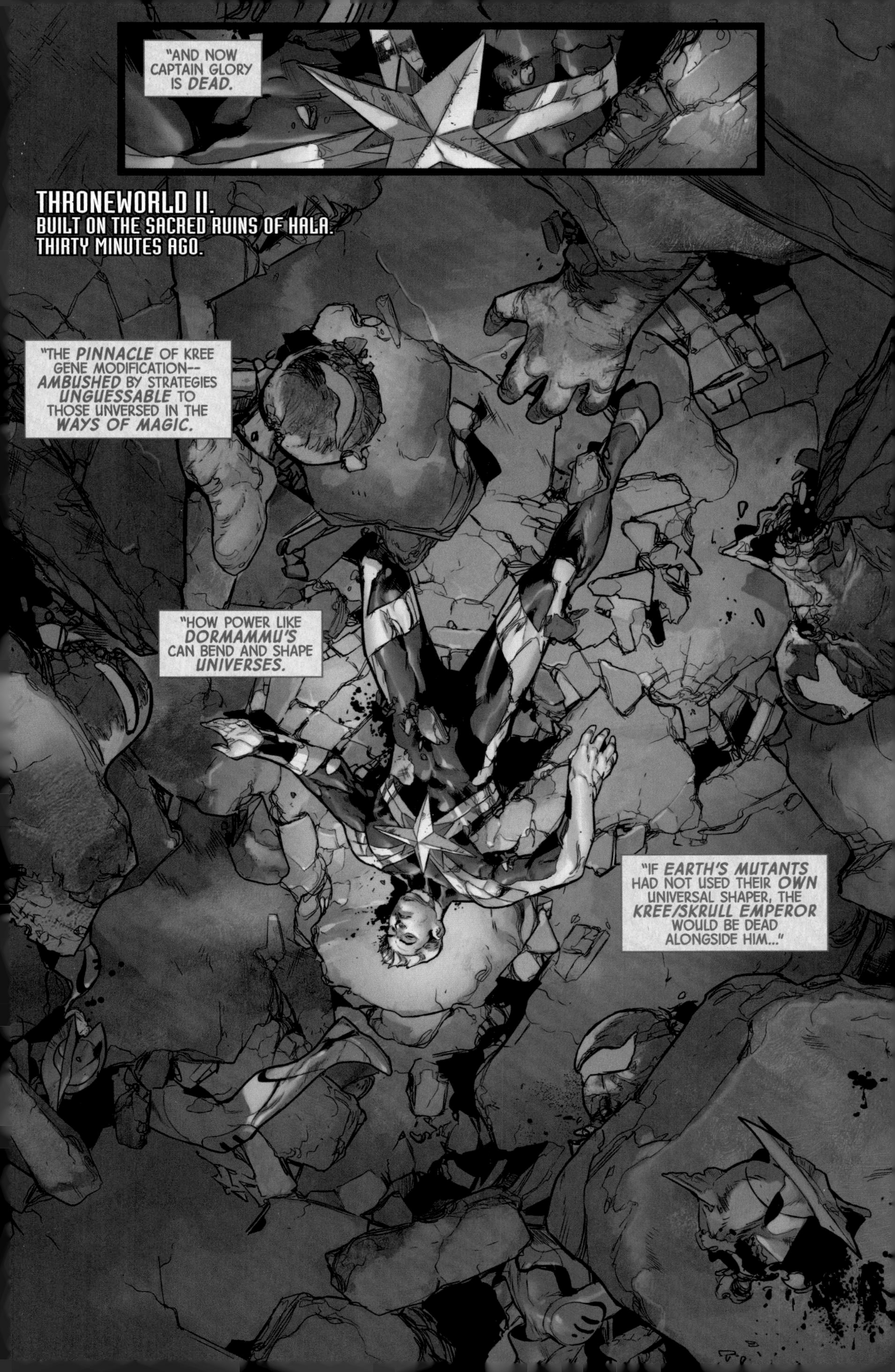
"AND NOW CAPTAIN GLORY IS DEAD.
THRONEWORLD II.
BUILT ON THE SACRED RUINS OF HALA.
THIRTY MINUTES AGO.
"THE PINNACLE OF KREE GENE MODIFICATION--AMBUSHED BY STRATEGIES UNGUESSABLE TO THOSE UNVERSED IN THE WAYS OF MAGIC.
"HOW POWER LIKE DORMAMMU'S CAN BEND AND SHAPE UNIVERSES.
"IF EARTH'S MUTANTS HAD NOT USED THEIR OWN UNIVERSAL SHAPER, THE KREE/SKRULL EMPEROR WOULD BE DEAD ALONGSIDE HIM..."

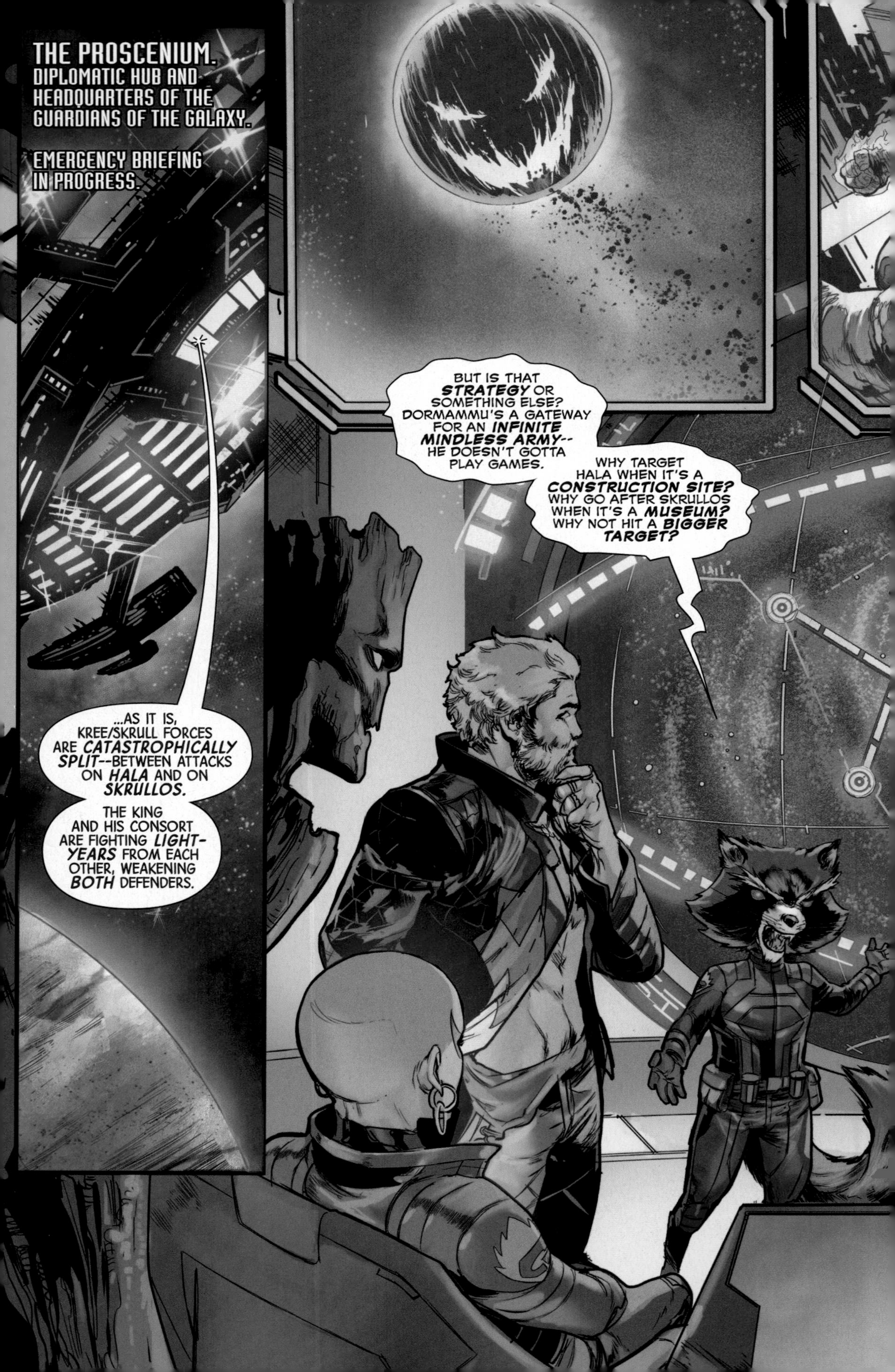
THE PROSCENIUM. DIPLOMATIC HUB AND HEADQUARTERS OF THE GUARDIANS OF THE GALAXY.
EMERGENCY BRIEFING IN PROGRESS.
...AS IT IS, KREE/SKRULL FORCES ARE CATASTROPHICALLY SPLIT--BETWEEN ATTACKS ON HALA AND ON SKRULLOS.
THE KING AND HIS CONSORT ARE FIGHTING LIGHT-YEARS FROM EACH OTHER, WEAKENING BOTH DEFENDERS.
BUT IS THAT STRATEGY OR SOMETHING ELSE? DORMAMMU'S A GATEWAY FOR AN INFINITE MINDLESS ARMY-- HE DOESN'T GOTTA PLAY GAMES.
WHY TARGET HALA WHEN IT'S A CONSTRUCTION SITE? WHY GO AFTER SKRULLOS WHEN IT'S A MUSEUM? WHY NOT HIT A BIGGER TARGET?

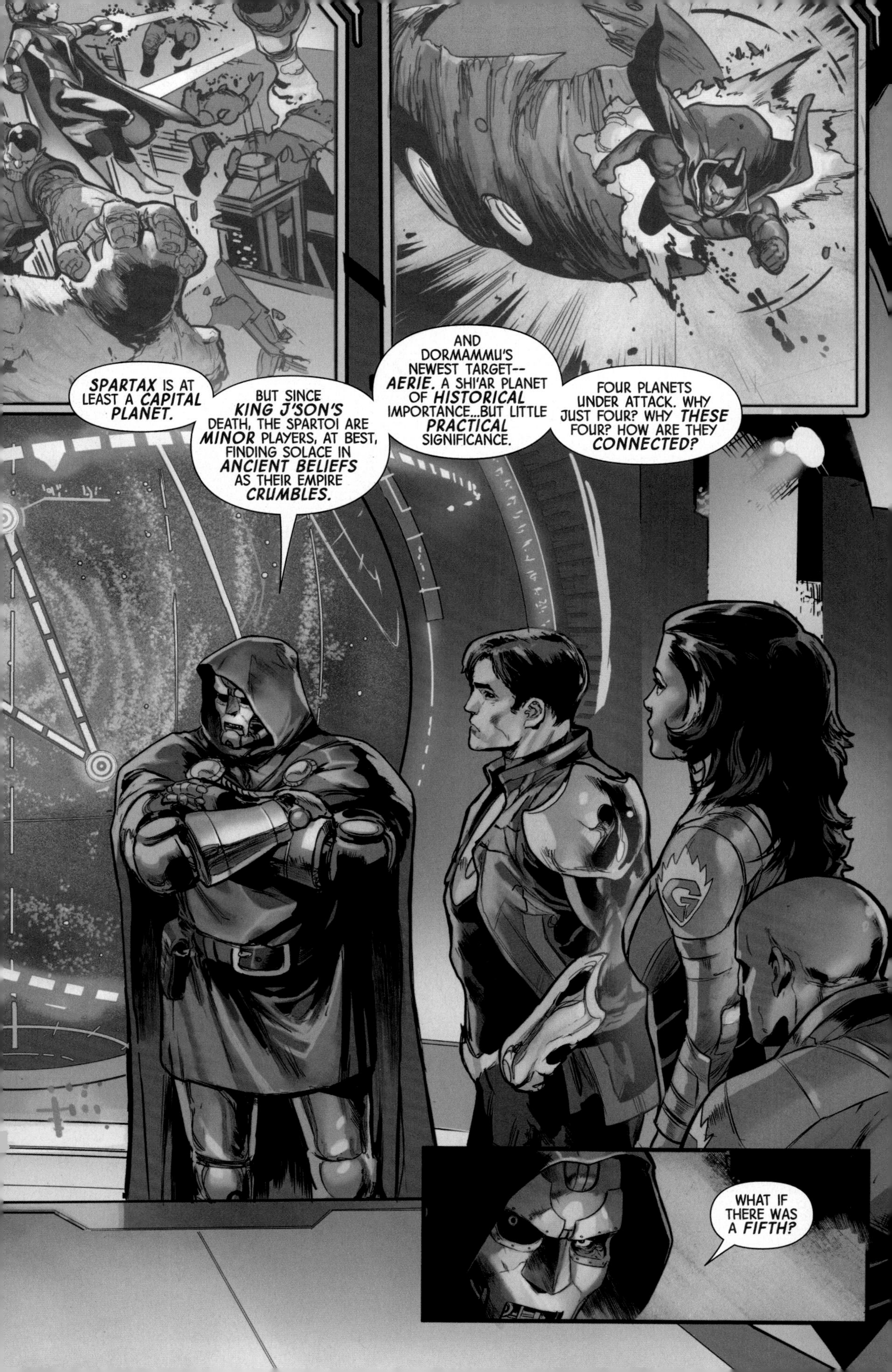
SPARTAX IS AT LEAST A CAPITAL PLANET.
BUT SINCE KING J'SON'S DEATH, THE SPARTOI ARE MINOR PLAYERS, AT BEST, FINDING SOLACE IN ANCIENT BELIEFS AS THEIR EMPIRE CRUMBLES.
AND DORMAMMU'S NEWEST TARGET-- AERIE. A SHI'AR PLANET OF HISTORICAL IMPORTANCE...BUT LITTLE PRACTICAL SIGNIFICANCE.
FOUR PLANETS UNDER ATTACK. WHY JUST FOUR? WHY THESE FOUR? HOW ARE THEY CONNECTED?
WHAT IF THERE WAS A FIFTH?

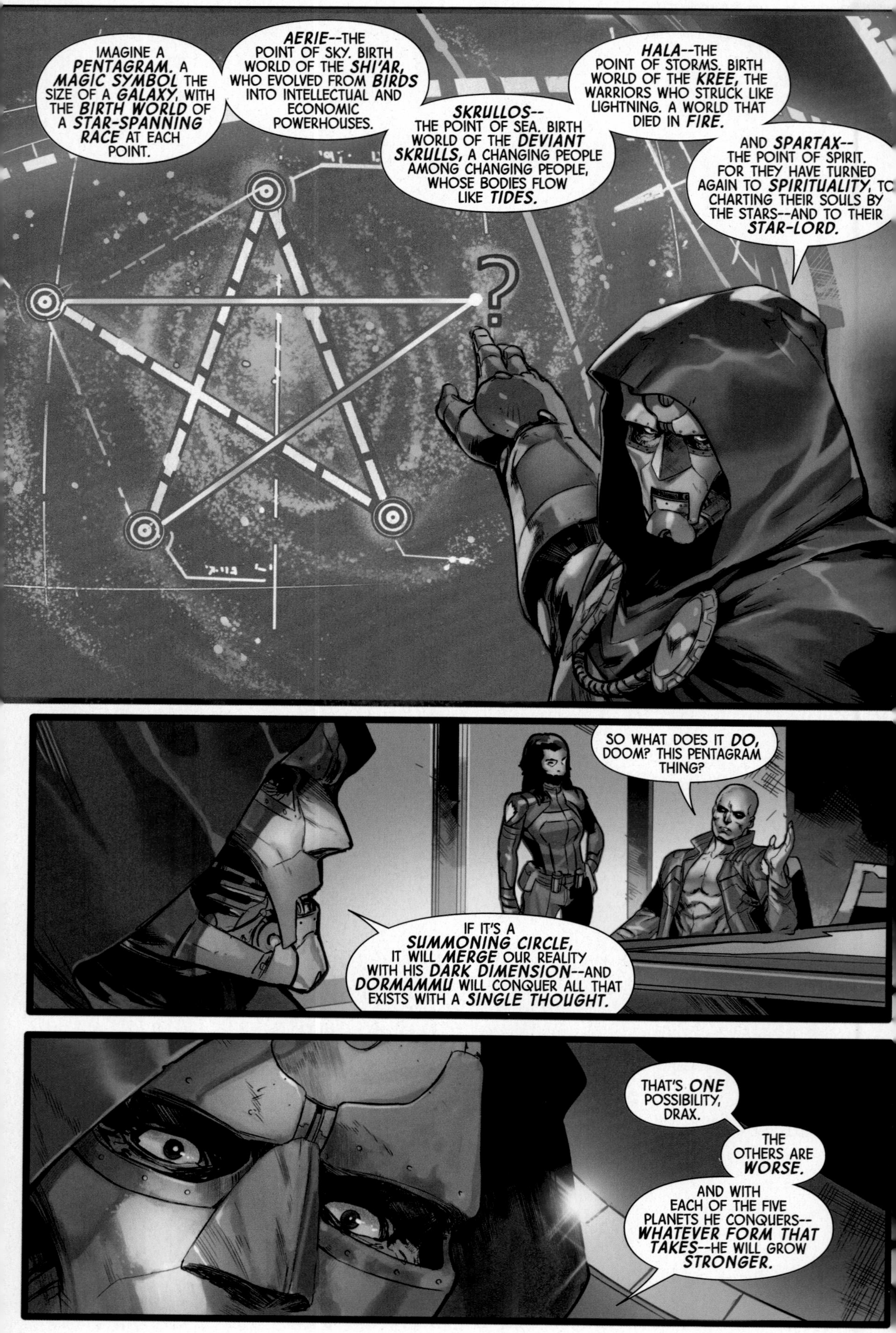
IMAGINE A PENTAGRAM. A MAGIC SYMBOL THE SIZE OF A GALAXY, WITH THE BIRTH WORLD OF A STAR-SPANNING RACE AT EACH POINT.
AERIE--THE POINT OF SKY. BIRTH WORLD OF THE SHI'AR, WHO EVOLVED FROM BIRDS INTO INTELLECTUAL AND ECONOMIC POWERHOUSES.
SKRULLOS--THE POINT OF SEA. BIRTH WORLD OF THE DEVIANT SKRULLS, A CHANGING PEOPLE AMONG CHANGING PEOPLE, WHOSE BODIES FLOW LIKE TIDES.
HALA--THE POINT OF STORMS. BIRTH WORLD OF THE KREE, THE WARRIORS WHO STRUCK LIKE LIGHTNING. A WORLD THAT DIED IN FIRE.
AND SPARTAX--THE POINT OF SPIRIT. FOR THEY HAVE TURNED AGAIN TO SPIRITUALITY, TO CHARTING THEIR SOULS BY THE STARS--AND TO THEIR STAR-LORD.
?
SO WHAT DOES IT DO, DOOM? THIS PENTAGRAM THING?
IF IT'S A SUMMONING CIRCLE, IT WILL MERGE OUR REALITY WITH HIS DARK DIMENSION--AND DORMAMMU WILL CONQUER ALL THAT EXISTS WITH A SINGLE THOUGHT.
THAT'S ONE POSSIBILITY, DRAX.
THE OTHERS ARE WORSE.
AND WITH EACH OF THE FIVE PLANETS HE CONQUERS--WHATEVER FORM THAT TAKES--HE WILL GROW STRONGER.

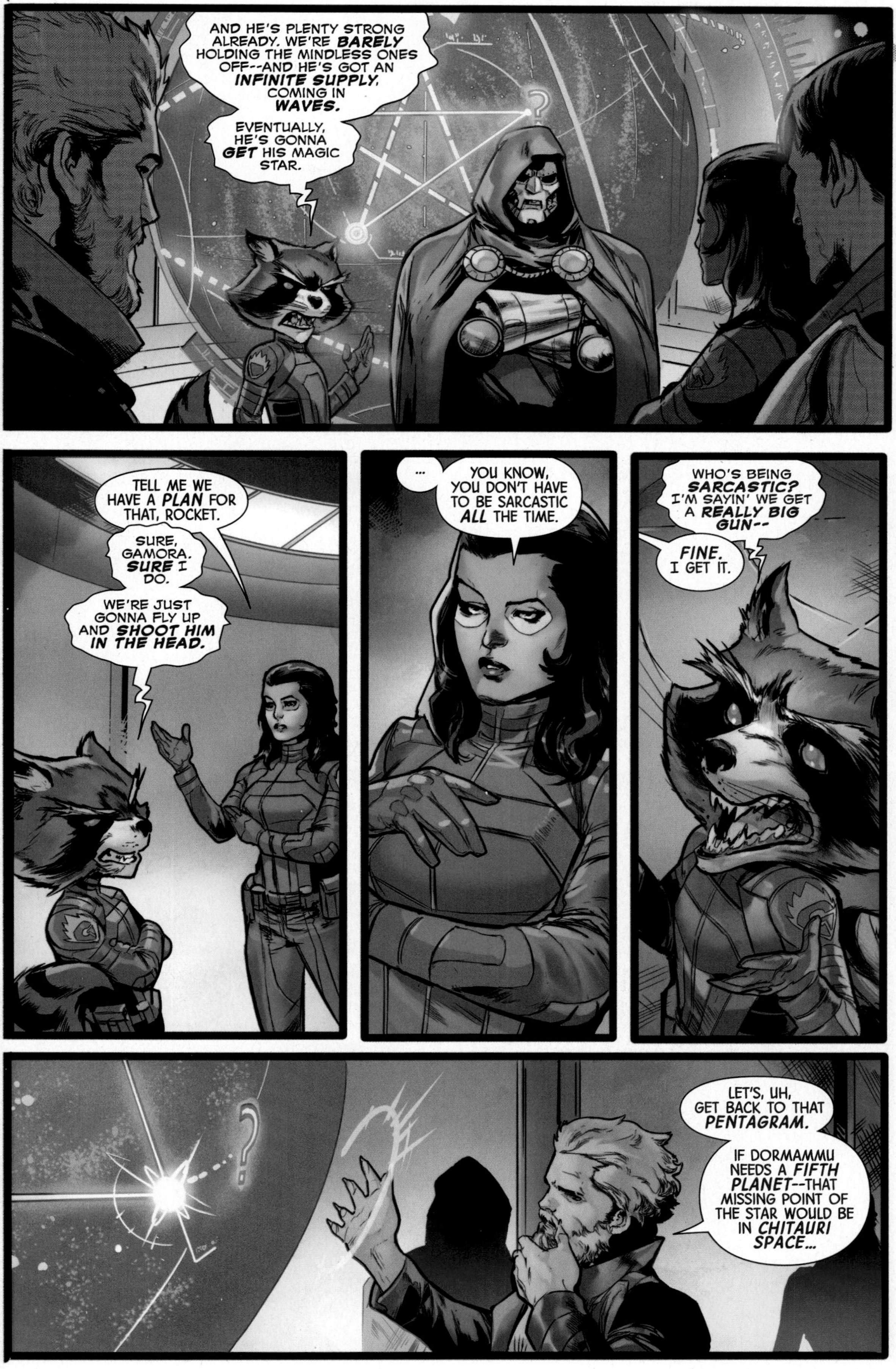

AND HE'S PLENTY STRONG ALREADY. WE'RE BARELY HOLDING THE MINDLESS ONES OFF--AND HE'S GOT AN INFINITE SUPPLY, COMING IN WAVES.
EVENTUALLY, HE'S GONNA GET HIS MAGIC STAR.
TELL ME WE HAVE A PLAN FOR THAT, ROCKET.
SURE, GAMORA. SURE I DO.
WE'RE JUST GONNA FLY UP AND SHOOT HIM IN THE HEAD.
...
YOU KNOW, YOU DON'T HAVE TO BE SARCASTIC ALL THE TIME.
WHO'S BEING SARCASTIC? I'M SAYIN' WE GET A REALLY BIG GUN--
FINE. I GET IT.
LET'S, UH, GET BACK TO THAT PENTAGRAM.
IF DORMAMMU NEEDS A FIFTH PLANET--THAT MISSING POINT OF THE STAR WOULD BE IN CHITAURI SPACE...

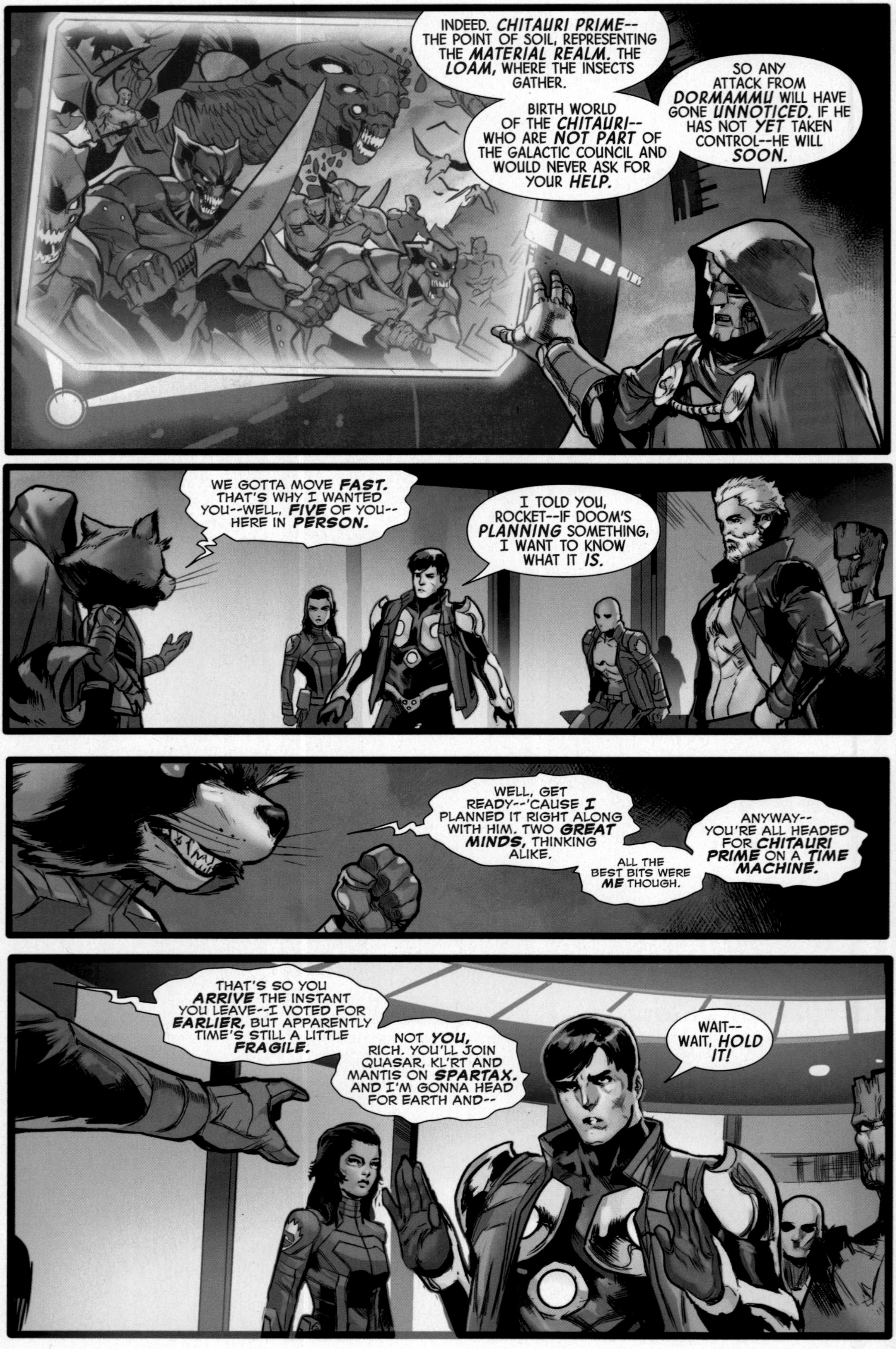
INDEED. CHITAURI PRIME--THE POINT OF SOIL, REPRESENTING THE MATERIAL REALM. THE LOAM, WHERE THE INSECTS GATHER.
BIRTH WORLD OF THE CHITAURI--WHO ARE NOT PART OF THE GALACTIC COUNCIL AND WOULD NEVER ASK FOR YOUR HELP.
SO ANY ATTACK FROM DORMAMMU WILL HAVE GONE UNNOTICED. IF HE HAS NOT YET TAKEN CONTROL--HE WILL SOON.
WE GOTTA MOVE FAST. THAT'S WHY I WANTED YOU--WELL, FIVE OF YOU--HERE IN PERSON.
I TOLD YOU, ROCKET--IF DOOM'S PLANNING SOMETHING, I WANT TO KNOW WHAT IT IS.
WELL, GET READY--'CAUSE I PLANNED IT RIGHT ALONG WITH HIM. TWO GREAT MINDS, THINKING ALIKE.
ALL THE BEST BITS WERE ME THOUGH.
ANYWAY--YOU'RE ALL HEADED FOR CHITAURI PRIME ON A TIME MACHINE.
THAT'S SO YOU ARRIVE THE INSTANT YOU LEAVE--I VOTED FOR EARLIER, BUT APPARENTLY TIME'S STILL A LITTLE FRAGILE.
NOT YOU, RICH. YOU'LL JOIN QUASAR, KL'RT AND MANTIS ON SPARTAX. AND I'M GONNA HEAD FOR EARTH AND--
WAIT--WAIT, HOLD IT!

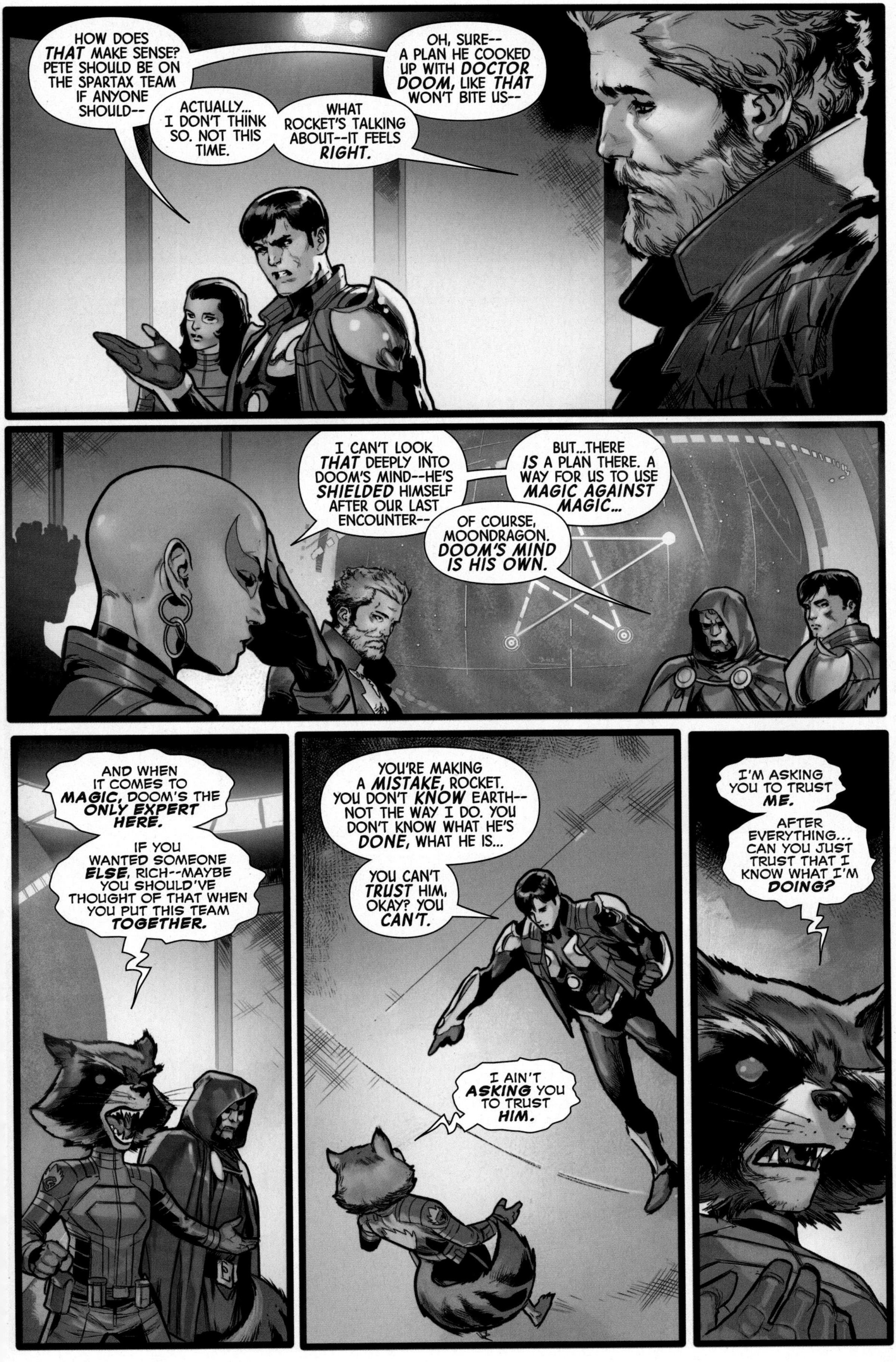
HOW DOES THAT MAKE SENSE? PETE SHOULD BE ON THE SPARTAX TEAM IF ANYONE SHOULD--
OH, SURE-- A PLAN HE COOKED UP WITH DOCTOR DOOM, LIKE THAT WON'T BITE US--
ACTUALLY... I DON'T THINK SO. NOT THIS TIME.
WHAT ROCKET'S TALKING ABOUT--IT FEELS RIGHT.
I CAN'T LOOK THAT DEEPLY INTO DOOM'S MIND--HE'S SHIELDED HIMSELF AFTER OUR LAST ENCOUNTER--
BUT...THERE IS A PLAN THERE. A WAY FOR US TO USE MAGIC AGAINST MAGIC...
OF COURSE, MOONDRAGON. DOOM'S MIND IS HIS OWN.
AND WHEN IT COMES TO MAGIC, DOOM'S THE ONLY EXPERT HERE.
IF YOU WANTED SOMEONE ELSE, RICH--MAYBE YOU SHOULD'VE THOUGHT OF THAT WHEN YOU PUT THIS TEAM TOGETHER.
YOU'RE MAKING A MISTAKE, ROCKET. YOU DON'T KNOW EARTH-- NOT THE WAY I DO. YOU DON'T KNOW WHAT HE'S DONE, WHAT HE IS...
YOU CAN'T TRUST HIM, OKAY? YOU CAN'T.
I AIN'T ASKING YOU TO TRUST HIM.
I'M ASKING YOU TO TRUST ME.
AFTER EVERYTHING... CAN YOU JUST TRUST THAT I KNOW WHAT I'M DOING?

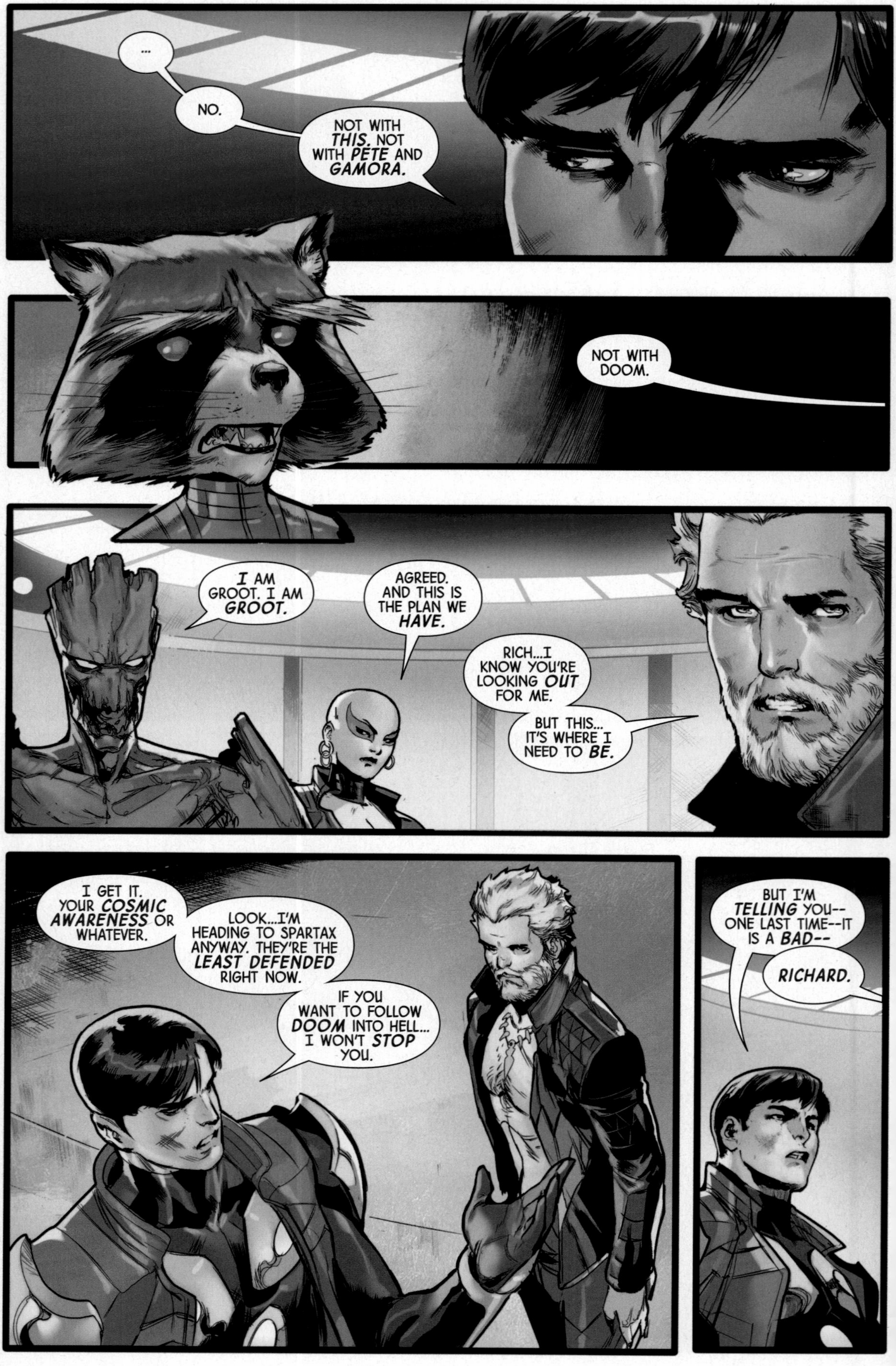
...
NO.
NOT WITH THIS. NOT WITH PETE AND GAMORA.
NOT WITH DOOM.
I AM GROOT. I AM GROOT.
AGREED. AND THIS IS THE PLAN WE HAVE.
RICH...I KNOW YOU'RE LOOKING OUT FOR ME.
BUT THIS... IT'S WHERE I NEED TO BE.
I GET IT. YOUR COSMIC AWARENESS OR WHATEVER.
LOOK...I'M HEADING TO SPARTAX ANYWAY. THEY'RE THE LEAST DEFENDED RIGHT NOW.
IF YOU WANT TO FOLLOW DOOM INTO HELL... I WON'T STOP YOU.
BUT I'M TELLING YOU-- ONE LAST TIME--IT IS A BAD--
RICHARD.

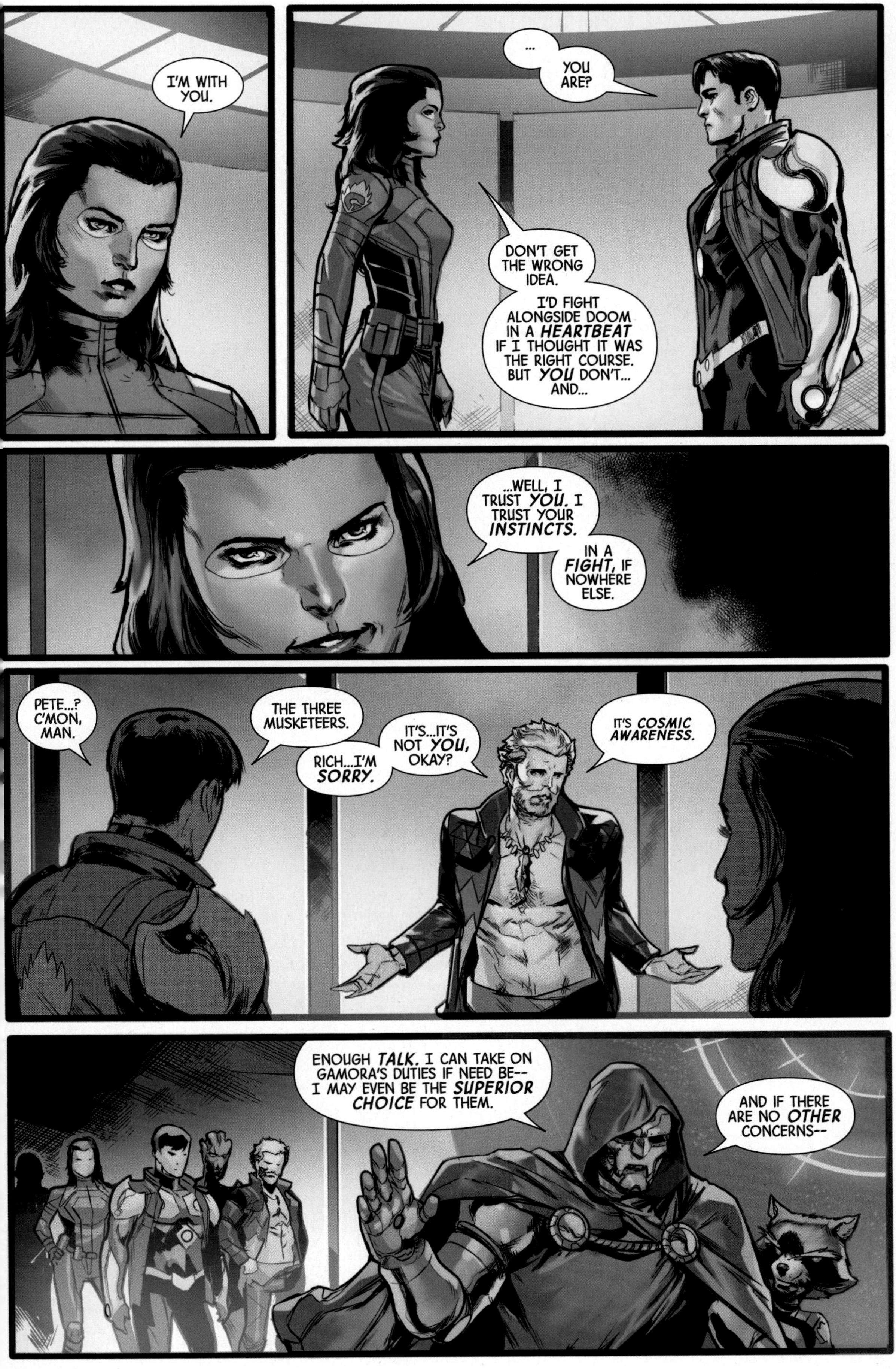
I'M WITH YOU.
... YOU ARE?
DON'T GET THE WRONG IDEA.
I'D FIGHT ALONGSIDE DOOM IN A HEARTBEAT IF I THOUGHT IT WAS THE RIGHT COURSE. BUT YOU DON'T... AND...
...WELL, I TRUST YOU. I TRUST YOUR INSTINCTS.
IN A FIGHT, IF NOWHERE ELSE.
PETE...? C'MON, MAN.
THE THREE MUSKETEERS.
RICH...I'M SORRY.
IT'S...IT'S NOT YOU, OKAY?
IT'S COSMIC AWARENESS.
ENOUGH TALK. I CAN TAKE ON GAMORA'S DUTIES IF NEED BE-- I MAY EVEN BE THE SUPERIOR CHOICE FOR THEM.
AND IF THERE ARE NO OTHER CONCERNS--

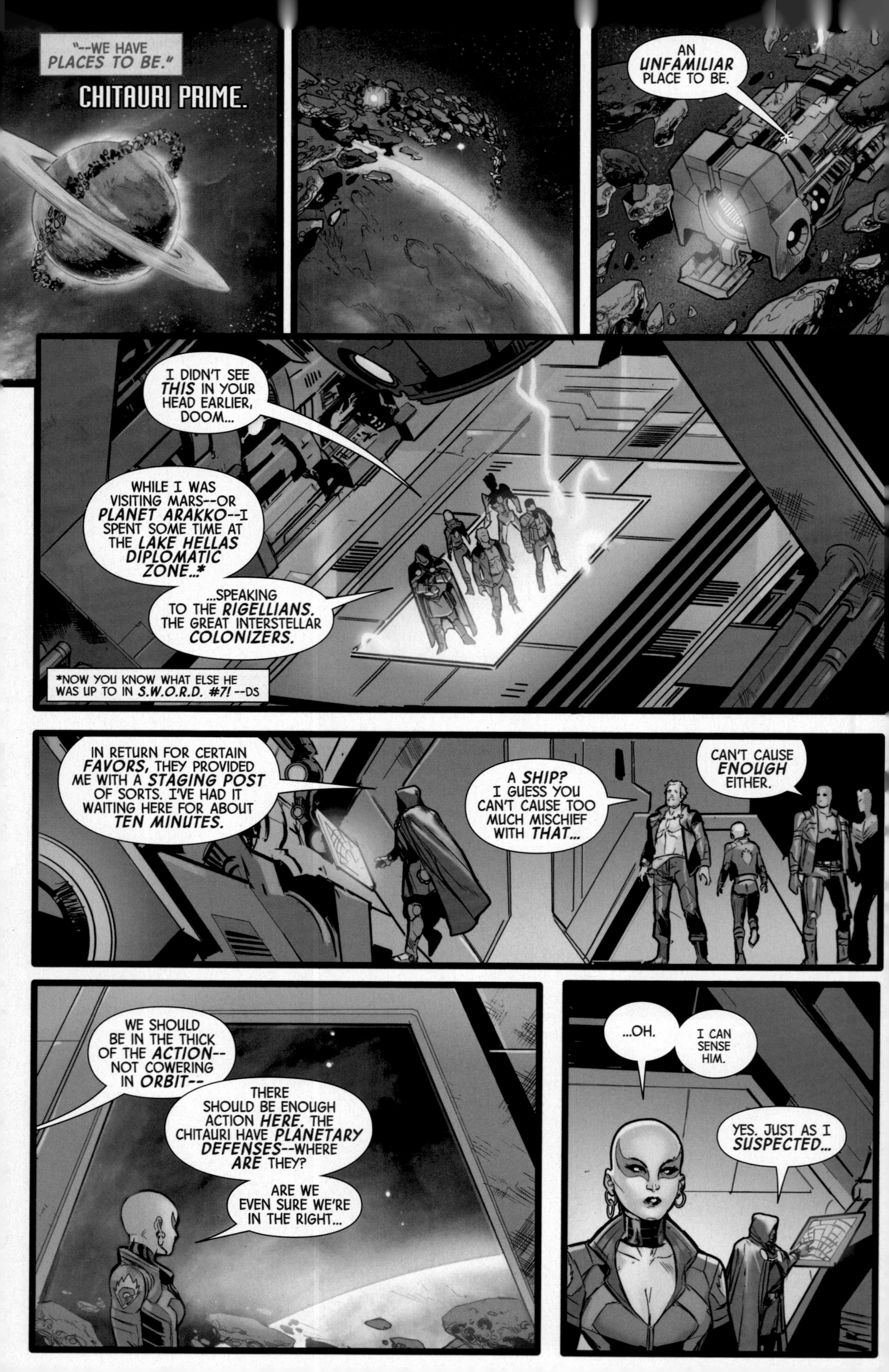
"--WE HAVE PLACES TO BE."
CHITAURI PRIME.
AN UNFAMILIAR PLACE TO BE.
I DIDN'T SEE THIS IN YOUR HEAD EARLIER, DOOM...
WHILE I WAS VISITING MARS--OR PLANET ARAKKO--I SPENT SOME TIME AT THE LAKE HELLAS DIPLOMATIC ZONE...*
...SPEAKING TO THE RIGELLIANS. THE GREAT INTERSTELLAR COLONIZERS.
*NOW YOU KNOW WHAT ELSE HE WAS UP TO IN S.W.O.R.D. #7! --DS
IN RETURN FOR CERTAIN FAVORS, THEY PROVIDED ME WITH A STAGING POST OF SORTS. I'VE HAD IT WAITING HERE FOR ABOUT TEN MINUTES.
A SHIP? I GUESS YOU CAN'T CAUSE TOO MUCH MISCHIEF WITH THAT...
CAN'T CAUSE ENOUGH EITHER.
WE SHOULD BE IN THE THICK OF THE ACTION--NOT COWERING IN ORBIT--
THERE SHOULD BE ENOUGH ACTION HERE. THE CHITAURI HAVE PLANETARY DEFENSES--WHERE ARE THEY?
ARE WE EVEN SURE WE'RE IN THE RIGHT...
...OH.
I CAN SENSE HIM.
YES. JUST AS I SUSPECTED...

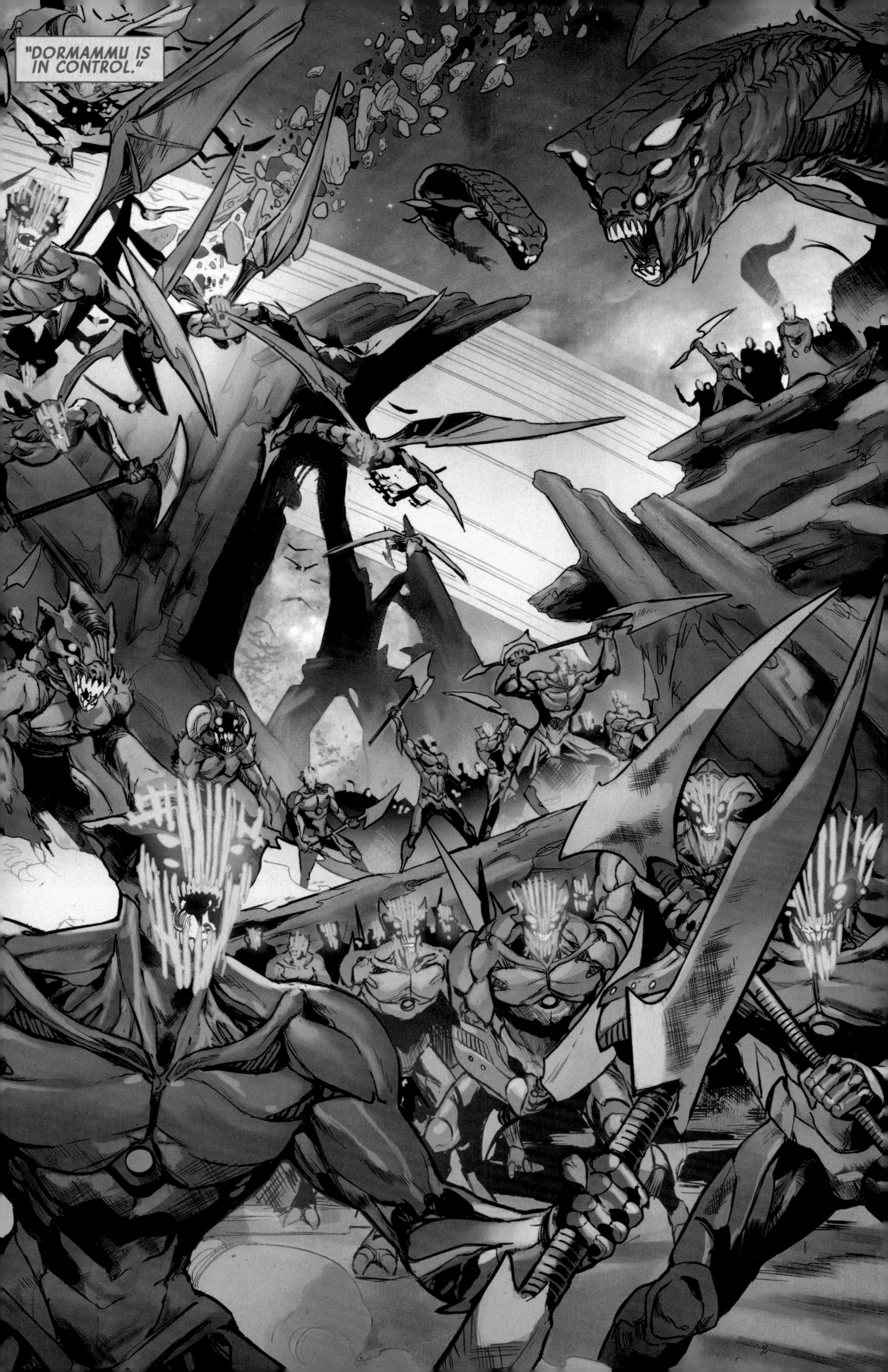
"DORMAMMU IS IN CONTROL."

A WHOLE *PLANET?* JUST LIKE THAT?

EACH PLANET DORMAMMU ATTACKS WILL HAVE ITS OWN *WEAKNESS.* ITS OWN UNIQUE MEANS OF *CONQUEST.* CONQUERING THE CHITAURI HAS *ALWAYS* BEEN SIMPLICITY ITSELF.

THEY HAVE A STRICT *HIERARCHY,* REMEMBER?

FROM THE TRULY MINDLESS *DRONES,* THROUGH THE RANKS OF SIMPLE-MINDED *SOLDIERS...* TO THEIR INTELLIGENT *WARBRINGER* CASTE...

...TO THE *QUEEN OF THE HIVE--*

--THE CENTRAL *MACRO-INTELLECT* THAT DICTATES TO ALL OTHERS. ONCE DORMAMMU POSSESSED HER--*INFECTED* HER--THE GAME WAS *OVER.*

WITHOUT A *MINDLESS ONE* BEING *DEPLOYED...*

I AM GROOT. I AM *GROOT...?*

TRANSLATION, PLEASE.

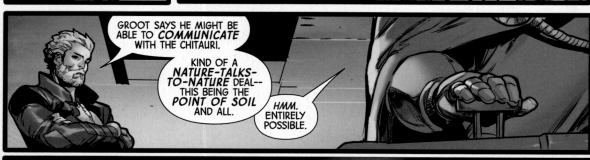

GROOT SAYS HE MIGHT BE ABLE TO *COMMUNICATE* WITH THE CHITAURI.

KIND OF A *NATURE-TALKS-TO-NATURE* DEAL-- THIS BEING THE *POINT OF SOIL* AND ALL.

HMM. ENTIRELY POSSIBLE.

BUT I PREFER A MORE...*DIRECT* APPROACH.

THIS IS NOT A *SHIP,* QUILL.

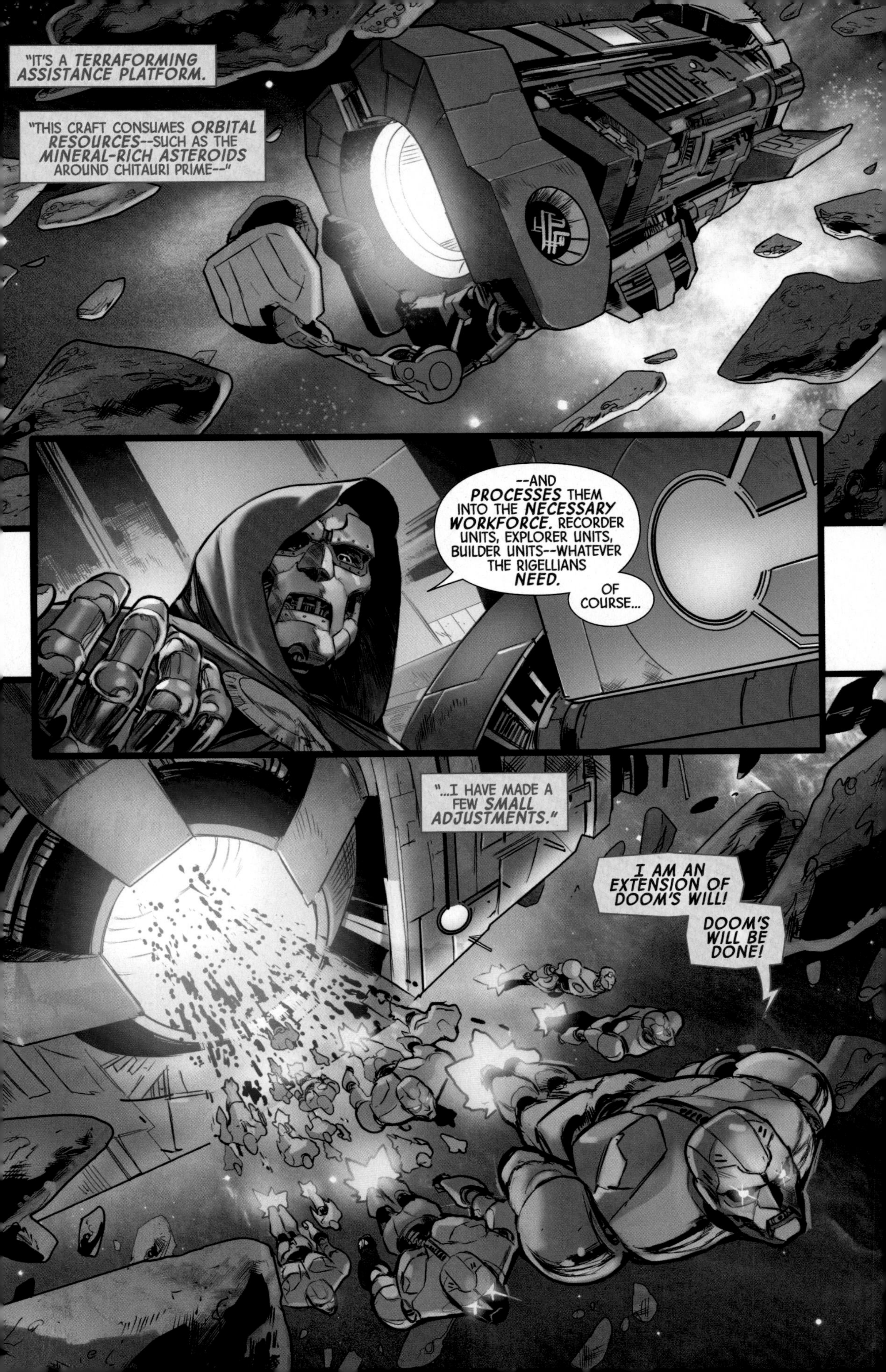
"IT'S A TERRAFORMING ASSISTANCE PLATFORM.
"THIS CRAFT CONSUMES ORBITAL RESOURCES--SUCH AS THE MINERAL-RICH ASTEROIDS AROUND CHITAURI PRIME--"
--AND PROCESSES THEM INTO THE NECESSARY WORKFORCE. RECORDER UNITS, EXPLORER UNITS, BUILDER UNITS--WHATEVER THE RIGELLIANS NEED.
OF COURSE...
"...I HAVE MADE A FEW SMALL ADJUSTMENTS."
I AM AN EXTENSION OF DOOM'S WILL!
DOOM'S WILL BE DONE!

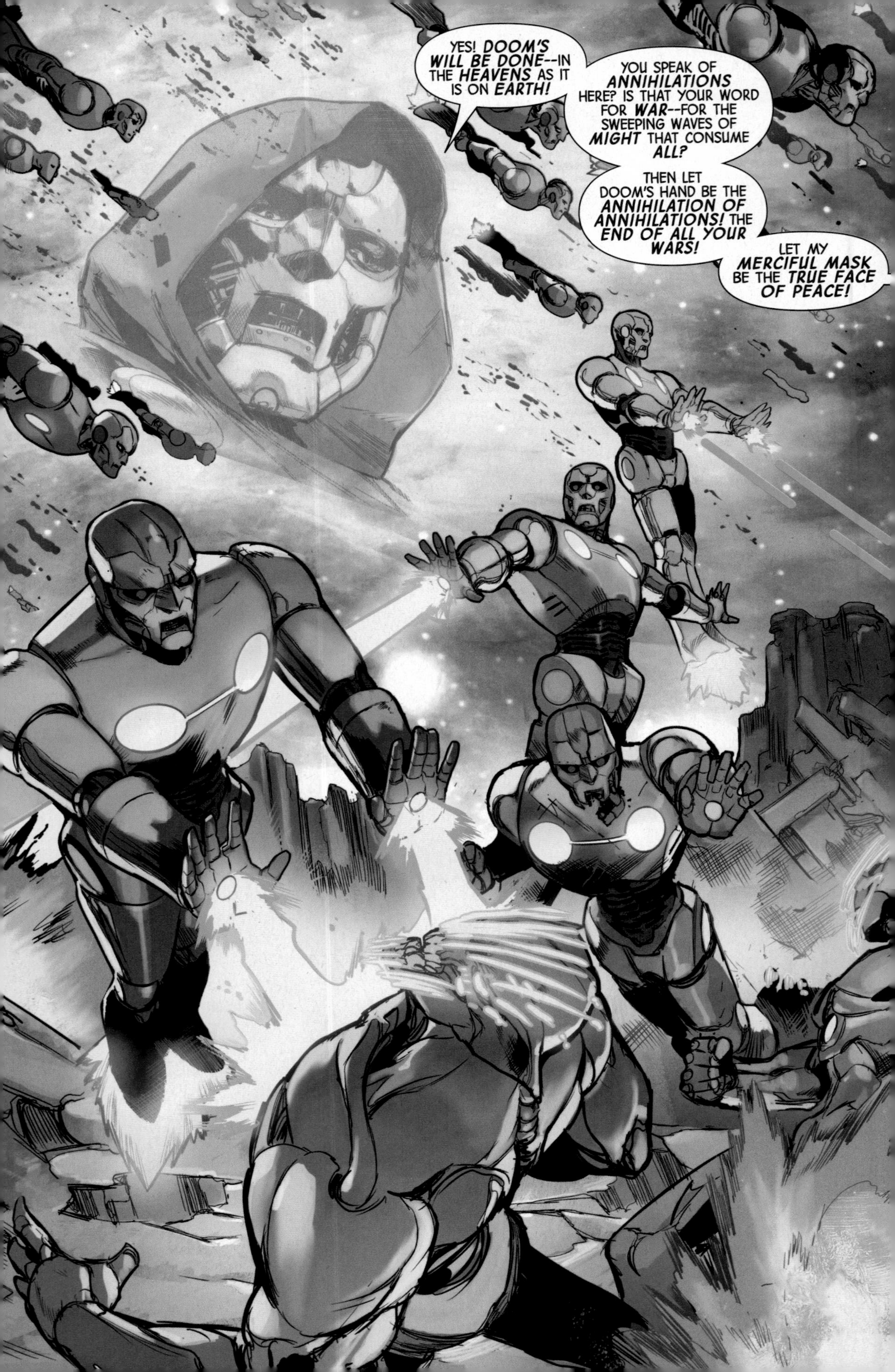
YES! DOOM'S WILL BE DONE--IN THE HEAVENS AS IT IS ON EARTH!
YOU SPEAK OF ANNIHILATIONS HERE? IS THAT YOUR WORD FOR WAR--FOR THE SWEEPING WAVES OF MIGHT THAT CONSUME ALL?
THEN LET DOOM'S HAND BE THE ANNIHILATION OF ANNIHILATIONS! THE END OF ALL YOUR WARS!
LET MY MERCIFUL MASK BE THE TRUE FACE OF PEACE!

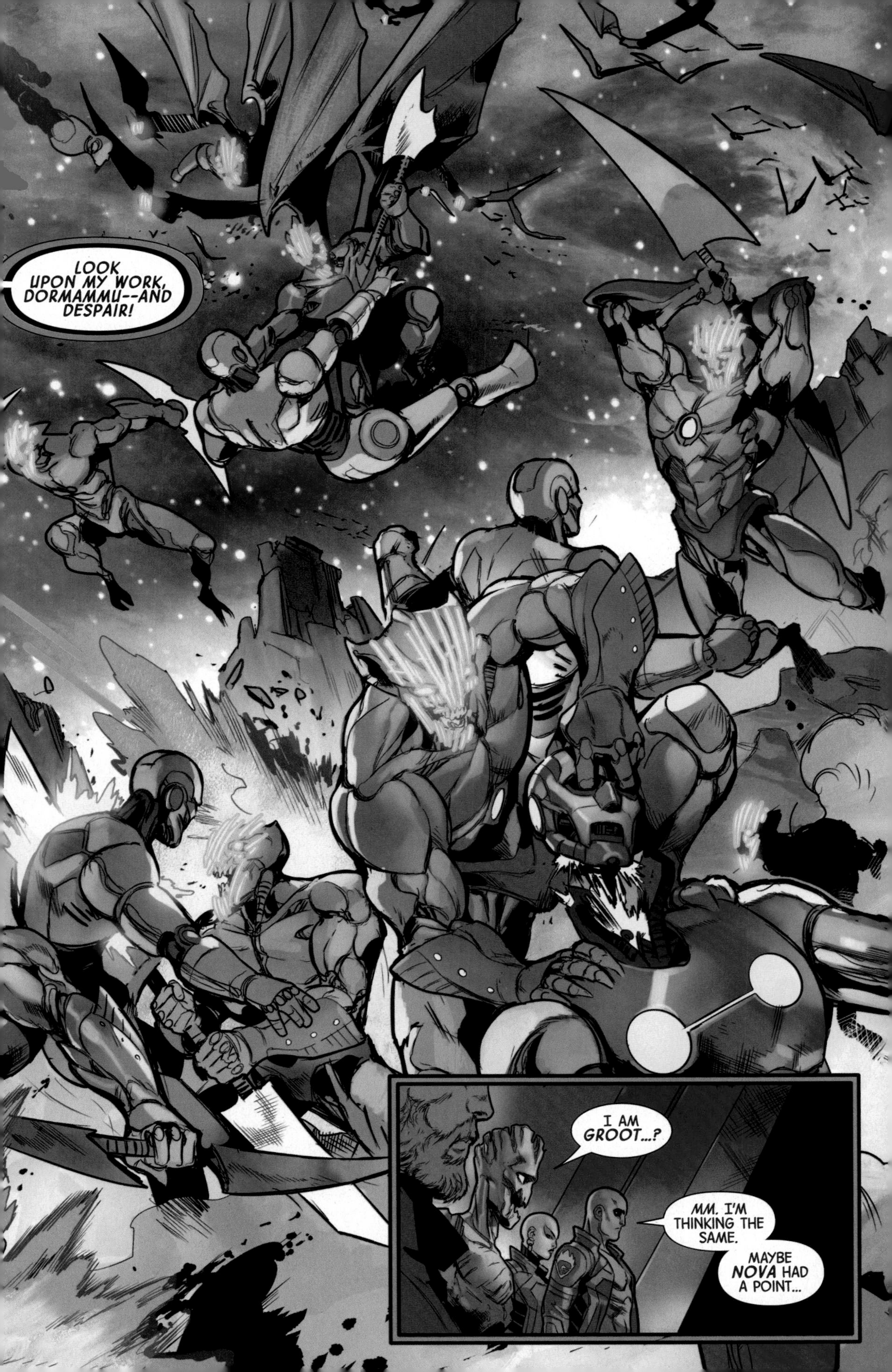
LOOK UPON MY WORK, DORMAMMU--AND DESPAIR!
I AM GROOT...?
MM. I'M THINKING THE SAME.
MAYBE NOVA HAD A POINT...

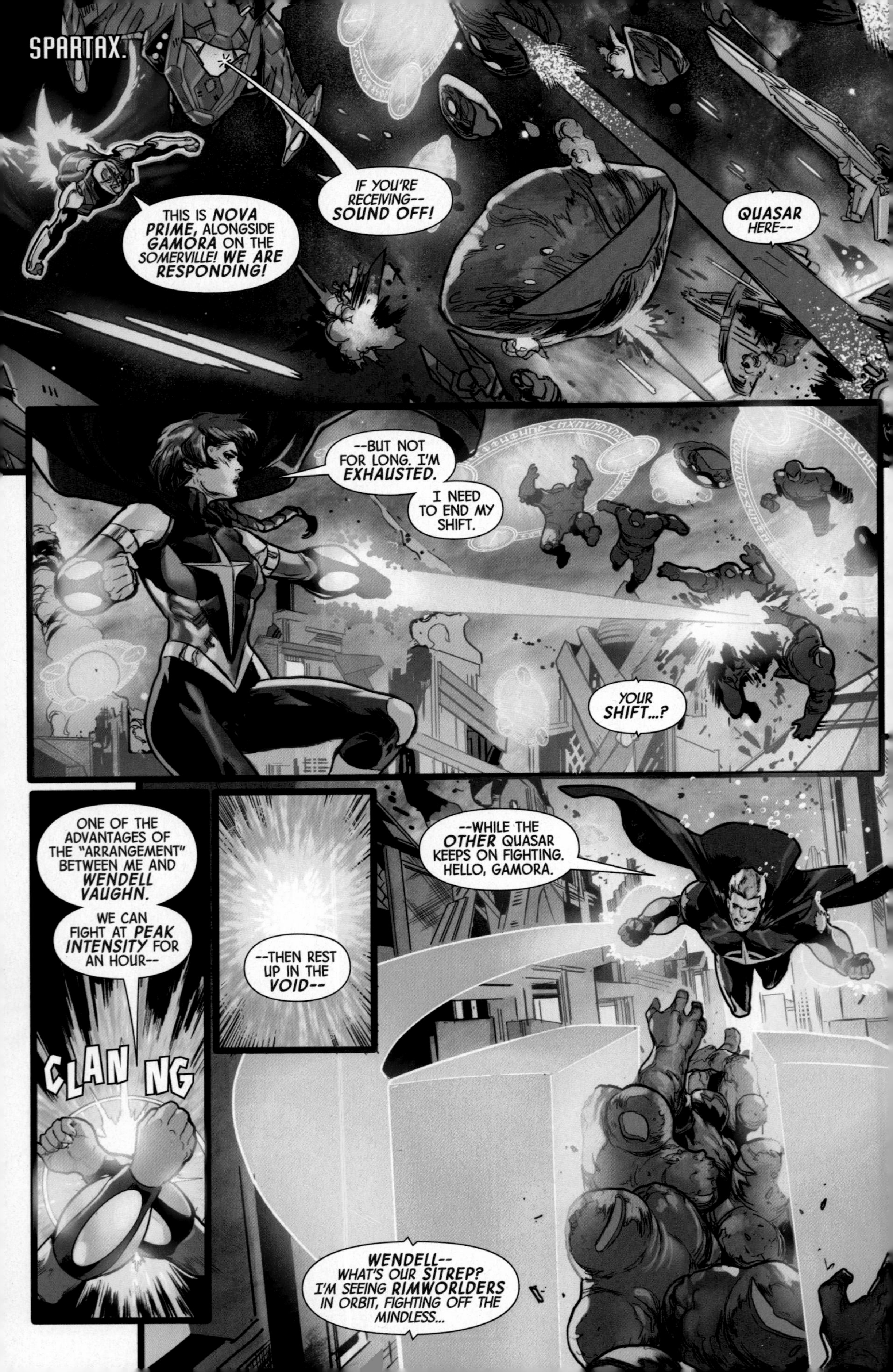

SPARTAX.
THIS IS NOVA PRIME, ALONGSIDE GAMORA ON THE SOMERVILLE! WE ARE RESPONDING!
IF YOU'RE RECEIVING-- SOUND OFF!
QUASAR HERE--
--BUT NOT FOR LONG. I'M EXHAUSTED.
I NEED TO END MY SHIFT.
YOUR SHIFT...?
ONE OF THE ADVANTAGES OF THE "ARRANGEMENT" BETWEEN ME AND WENDELL VAUGHN.
WE CAN FIGHT AT PEAK INTENSITY FOR AN HOUR--
--THEN REST UP IN THE VOID--
--WHILE THE OTHER QUASAR KEEPS ON FIGHTING. HELLO, GAMORA.
CLAN NG
WENDELL-- WHAT'S OUR SITREP? I'M SEEING RIMWORLDERS IN ORBIT, FIGHTING OFF THE MINDLESS...

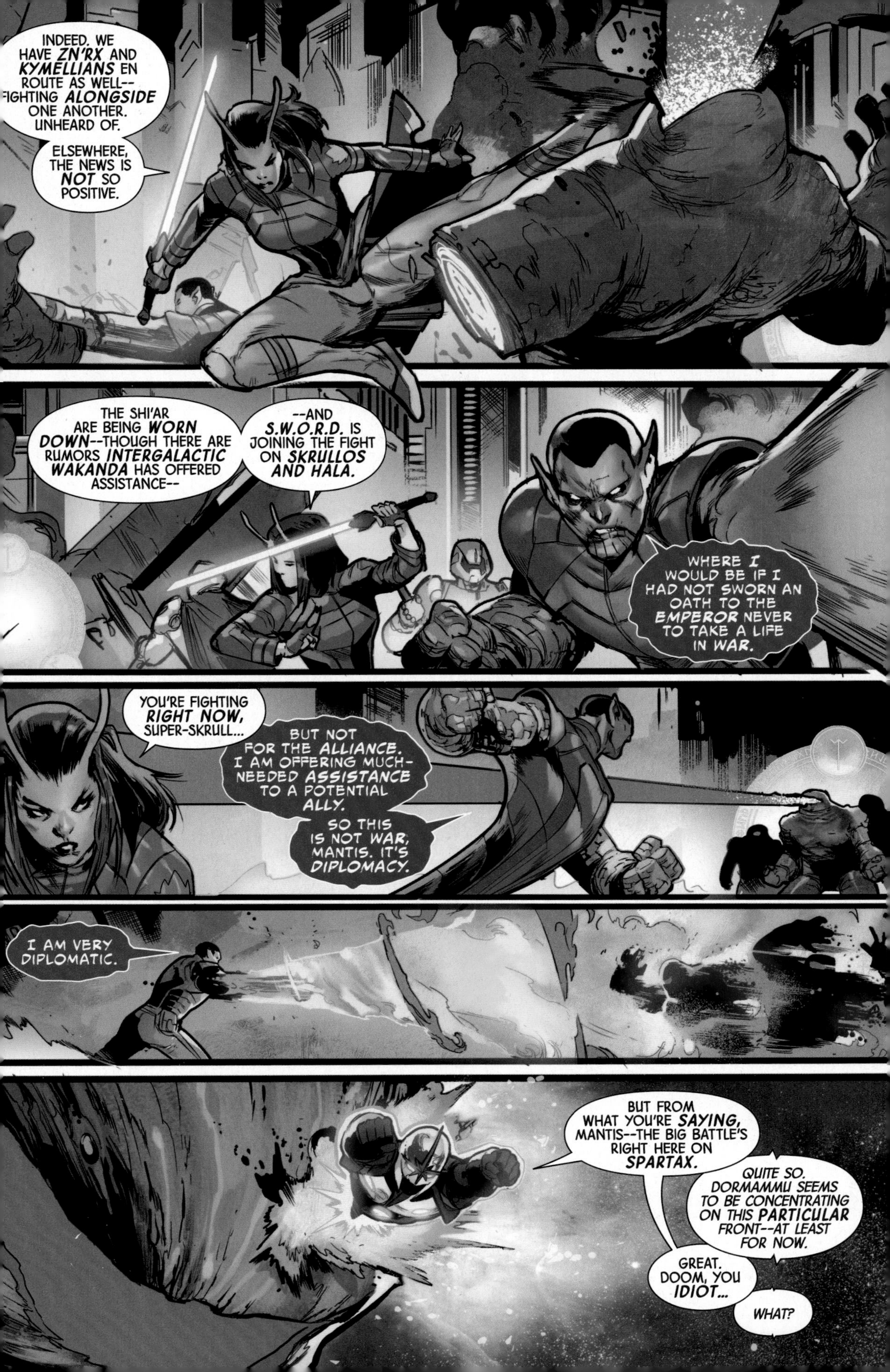
INDEED. WE HAVE ZN'RX AND KYMELLIANS EN ROUTE AS WELL--FIGHTING ALONGSIDE ONE ANOTHER. UNHEARD OF.
ELSEWHERE, THE NEWS IS NOT SO POSITIVE.
THE SHI'AR ARE BEING WORN DOWN--THOUGH THERE ARE RUMORS INTERGALACTIC WAKANDA HAS OFFERED ASSISTANCE--
--AND S.W.O.R.D. IS JOINING THE FIGHT ON SKRULLOS AND HALA.
WHERE I WOULD BE IF I HAD NOT SWORN AN OATH TO THE EMPEROR NEVER TO TAKE A LIFE IN WAR.
YOU'RE FIGHTING RIGHT NOW, SUPER-SKRULL...
BUT NOT FOR THE ALLIANCE. I AM OFFERING MUCH-NEEDED ASSISTANCE TO A POTENTIAL ALLY.
SO THIS IS NOT WAR, MANTIS. IT'S DIPLOMACY.
I AM VERY DIPLOMATIC.
BUT FROM WHAT YOU'RE SAYING, MANTIS--THE BIG BATTLE'S RIGHT HERE ON SPARTAX.
QUITE SO. DORMAMMU SEEMS TO BE CONCENTRATING ON THIS PARTICULAR FRONT--AT LEAST FOR NOW.
GREAT. DOOM, YOU IDIOT...
WHAT?

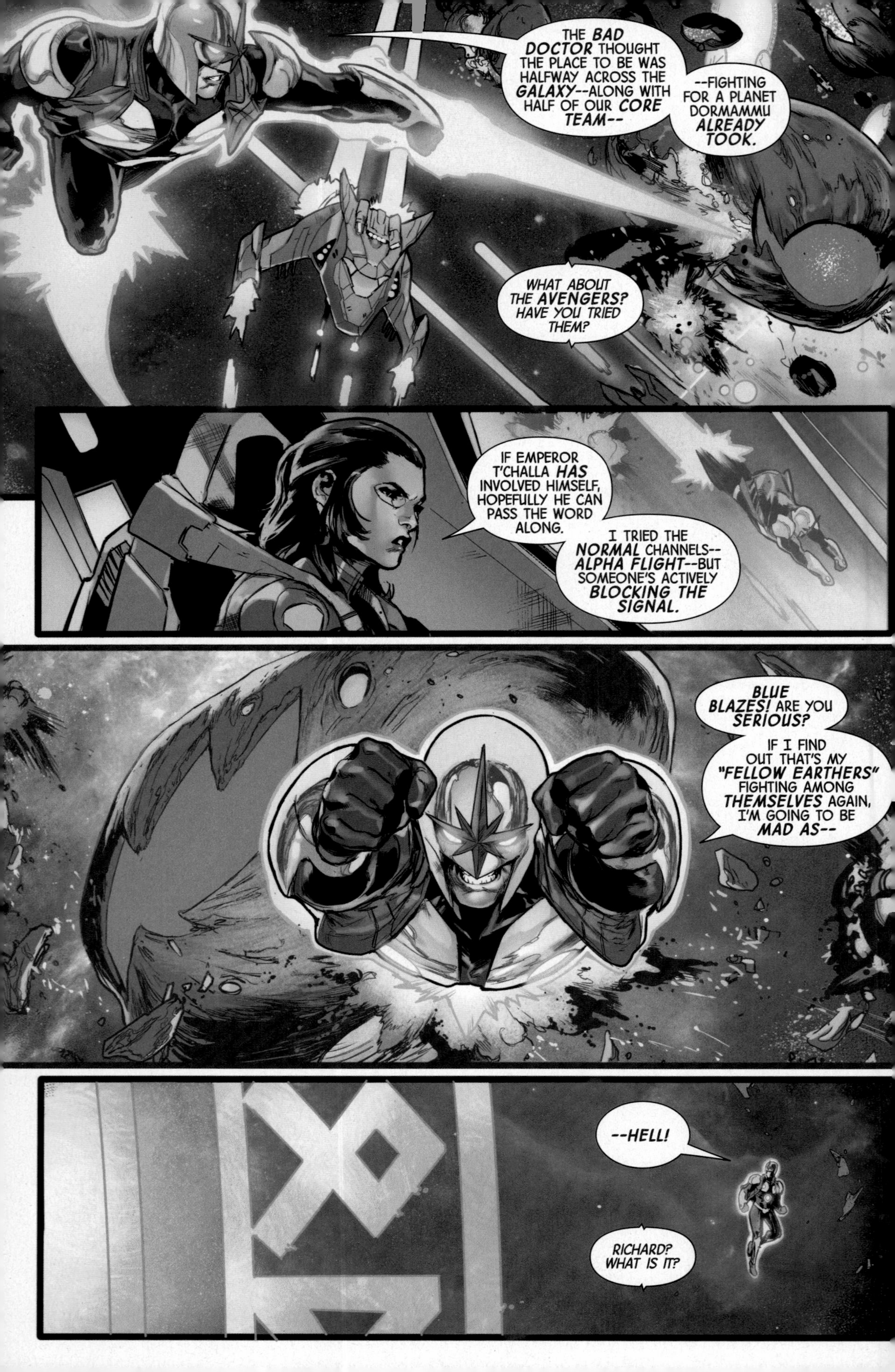
THE BAD DOCTOR THOUGHT THE PLACE TO BE WAS HALFWAY ACROSS THE GALAXY--ALONG WITH HALF OF OUR CORE TEAM--
--FIGHTING FOR A PLANET DORMAMMU ALREADY TOOK.
WHAT ABOUT THE AVENGERS? HAVE YOU TRIED THEM?
IF EMPEROR T'CHALLA HAS INVOLVED HIMSELF, HOPEFULLY HE CAN PASS THE WORD ALONG.
I TRIED THE NORMAL CHANNELS--ALPHA FLIGHT--BUT SOMEONE'S ACTIVELY BLOCKING THE SIGNAL.
BLUE BLAZES! ARE YOU SERIOUS?
IF I FIND OUT THAT'S MY "FELLOW EARTHERS" FIGHTING AMONG THEMSELVES AGAIN, I'M GOING TO BE MAD AS--
--HELL!
RICHARD? WHAT IS IT?

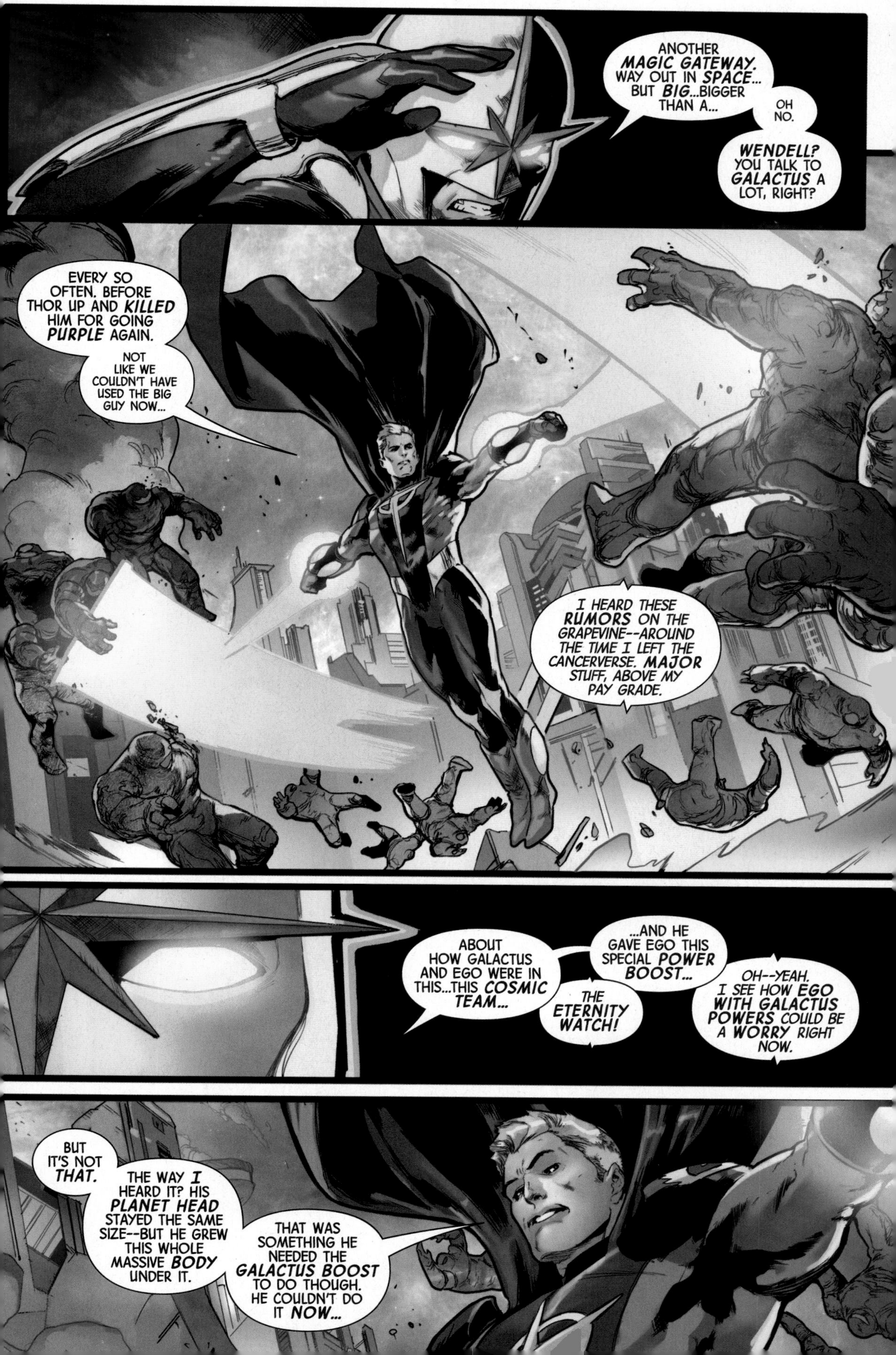
ANOTHER MAGIC GATEWAY. WAY OUT IN SPACE... BUT BIG...BIGGER THAN A...
OH NO.
WENDELL? YOU TALK TO GALACTUS A LOT, RIGHT?
EVERY SO OFTEN. BEFORE THOR UP AND KILLED HIM FOR GOING PURPLE AGAIN.
NOT LIKE WE COULDN'T HAVE USED THE BIG GUY NOW...
I HEARD THESE RUMORS ON THE GRAPEVINE--AROUND THE TIME I LEFT THE CANCERVERSE. MAJOR STUFF, ABOVE MY PAY GRADE.
ABOUT HOW GALACTUS AND EGO WERE IN THIS...THIS COSMIC TEAM...
THE ETERNITY WATCH!
...AND HE GAVE EGO THIS SPECIAL POWER BOOST...
OH--YEAH. I SEE HOW EGO WITH GALACTUS POWERS COULD BE A WORRY RIGHT NOW.
BUT IT'S NOT THAT.
THE WAY I HEARD IT? HIS PLANET HEAD STAYED THE SAME SIZE--BUT HE GREW THIS WHOLE MASSIVE BODY UNDER IT.
THAT WAS SOMETHING HE NEEDED THE GALACTUS BOOST TO DO THOUGH. HE COULDN'T DO IT NOW...

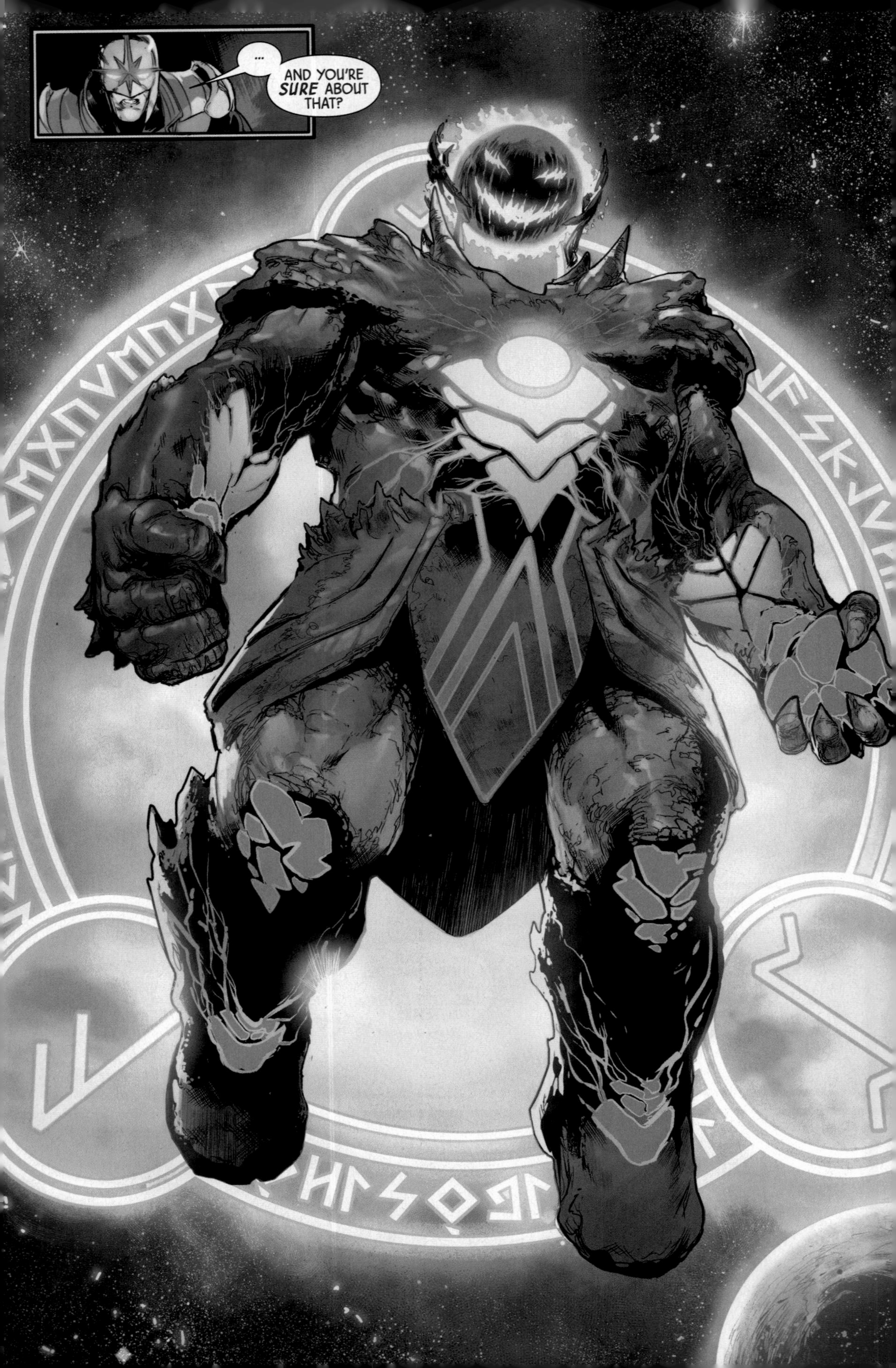
...
AND YOU'RE SURE ABOUT THAT?

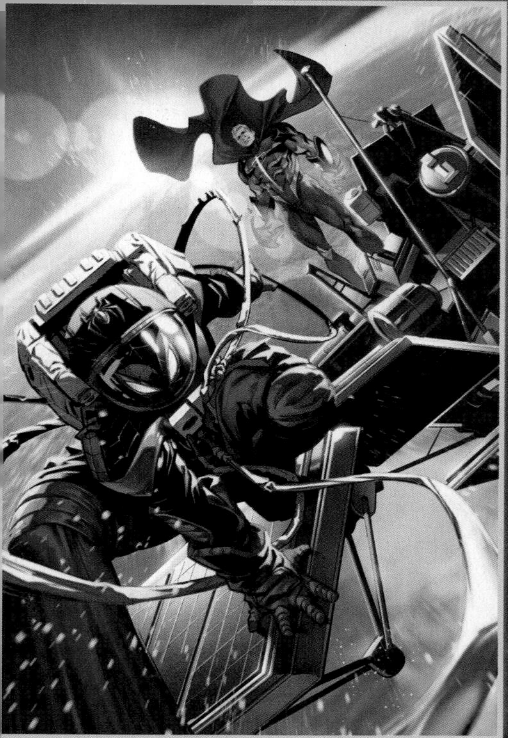

MILES MORALES: SPIDER-MAN 10TH ANNIVERSARY VARIANT BY:
FRANCESCO MANNA & FLAVIO DISPENZA

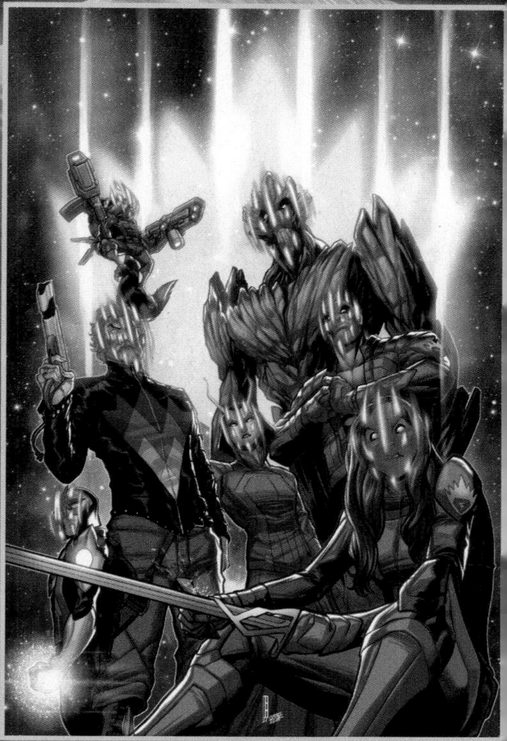

#18 VARIANT BY:
DAVID BALDEON & ISRAEL SILVA

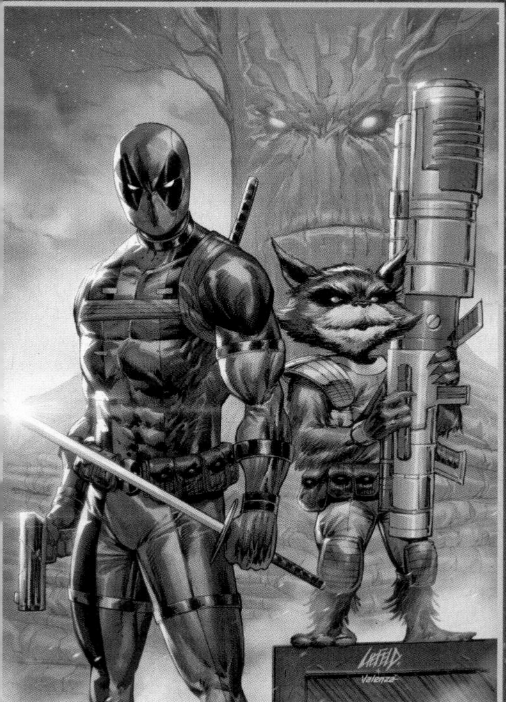

#13 DEADPOOL 30TH ANNIVERSARY VARIANT BY:

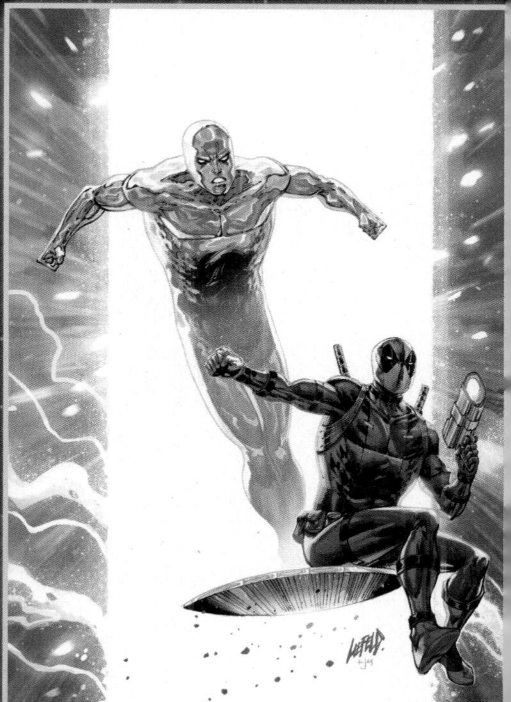

#15 DEADPOOL 30TH ANNIVERSARY VARIANT BY:

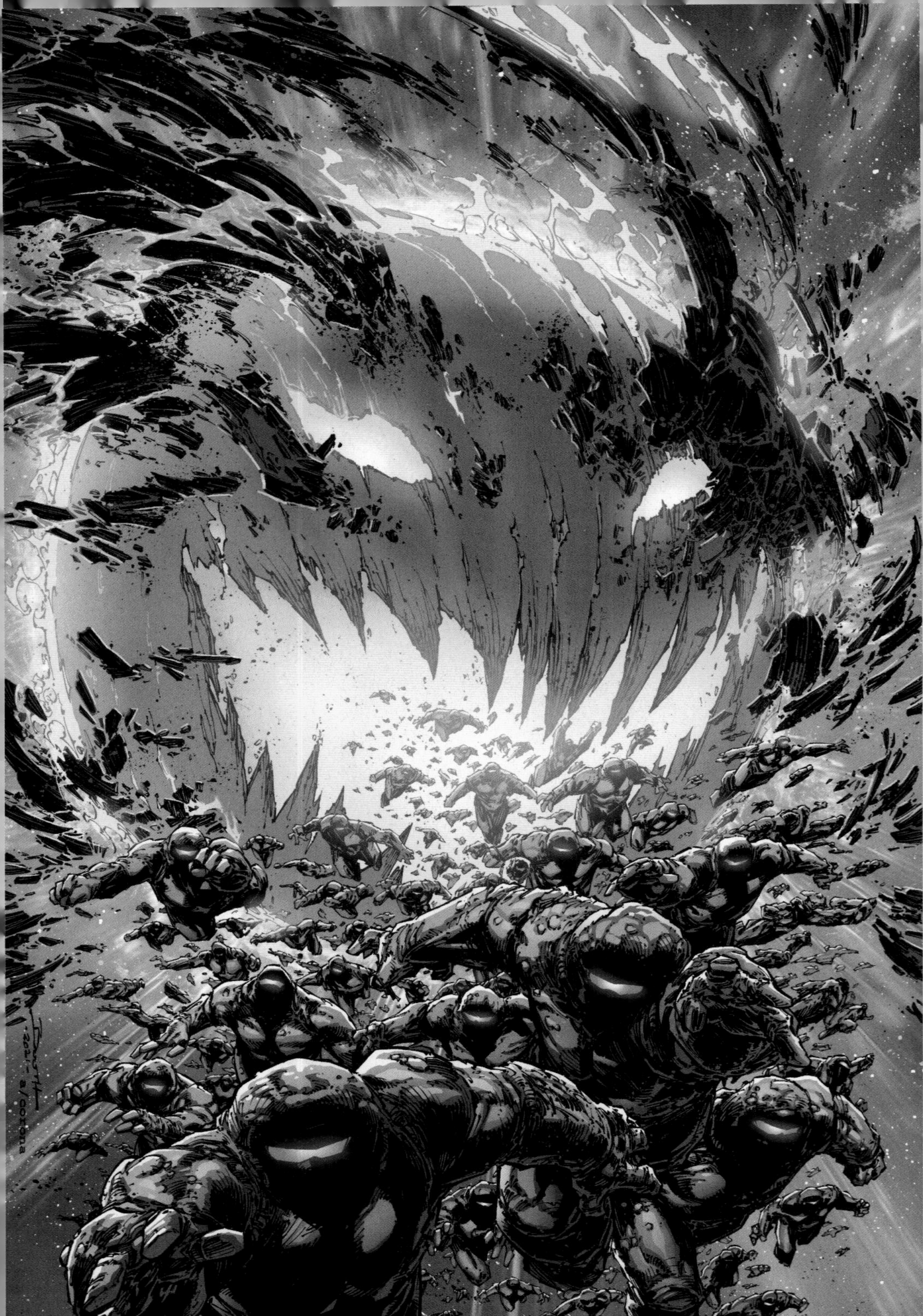

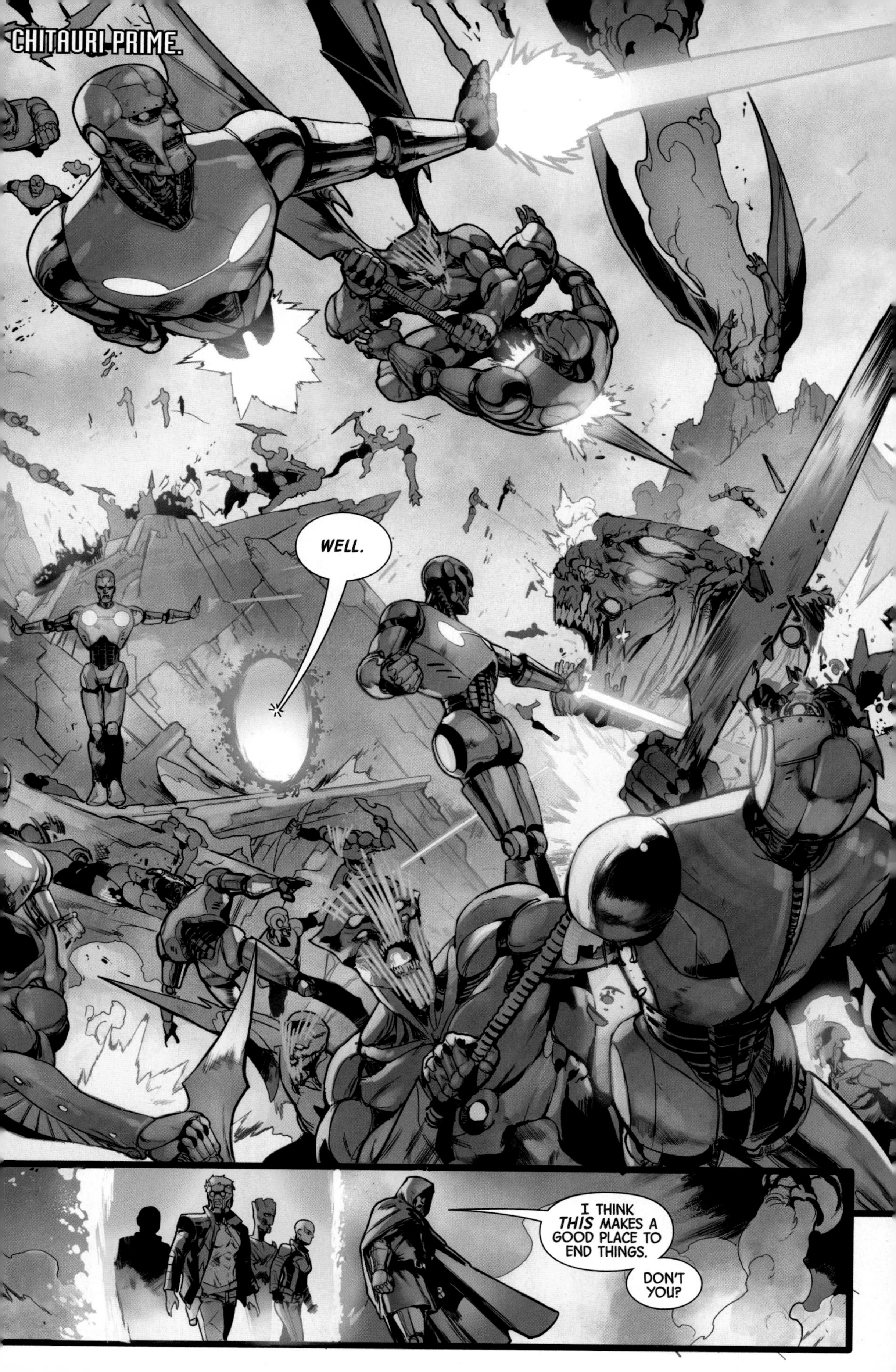
CHITAURI PRIME.
WELL.
I THINK THIS MAKES A GOOD PLACE TO END THINGS.
DON'T YOU?

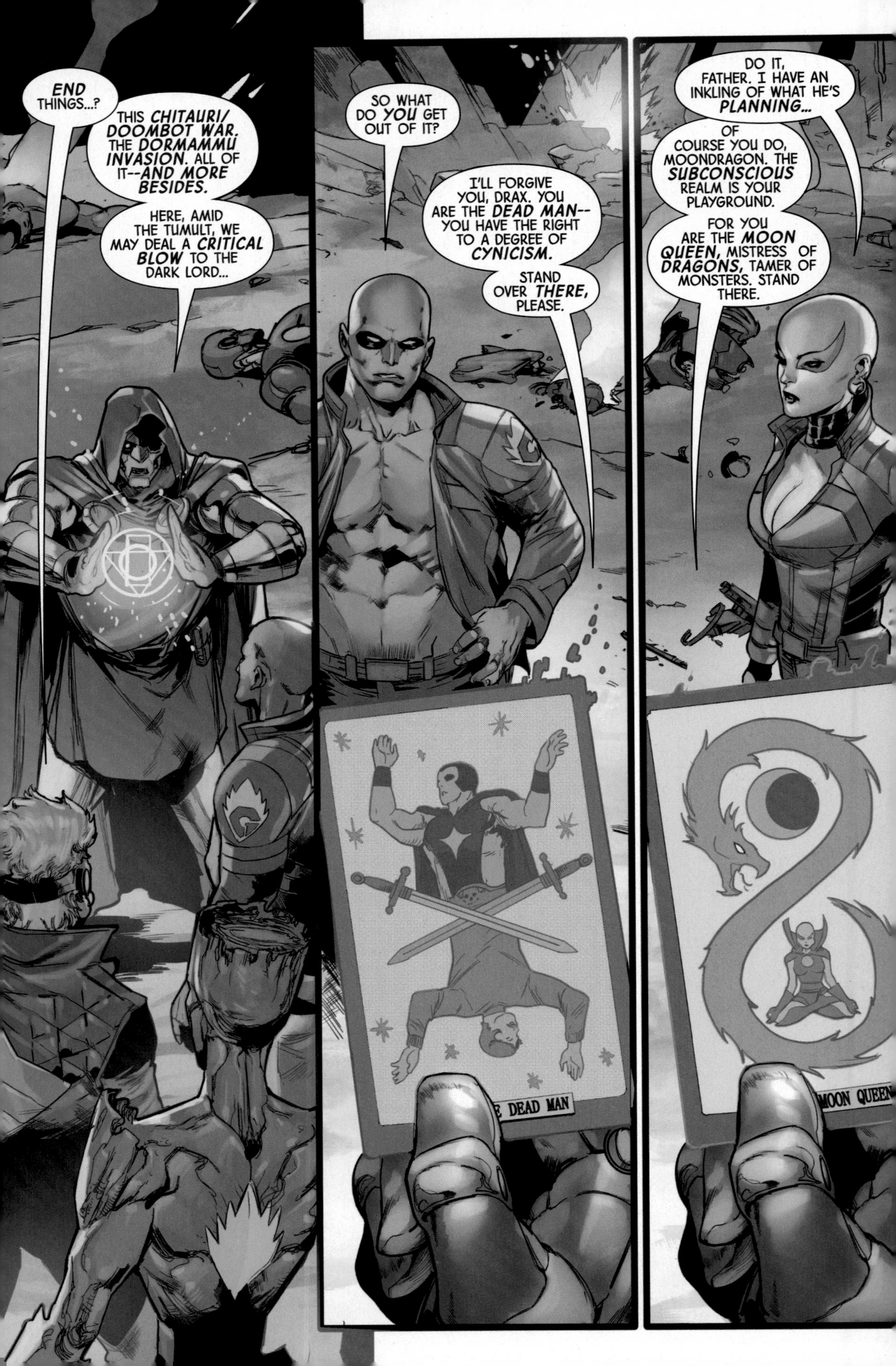

END THINGS...?
THIS CHITAURI/ DOOMBOT WAR. THE DORMAMMU INVASION. ALL OF IT--AND MORE BESIDES.
HERE, AMID THE TUMULT, WE MAY DEAL A CRITICAL BLOW TO THE DARK LORD...
SO WHAT DO YOU GET OUT OF IT?
I'LL FORGIVE YOU, DRAX. YOU ARE THE DEAD MAN--YOU HAVE THE RIGHT TO A DEGREE OF CYNICISM.
STAND OVER THERE, PLEASE.
DEAD MAN
DO IT, FATHER. I HAVE AN INKLING OF WHAT HE'S PLANNING...
OF COURSE YOU DO, MOONDRAGON. THE SUBCONSCIOUS REALM IS YOUR PLAYGROUND.
FOR YOU ARE THE MOON QUEEN, MISTRESS OF DRAGONS, TAMER OF MONSTERS. STAND THERE.
MOON QUEEN

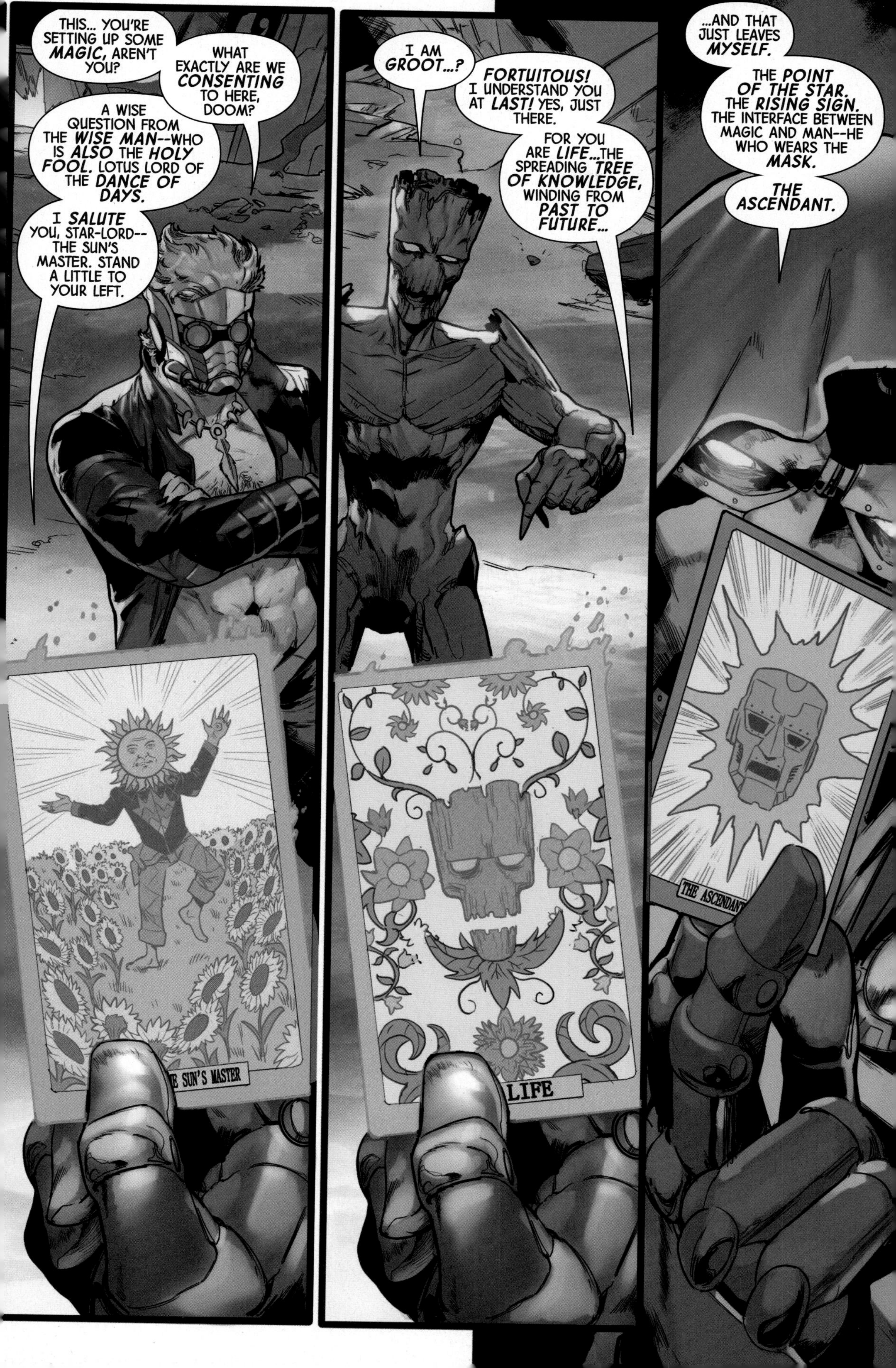

THIS... YOU'RE SETTING UP SOME MAGIC, AREN'T YOU?
WHAT EXACTLY ARE WE CONSENTING TO HERE, DOOM?
A WISE QUESTION FROM THE WISE MAN--WHO IS ALSO THE HOLY FOOL. LOTUS LORD OF THE DANCE OF DAYS.
I SALUTE YOU, STAR-LORD--THE SUN'S MASTER. STAND A LITTLE TO YOUR LEFT.
THE SUN'S MASTER
I AM GROOT...?
FORTUITOUS! I UNDERSTAND YOU AT LAST! YES, JUST THERE.
FOR YOU ARE LIFE...THE SPREADING TREE OF KNOWLEDGE, WINDING FROM PAST TO FUTURE...
LIFE
...AND THAT JUST LEAVES MYSELF.
THE POINT OF THE STAR. THE RISING SIGN. THE INTERFACE BETWEEN MAGIC AND MAN--HE WHO WEARS THE MASK.
THE ASCENDANT.
THE ASCENDANT

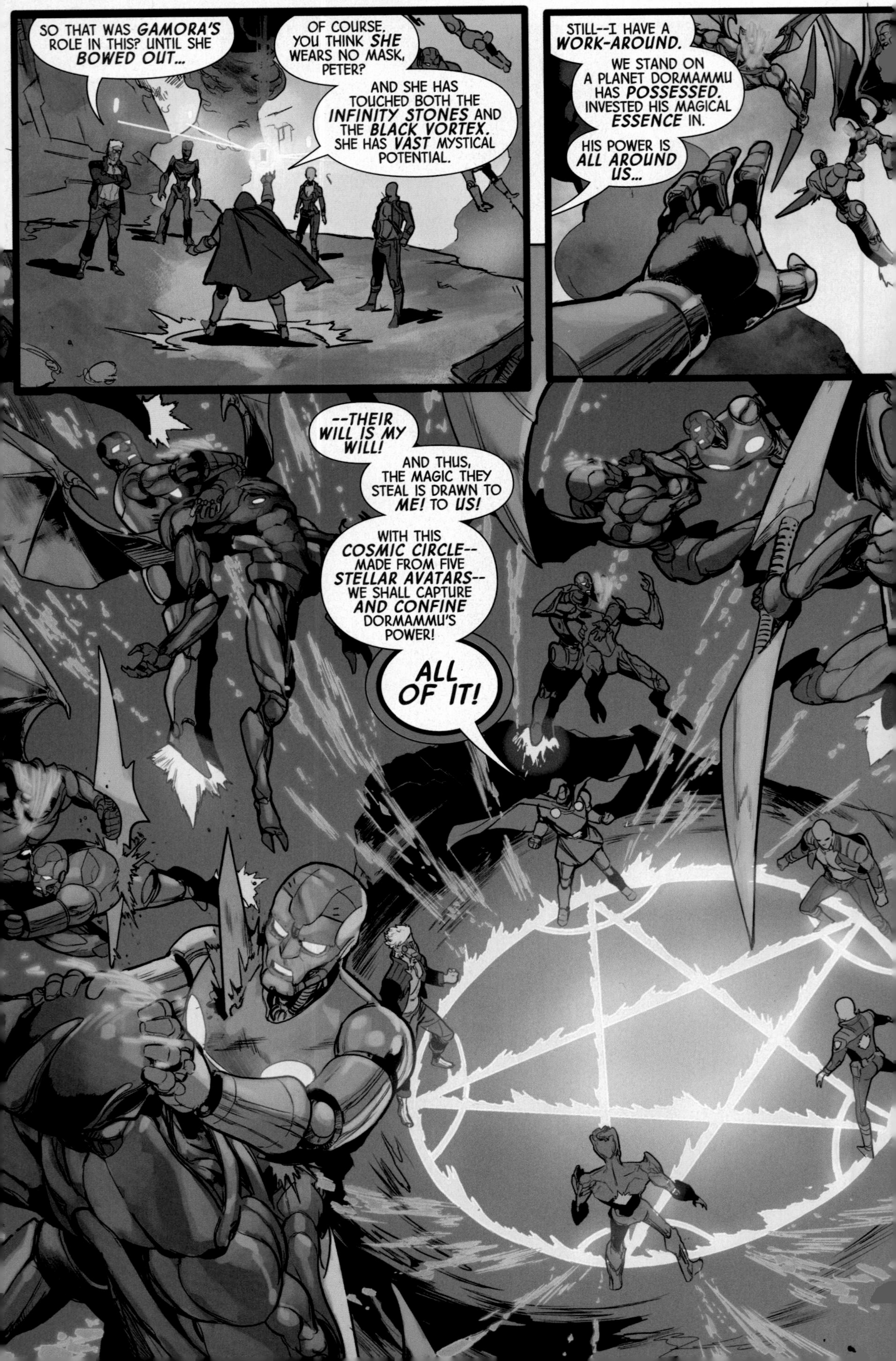
SO THAT WAS GAMORA'S ROLE IN THIS? UNTIL SHE BOWED OUT...
OF COURSE. YOU THINK SHE WEARS NO MASK, PETER?
AND SHE HAS TOUCHED BOTH THE INFINITY STONES AND THE BLACK VORTEX. SHE HAS VAST MYSTICAL POTENTIAL.
STILL--I HAVE A WORK-AROUND.
WE STAND ON A PLANET DORMAMMU HAS POSSESSED. INVESTED HIS MAGICAL ESSENCE IN.
HIS POWER IS ALL AROUND US...
--THEIR WILL IS MY WILL!
AND THUS, THE MAGIC THEY STEAL IS DRAWN TO ME! TO US!
WITH THIS COSMIC CIRCLE-- MADE FROM FIVE STELLAR AVATARS-- WE SHALL CAPTURE AND CONFINE DORMAMMU'S POWER!
ALL OF IT!

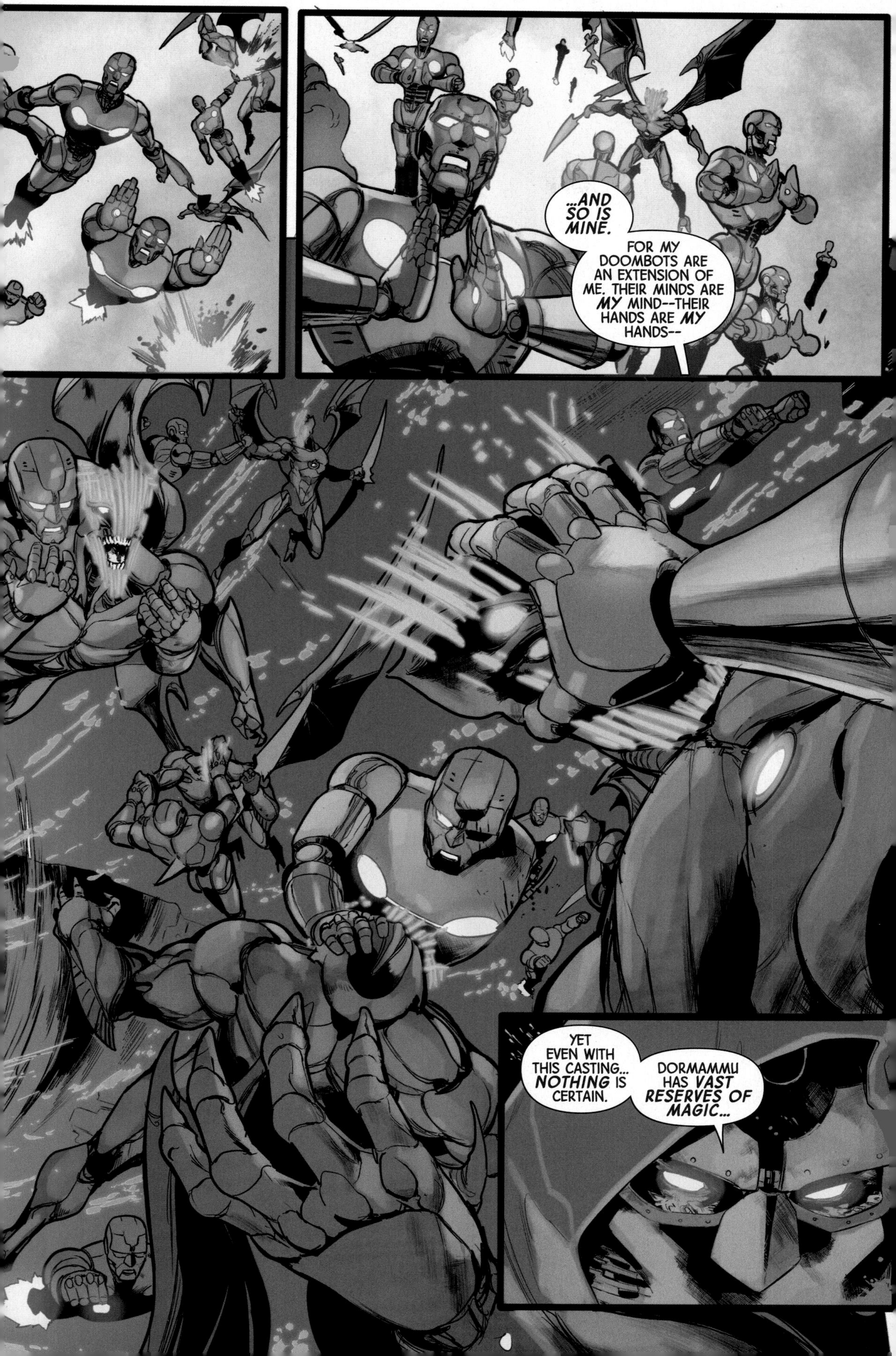
...AND SO IS MINE.
FOR MY DOOMBOTS ARE AN EXTENSION OF ME. THEIR MINDS ARE MY MIND--THEIR HANDS ARE MY HANDS--
YET EVEN WITH THIS CASTING... NOTHING IS CERTAIN.
DORMAMMU HAS VAST RESERVES OF MAGIC...

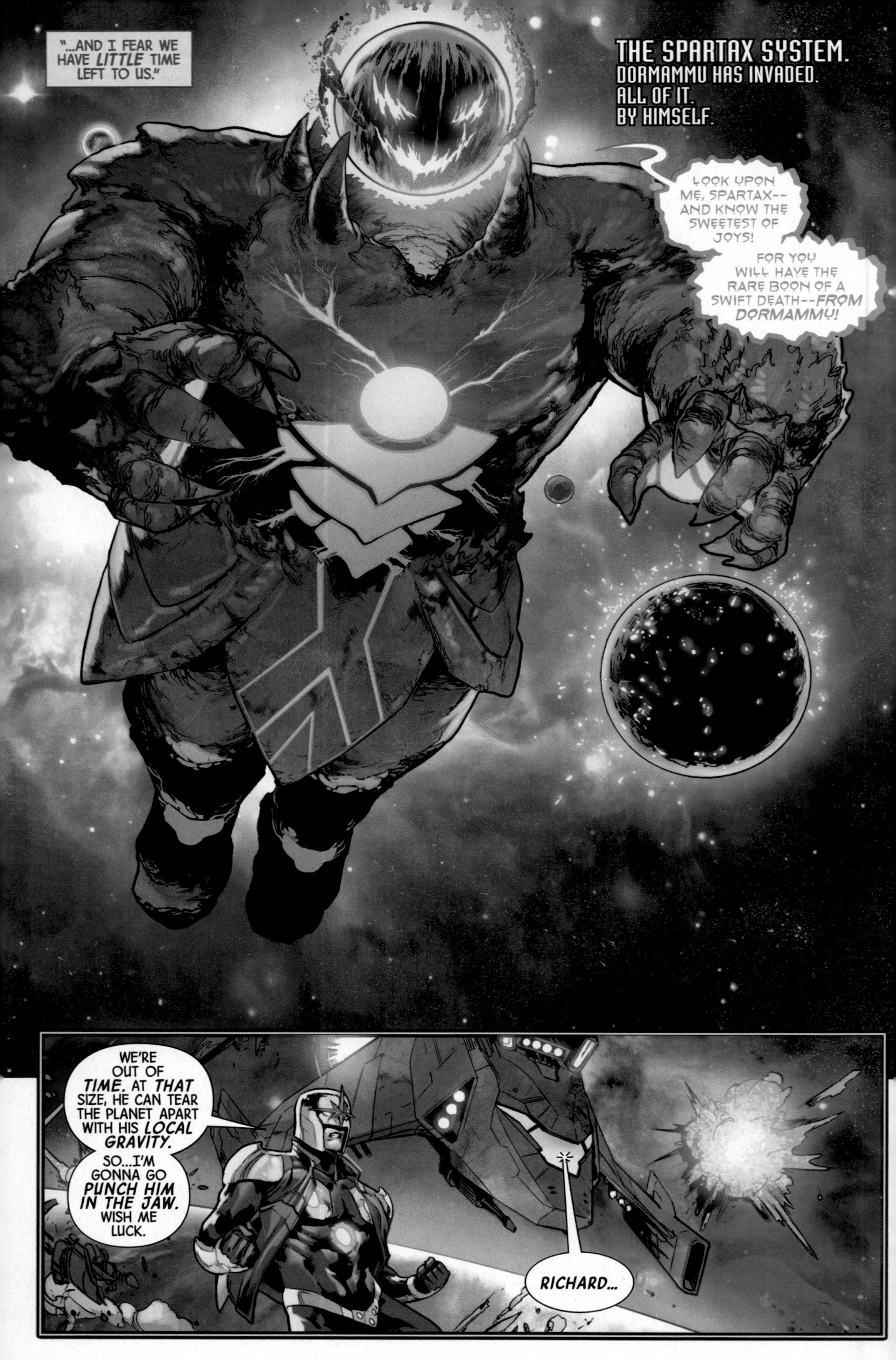
"...AND I FEAR WE HAVE LITTLE TIME LEFT TO US."
THE SPARTAX SYSTEM.
DORMAMMU HAS INVADED.
ALL OF IT.
BY HIMSELF.
LOOK UPON ME, SPARTAX-- AND KNOW THE SWEETEST OF JOYS!
FOR YOU WILL HAVE THE RARE BOON OF A SWIFT DEATH--FROM DORMAMMU!
WE'RE OUT OF TIME. AT THAT SIZE, HE CAN TEAR THE PLANET APART WITH HIS LOCAL GRAVITY.
SO...I'M GONNA GO PUNCH HIM IN THE JAW. WISH ME LUCK.
RICHARD...

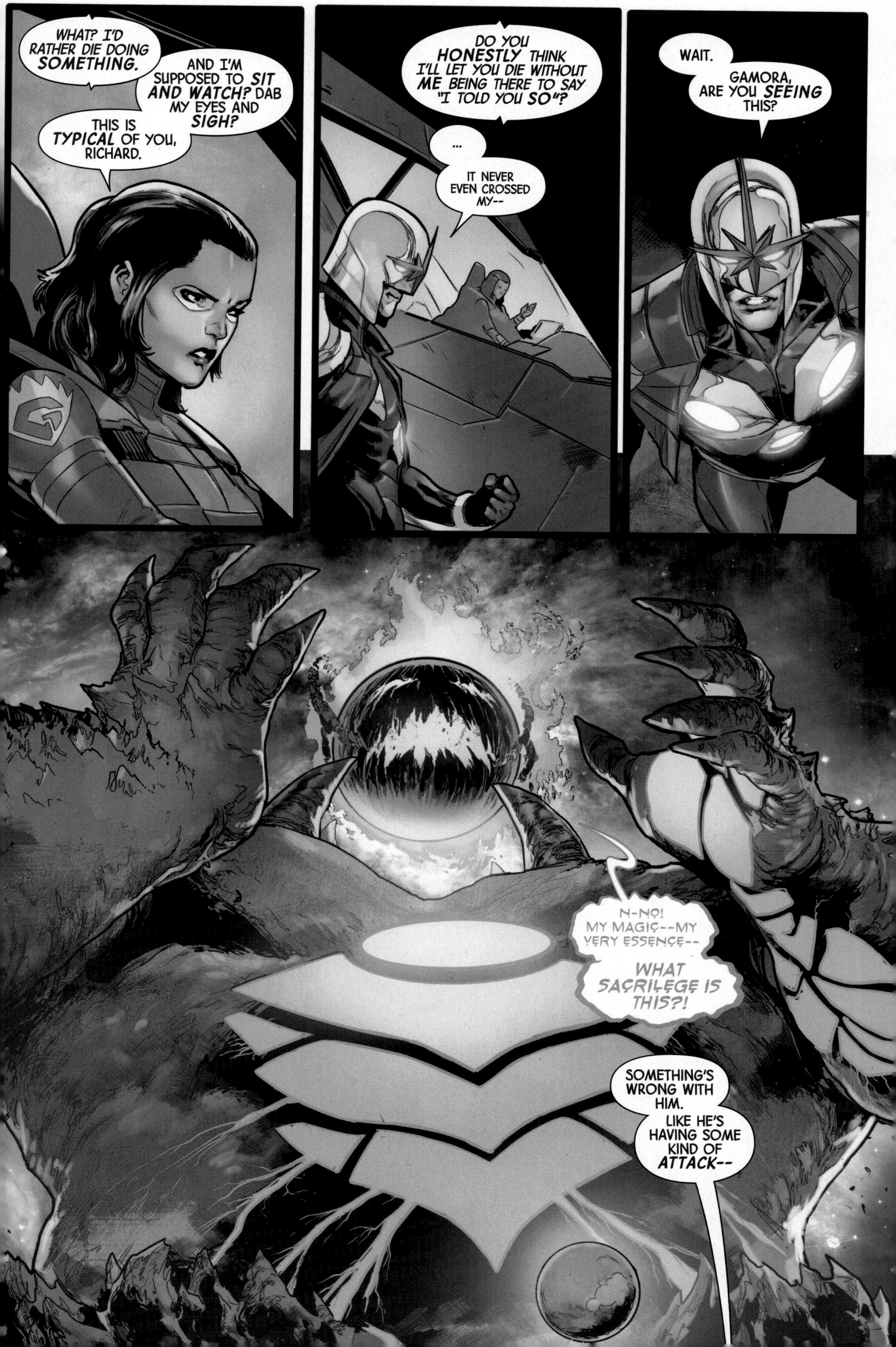
WHAT? I'D RATHER DIE DOING SOMETHING.
AND I'M SUPPOSED TO SIT AND WATCH? DAB MY EYES AND SIGH?
THIS IS TYPICAL OF YOU, RICHARD.
DO YOU HONESTLY THINK I'LL LET YOU DIE WITHOUT ME BEING THERE TO SAY "I TOLD YOU SO"?
...
IT NEVER EVEN CROSSED MY--
WAIT.
GAMORA, ARE YOU SEEING THIS?
N-NO! MY MAGIC--MY VERY ESSENCE--
WHAT SACRILEGE IS THIS?!
SOMETHING'S WRONG WITH HIM.
LIKE HE'S HAVING SOME KIND OF ATTACK--

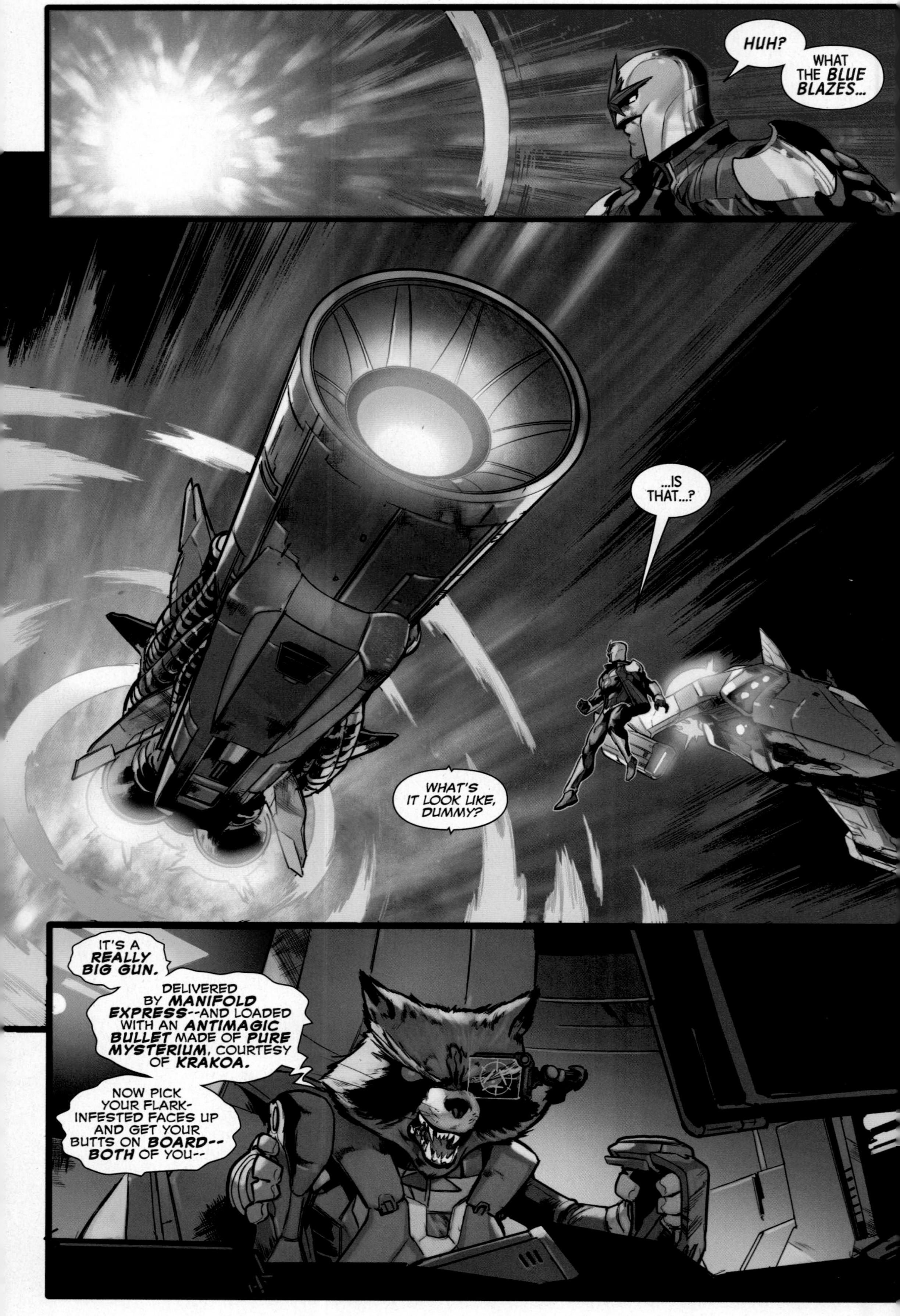
HUH?
WHAT THE BLUE BLAZES...
...IS THAT...?
WHAT'S IT LOOK LIKE, DUMMY?
IT'S A REALLY BIG GUN.
DELIVERED BY MANIFOLD EXPRESS--AND LOADED WITH AN ANTIMAGIC BULLET MADE OF PURE MYSTERIUM, COURTESY OF KRAKOA.
NOW PICK YOUR FLARK-INFESTED FACES UP AND GET YOUR BUTTS ON BOARD--BOTH OF YOU--

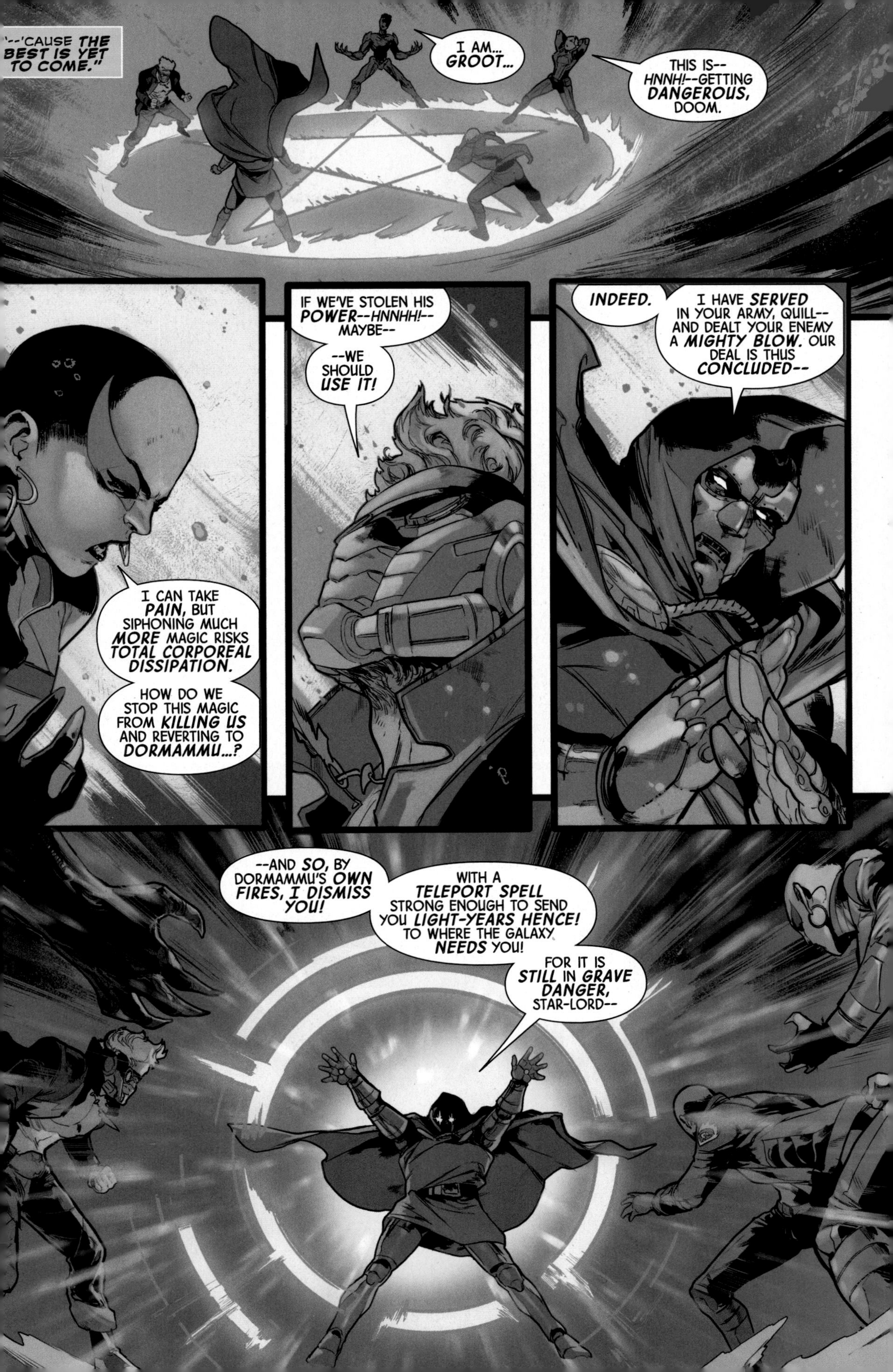
"--'CAUSE THE BEST IS YET TO COME."
I AM... GROOT...
THIS IS-- HNNH!--GETTING DANGEROUS, DOOM.
I CAN TAKE PAIN, BUT SIPHONING MUCH MORE MAGIC RISKS TOTAL CORPOREAL DISSIPATION.
HOW DO WE STOP THIS MAGIC FROM KILLING US AND REVERTING TO DORMAMMU...?
IF WE'VE STOLEN HIS POWER--HNNHH!-- MAYBE--
--WE SHOULD USE IT!
INDEED.
I HAVE SERVED IN YOUR ARMY, QUILL-- AND DEALT YOUR ENEMY A MIGHTY BLOW. OUR DEAL IS THUS CONCLUDED--
--AND SO, BY DORMAMMU'S OWN FIRES, I DISMISS YOU!
WITH A TELEPORT SPELL STRONG ENOUGH TO SEND YOU LIGHT-YEARS HENCE! TO WHERE THE GALAXY NEEDS YOU!
FOR IT IS STILL IN GRAVE DANGER, STAR-LORD--

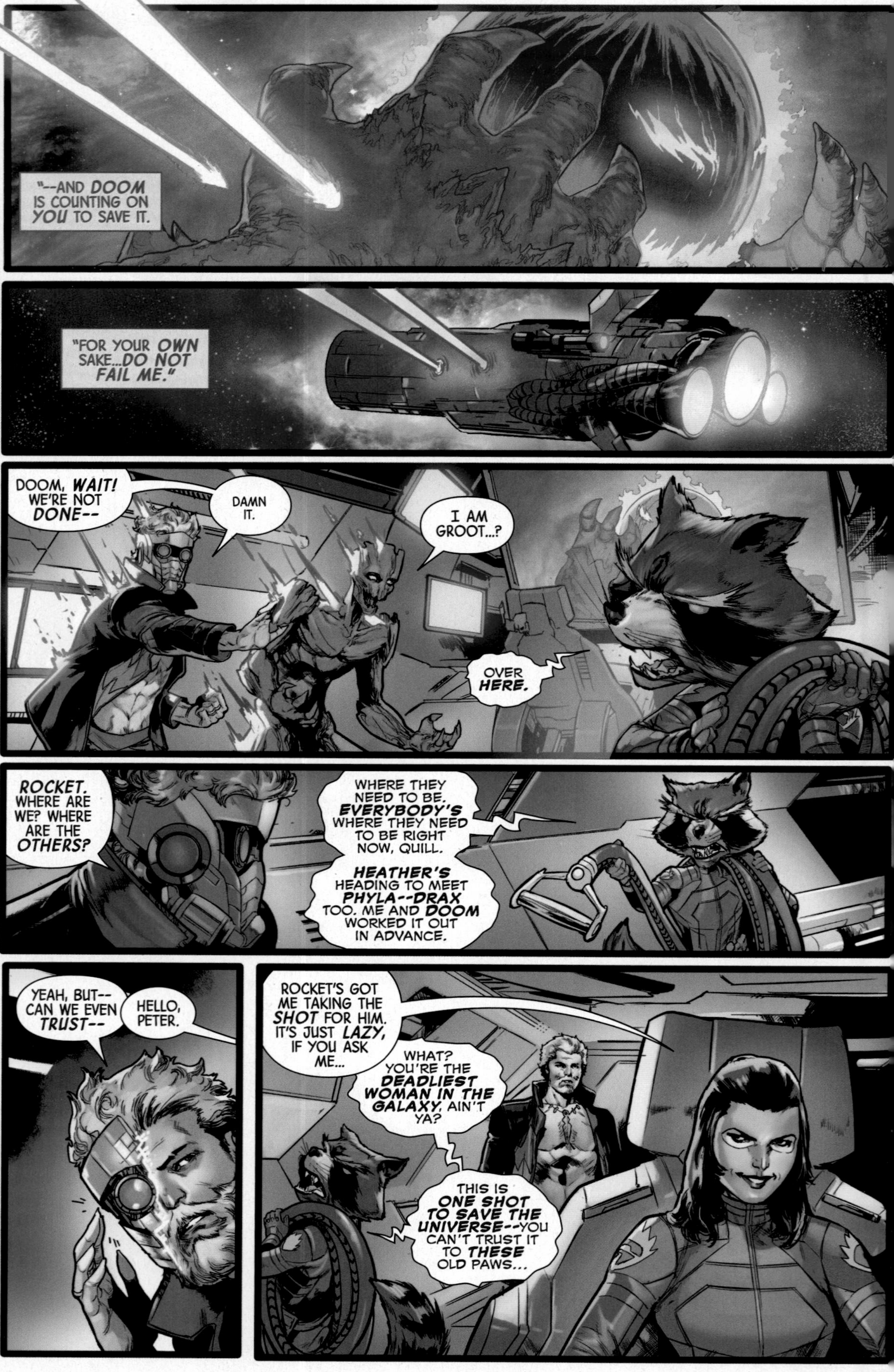
"--AND DOOM IS COUNTING ON YOU TO SAVE IT.
"FOR YOUR OWN SAKE...DO NOT FAIL ME."
DOOM, WAIT! WE'RE NOT DONE--
DAMN IT.
I AM GROOT...?
OVER HERE.
ROCKET. WHERE ARE WE? WHERE ARE THE OTHERS?
WHERE THEY NEED TO BE. EVERYBODY'S WHERE THEY NEED TO BE RIGHT NOW, QUILL.
HEATHER'S HEADING TO MEET PHYLA--DRAX TOO. ME AND DOOM WORKED IT OUT IN ADVANCE.
YEAH, BUT-- CAN WE EVEN TRUST--
HELLO, PETER.
ROCKET'S GOT ME TAKING THE SHOT FOR HIM. IT'S JUST LAZY, IF YOU ASK ME...
WHAT? YOU'RE THE DEADLIEST WOMAN IN THE GALAXY, AIN'T YA?
THIS IS ONE SHOT TO SAVE THE UNIVERSE--YOU CAN'T TRUST IT TO THESE OLD PAWS...

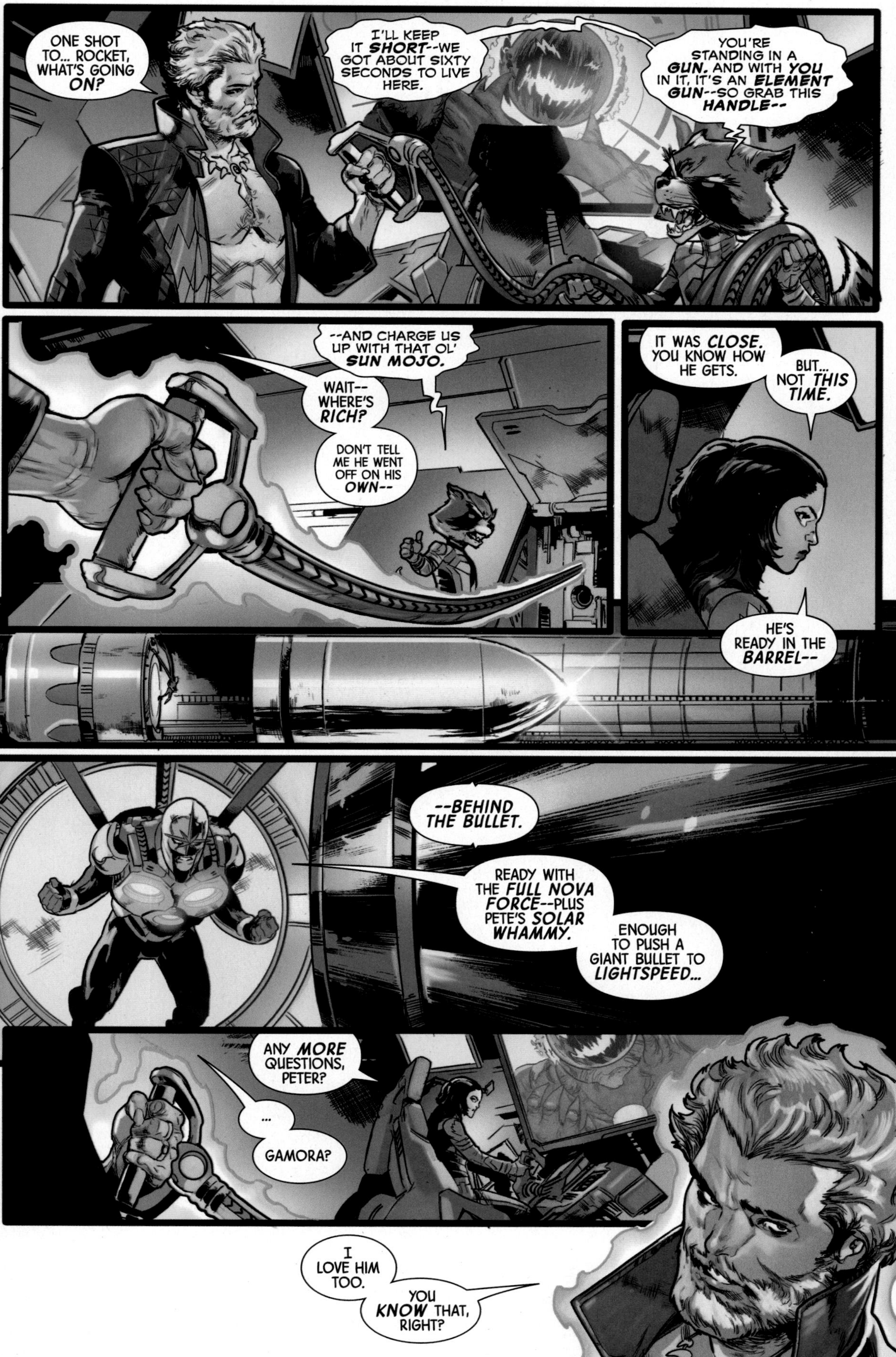
ONE SHOT TO... ROCKET, WHAT'S GOING ON?
I'LL KEEP IT SHORT--WE GOT ABOUT SIXTY SECONDS TO LIVE HERE.
YOU'RE STANDING IN A GUN. AND WITH YOU IN IT, IT'S AN ELEMENT GUN--SO GRAB THIS HANDLE--
--AND CHARGE US UP WITH THAT OL' SUN MOJO.
WAIT-- WHERE'S RICH?
DON'T TELL ME HE WENT OFF ON HIS OWN--
IT WAS CLOSE. YOU KNOW HOW HE GETS.
BUT... NOT THIS TIME.
HE'S READY IN THE BARREL--
--BEHIND THE BULLET.
READY WITH THE FULL NOVA FORCE--PLUS PETE'S SOLAR WHAMMY.
ENOUGH TO PUSH A GIANT BULLET TO LIGHTSPEED...
ANY MORE QUESTIONS, PETER?
...
GAMORA?
I LOVE HIM TOO.
YOU KNOW THAT, RIGHT?

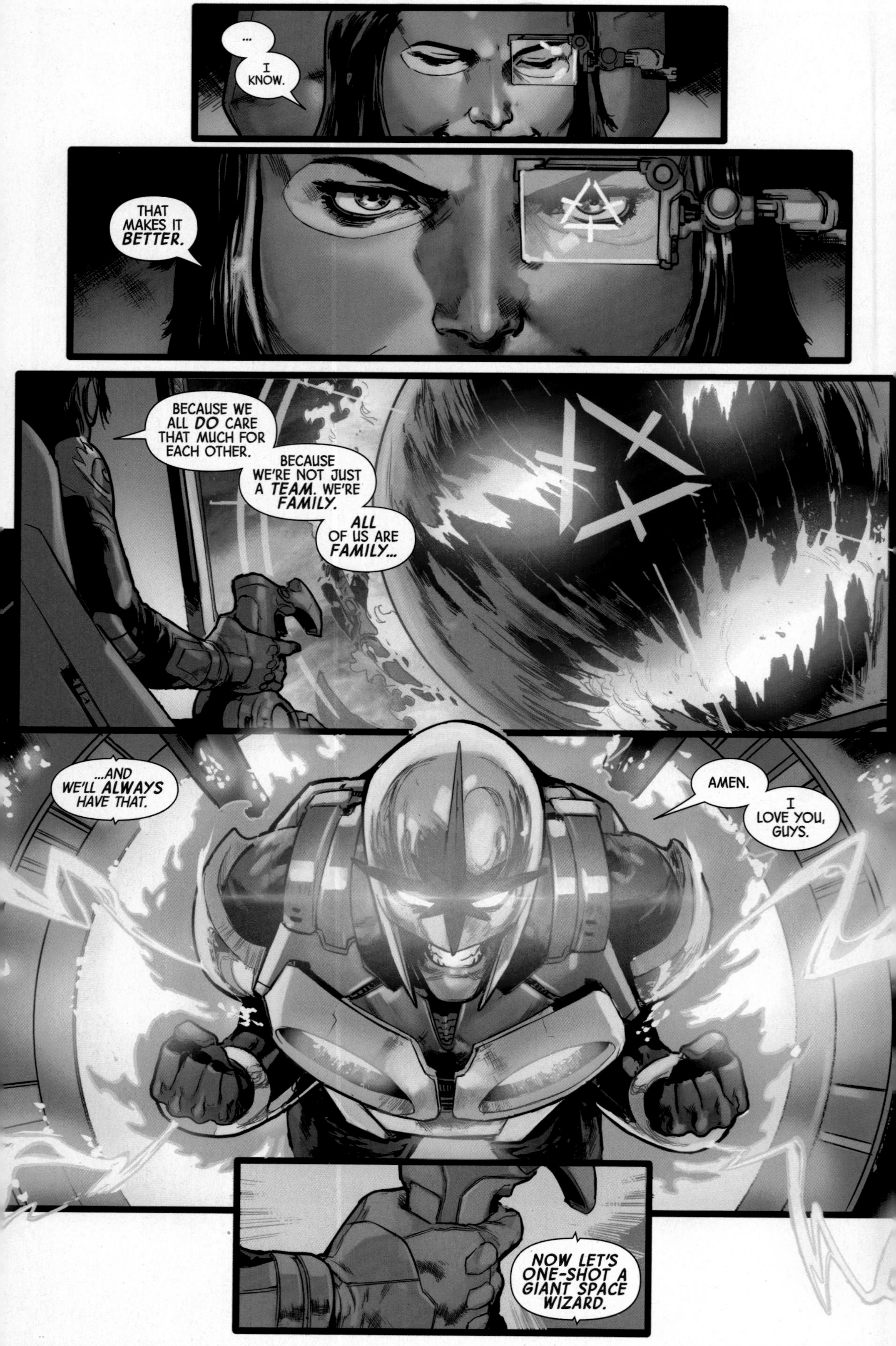
...
I KNOW.
THAT MAKES IT BETTER.
BECAUSE WE ALL DO CARE THAT MUCH FOR EACH OTHER.
BECAUSE WE'RE NOT JUST A TEAM. WE'RE FAMILY.
ALL OF US ARE FAMILY...
...AND WE'LL ALWAYS HAVE THAT.
AMEN.
I LOVE YOU, GUYS.
NOW LET'S ONE-SHOT A GIANT SPACE WIZARD.

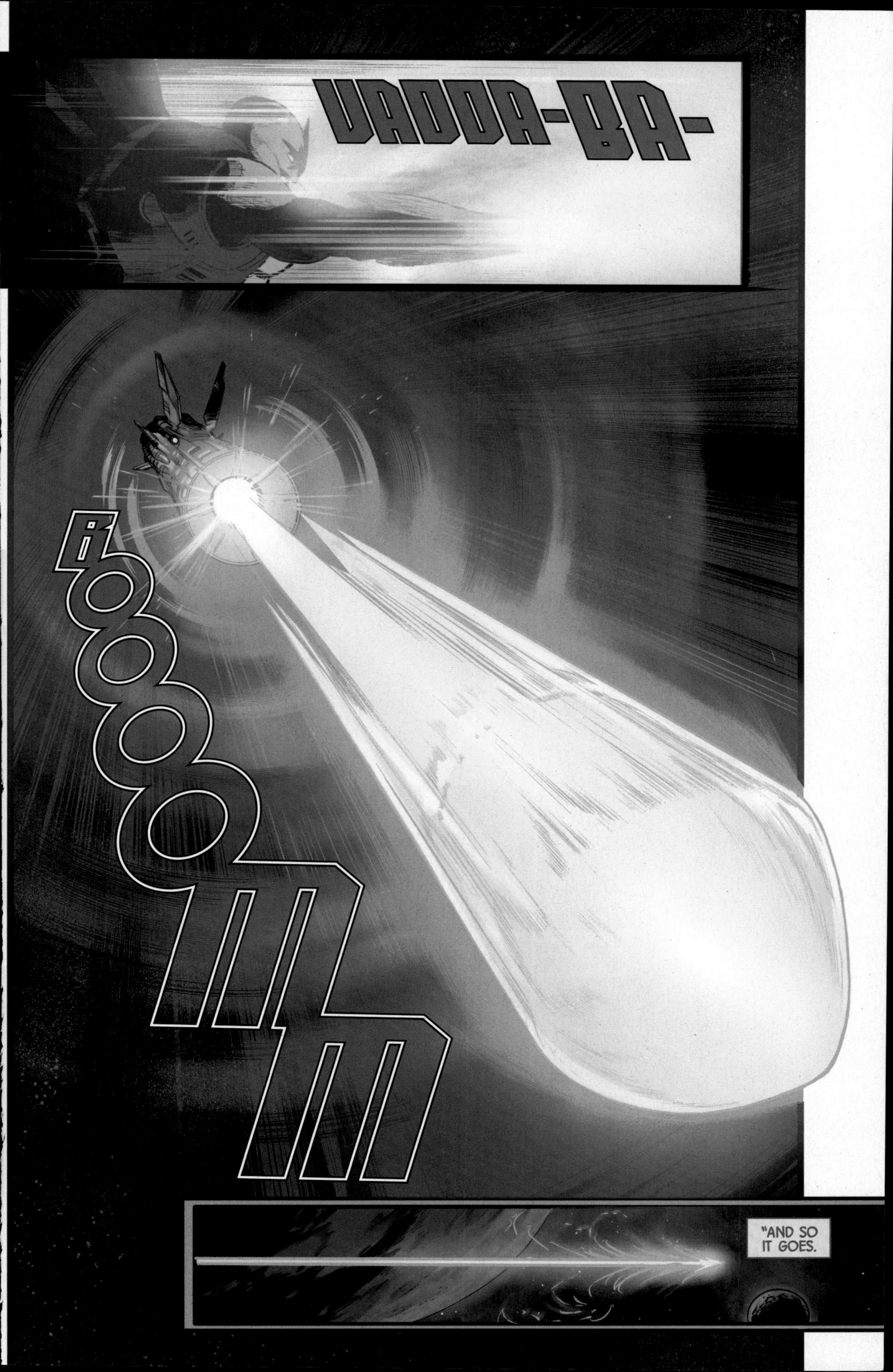
VADDA-BA-
BOOOOOMMM
"AND SO IT GOES.

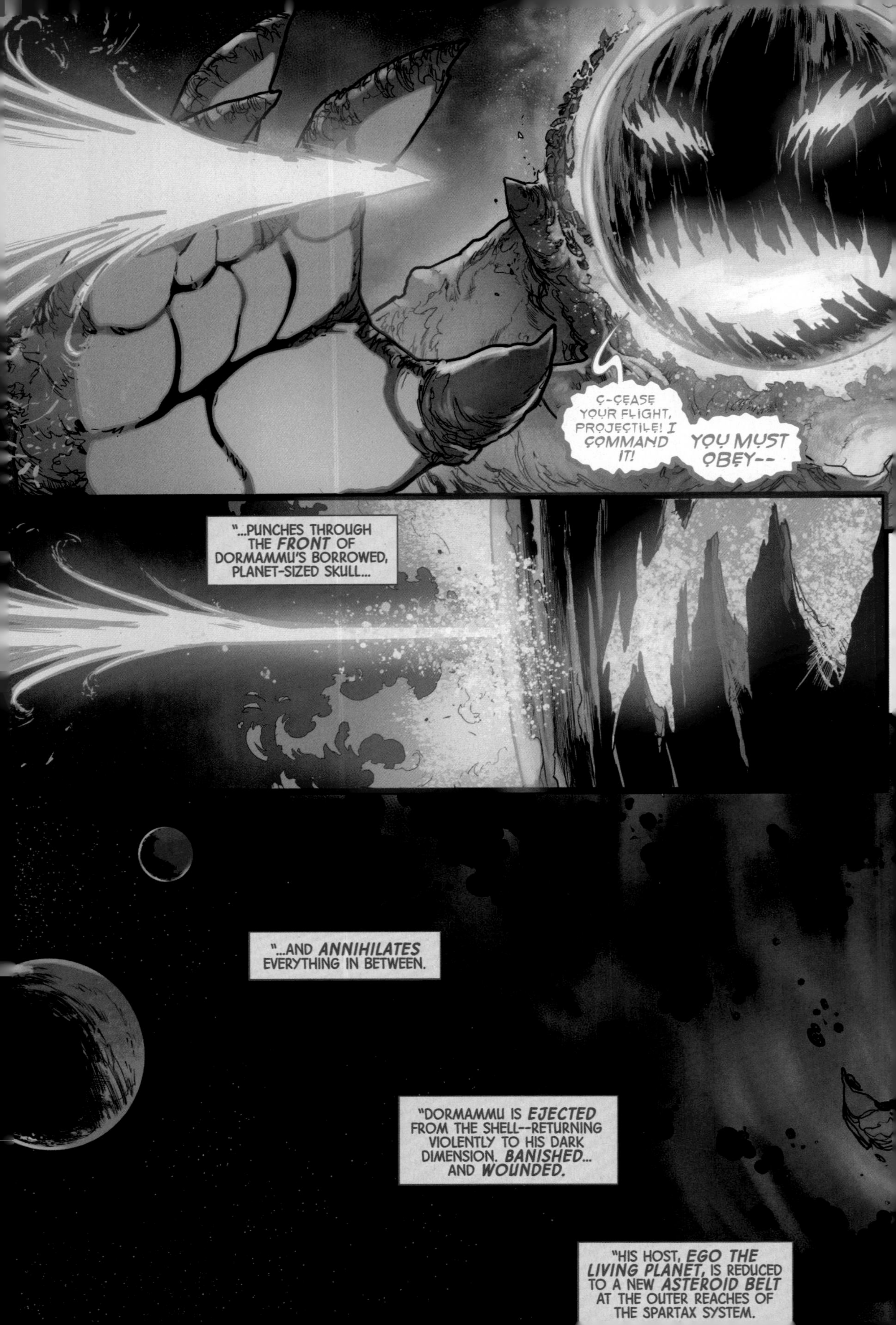
C-CEASE YOUR FLIGHT, PROJECTILE! I COMMAND IT!
YOU MUST OBEY--
"...PUNCHES THROUGH THE FRONT OF DORMAMMU'S BORROWED, PLANET-SIZED SKULL...
"...AND ANNIHILATES EVERYTHING IN BETWEEN.
"DORMAMMU IS EJECTED FROM THE SHELL--RETURNING VIOLENTLY TO HIS DARK DIMENSION. BANISHED... AND WOUNDED.
"HIS HOST, EGO THE LIVING PLANET, IS REDUCED TO A NEW ASTEROID BELT AT THE OUTER REACHES OF THE SPARTAX SYSTEM.

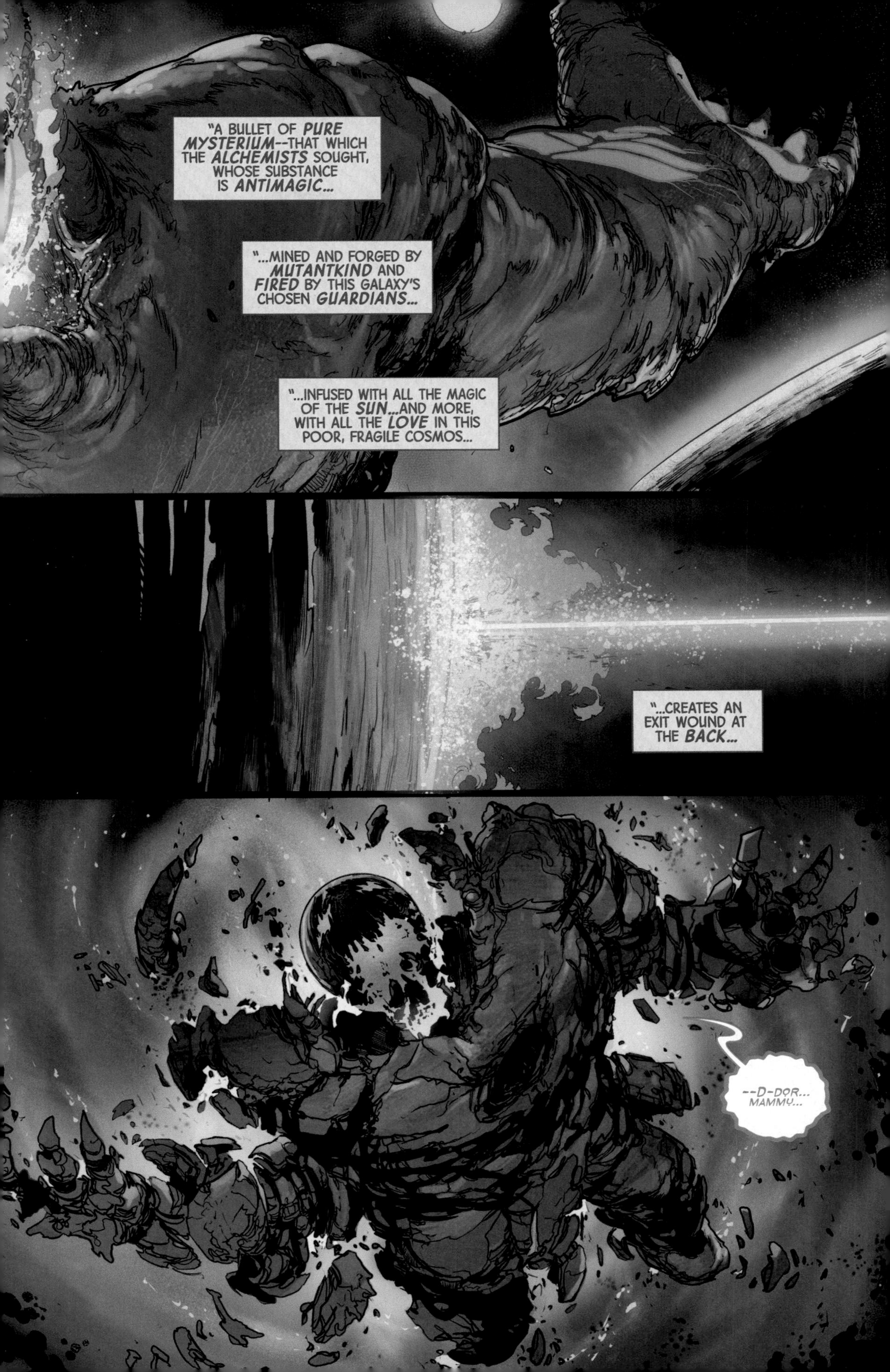
"A BULLET OF PURE MYSTERIUM--THAT WHICH THE ALCHEMISTS SOUGHT, WHOSE SUBSTANCE IS ANTIMAGIC...
"...MINED AND FORGED BY MUTANTKIND AND FIRED BY THIS GALAXY'S CHOSEN GUARDIANS...
"...INFUSED WITH ALL THE MAGIC OF THE SUN...AND MORE, WITH ALL THE LOVE IN THIS POOR, FRAGILE COSMOS...
"...CREATES AN EXIT WOUND AT THE BACK...
--D-DOR... MAMMY...

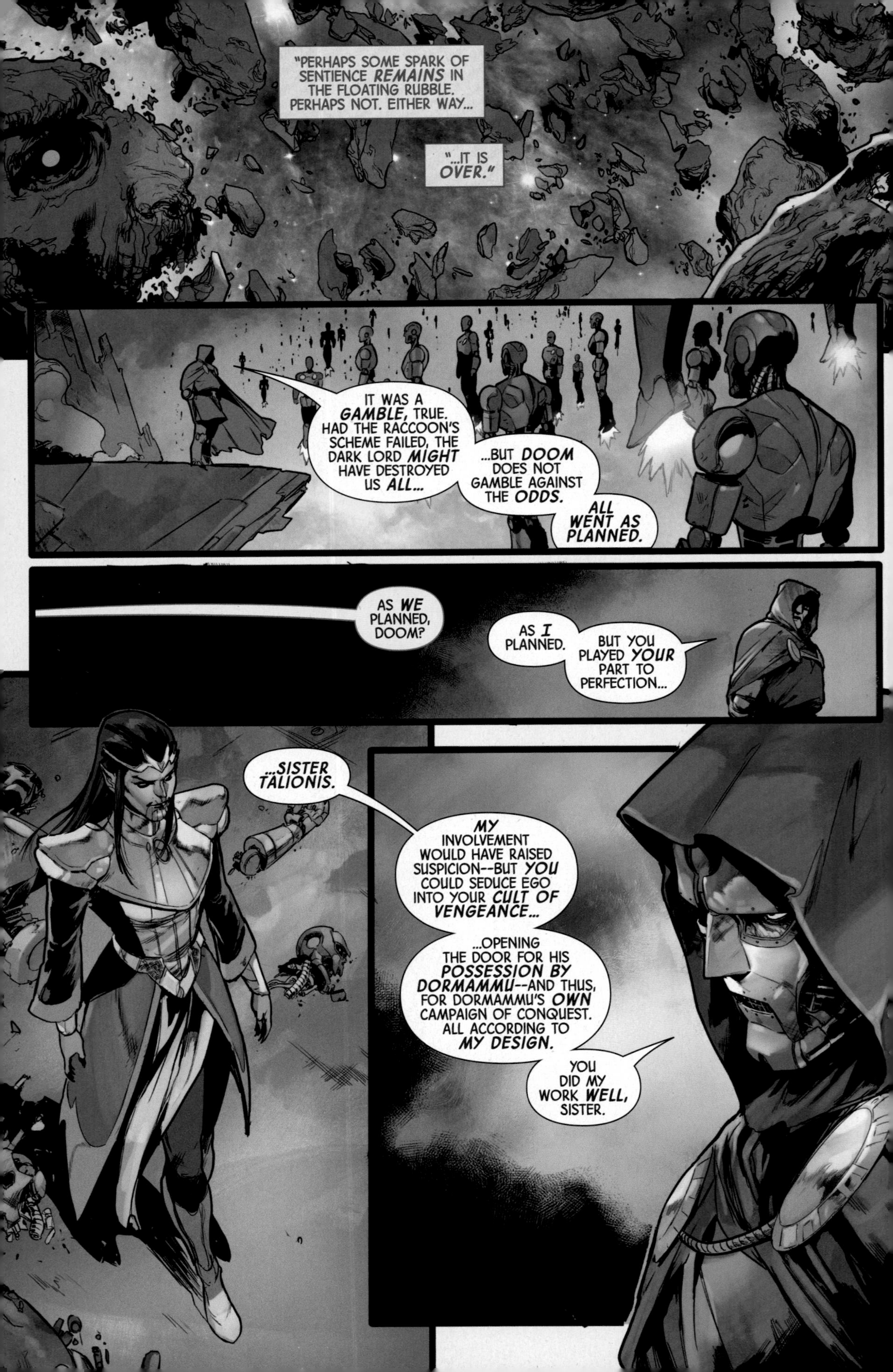
"PERHAPS SOME SPARK OF SENTIENCE REMAINS IN THE FLOATING RUBBLE. PERHAPS NOT. EITHER WAY...
"...IT IS OVER."
IT WAS A GAMBLE, TRUE. HAD THE RACCOON'S SCHEME FAILED, THE DARK LORD MIGHT HAVE DESTROYED US ALL...
...BUT DOOM DOES NOT GAMBLE AGAINST THE ODDS.
ALL WENT AS PLANNED.
AS WE PLANNED, DOOM?
AS I PLANNED.
BUT YOU PLAYED YOUR PART TO PERFECTION...
...SISTER TALIONIS.
MY INVOLVEMENT WOULD HAVE RAISED SUSPICION--BUT YOU COULD SEDUCE EGO INTO YOUR CULT OF VENGEANCE...
...OPENING THE DOOR FOR HIS POSSESSION BY DORMAMMU--AND THUS, FOR DORMAMMU'S OWN CAMPAIGN OF CONQUEST. ALL ACCORDING TO MY DESIGN.
YOU DID MY WORK WELL, SISTER.

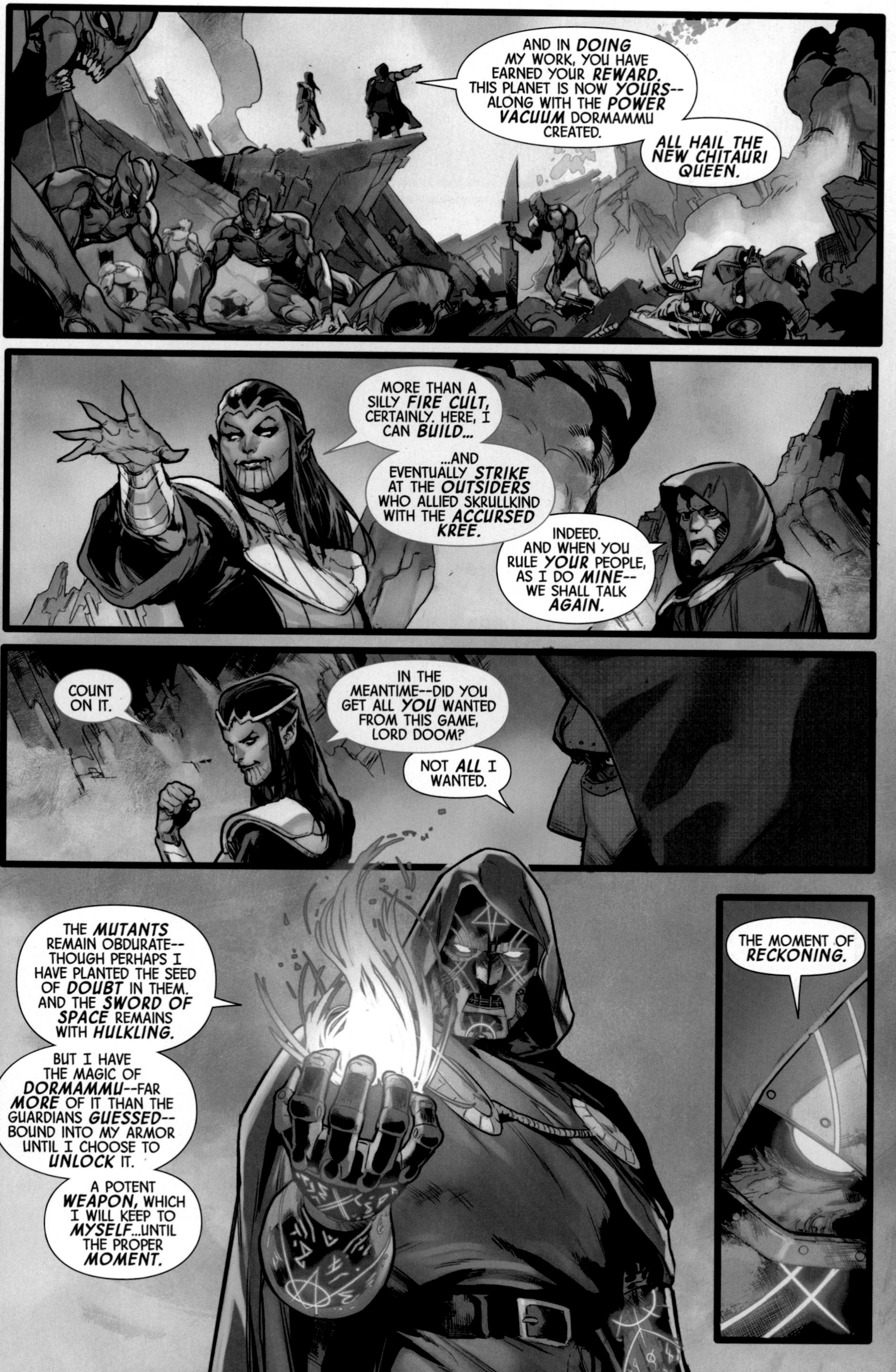
AND IN DOING MY WORK, YOU HAVE EARNED YOUR REWARD. THIS PLANET IS NOW YOURS--ALONG WITH THE POWER VACUUM DORMAMMU CREATED.
ALL HAIL THE NEW CHITAURI QUEEN.
MORE THAN A SILLY FIRE CULT, CERTAINLY. HERE, I CAN BUILD...
...AND EVENTUALLY STRIKE AT THE OUTSIDERS WHO ALLIED SKRULLKIND WITH THE ACCURSED KREE.
INDEED. AND WHEN YOU RULE YOUR PEOPLE, AS I DO MINE--WE SHALL TALK AGAIN.
COUNT ON IT.
IN THE MEANTIME--DID YOU GET ALL YOU WANTED FROM THIS GAME, LORD DOOM?
NOT ALL I WANTED.
THE MUTANTS REMAIN OBDURATE--THOUGH PERHAPS I HAVE PLANTED THE SEED OF DOUBT IN THEM. AND THE SWORD OF SPACE REMAINS WITH HULKLING.
BUT I HAVE THE MAGIC OF DORMAMMU--FAR MORE OF IT THAN THE GUARDIANS GUESSED--BOUND INTO MY ARMOR UNTIL I CHOOSE TO UNLOCK IT.
A POTENT WEAPON, WHICH I WILL KEEP TO MYSELF...UNTIL THE PROPER MOMENT.
THE MOMENT OF RECKONING.

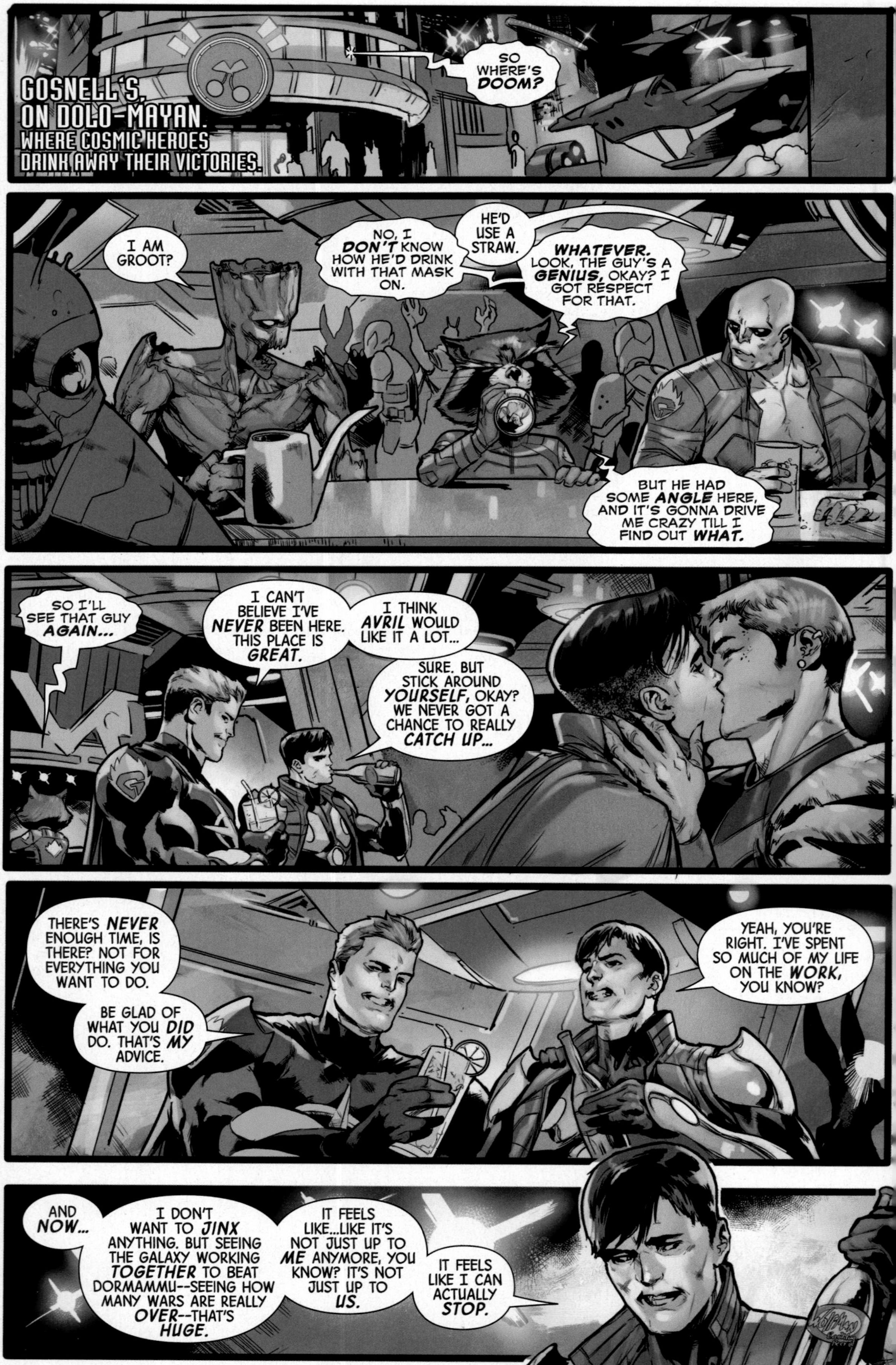
GOSNELL'S, ON DOLO-MAYAN.
WHERE COSMIC HEROES DRINK AWAY THEIR VICTORIES.
SO WHERE'S DOOM?
I AM GROOT?
NO, I DON'T KNOW HOW HE'D DRINK WITH THAT MASK ON.
HE'D USE A STRAW.
WHATEVER. LOOK, THE GUY'S A GENIUS, OKAY? I GOT RESPECT FOR THAT.
BUT HE HAD SOME ANGLE HERE, AND IT'S GONNA DRIVE ME CRAZY TILL I FIND OUT WHAT.
SO I'LL SEE THAT GUY AGAIN...
I CAN'T BELIEVE I'VE NEVER BEEN HERE. THIS PLACE IS GREAT.
I THINK AVRIL WOULD LIKE IT A LOT...
SURE. BUT STICK AROUND YOURSELF, OKAY? WE NEVER GOT A CHANCE TO REALLY CATCH UP...
THERE'S NEVER ENOUGH TIME, IS THERE? NOT FOR EVERYTHING YOU WANT TO DO.
BE GLAD OF WHAT YOU DID DO. THAT'S MY ADVICE.
YEAH, YOU'RE RIGHT. I'VE SPENT SO MUCH OF MY LIFE ON THE WORK, YOU KNOW?
AND NOW...
I DON'T WANT TO JINX ANYTHING. BUT SEEING THE GALAXY WORKING TOGETHER TO BEAT DORMAMMU--SEEING HOW MANY WARS ARE REALLY OVER--THAT'S HUGE.
IT FEELS LIKE...LIKE IT'S NOT JUST UP TO ME ANYMORE, YOU KNOW? IT'S NOT JUST UP TO US.
IT FEELS LIKE I CAN ACTUALLY STOP.

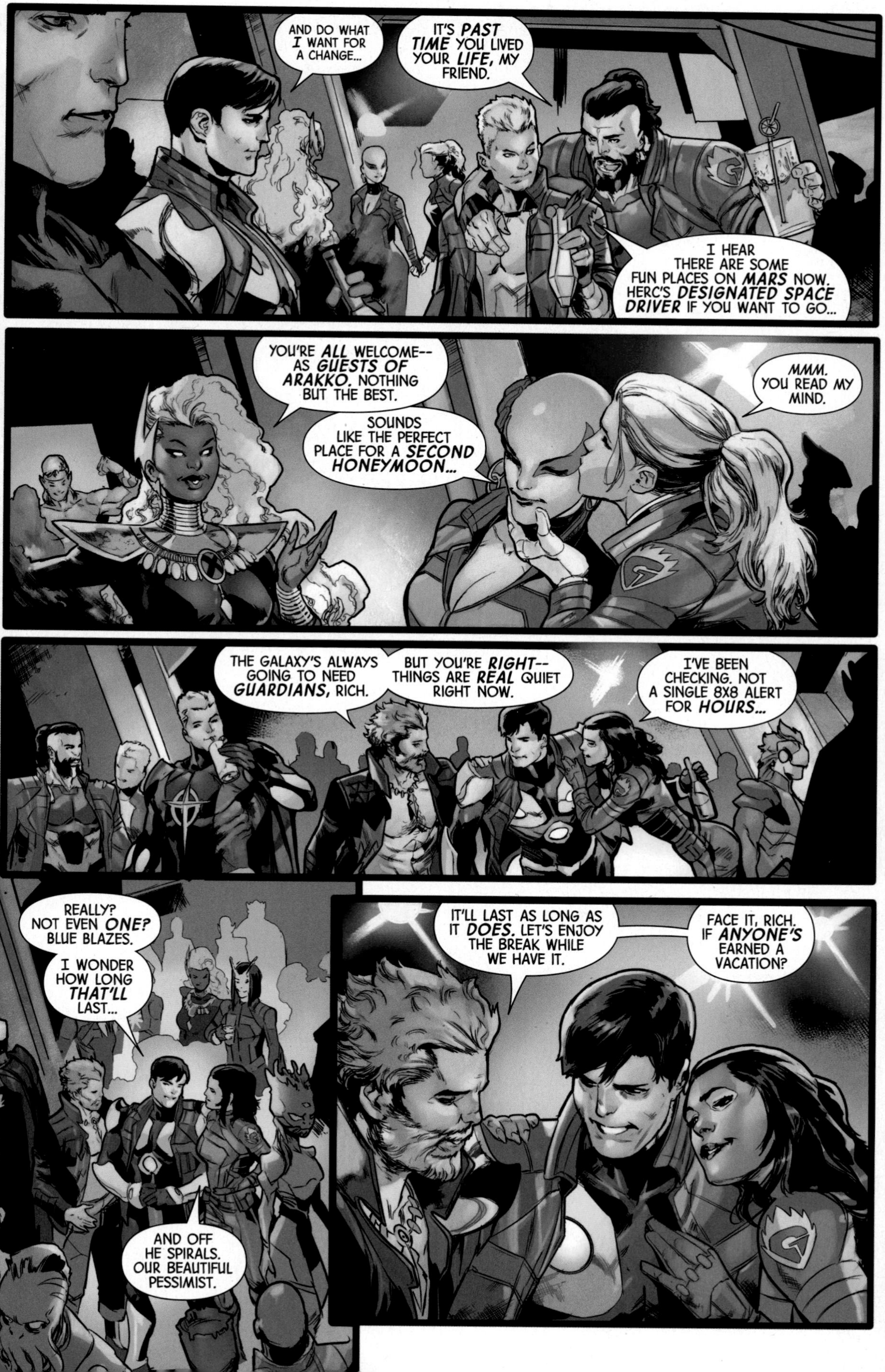
AND DO WHAT I WANT FOR A CHANGE...
IT'S PAST TIME YOU LIVED YOUR LIFE, MY FRIEND.
I HEAR THERE ARE SOME FUN PLACES ON MARS NOW. HERC'S DESIGNATED SPACE DRIVER IF YOU WANT TO GO...
YOU'RE ALL WELCOME-- AS GUESTS OF ARAKKO. NOTHING BUT THE BEST.
SOUNDS LIKE THE PERFECT PLACE FOR A SECOND HONEYMOON...
MMM. YOU READ MY MIND.
THE GALAXY'S ALWAYS GOING TO NEED GUARDIANS, RICH.
BUT YOU'RE RIGHT-- THINGS ARE REAL QUIET RIGHT NOW.
I'VE BEEN CHECKING. NOT A SINGLE 8X8 ALERT FOR HOURS...
REALLY? NOT EVEN ONE? BLUE BLAZES.
I WONDER HOW LONG THAT'LL LAST...
AND OFF HE SPIRALS. OUR BEAUTIFUL PESSIMIST.
IT'LL LAST AS LONG AS IT DOES. LET'S ENJOY THE BREAK WHILE WE HAVE IT.
FACE IT, RICH. IF ANYONE'S EARNED A VACATION?

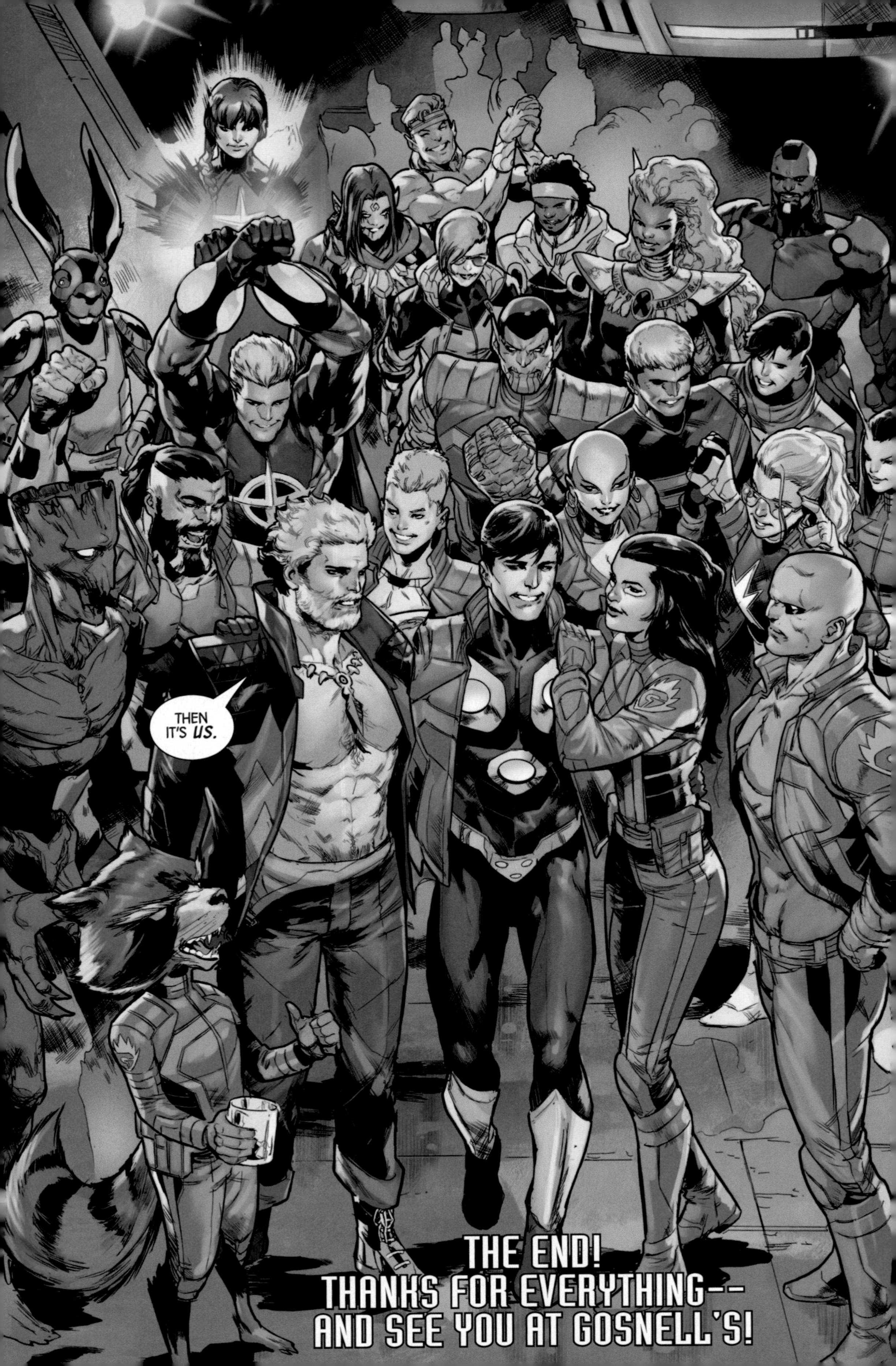
THEN IT'S US.
THE END!
THANKS FOR EVERYTHING--
AND SEE YOU AT GOSNELL'S!

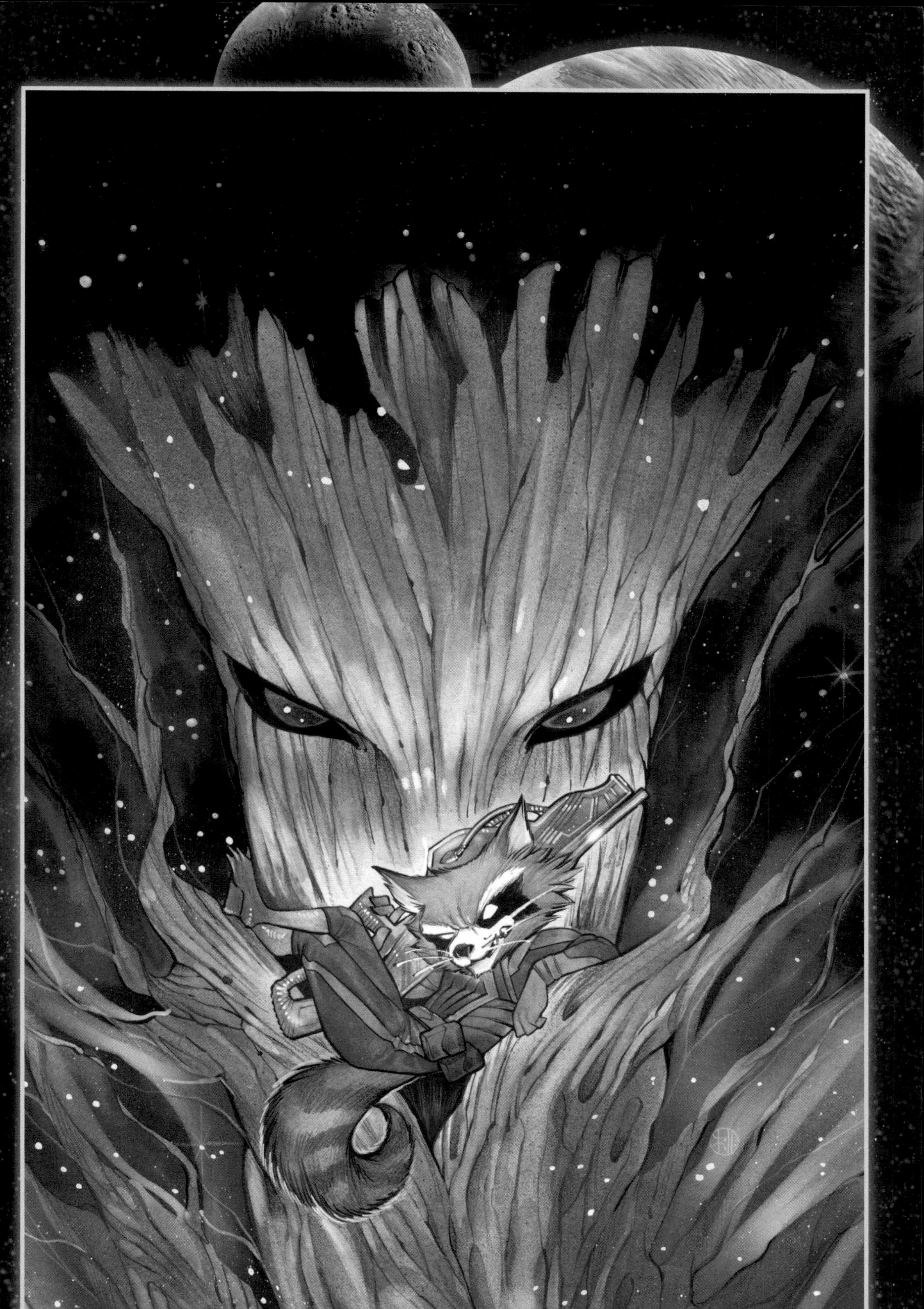

#13 VARIANT BY:
PEACH MOMOKO

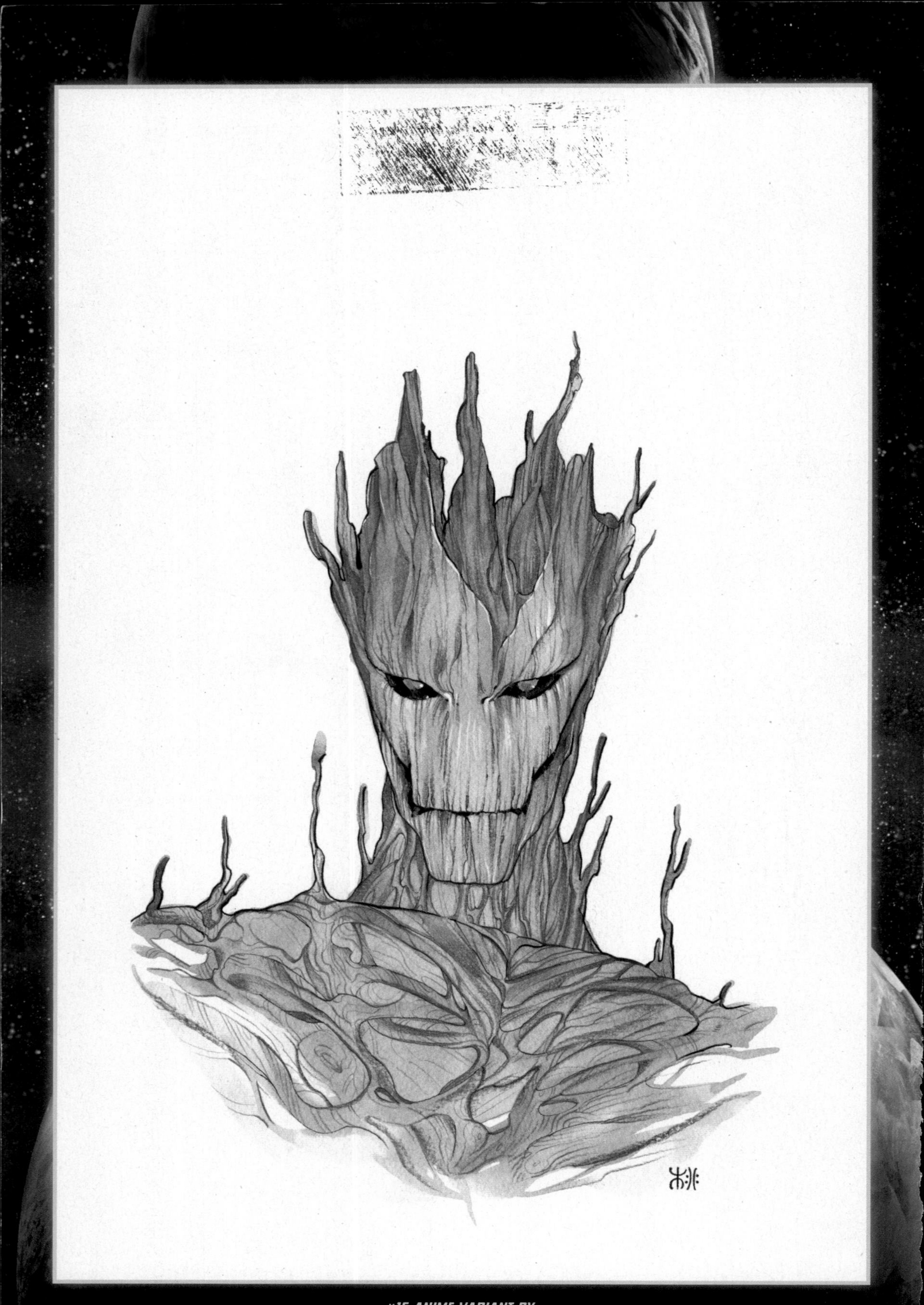

#16 ANIME VARIANT BY:
PEACH MOMOKO